REFLECTIONS OF WOMEN IN ANTIQUITY

REFLECTIONS OF WOMEN
IN ANTIQUITY

HELENE P. FOLEY

BARNARD COLLEGE, COLUMBIA UNIVERSITY

GORDON AND BREACH SCIENCE PUBLISHERS
NEW YORK   LONDON   PARIS

Gordon and Breach, Science Publishers, Inc.
One Park Avenue
New York, NY 10016

Gordon and Breach Science Publishers Ltd.
42 William IV Street
London, WC2N 4DE

Gordon and Breach
58 rue Lhomond
75005 Paris

Library of Congress catalog card number 81–13352.
ISBN 0 677 16370 3.

To the memory of my mother and sister

Epigraph

Let the sacred rivers run uphill to their springs;
All principles of order are reversed.
For it is men whose thoughts are treacherous,
Who break their oaths sworn on the gods.
But songs of praise will turn my life to good
   repute,
Since honor comes to the race of women
And insults shall cease to defame us.

Now the ancient poets' muses can stop
their hymn on our unfaithfulness.
Our understanding has no holy gift
Of lyre and song from Apollo,
Master of music. Otherwise I would have made
a counter-hymn to answer the male race.
For time has much to say about the lot
of us and men throughout the years.

Euripides' *Medea*, 410–430

Contents

Preface

THIS VOLUME of essays grew out of a double issue of *Women's Studies* (Vol. 8, Nos. 1–2, 1981), which was the first special issue on Women in Antiquity in a major women's studies journal. It came as a sequel to two issues on Women in Antiquity in the classical journal *Arethusa* (Vol. 6, No. 1 and Vol. 11, Nos. 1 and 2) which also contained many important articles and a useful bibliography by Sarah B. Pomeroy, author of *Goddesses, Whores, Wives and Slaves: Women in Classical Antiquity* (New York, 1975). The present volume, which includes a number of new papers in addition to those in the journal, is the first book in English to offer classical and non-classical readers alike an opportunity to learn about the research being done in this field.

The documentary evidence for the lives of women in antiquity is fragmentary and difficult to interpret. With the exception of poems composed by female lyric poets, our knowledge is confined to a male perspective. The papers on Sappho by Stigers and Winkler in this volume take advantage of this rare opportunity to explore a specifically feminine poetic consciousness.

Research on women in antiquity has tended to move in two directions. The first line of research has emphasized the methodological problems involved in studying women in the literary texts: one such problem is the dichotomy between women's apparent confinement to the private sphere in everyday life, and their dominant, often public role in Attic drama. I chose to examine this problem in my paper in order to epitomize and emphasize the general difficulties inherent in studying women in classical literature, and the interdisciplinary perspectives that must be brought to bear on the issue.

In fact, life and imagination seem consistently to contradict each

xi

other on the subject of women throughout ancient literature. Griffiths and Cameron explore this dichotomy, and revise previous assumptions about the relation between life and poetry in the Hellenistic period. The papers in this volume by Arthur, Zeitlin, Perkell and myself share with earlier scholars a sense that the role of women in ancient literature can only be understood by examining the larger cognitive and symbolic systems through which epic and dramatic poets apprehended and structured their world and by placing the concept of women in these texts into the context of a full reading of the individual works being interpreted. In studying these literary texts carefully we examine, in effect, the origins of the Western attitude towards women.

The rest of the papers in this book, however, adopt the second major line of research and explore aspects of the social, economic or legal place of women in Mycenaean Greece (Billigmeier and Turner), Etruscan Italy (Bonfante), Roman Egypt (Pomeroy) and Republican and Imperial Rome (Carp and Richlin), the literacy of Greek women (Cole), and the evaluation of women's role in history by Herodotus, the first Greek historian (Dewald). The authors of these papers emphasize the methodological problems involved in using such relatively untapped sources as the economic records of the Linear B tablets, Etruscan art or the private correspondence of Cicero for women's history. They explore the conflicting picture of literacy, female land ownership, or adultery, for example, given in literary, historical, epigraphical, papyrological or legal sources. The Herodotus of Dewald's study treats women in an extraordinarily different fashion from the contemporary Attic dramatic poets, and raises further questions about the relation between life, genre and ideology in classical Greece.

The number and quality of the papers submitted to this volume testify to the growing excitement and sophistication of research in this area. Much remains to be done — art, philosophy, and the medical texts, for example, remain relatively untapped, while the present volume raises further difficult literary and historical questions to be answered with the help not only of the precise technical skills of the classicist, but of work done in other related disciplines like anthropology or psychology.

I want to express my gratitude to Wendy Martin, editor of *Women's Studies*, to the many anonymous referees whose comments and criticisms helped to shape and improve the *Women's Studies* issue, and to all those who submitted papers for consideration in this volume, many of whose papers deserved to be published here had space permitted.

Helene P. Foley
New York

Contributors

MARYLIN ARTHUR — Assistant Professor, Wesleyan University, Middletown, Connecticut. "The Tortoise and the Mirror: Erinna P.S.I. 1090," *Classical World* **74**.2 (1980), and "The Limits of Transcendence: Male and Female in Hesiod's *Theogony*," forthcoming in *La Donna Antica*, eds. Vegetti and Lanza (in Italian).

JON-CHRISTIAN BILLIGMEIER — Johns Hopkins University, Maryland — formerly at Center for Hellenic Studies, Washington, D.C. Two articles in *Talanta* and "Towards a Decipherment of Cypro-Minoan," AJA **80** (1976).

LARISSA BONFANTE — Professor of Classics and Chairman of the Department of Classics at New York University. *Etruscan Dress*, a translation of *The Plays of Hrotswitha of Ganderheim* and *Out of Etruria* (forthcoming).

ALAN CAMERON — Anthon Professor of Latin Languages and Literature and Chairman of the Department at Columbia University, New York City, N.Y. *Claudian: Poetry and Propaganda in the Court of Honorius, Porphyrius the Charioteer Circus Factions: Blues and Greens at Rome and Byzantium*, the forthcoming *The Greek Anthology: from Meleager to Planudes*.

TERESA CARP — Assistant Professor of Classics at the University of Oregon. "*Puer Senex* in Ancient and Medieval Thought" (forthcoming in *Latomus*) and "Samuel, Teiresias and the Way Home" (forthcoming in *California Studies in Classical Antiquity*).

SUSAN COLE — Assistant Professor, University of Illinois at

Chicago Circle, Chicago, Ill. Forthcoming book on the *Samothracian Mysteries.*

CAROLYN DEWALD — Assistant Professor at University of Southern California — formerly at Stanford University. An article on Horace in *Pacific Coast Philology.*

HELENE P. FOLEY — Assistant Professor at Barnard College, Columbia University, New York, New York — formerly at Stanford University. "Sex and State in Ancient Greece," *Diacritics* **5** (Winter 1975), "'Reverse Similes' and Sex Roles in the *Odyssey*," *Arethusa* **11**, Nos. 1 and 2 (Spring and Fall, 1978), "'The Female Intruder' Reconsidered: Women in Aristophanes' *Lysistrata* and *Ecclesiazusae*," forthcoming in *Classical Philology*, and "Marriage and Death in Euripides' *Iphigeneia at Aulis*," forthcoming in *Arethusa.*

FREDERICK GRIFFITHS — Associate Professor at Amherst College, Amherst, Massachusetts. *Theocritus at Court*, and many articles on Hellenistic poetry and on classical influences in modern literature.

CHRISTINE PERKELL — Assistant Professor of Classics at Dartmouth College, New Hampshire. "A Reading of Virgil's Fourth *Georgic*," *Phoenix* **32** (1978).

SARAH B. POMEROY — Associate Professor of Classics at Hunter College and the Graduate School, CUNY and Coordinator of the Women's Studies Program at Hunter. *Goddesses, Whores, Wives, and Slaves: Women in Classical Antiquity.*

AMY RICHLIN — Assistant Professor at Dartmouth College, formerly at Rutgers University, New Brunswick, New Jersey. "The Meaning of *irrumare* in Catullus and Martial," *Classical Philology*, October 1980.

EVA S. STIGERS — Wheaton College, Norton, Massachusetts. "Retreat from the Male: Catullus 62 and Sappho's Erotic Flowers," *Ramus* **6** (1977).

JUDITH TURNER — completing her Ph.D. in Ancient History at University of California at Santa Barbara with a dissertation on "Priestesses in Ancient Greece".

JACK WINKLER — Assistant Professor at Stanford University, Palo Alto, California — formerly at Yale University. "Lollianus and the Desperadoes," *Journal of Hellenic Studies* **100** (1980).

FROMA I. ZEITLIN — Associate Professor of Classics at Princeton University, New Jersey. "Language, Structure, and the Son of Oedipus in Aeschylus' *Seven Against Thebes*: a Semiotic Study of the Shield Scene." Also, numerous articles on Greek and Roman literature and on women in antiquity.

The socio-economic roles of women in Mycenaean Greece: A brief survey from evidence of the Linear B tablets

JON-CHRISTIAN BILLIGMEIER

Center for Hellenic Studies

and JUDY A. TURNER

University of California, Santa Barbara

OUR KNOWLEDGE of the social and economic life of Bronze Age Greece comes mainly from four sources:[1]

1)   from archaeology in the narrow sense, the study of the material remains (buildings, artifacts, utensils, tools, cult objects, plant and animal remains);[2]

2)   from works of art, which include vivid portraits of Minoans and Mycenaeans involved in activities ranging from hunting to religion, from war to athletics;[3]

3)   from literary sources, the most important of which are the Homeric poems and the works of Hesiod;

4)   from contemporary documents, the Linear B tablets.

The evidence of art and of the physical remains is rarely clear enough to permit an adequate assessment of social relationships. A fresco can be interpreted several different ways; a new pottery style may be due to importation, imitation of foreign models, or the immigration of a new people. Language is so central to human experience that non-linguistic evidence must always be inexact in illuminating social realities.

The evidence of literature is verbal and very precise, but it is also highly suspect. The *Iliad* and the *Odyssey* are based on centuries of oral composition; so too is much of Hesiod's poetry. Some may see "Homeric society" as basically Mycenaean,[4] while others maintain that it represents Greek social realities during the Dark Ages after the fall of Mycenae,[5] but it seems safest to assume that the society portrayed by Homer is a mixture of Bronze Age, Dark Age, and Lyric Age elements combined by the imagination of generations of oral poets. One should not use the poems as sources for understanding the social and economic realities of any period unless there is strong supporting evidence from art, archaeology, or contemporary documents.[6]

The fourth main source, the Linear B tablets, offers the best hope for understanding Mycenaean Greek society and is an indispensible tool in elucidating the religion, economics, geography, and demography of Greece during the Late Helladic period. These documents are as contemporary as the art and the material remains and as verbal and precise as Homer. Despite their exclusive focus on the immediacies of everyday life, they give us a glimpse at complexities that cannot be imagined from other sources.[7]

This study of the socio-economic roles of women in Mycenaean Greece will confine itself to evidence gleaned from the Linear B documents. We do not suggest that archaeological, artistic, and even literary testimony have no worth; on the contrary, a study integrating information from all these sources with what is known from the tablets would have great value. Since, however, Linear B does give the most precise and accurate information available on Bronze Age Greek society, this brief inquiry will be restricted to data from the Linear B tablets.

The Linear B texts from Knossos, Pylos, Mycenae, and Thebes involve only public activities of concern to palace authorities. Parentage of individuals is sometimes mentioned, but family life is not discussed; thus we learn nothing about women's work in the home. On the other hand, numerous women's occupations outside the home appear in the tablets. These occupations fall into two main groupings:

1) craftswomen and other women who do skilled and un-skilled manual labor and
2) sacerdotal women.

Craftswomen who work for the *woikos* of a divinity,[8] such as the textile workers in the service of Potnia at Thebes, could be in-cluded in either group, but are best placed in the first, since their activities involve their crafts and not ritual cult functions. A hand-ful of women belong in neither group, for they seem to enjoy high social status but have secular rather than religious connections.

The great majority of women mentioned in the tablets are skilled workers; at Pylos they number over 1400, roughly twice the number of craftsmen.[9] Women in crafts are usually listed by occupation, followed by the ideogram WOMAN plus numeral, rather than by personal name. Unlike the sacerdotal women, the craftswomen appear to hold no land, either as groups or as indivi-duals. Most of the more than thirty women's occupations specified are connected with textiles and clothing, including *ālakateiai* "spinners," *histeiai* "weavers," *pektriai* "wool-carders," and *lineiai* "flax-workers." Leather-working occupies both men and women, as is shown by the Pylos tablet Ub 1318, where five individuals receive hides to work into leather items such as saddle-bags and sandals. The three men (Augeiateus, Mestianor, Myrteus) and two women (Wordieia, Amphehia) are mentioned by personal name on Ub 1318, a rarity for craftspeople and a possible indica-tion of their importance. The male *raptēres* and female *raptriai* "stitchers" also seem to be engaged in the making of leather items; on Ub 1315 reins, halters, and headbands for horses are men-tioned.[10] Grain-processing involves *meletriai* "grain-grinders" and *sitokhowoi* "grain-pourers" (= measurers). Household chores (pre-sumably in the palace) employ the *amphiquoloi* "attendants," a term with religious connections, as well as *lewotrokhowoi* "bath-pourers," whose numbers — 38 — on one Pylos tablet suggest that the Pylians kept themselves squeaky-clean, though an alternative explanation is offered below. Most of the names of these women's occupations have no male counterpart; exceptions are *raptēr* and *raptria* discussed above and *histeus* and *histeia*, male and female weaver. This would seem to imply that most of these trades were followed only by women.

Many working women are classified by ethnic adjectives in addition to or instead of occupational terms. Several ethnics at Pylos refer to places in the eastern Aegean: Lemnos, Miletos, Knidos, and possibly Asia (Lydia), Khios, and Zephyria (identified by some with Halikarnassos) as well.[11] Were these women captured by the Achaean expedition to Asia Minor described by Homer and by Hittite sources? Certainly Homer mentions frequently the practice of taking captives, mainly women, in war and putting them to work back home. Ventris and Chadwick believed them to be war captives and supported this contention by connecting the Linear B word *ra-wi-ja-ja*, which occurs on three Pylos tablets (Aa 807, Ab 586, Ad 686) with Doric *lāiā*, Ionic *lēiē* "booty."[12] Even if we accept this equation, based on a highly speculative etymology, it does not prove that the women described by ethnics and/or occupational terms are captives.[13] On the contrary, the latter are never described as *ra-wi-ja-ja*, a word used but thrice in all the Pylos archives, in each case referring to women at *pu-ro ke-re-za*, apparently a part or suburb of Pylos, and nowhere else. Is it likely that the term would be used for captives at only one place, when *all* working women were captives? To avoid this difficulty, Chadwick subsequently proposed that the ethnic women be considered slaves bought at places to which the ethnics refer.[14] Two of the ethnics, however, demonstrably refer to places within the Pylian kingdom: the *ti-nwa-si-ja*, women of Tinwatos, described as weavers on Ad 684, and *e-wi-ri-pi-ja* on Aa 60, women of *e-wi-ri-po*, Euripos.[15] This makes the identification of all the ethnic women as either war captives or slaves highly improbable.

The women described by ethnic adjectives are more likely to be refugees than captives or slaves. The lack of occupational designation may suggest that they were engaged in unskilled labor, but nothing indicates servile status. This was a time of wars and of large movements of peoples, including the famous "Peoples of the Sea"; Pylos itself was about to be successfully attacked. The presence at Pylos of refugees from places within the Messenian kingdom and from Mycenaean Greek colonies in Asia Minor would

not be surprising.[16] Xenophon mentions (*Memorabilia* 117. 2-8)
free women refugees being put to work making clothing and baking bread to support themselves in besieged Athens during the
Peloponnesian War. In late antiquity, in Alexandria and elsewhere,
"bath attendants" take care of the sick and the wounded.[17] Thus
the occupational categories on the tablets are consistent with what
we would expect refugees to be doing from the evidence of late
periods. Refugee women would do the same work as native
women who are named by occupation; the men would be at the
front. It is noteworthy in this regard that the gap between the
number of male and female workers can be largely filled by adding
to the working males the soldiers and rowers listed in the Pylos An
tablets as having been mobilized to prepare for an attack by sea.

An alternative suggestion is that the ethnics designate guilds of
skilled craftswomen whose ancestors came from abroad, pursuing
crafts for which their places of origin were famous.[18] Thus Aswian
and Zephyrian women were known as flax-workers (Ad 326, Ad
664), Khians as *o-nu-ke-ja* (Ab 194, Ad 675), Milesians as spinners,
and Tinwasians as weavers (Ad 684). Usually the occupation is not
mentioned, as it would be obvious to the scribe, but fortunately
for us it occasionally is. These women — or their forebears —
would have been drawn to Pylos by its emergence as a textile-
making center.[19]

The tablets list some men as sons of women with specific occupational or ethnic designations, as for example "sons of the flax-
workers" or "sons of the Tinwasian weavers." Ventris and Chadwick originally compared these phrases with an alleged Ugaritic
bn amht kt, "sons of the slave-women of Kition," a parallel seemingly supportive of their assumption that Pylian working women
are slaves.[20] The reading is, however, a mirage; Dussaud now reads
the last word as *rt*, not *kt*; *rt* is a personal name occurring elsewhere at Ugarit.[21] There is no evidence that the mothers of these
Pylian men are anything but free craftswomen, whether of native
or of foreign extraction.

A few men are listed as sons of male workers, as are the "sons
of rowers" on Ad 684, but the metronymics are far commoner.
On tablets Oe 106 and V 659 from Mycenae, women are described

as daughters of other women. It is conceivable that descent was reckoned matrilineally among the humbler segments of society, whereas patronymics following the personal names of male aristocrats, such as *Alektruōn Etewoklewehios* (Alektryon, son of Eteokles), show that the upper classes were patrilineal, at least as regards the ancestry of men.

A considerable controversy raged for some years over the size of monthly rations given men, women, and children of both sexes in work groups.[22] There seems no doubt now that ordinary men and women alike were given a ration of T2 of wheat or double that of barley (exact modern equivalents of Mycenaean measures are uncertain), while children received half that.[23] Thus on the Pylos tablet Ab 899, 8 women, 3 girls, and 3 boys receive T22 (8 × 2 + 6) of wheat and figs. On Ab 789, 6 women and 9 children draw T21 (6 × 2 + 9) and on Ab 745, 2 women and one child are given T5 (2 × 2 + 1). On Au 658 from Mycenae, 20 men receive rations of T40 (20 × 2) of wheat. On Am 819 from Knossos, 18 men and 8 boys draw a total ration of T97 3/4 of barley for a month. The only way to get exact figures from this equation is to assume that these boys (significantly listed with men and not with women) are old enough to receive adult rations. Dividing T97 3/4 by 26 (18 + 8), we get T3 3/4 of barley for each worker.[24] Since barley rations in antiquity were generally double those of wheat, we have here further evidence that the basic monthly wheat ration for men as well as women was T2.[25] This equality among the sexes in the matter of rations distinguishes Mycenaean Greece sharply from contemporary Near Eastern civilizations such as Babylonia, where a man received three times the rations of a woman, and may reflect the greater importance of women in the Mycenaean labor force and perhaps in the society in general.[26]

Sacerdotal women — priestesses and other female religious personnel — constitute the second main group of women in the Mycenaean tablets. They differ from the craftswomen in that they are fewer in number and are customarily named, have aristocratic connections, hold tracts of land, and are probably of high status.[27]

The most prestigious sacerdotal women appear to be the priestesses (*hiereiai*) who number four at Pylos and at least three at

Knossos. Compared with this there are seven or possibly eight priests documented at Pylos and only one doubtful reference to a priest at Knossos.[28] At Pylos one priestess's name cannot be read; the names of the other three are Ka-wa-ra (Qa 1289), Ke-i-ja (Qa 1303), and Erita, the priestess of Pa-ki-ja-na. The cult of Pa-ki-ja-na seems to be connected with the goddess Potnia, the chief female deity at Pylos. At Knossos there is a priestess of the Winds (*a-ne-mo i-je-re-ja*, KN Fp 1). Another priestess of the Winds serves the cult at Utanos (Ed 317). This cult seems to be popular on Krete, for the third known priestess, whose sanctuary is at Mt. Dikte, may also be a priestess of the Winds.

Some priestesses, such as Erita, are wealthy land owners. At Pylos, Erita appears on several tablets (Ep 704) and not only owns land, but also has her own assistants (*do-e-ra*) who in turn are prosperous and are landholders. One *do-e-ra*, listed on the same tablet, owns nearly as much land as Erita. Erita's dispute with the local *dāmos* over land-leases suggests that priestly women are legally independent.

The tablets document other female religious personnel including the Keybearers (*klāwiphoroi*), the *ki-ri-te-wi-ja*, unnamed women forming a kind of religious corporation, and the *do-e-ra*, or assistants. Tablet Ep 704 mentions all of the above-listed types of sacerdotal women in connection with the sanctuary at Pa-ki-ja-na.

Another group, the *ma-ri-ne-we-ja* (perhaps semi-sacerdotal women) is known from Thebes and seems to be linked to textile manufacture on the sacred precincts of Potnia there.[29]

The Keybearers are important cult officials. They joined in donating temple-bronze for military purposes during the emergency before the fall of Pylos. Their ability to dispense the sacred treasure suggests that their duties involve the economic concerns of the deity's estate. Karpatia, a Keybearer of the sanctuary at Pylos, appears on several tablets (Ed 714, Eb 338). This fact probably reflects her importance in the cult. Characteristically, she associates with aristocrats and has land holdings.

The *ki-ri-te-wi-ja* (the etymology of whose name is uncertain)[30] appear only on the tablets at Knossos and Pylos. *Ki-ri-te-wi-ja* are unnamed as individuals, but comprise a board of women collectively possessing wealth and prestige. Tablet Ep 704 records their extensive land holdings between two notations of the priestess Erita's holdings. Their close association with the priestess and their position of responsibility for a valuable, large supply of wheat at the sanctuary imply that the *ki-ri-te-wi-ja* are upper class.

Pylian tablet An 607 gives the parentage of the *ki-ri-te-wi-ja* of the goddess Do-qe-ja. In each case the women who are *ki-ri-te-wi-ja* have mothers who are *do-e-ra* of Do-qe-ja or fathers who are her *do-e-ro*. This suggests that sacerdotal status was hereditary in either the female or the male line, but that a person could belong to a different priestly group than her/his parent(s), though serving the same deity.[31]

The *do-e-ra* are female attendants or servants who are mentioned only in a religious context and should be considered among the sacerdotal women of possibly high status. The etymological connection of *do-e-ra* with *doulē*,[32] even if sound, does not prove a servile or slave status for these women (cf. θεράπων "henchman," "attendant," later Attic "slave").[33] Many *do-e-ra* appear in the Knossos and Pylos tablets; Huamia (Eb 416, Ep 704), E-ra-ta-ra, Po-so-re-ja (En 609, Eo 224), I-ni-ja, and Sima (En 609) are but a few examples. *Do-e-ra* are categorized according to whom they serve. Some may be directly in the service of the individual, such as a priestess; others directly serve the god and are called *te-o-jo do-e-ra/ro*, servants of the god(dess). One, a woman named Huamia, is associated with the Keybearer Karpatia and a priestess. *Do-e-ra* and *do-e-ro* are (frequently) described as belonging to various named deities (Artemis, Diwia, Do-qe-ja) and to "the priestess" and other prominent persons. Some hold land and are named — usually characteristics of persons of religious affiliation and/or high social position.

The duties of the *do-e-ra* seem to involve sacred metals, such as gold and bronze. Tablet An 607 documents the parentage of *ki-ri-te-wi-ja*: two mothers are *do-e-ra* who are married to bronze-smiths. On tablet Ae 303 *do-e-ra* of the priestess appear to have charge over sacred gold (or gold of the *hieron*), perhaps serving in a custodial capacity. The important responsibility for the sanctuary's treasure argues against the opinion that *do-e-ra* are of low or slave status because the *do-e-ra* in tablet An 607 are grouped in relation to the status of their parents. On the tablet at least one parent of each woman is a *do-e-ra/ro*; several women have both parents as *do-e-ra/ro*. Four *ki-ri-te-wi-ja* are daughters of *do-e-ra* of Do-qe-ja and have fathers who are bronze-smiths.

Contrary to the view that these family relationships indicate low status, there may be a requirement that a *ki-ri-te-wi-ja's* parent be a *do-e-ra/ro* of a divinity in order to insure the high or noble status of the sanctuary personnel. The connection of the *do-e-ra* with bronze-smiths may be an indication of high status as well, since smithery associated with the sanctuary's sacred bronze or gold seems to be a privileged, high-ranking, or even hereditary occupation. Some bronze-smiths had *do-e-ro* as assistants or servants of their own (the Jn tablets). Several bronze-smiths are designated *po-ti-ni-ja-we-jo* "dedicated to the Divine Mistress." Thus these smiths are consecrated directly to the chief deity in the same way the *te-o-jo do-e-ra* belong to her. In a society which has bronze as a pre-eminent metal used for religious and practical purposes, the bronze-smiths and the above-mentioned sacerdotal women probably are among the most important of the sanctuary personnel.

Secular women of high social status appear in a few places in the tablets. At Knossos, Perieia holds an orchard plot (Uf 1031); nothing indicates that she has religious connections. In fact, the context argues against it. The same is true of the landholder Kessandra at Pylos (Fg 368, 828). We must certainly reject the assertion of C.J. Thomas that "women held property only in their capacity of religious functionaries."[34] At Pylos, tablet Vn 1191 lists women's names preceded by those of men in the genitive, presumably representing their husbands. One of these men, Kaesamenos, is a member of the King's *hequetai* or Followers, an indication that some of these couples are aristocrats. One pair, Mestianor and Wordieia, are elsewhere (Ub 1318) involved with leather-making, an occupation which is not commonly considered suitable for aristocrats. Consequently, the aristocratic associations of all the members of the group are unclear. Pu_2-ke-qi-ri, who is probably a woman,[35] appears as an inspector (Ta 711) of vessels designated as belonging to the Queen. Perhaps the Queen had a staff of female officials to look after her property. All things considered, however, the number of such secular female officials was probably small.

This survey of the evidence for the socio-economic status of women in the Linear B tablets suggests that women were an essential part of the Mycenaean Greek labor force, skilled and unskilled. In the upper class, priestesses and other sacerdotal women were as prominent as their male counterparts. These facts, along with the equal rations given to women and men and the metronymic designations of some men, suggest that women in Mycenaean Greece may have enjoyed a more equal socio-economic status than they did in Classical Hellas.

Acknowledgements

We wish to thank David Young of the University of California, Santa Barbara, and Susan Cole of the University of Illinois, Chicago Circle, for reading our manuscript and making helpful suggestions. We express here our appreciation to Sarah Pomeroy, Marilyn Skinner, and Helene Foley for their help and encouragement on the way. We are also grateful to Bernard Knox, Director of the Center for Hellenic Studies for permission to quote from a recent lecture.

Orthographical note

Transliterations of Linear B words employ dashes to divide one group of letters, representing one syllabic sign, from another. Thus, for example, *ki-ri-te-wi-ja*, written with five syllabograms in Linear B. Normalized transcriptions, such as *hiereia* for *i-je-re-ja*, are not written with dashes, for they are not a sign by sign transliteration of the Linear B. Proper names, such as Do-qe-ja and Po-so-re-ja, are not italicized.

Bibliographical note

The following abbreviations are used for works referred to in the Notes:
1. Vermeule, *Greece* = Emily Vermeule, *Greece in the Bronze Age* (Chicago 1964, 1972).
2. Tritsch, *Minoica* = Franz Josef Tritsch, "The women of Pylos," in *Minoica* (Festschrift for Johannes Sundwall) Ernst Grumach, ed., 402-445.
3. *Documents* = Michael Ventris and John Chadwick, *Documents in Mycenaean Greek* (1st edition, Cambridge 1956).

4. *Documents II* = John Chadwick, *Documents in Mycenaean Greek* (2nd edition, Cambridge 1973).
5. AJA = *American Journal of Archaeology*.

Notes

1. The physical sciences are now making an important contribution to knowledge of the Bronze Age. Palaeobotany and palaeozoology can tell us what people ate, spectroscopy can elucidate the structure and origin of clay in pottery, while vulcanologists can judge the effects of the Thera/Santorini eruption, dated to the middle of the Second Millennium B.C.

      The application of these sciences to efforts to understand the nature of Mycenaean *society* is, however, still in its infancy.
2. A standard work is Vermeule's *Greece*.
3. For a succinct overview, see Reynold Higgins, *Minoan and Mycenaean Art* (London 1967).
4. As for example, Martin P. Nilsson, *Homer and Mycenae* (London 1933).
5. See for example, M.I. Finley, *The World of Odysseus* (New York 1954, 1965).
6. Emily Vermeule remarks (*Greece*, 312): "whatever the Greeks knew about their own past was surely very different from reality." Bernard Knox put it thus in a recent talk at the Smithsonian Institution (May 28, 1980): "The memory of Kalliope, the epic Muse, is erratic and selective . . . She sings, like Achilles, *klea andrōn*, the famous deeds of men, but magnificent though her song may be, we cannot take it as truth unless it is confirmed by her sister Kleio, the Muse of History. Without external supporting evidence, a comparative study of epic traditions suggests, we should suspend judgement not only about the heroes' deeds, but even about their existence."
7. Vermeule, *Greece*, 297.
8. The *woikos*, literally "household," is defined by L.R. Palmer (*Nestor*, February 1979, 1138) as an industrial complex with divine connections.
9. Tritsch, *Minoica*, 428.
10. *Documents II*, 413, 489-493.
11. *Documents*, 145, 156; *Documents II*, 410, 417.
12. *Documents*, 156, 162.
13. Tritsch, *Minoica*, 428.
14. *Documents II*, 410, 417.
15. For discussions of the Tinwasians and Euripians, especially the former, see Alan P. Sainer, "An Index of the Place Names at Pylos," *Studi Micenei ed Egeo-Antalolici* 17 (1976) 17-63, especially 17, 40, and 59, as well as Tritsch, *Minoica*, 429, and *Documents II*, 410. Sainer's confusing suggestion that *Tinwatos may be "outside the borders of the kingdom, though subject to the king of Pylos" (17) should be set aside, as it is contradicted by his discussion on pages 40 and 59 as well as by

tablets Jo 438.21 and On 300.12, which show that a certain *Te-po-se-u* was *ko-re-tēr* (roughly the equivalent of mayor) of *Tinwatos (the ethnic adjective is used). The *ko-re-tēres* of other Pylian towns, such as *Pa-ki-ja-ne* (the ethnic adjective is used here too in place of the actual place name), the religious center, *A-ke-re-wa* and *Ti-mi-ti-ja*, also appear on Jo 438, which is apparently a record of "a tribute of gold from the chieftains (*basileus*, *ko-re-te*, *mo-ro-pa₂*) of surrounding villages" (*Documents*, 359). Chadwick further suggests (*Documents II*, 514) that *Te-po-se-u* and *Tinwatos are to be located at the "end" of the Further Province (*pe-ra₃- ko-ra-i-ja*), agreeing in this with Tritsch. Thus the Tinwasians are definitely within the Pylian kingdom and probably part of the Further Province.

Sainer's location of *Tinwatos as possibly on the east coast of the Messenian Gulf fits well with the position of the Further Province ("beyond Aigolaion") in the Pamisos valley. Euripos, given its name, is surely on the sea; Ventris and Chadwick (*Documents*, 145) tentatively situate it near the Methoni Strait, which divides the island of Sapientsa from the mainland. Since "women of Kythera" are mentioned at Pylos (Aa 506+), we may perhaps assume that the attack that the Pylians were preparing for (see *Documents*, 183-194, for these preparations) was coming from sea-borne raiders operating off the southern coasts of the Peloponnesos. Civilians, or at least the women and children, had been evacuated from exposed places along these coasts.

16. See the discussion in *Documents II*, 410. For archaeological evidence for a Greek colony at Miletos in the Mycenaean period, see C. Weichert, "Die Ausgrabungen beim Athena-Tempel in Milet," in *Istanbuler Mitteilungen* 7 (1957) 102-132, 9-10 (1959-1960) 1-96 and by the same author *Neue Deutsche Ausgrabungen im Mittelmeer Gebiet* (1959).

17. Tritsch, *Minoica*, 438.

18. Margareta Lindgren, in her invaluable prosopographical work, *The People of Pylos* (Uppsala Studies in Ancient Mediterranean and Near Eastern Civilizations 3: 1973), agrees (II, 92): "it may also be possible to assume the conversion of an original ethnical designation into a sort of occupational designation for specialists with a common province (at least originally — the group being renewed by people from elsewhere in the course of time)."

19. For a detailed study of the linen industry at Pylos, see A.L.H. Robkin's new study, "The Agricultural Year, the Commodity *SA* and the Linen Industry of Mycenaean Pylos," *AJA* 83 (1979) 469-474. Robkin estimates Pylos' production of fiber at 1696 talents, equal to 108,342 lbs. or 49,184 kg. and concludes that the existence of "a thriving linen industry is likely . . ."

20. *Documents*, 156.

21. Tritsch, *Minoica*, 435. *Rt* occurs in the phrase *bn rt*, "son of *Rt*" in Text 400.iii.19 (Cyrus Gordon, *Ugaritic Handbook*, 178).

22. The principal antagonists were John Chadwick and L.R. Palmer. For the controversy between them see *Documents*, *Documents II*, Palmer's *The Interpretation of Mycenaean Greek Texts* (Oxford 1963), as well as

letters to the editor of *Nestor* between August 1, 1975 and August 1, 1977 by a number of scholars, including Palmer and Chadwick. Palmer seeks to prove that certain supervisors denoted by the ideogram or abbreviation DA were men and received T5. On Knossos tablet Am 819, where 18 men and 8 "boys" receive T97 3/4 of barley, he allots T5 to the 18 men for a total of 90, one each to seven boys, and 3/4 to the eighth boy, whom he assumes to have been especially small. Even if all this were true (for a better explanation see the text of this article), it would not prove that the *normal* rations in a given type of grain are any different for men than for women. For T5 of barley is the equivalent of T2 1/2 of wheat, which is close to what women in Pylos (Ab 745+) and men at Mycenae (Au 658) receive. As for the DA (and TA), their rations are extra large because they are supervisory personnel. There is no good evidence that the DA are men; Chadwick suggests (*Documents II*, 418) that they are women workers charged with additional supervisory responsibilities and are rewarded with extra payments.

23.   As one can see from Pylos tablets Ab 745, Ab 789, and Ab 899. The smaller children would still be with their mothers. The *ko-wo* on Am 819 are working with the men and are probably teenagers, easily able to outeat adults! Thus it is not surprising to find them receiving men's rations. See the discussion by Yves Duhoux in *Nestor*, December 1, 1976, 1087-1088.

24.   T3 3/4 is equal to Z90, where Z, the smallest Mycenaean measure of capacity, is represented by an ideogram in the shape of a cup. Dividing Z90 by 30, the number of days in an average month, we get Z3 as a daily ration. See Duhoux's letter in *Nestor* cited above (note 23). He regards this as the only correct explanation of the figures on Am 819.

25.   For the ratio of barley to wheat, see *Documents II*, 420 and, *inter alia*, the letters of Yves Duhoux (*op. cit.*, note 23) and Daniel A. Was (February 1, 1976, 1031-1032) to *Nestor*.

26.   Figures given by Palmer in *Nestor*, November 1, 1082-1083.

27.   As on Pylos tablet Eb 317, where a priestess and a Keybearer hold leases with the Followers and Westreus, a prominent priest and noble. A priestess, probably Erita, claims on Eb 297 that she has an *etonion* — a privileged type of land-holding — on behalf of her god. The only other Pylian to have an *etonion* is Amphimedes on Ep 539.14; he is one of the most powerful men in the kingdom.

28.   Margareta Lindgren, (*op. cit.*, note 18) 56, for Pylos; for Knossos we made our own count.

29.   L.R. Palmer, *Nestor* (February, 1979), 1338-1339, proposes (rightly, we believe) that the *ma-ri-ne-we-ja* are connected with the god Ma-ri-ne-u, who is associated with cloth at Mycenae (X 508) and at Knossos possesses his own *woikos*. He reads Ma-ri-ne-u as *Mallineus*, "God of Woolens," a functional deity.

30.   From *krithai* "barley," *chriō* "anoint" or *kritai* "chosen, exquisite." The last is the most likely of the etymologies. Compare the Linear B word *ki-ri-ta*. For a full discussion, see Lindgren, (*op. cit.*, note 18) 81-82. We follow her suggestion to translate "corporation of religious women."

31. See Appendix I for the exact genealogies.
32. For a brief discussion and bibliography, see Lindgren (*op. cit.*, note 18) 36. Since the series of Linear B syllabic signs transliterated with *r* stand for *l*, as well, *do-e-ra/ro* could be *do(h)erā/ros* or *do(h)elā/los*. Or the latter could be a possible ancestor of *doulos* and *doulē*, with vowel contraction (but Homer never uses uncontracted forms of this word, which is very rare, and not the usual word for servant or slave in the *Iliad* and *Odyssey*). An alternative etymology derives *doulos* and *doulē* from Akkadian *dullu*, "Arbeit, Dienst, Ritual." If a **no-e-ra/ro* had appeared in Linear B everywhere *do-e-ra/ro* does, no one would have ever translated the word as "servant" or "slave," for the context suggests a more exalted status.
33. Robert Renehan, *Greek Lexicographical Notes* (= *Hypomnemata*, Heft 45) [Göttingen 1975] s.v. θεράπων. If the words *do-e-ro* and *do-e-ra* are connected with *doulos* and *doulē* at all, we must assume that the words meant "assistant," "subordinate" in Mycenaean times and only later "slave," "servant," thus paralleling the development of *therapōn*: in Homer, "henchman," "attendant," but in later Attic often "slave". There is no definite evidence for anything like slavery in Mycenaean texts.
34. C.G. Thomas, "Matriarchy in Early Greece: The Bronze and Dark Ages," *Arethusa*, 6, no. 2 (1973) 183. Thomas is speaking of Pylos, but there is no reason to believe the situation would have been different there than at Knossos. Except for a few magnates, all the male Pylian landholders seem to have religious connections, too, yet we must not imagine that land was exclusively in the control of the clergy.
35. Among the personal names ending in *-i*, ten are clearly those of women, but only three of men (*Documents*, 95-96, 101). The association with the *qe-ra-na wa-na-se-wi-ja*, vessels belonging to the Queen, strengthens the probability that Pu₂-ke-qi-ri is a woman.

Appendix I

GENEALOGY OF THE KI-RI-TE-WI-JA OF DO-QE-JA (PYLOS TABLET AN 607)

I.   *do-qe-ja* do-e-ro *pa-te* = ma-te-de ku-te-re-u-pi
     6 *do-qe-ja* ki-ri-te-wi-ja

II. *do-qe-ja* do-e-ro *pa-te* = ma-te-de di-wi-ja do-e-ra
     3 *do-qe-ja* ki-ri-te-wi-ja

III. *do-qe-ja* do-e-ra *ma-te* = pa-te-de ka-ke-u
     1 *do-qe-ja* ki-ri-te-wi-ja

IV. *do-qe-ja* do-e-ra *ma-te* = pa-te-de ka-ke-u
    3 *do-qe-ja* ki-ri-te-wi-ja

N.B. pa-te = patēr "father"; ma-te = mātēr "mother"; ka-ke-u = khalkeus "bronze-smith."

Conclusions: Twice the ki-ri-te-wi-ja of Do-qe-ja derive their status as devotees of that deity from their fathers (I-II) and twice from their mothers (III-IV). The parent who served Do-qe-ja is listed first, the other parent, followed by enclitic *-de*, is mentioned second. It may be concluded that in religious matters, at least, status could be inherited either through the male or female line.

Appendix II

LIST OF WOMEN'S OCCUPATIONAL DESIGNATIONS FOUND IN THE LINEAR B TABLETS

1. a-ke-ti-ra$_2$, PY TH, nom. pl.: *askētriai* "practitioners of a trade" or *akestriai* "seamstresses?"
   a-ke-ti-ri-ja, KN PY, nom. pl.: variant of the above.
   a-ke-ti-ra$_2$-o, PY, gen. pl.
   a-ke-ti-ri-ja-i, PY MY, dat. pl.
   cf. a-ze-ti-ri-ja?
2. a-ne-mo-i-je-re-ja, KN, gen. pl. nom. sing.: *anemōn hiereia* "priestess of the winds."
3. a-pi-qo-ro, PY TH, nom. & gen. pl., dat. sing.?: *amphiquoloi* "attendants."
4. a-pu-ko-wo-ko, PY, nom. & gen. pl.: *ampuk(o)worgoi* "headband makers."
5. a-ra-ka-te-ja, KN PY TH, nom. pl.: *ālakateiai* "spinning-women."
   a-ra-ka-te-ja-o, PY, gen. pl.
6. a-ze-ti-ri-ja, KN, nom. pl.: variant of a-ke-ti-ri-ja?
7. DA (ideogram), KN PY: supervisor? Associated with WOMAN

ideogram in some places, with MAN in others. See discussion in note 21.

8. do-e-ra, KN PY, nom. sing, & pl.: *dohelā, -ai* (?) "attendant," "assistant" (a better translation than "slave," "servant").

9. e-ke-ro-qo-no, PY, nom. & gen. pl.: *enkhêro-quoinoi* "wage-earners" (men and women).

10. e-ne-re-ja, KN, nom. pl.: *enereiai* (?) "makers of e-ne-ra (underclothes??)"

11. e-ro-pa-ke-ja, KN MY, nom. pl.: class of women cloth-workers.

12. i-je-re-ja, KN PY, nom. & gen. sing.: *hiereia, -ās* "priestess."

13. i-te-ja-o, PY, gen. pl.: *histeiāōn* "weavers."

14. ka-pa-ra$_2$, KN, nom. sing. in -*as*: class of women textile-workers.
    ka-pa-ra$_2$-de, PY, nom. pl. in -*ades*.
    ka-pa-ra$_2$-do, PY, gen. pl., -*adōn*.

15. ka-ra-wi-po-ro, PY, nom. & dat. sing., nom. pl.: *klāwiphoros, -ō, -oi*, literally "keybearer(s)," a type of sacerdotal woman.
    ka-ra-wi-po-ro-jo, PY, gen. sing.

16. ka-ru-ti-je-ja-o, PY, gen. pl.: "sweepers"?

17. ke-re-me-ja, KN, nom. sing.: *kerameia* "potter" (fem. of *kerameus*) or personal name.

18. ke-ri-mi-ja, PY, nom. pl.?: adj. describing the do-e-ra of Do-qe-ja on Pylos tablet An 607. Also KN.

19. ki-ma-ra, PY, nom. pl.: description of women; occupation or ethnic.
    ki-ma-ra-o, PY, gen. pl.

20. ki-ri-te-wi-ja, KN PY, nom. pl.: a class of sacerdotal women.

21. ko-ru-we-ja, KN, nom. (?) pl.: description of women textile workers.
    cf. ko-ro-we-ja, KN, no context?
    cf. ko-we-ja, KN.

22. ko-u-re-ja, KN, nom. pl.: "makers of ko-u-ra (a type of textile)."

23. ma-ri-ne-we-ja-i, TH, dat. pl.: women with textile connections; name is connected with that of god Ma-ri-ne-u (KN MY), whom Palmer connects with *mallos* "flock of wool."

Mallineus would then be patron deity of the wool industry.

24. me-re-ti-ri-ja, PY, nom. pl.: *meletriai* "grain-grinders" (lit. "flour-makers") (me-re-u-ro = *meleuron* "flour," Classical *aleuron, maleuron,* all from proto-Greek *$\underset{o}{m}leuron/meleuron$,* cf. English *mill*, etc.).

me-re-ti-ra$_2$, PY: Alternative spelling of above.

me-re-ti-ra$_2$-[o], PY, gen. pl.

25. ne-ki-ri-de, KN, nom. pl.: description of women with textile connections.

ne-ki-ri-si, KN, dat. pl.

26. ne-we-wi-ja, KN PY, nom. pl.: class of women textile workers.

ne-we-wi-ja-o, PY, gen. pl.

27. no-ri-wo-ko, PY, nom. pl.: *noriworgoi*, a trade; "makers of no-ri."

no-ri-wo-ko-jo, PY, gen. sing.: *noriworgoio.*

no-ri-wo-ki-de, TH, dat. sing. of derivative of above in *-is, -idos.*

28. o-nu-ke-ja, PY, nom. pl.: "women who make o-nu-ke (a textile?)."

o-nu-ke-ja-o, PY, gen. pl.

29. o-ti-ri-ja, PY, nom. pl.: members of a women's trade.

o-ti-ra$_2$, PY: Alternative spelling of above.

o-ti-ra$_2$-o, PY, gen. pl.

30. pa-ke-te-ja, PY, nom. pl.: "makers of pa-ko-to (a type of vessel)."

pa-ke-te-ja-o, PY, gen. pl.: *panworgōn, parworgōn.*

31. pa-wo-ke, PY, nom. pl.: *panworges* "maids of all work" or *parworges* "supplementary workers."

pa-wo-ko, PY, gen. pl.: *panworgōn, parworgōn.*

32. pe-ki-ti-ra$_2$, PY, nom. pl.: *pektriai* "wool-carders."

pe-ki-ti-ra$_2$-o, PY, gen. pl.: *pektriāōn.*

pe-ki-ti-[, KN, probably to be restored as this word.

33. ra-pi-ti-ra$_2$, PY, nom. pl.: *raptriai* "sewing-women," "seamstresses" (possibly in leather).

34. ra-qi-ti-ra$_2$, PY, nom. pl.: *laqutriai* (?) [cf. *lazomai*], class of women of uncertain function.

ra-qi-ti-ra$_2$-o, PY, gen. pl.

35. ra-wi-ja-ja, PY, nom. pl.: *lāwiaia* (?). Tritsch's "plant-culti-vators" (cf. Greek *lēïon* from **lāwion* "standing crop," "cornfield"), rather than Chadwick's "captives."
    ra-wi-ja-ja-o, PY, gen. pl.: *lāwiaiāōn* (?).
36. re-wo-to-ro-ko-wo, PY, nom. & gen. pl.: *lewotrokhowoi, -ōn*, "bath attendants" (cf. Homeric *leotrokhoos* with inversion).
37. ri-ne-ja, PY, nom. pl.: *lineiai* "flax-workers" or "linen-weavers."
    ri-ne-ja-o, PY, gen. pl. *lineiāōn*.
38. si-to-ko-wo, PY, nom. pl.: *sītokhowoi* "grain-pourers," "baking women."
39. te-o-jo do-e-ra, PY, nom. sing.: *theoio dohelā* "do-e-ra of the god(dess)," an important type of female religious functionary.
40. te-pe-ja, KN TH, nom. pl. & dat. sing. (?): makers of te-pa (a type of cloth)" te-pe-ja-o, PY, gen. pl.: trade designation of women.
42. to-te-ja, KN, nom. pl.: members of a women's trade.
43. we-we-si-je-ja, PY, nom. pl.: *werwesieiai* "wool-workers."
    we-wi-si-je-ja-o, gen. pl.

Note: KN = Knossos, TH = Thebes, PY = Pylos, MY = Mycenae. Craftspeople of uncertain sex, such as the *kuwanoworgoi* "kyanos-workers" of Mycenae, are not listed, though they may well be women. Certain doubtful or fragmentary craft titles are also omitted.

The divided world of *Iliad* VI

MARYLIN B. ARTHUR

Wesleyan University, Middletown, Conn.

THE ANCIENT GREEKS of the classical period inhabited what anthropologists call "a divided world,"[1] and the principle of division was the opposition between masculine and feminine. As in many contemporary traditional societies, male and female space, male and female attributes, roles, modes of behavior, and the like, are both conceived and acted out as opposites and as complements of each other.[2] Although Xenophon's *Oeconomicus* is the earliest explicit articulation of this system of dual classification, its force pervades many texts of the classical period[3] and informs the structure of Greek mythological thought.[4]

In the Homeric poems, by contrast, the dichotomization of roles, attributes, and spheres of activity is far less rigid,[5] and the opposition between "public" and "private"[6] domains is arguably non-existent. Instead, we find in the *Iliad* and the *Odyssey* a certain plasticity in the conception of male and female sex roles which is manifested, for example, in the "reverse similes" of the Odyssey studied recently by Helene Foley.[7] A similar spirit pervades the *Iliad*, and the *homilia* ("meeting and conversation") between Hector and Andromache in *Iliad* VI represents the climax of a thematic movement in the first five books which explores the contrast between male and female modes of being. *Iliad* VI, in turn, establishes the focal point from which the enmity between Hector and Achilles is developed in the ensuing narrative.[8]

The *homilia* takes place at the Scaean gates through which Hector enters the city of Troy in the middle of Book VI, and through which he exits at the beginning of VII to rejoin the battle.

The Scaean gates separate two radically different worlds, and they are the dividing line between city and battlefield. Book VI is structured[9] so as to emphasize and highlight this opposition, but also so as to suggest a merging or meeting of the two worlds. In Book VI the contrast is suggested primarily by the opposing figures of Hector and Andromache, and so it is formulated as a contrast between the male and female spheres. But, just as Hector and Andromache meet, embrace, and exchange discourses, so the thematic movement of the book suggests an interpenetration of these two spheres, and a dialectical rather than strictly polarized relationship between them. Earlier scenes in the first five books of the *Iliad* have prepared us to read this encounter as a resolution of the opposition between male and female, battlefield and city, in the form of a new heroic code. For in the first part of the *Iliad* the male and female characters are developed as polar opposites within the larger opposition between male and female spheres of activity.

Diomedes and Paris appear in the *Iliad* in a way that complements and anticipates the opposition between the worlds of the city and battlefield. Each is characterized in terms of his relationship to Aphrodite, the symbol of female sexuality and the polar opposite to her fellow god Ares.

Diomedes calls her an "unwarlike goddess" (V.331) and contrasts her in this respect with Athena in the same passage, whom he characterizes as, like Enyo, one of the goddesses "who lead men into battle" (V.332). When Aphrodite returns wounded to Olympus, Zeus reminds her that her province is not the works of war but the antipathetic sphere:

> No, my child, not for you are the works of warfare. Rather
> concern yourself only with the lovely secrets of marriage,
> while all this [warfare] shall be left to Athene and sudden Ares.[10]
> V.428-430

Diomedes, up to and through the first third of Book VI, and especially in the section immediately preceding the *homilia*, is the most important and fully drawn of the Greek heroes. As V opens, Athena in her function as war-goddess gives him a strength and daring which will distinguish his excellence among the Greeks

(V.1-8). Her support of Diomedes is renewed at several points in the course of his *aristeia* ("account of heroic deeds"): in V.124-132 she speaks to him directly and encourages him, and in V.826 she addresses him as "the one in whom my heart delights" and goes on to urge him to confront Ares, the god of war.[11]

Athena's sponsorship of Diomedes' *aristeia* is one of the ways in which this hero's excellence is pointed up. In addition, when Hector enters the city, he remarks that Diomedes, "the savage spear-fighter," as Helenus describes him, had become the strongest of the Greeks:

> that wild spear-fighter, the strong one who drives men to thoughts of terror,
> who I say now is become the strongest of all the Achaians.
>
> VI.97-98

He is more fearsome even than Achilles himself (VI.99-100), and he is irresistible: "This man has gone clean / berserk, so that no one can match his warcraft against him" (VI.101).

The similes applied to Diomedes anticipate those which figure when Achilles re-enters the battle and fights with such savage fury: the comparison to the dog-star is particularly remarkable, since it occurs just as the point when Diomedes rises into prominence in the narrative (V.4-8). When the same simile is applied to Achilles (in XXII.26ff.) its place in the narrative gives it special prominence among all the other occurrences in the later books of the *Iliad* where Achilles' destructive battle-fury is likened to the ravages of fire (e.g. XIX.365ff., 375ff., XX.371f., 490ff.).[12]

But Diomedes, terrible fighter though he is, is above all the typical warrior-hero. He adheres unflinchingly to the warrior's code which enjoins upon him the duty to fight in the forefront and not to yield before the onslaught of the enemy. He will not withdraw before the challenge of Aeneas and Pandarus, though Sthenelus urges him to:

> Argue me not toward flight, since I have no thought of obeying you.
> No, for it would be ignoble for me to shrink back in the fighting
> or to lurk aside, since my fighting strength stays forever.
>
> V.252-4

In V.96ff. he fights on though he is wounded, and when he finally does yield on the battlefield, it is only because he is confronted with overwhelming odds (V.589ff.: Hector and Ares). One of the signs that Diomedes is a typical hero is that does not challenge the gods or overstep his limits as a mortal.[13] Achilles, by contrast, arrogantly challenges the divine river Scamandrios in XXI.223, and asserts that he would willingly fight with Apollo if only he had the strength (*dynamis*: XXII.15ff.).

Diomedes not only observes the conventional limits which separate men and gods, but acts similarly in the human sphere. In contrast to Achilles (and even to Odysseus: see IV. 350ff.). Diomedes does not question Agamemnon's right to insult him and accuse him, however unjustly, of cowardice. Diomedes himself does not reply ("So he spoke, and strong Diomedes gave no answer / in awe before the majesty of the king's rebuking." IV.401-2), and restrains Sthenelus when he objects (IV.411ff.).

A very significant feature of Diomedes' characterization is his encounter on the battlefield with, first, Aphrodite, and then, Ares. Diomedes encounters Aphrodite as the enemy, the other, the hostile one whom he easily subdues. As Diomedes at this point in the narrative is the primary warrior, and the symbol of war's raging force, so Aphrodite is his natural opposite. When he wounds her, he invites her to draw the lesson that war is not her sphere:

> Give way, daughter of Zeus, from the fighting and the terror. It is
> not then enough that you lead astray women without warcraft?
> Yet, if still you must haunt the fighting, I think that now you
> will shiver even when you hear some other talking of battles.
> V.348-351

Diomedes overpowers Ares as well, also under Athena's guidance and at her instigation (V.792-863). But by this episode Diomedes' excellence as a warrior, his abilities in the works of war, his superiority to even Ares, the god of war, is shown.

Diomedes, then, at the point in the narrative where Hector enters Troy, has been established as the typical Greek warrior, the symbol of the masculine sphere. An essential feature of this definition of his character is the exclusion of the *himeroenta erga*, the works of Aphrodite, from his sphere of activity — not only directly and explicitly, in the form of a hostile encounter with the goddess, but implicitly, in the irrelevance of his wife and children to his martial activity. They exist, because Dione mentions them when she comforts Aphrodite (V.460ff.).[14] And they are not absent from consideration just because Diomedes is fighting far from his homeland; for Sarpedon, in the same section of the poem, twice remarks to Hector that he misses his dear wife, baby son, and many possessions which he last left behind in Lycia:

> Lykia lies far away, by the whirling waters of Xanthos;
> there I left behind my own wife and my baby son, there
> I left my many possessions which the needy man eyes longingly.[15]
> V.479-81

But for Diomedes, his wife and child are simply irrelevant.

Paris, in VI, is the only man in a world of women. This is consonant with his characterization when he first appears in the narrative. There, Hector calls him "evil Paris, beautiful, woman-crazy, cajoling" (III.39). Paris acknowledges the insult, but warns Hector not to begrudge him his special sphere, the gifts of golden Aphrodite (III.64). Book III is Paris' *aristeia*, just as V celebrates the excellence of Diomedes. In the course of the book the original quarrel between Menelaus and Paris is re-enacted in reverse, so that the warriors first compete over "Helen and all her possessions," and then Paris is literally carried away by Aphrodite. Helen yields to the goddess' enticements less readily, with a reticence and concern for social propriety which is hardly appropriate after nine years, but which is clearly a revival of her original ambivalence:

> Not I. I am not going to him. It would be too shameful.
> I will not serve his bed, since the Trojen women hereafter
> would laugh at me, all, and my heart even now is confused with
> sorrows.
> III.410-412

In order to seduce her away to Paris' bedroom Aphrodite assumes the guise of an old woman, a wool-dresser who was especially dear to Helen "when she was living in Lakedaimon" (III.387). Although we are clearly meant to assume that this woman had accompanied Helen to Troy, both this detail and Paris' reminiscence at the end of Book III of the first time that passion overwhelmed him (III.442) and he and Helen first made love together on the island of Cranae (III.445), invite us to picture to ourselves the emotions and circumstances of the first seduction. Then, the old woman must have acted as confidante and go-between in much the same way as Eurycleia serves Penelope in the *Odyssey*.[16] And, finally, Paris' confession of love to Helen, with which he overcomes her resistance, is a fitting conclusion to a book which has shown Paris' particular area of excellence.

Paris can also, to be sure, perform on the battlefield as a good warrior. In both III and VI, when Hector recalls him to his martial duties, he joins in the fray wholeheartedly and bravely. But Paris' primary identification is with the world of Aphrodite, the antipathetic sphere to the battlefield, and he must be either rebuked (as above, in Book III) or cajoled by Hector (as in Book VI) before he can re-focus his energies on the specifically masculine field of endeavor.[17]

The women of the first five books of the *Iliad* present a contrast that is analogous to that between Diomedes and Paris. Briseis and Helen, the principal female characters up to Book VI, are characterized in terms of their relationship to the male world of war.

Briseis is the symbol of the dehumanizing effects of war, the living example of the way in which women, considered only from the perspective of the battlefield, become objectified as possessions and war-booty. The term which describes Briseis throughout almost all of Book I is *geras* ("prize"), a neuter noun. She is the symbol of Achilles' honor and the reward for his labor ("whom, after much hard work he had taken away from Lyrnessos / after he had sacked Lyrnessos and the walls of Thebe" [II.690-691]). In the competive world of masculine values women exist only as chattel — whether the activity is war or funeral games. In wartime the prizes are, as Thersites lists them, bronze, women, and gold (II. 225ff.); in the funeral games for Patroclus, Achilles offers as prizes cauldrons, tripods, horses, mules, cattle, women and iron (XXIII.259ff.).

Achilles' attitude toward Briseis in I contrasts markedly with his later display of affectionate regard for her:

> Since any who is a good man, and careful,
> loves her who is his own and cares for her, even as I now
> loved this one from my heart, though it was my spear that won her.
>   IX.341-343

This is a statement which Achilles makes as part of a larger refusal to take part in the war, and as part of a rejection of the world of Ares. When, at a later point in the *Iliad*, Patroclus has been killed and Achilles re-enters the battle, one of the ways in which he asserts his recovered sense of community with the Greek warriors is through the expression of a wish that Briseis had been killed:

> Son of Atreus, was this after all the better way for
> both, for you and me, that we, for all our hearts' sorrow,
> quarrelled together for the sake of a girl in soul-perishing hatred?
> I wish Artemis had killed her beside the ships with an arrow
> on that day when I destroyed Lyrnessos and took her . . .
>   XIX.56-60

In the first books of the *Iliad* as here, Briseis is a *geras* only, a pawn in the men's disputes.

Briseis' unlucky fate is also an ominous foreshadowing of the doom that awaits the women of Troy. As we shall see, this feature of war figures importantly in the dialogue between Hector and Andromache in Book VI, and several passages in the first books of the *Iliad* draw attention to it. The Greek leader's incitement of their men to war in Book II includes the vision of revenge to be exacted from the Trojans' wives:

> Therefore let no man be urgent to take the way homeward
> until after he has lain in bed with the wife of a Trojan
> to avenge Helen's longing to escape and her lamentations.
>   II.354-356

Agamemnon, in his prayer for victory to Zeus in III, includes the wish that they might rape the Trojan's wives (III.301).[18] Such passages, with their vision of the violence and abuse to which the women of the defeated warriors will be subjected, crystallize the vicious, dehumanizing aspects of war, and associate them with the fate of women. After Book VI there are no examples of such exhortations as those of Nestor in II or Agamemnon in II, IV, and VI. This is largely because the tragic effects of war, after VI, encompass the men of the poem (Patroclus and Hector especially) as well as the women. But, fittingly, the last exhortation to brutalize the women of Troy is the most savage:

> No, let not one of them [the Trojans] go free of sudden
> death and our hands; not the young man child that the mother carries
> still in her body, not even he . . .
>
> VI.57-59

Up to Book VI, then, one of the two kinds of women who appear in the poem is the woman as victim of war, the pawn in men's disputes and the innocent sufferer of all the degrading effects of war.

The other type of woman is Helen. She is the woman who subjugates warriors instead of being subject to them; instead of being the pawn in the men's disputes she plays a more active role — inciting them to hostility against each other on her behalf. When we first see her in III she is commemorating her powers in a woven robe depicting the struggles of the Greeks and Trojans which they underwent "for her sake" (128). She is shortly to venture forth to the Scaean gates to witness the duel between Paris and Menelaus — to see once more how the effects of her beauty and appeal are to set men at variance with one another. And in the end of III Paris confesses that he is "overwhelmed" by desire for Helen.[19]

Helen enters the world of war, then, as a disruptive force, in a fashion that is analogous to the warrior's destruction of the female world through conquest. Briseis and Helen, the two opposite types of women, are related to opposite ways to the male sphere of the battlefield. Similarly, Diomedes and Paris, the two opposite types of warriors, are related in opposite ways to the exclusively female sphere, the world of Aphrodite.

The development of this dual polarity conditions our response to Book VI, when Hector enters the city of Troy and meets

Andromache. Book VI is the first point in the *Iliad* which shows an affectionate rather than hostile relationship between male and female, the first point in the narrative where there is presented an encounter which is free from the domination of one sphere of interests by the other.[20] But Hector encounters Andromache only at the end of his visit within the walls, and only after he has first met the women of Troy, his mother, and Helen and Paris. Thus, he makes his way through the city in stages, each of which is represented by a single encounter, and which, taken together, make up a representation of what J.T. Kakridis has called "the ascending scale of affections."[21] This is a typical motif found in epic and tragedy and derived from folk-tale; its outstanding feature is the elevation of conjugal love over the love of friends and relatives. The order in which the persons appear is typical, and there are two principal patterns:

1) a) friends (compatriots)
    b) parents
    c) husband / wife

2) a) friends (compatriots)
    b) mother
    c) father
    d) brothers and sisters
    e) husband / wife

In Book VI the second pattern, with modifications, predominates. Hector encounters the Trojan women (VI.238; 2.a), his mother (VI.251; 2.b), his brother Paris and sister-in-law Helen (VI.313; 2.d), and at last Andromache, his wife (VI.394; 2.e). The encounter with the father (2.c) is omitted, since Troy in Book VI is a world inhabited by women alone (with the exception of Paris, a figure whose masculinity is always under scrutiny, as we have seen). The presence of this pattern is underscored by the use of formulaic parallels in the three principal encounters.[22]

As Hector proceeds through these encounters he becomes increasingly immersed in a world which, as the narrative presents it, is a direct contrast to that of the battlefield. The lengthy initial description of Priam's house, called *perikallea* (VI.242; "very lovely"), and the product of a long and careful labor ("wonder-fully built" [242]; "fashioned with smooth-stone cloister walks" [243]; "sleeping chambers of smoothed stone" [244]; "close smooth-stone sleeping chambers" [248]), suggests that form of work which occupies men during peacetime. A little later in the narrative, when Hector reaches Paris' dwelling, the poet tells us that it was a lovely (kala) one, which Paris himself had con-structed, together "with the men who at that time / were the best men (aristoi) for craftsmanship in the generous Troad" (VI.314-315) — men distinguished by virtue of their abilities as builders rather than warriors.

Troy is not only a world of women, but of beautiful women. Laodice, the most beautiful of Priam's daughters (VI.252), accom-panies her mother when Hector meets them, and he is soon to encounter Helen, the woman whose beauty the elders on the wall in III had likened to that of the goddesses (III.158).

Troy is a world of rest and relaxation. Hecuba offers Hector wine to help relieve his exhaustion (VI.261f.), and in the descip-tion of Priam's palace (see above) the poet focuses on the bed-rooms (thalamoi) where men and women sleep together (VI.245-246, 249-250).

Troy is a world of the works of women: the storage room holds the erga gynaikōn, the elaborate peploi ("woven cloths or robes") which Paris had brought back to Troy together with Helen (VI.289ff.). When Hector comes upon Helen she is overseeing the work of her serving-women (VI.323f.), and this is the task to which Hector directs Andromache at the end of the homilia (VI.490ff.). Supervision of the spinning and weaving is the work with which Andromache is in fact occupied when, in Book XXII, the sound of lamentation calls her forth once more to the walls: "but she was weaving a web in the inner room of the high house, / a red folding robe, and inworking elaborate figures" (XXII.440-441). The ritual which the women of the city perform also tradi-tionally belongs to their sphere of activity; prayers to the gods for salvation are the office of the women of the city in time of war.[23]

When Hector reaches the home, and enters the bedroom (thalamos, VI.321) of Helen and Paris, there is once more an offer of rest. Helen invites Hector to sit down on the chair beside her and relax:

> But come now, come in and rest on this chair, my brother,
> since it is on your heart beyond all that the hard work has fallen.
> VI.354-355

The invitation clearly has sexual overtones, although they are presented with delicacy. When Helen earlier refused Aphrodite's suggestion that she return to the bedroom where Paris was awaiting her "in the bed with its circled pattern" (III.391), Helen's initial refusal included the outrageous proposal, "go yourself and *sit beside him*" (III.406). And when Helen does enter the bedroom, she first sits down with Paris on an "armchair" (*diphros* [III.424-6]), a type of chair which ordinarily seats two,[24] and which is the chair which Helen invites Hector to share with her in our passage (VI.354). In addition, Helen's description of the "perfect" husband, which she addresses to Hector in the context of a disparagement of Paris (III.350ff.), fits Hector precisely. He is above all the man "who [knows] modesty and all things of shame that men say" (III.351). This is indicated especially by the famous line "I would feel deep shame / before the Trojans, and the Trojan women with trailing garments" (VI.441), in which he explains to Andromache his reasons for fighting in the forefront of the Trojan ranks, and which he repeats at the significant point when he makes the decision to remain outside the walls and face Achilles (XXII.105).

In the first two principal encounters with women in VI, then, Hector meets them as representatives of the domain with which they are traditionally associated — the activities of nurturing, of the sustenance of life as both a daily activity and as the act of generation. Between them, Hecuba and Helen offer Hector gratification of his primary needs: Hecuba, as mother, wants to satisfy his thirst, and Helen's offer has overtones of a sexual enticement.[25] In addition, the descriptions in VI remind us of the cultural activities of peacetime — the building of homes by the men and the weaving of clothes by the women.

Hector is out of place in this world. He rejects Hecuba's cup of wine out of worry that it might take away his fighting strength: "My honoured mother, lift not to me the kindly sweet wine, / for fear you stagger my strength and make me forget my courage" (VI.264-265). He is covered with blood and muck and so cannot engage in ritual activity (VI.266ff.). When he enters the bed-chamber of Paris and Helen, a description of two lines' length (VI.319-320) highlights the long spear which he brings; Paris, by contrast, is not dressed in his armor but is holding it, turning it over and admiring it, but not using it (VI.321-322). And when Hector refuses Helen's offer of relaxation and rest, he counter-poses to her desire for him his troops' longing (*pothē* [VI.362]) for him.

Andromache is also temporarily dislocated in this book. She is absent from her home: "[he] failed to find in the house Andro-mache of the white arms" (VI.371); she is not with her sisters-in-law: "she is not / with any of the sisters of her lord or the wives of his brothers" (VI.382-383); nor has she gone to share in the ritual sacrifice in which all of the other highborn women of the city take part: "nor has she gone to the house of Athene, where all the other / lovely-haired women of Troy propitiate the grim goddess" (VI.384-385). These are the places where Hector expects to find Andromache when he discovers her absence from his home, and these are the proper and traditional places and activities for her. Instead, she has run forth to the walls "like a woman gone mad" (VI.389).

Women, when they were possessed by Dionysus, acted like maenads (of whose existence Homer knew: see XXII.460[26]), rush-ing to the mountains and abandoning their traditional activities. This is the thrust of Pentheus' complaints and the cause of his outrage against Dionysus and the women in Euripides' *Bacchae*.[27] If, as seems likely, μαινομένηι εἰκυῖα is a metrical variant for μαινάδι ἴση,[28] then the force of the simile here is to underscore Andro-mache's dislocation. She is not only in a condition of heightened emotionality, but she is experiencing a transport that delivers her out of the world with which she is normally associated.

Hector and Andromache move toward one another, then, by a

process in which each dissociates himself from the world to which he or she normally belongs, and assimilates himself to the sphere of the other. At the same time, a tension is developed as the narrative focuses on the abnormality of this process: Hector enters the world of Troy but does not really belong there; Andromache's ability to function in this world, which is her proper sphere, is temporarily suspended.

The climax comes at the wall, when Hector removes his helmet in order to embrace his son. Since one of his principal epithets is *korythaiolos* ("of the shining helmet"), and since it is used of him frequently in VI,[29] the act takes on symbolic importance, and marks the moment of Hector's furthest distance from the world of the battlefield. Andromache, for her part, gives Hector advice about the conduct of the war — a move so inappropriate as to have led Aristarchus to athetize the passage on the grounds that it was unfitting for Andromache "to compete with Hector's generalship" (*antistratēgein*).

The speeches at the wall, and especially that of Hector, treat a dichotomy which has been building, not only throughout the entire first section of the *Iliad*, but in the course of VI, where the opposition between the city and the battlefield, between the feminine and masculine worlds, is developed. The *homilia* takes place at a point in time and space where both Hector and Andromache have been dissociated from their proper spheres and have each partially entered the world of the other. For this reason the Scaean gates, the dividing line between the two worlds, is an appropriate meeting place. The speeches which, like Hector's passage through Troy, make use of the ascending scale of affections, present a correlate; for in them the poet attempts a resolution of the polarity which affirms the possibility of their compatibility and, indeed, asserts the basic continuity between the two worlds.

Andromache's use of the ascending scale of affections constitutes something of a departure from the pattern which usually presents the husband loving his wife above all others or the wife loving her husband *more than others do*[30] (i.e. not more than she loves all others). Thus the pattern as it is applied to the wife is not normally analogous, but correlative. However, Homer has

Andromache employ the scale of affections in exactly the form in which Hector used it — only she does it in reverse.

Andromache begins by rebuking Hector for his battle-thirst and for endangering his life. For, she goes on, if he is killed, life would be worthless for her: "for there is no other consolation for me after you have gone to your destiny — / only grief" (VI.411-412). The word that Andromache uses, *thalpōrē* ("consolation"), covers the whole range of human affections and the warmth and pleasure to be derived from them. It is used by Telemachus to signify his longing for his absent father (1.167), and by Odysseus (X.223) when he explains to Nestor his need for a companion on the expedition into the Trojan camp. It is a good word to express the range of meaning of Andromache's love for her husband: he is the source of comfort, companionship, and protection for her.

As the progression continues, Andromache explains that she lost both her father, Eetion (2.c), and mother (2.b), when Achilles sacked her town, Thebe (2.a). The poet then resumes the use of the pattern to explain that Eetion (2.c) and Andromache's seven brothers (2.d) were killed, but that her mother (2.b) was ransomed but perished shortly thereafter. Hector is therefore father, mother, brother, and tender husband to Andromache (2.b, c, d, e):

> Hektor, thus you are father to me, and my honoured mother,
> you are my brother, and you it is who are my young husband.
> VI.429-430

In the space of twenty lines Homer has used the scale of affections three times, and this repetition effectively conveys Andromache's extraordinarily strong love for Hector.

In the remaining lines of her speech (VI.431-439) Andromache gives to Hector the advice on military strategy which Aristarchus condemned. If we look carefully at these lines, it will be clear that Andromache does not, as she has often been thought to do, ask Hector to refrain from going out to battle. Although she does say, "stay here on the rampart" (VI.431), the lines that follow constitute an explanation that what she wants is for Hector to adopt

a more defensive strategy. This wish accords with her reproach in
the opening lines of her speech, where she had said, "your own
great strength will be your death" (VI.407), and with her dire pre-
monition in Book XXII where she fears for him because "[Hector]
would never stay back where the men were in numbers / but break
far out in front, and give way in his fury to no man" (XXII.458-
459).

Andromache, then, does not ask that Hector play the coward,
but that he give up his quest for *kleos* ("glory"[31]) — that he not
fight in the forefront where, as Sarpedon explains it to Glaucus in
XX.322ff., men win glory and fame. Andromache's speech, therefore, is not only an expression of sincerely felt emotion; it is also
a suggestion for a course of action by which Hector can honor his
commitment to her and his responsibility as the defender of Troy.

Hector, in his response, also makes use of the ascending scale of
affections (2.a.b.c.d.e):

> But my concern is not so much for the sufferings of the Trojans
> nor [of my mother and father and brothers],
> but for your suffering [on the day when some Achaean
> leads you away as his slave].
>
> VI.450-455 (abridged)

But Hector precedes his confession of love for Andromache with a
firm rejection of her appeal. Both his regard for the Trojans (his
public standing) and his own heart (*thymos*-VI.444) enjoin upon
him the necessity of fighting in the front ranks and seeking glory:

> and the spirit [*thymos*] will not let me, since I have learned to be
>   valiant
> and to fight always among the foremost ranks of the Trojans,
> winning for my own self great glory [*kleos*], and for my father.
>
> VI.444-446

Hector's use of the scale of affections, like Andromache's, is tailored
to the particular message which he wants to convey. Whereas
Andromache had asserted simply that life for her had no joy without Hector, Hector paints a dismal picture in which he combines
the two aspects of his dread: his anguish over her suffering and his
sorrow at his own loss of honor (VI.454-461). He concludes:

> But may I be dead and the piled earth hide me under before I
> hear you crying and know by this that they drag you captive.
>   VI.464-465

For both Hector and Andromache their exchange has emerged
as a statement of the doom that awaits them both,[32] and the
mood at the end of Hector's speech is one of profound despair.
The exchange with his son which follows is the turning point of
mood in the episode and the occasion for Hector to formulate a
resolution between the conflicting demands of *eleos* ("pity") and
kleos, the demands of the female and male spheres (cf. Andromache's appeal in VI.431: "Please take pity upon me."). This
Hector does in the form of an address to his son which, since it
takes the form of a prayer just preceding his re-entrance into
battle, is the structural parallel to the hero's traditional prayer for
strength and courage (e.g. V.115ff.).

In a brief six lines Hector counteracts the mood of despair by
constructing a fantasy which both Andromache ("your own great
strength will be your death" [VI.407]) and Hector himself ("For
I know this thing well in my heart, and my mind knows it: / there
will come a day when sacred Ilion shall perish" [VI.447-448])
realize will never be brought to fulfillment. Under the guise of a
prayer he projects a picture of joyous harmony, delinated in terms
which have specific reference to the family: his son fights bravely
(and presumably beside his father), bringing fame to his father and
joy to his mother:

> Zeus, and you other immortals, grant that this boy who is my son,
> may be as I am, pre-eminent among the Trojans,
> great in strength, as am I, and rule strongly over Ilion;
> and some day let them say of him: "He is better by far than his
>   father,"
> as he comes in from the fighting; and let him kill his enemy
> and bring home the blooded spoils, and delight the heart of his
>   mother.
>   VI.476-481

It is a portrait of mutual cooperation, in which the traditional
competition between father and son (cf. Sthenelus' boast on

behalf of Diomedes and himself in IV.405: "We two claim we are better men by far than our fathers."[33]) does not function. In addition, it is a situation in which the wife/mother is not only reconciled to her son's (and presumably husband's) martial activity — she too derives pleasure and satisfaction from it. This is a utopian vision of the nuclear family as the ideal reconciliation between opposing interests; it is a unity in which war is not a threat for women and children, and where women are a support in this venture for their husbands. The worlds of men and women do not exclude, but include each other; there is not opposition, but fusion and cooperation between the two spheres. It is an ideal which finds its fullest expression in the *Odyssey*, which culminates in a battle that fulfills every aspect of the fantasy which Hector projects in the Iliad — father and son fight alongside one another and bring joy to the heart of Penelope.[34] And at the very end of the *homilia*, when Hector returns the child to Andromache, directs Andromache to her loom and her woman's world, and himself returns to battle, the formulaic lines which delineate the separate spheres dissolve the contradictions and confusions of the halfway world of the wall:

> Go therefore back to our house, and take up your own work,
> the loom and the distaff, and see to it that your handmaidens
> ply their work also; but the men must see to the fighting,
> all men who are the people of Ilion, but I beyond others.
> VI.490-493

As the climax to the *homilia*, the lines must be understood in context, and must be seen as a resolution of competing interests.

But in the *Iliad*, this vision is a false resolution. In XXII, when Hector is killed and Andromache is called forth to the walls by the sound of lamenting, there are formulaic and other parallels with VI. Segal has discussed these fully in an article which argues that the scene which he characterizes as "Andromache's *Anagnorisis*" (XXII.437-476) describes Andromache "in terms of the stricken warrior . . . [and thus] equates her sufferings with the more 'public' sufferings of the heroes themselves."[35] In this episode of the *Iliad*, as in VI, Segal finds that one of the characterizing features is "the confrontation between war and peace, battles and domesticity,"[36] which provide the background against which the action takes place.

In addition to this aspect of the scene, there is another important dimension. After Andromache returns to consciousness in XXII.475-476, she constructs a picture which constitutes a counter-fantasy to that of Hector in his prayer for his son. Andromache first laments Hector's death and then turns to contemplation of the fate that awaits her and their child. Instead of imagining their enslavement (the likely outcome, as they had both recognized earlier), she passes over this possibility in one brief line (XXII.487) and instead pictures to herself life as the widowed mother of an orphaned child.

The child is reduced to the status of a little beggar, tugging pitifully at the fine cloaks of his father's former companions in order to procure a few scraps from the table. This picture is the analogue to the one that Hector had imagined in VI, where Andromache is forced into the slavish tasks of working at the looms and fetching water. And in Andromache's vision there is an analogue to the abuse to which Hector imagined her subjected. The more fortunate child (the *amphithalēs*, "child with both parents living" [XXII.496]) chases Hector's son from the halls in disgrace, and the child cries (Andromache wept in VI.459) and seeks the consolation of his mother's embrace. A reminiscence of Astyanax's former position of carefree comfort and luxury (XXII.504) closes the passage.

This picture is a highly improbable one. It is scarcely thinkable that, given Hector's forty-nine brothers and twelve brothers-in-law, one at least (and most probably Deiphobus, who according to tradition survives the deaths of both Hector and Paris — see *Odyssey* 4.276 and 8.518 — and in the *Iliad* is close to Hector) would not have taken this favored child under his protection. Although there is no model for this in the Homeric poems themselves, it is appropriate to invoke the example of Eurysaces in the *Ajax* of Sophocles, since the dramatist was consciously imitating the circumstances and the action of the drama involving Hector, Andromache, and Astyanax.[37] In that play the dying Ajax entrusts his son to his half-brother Teucer's care (558ff.; esp. 560-561), and thus avoids the reproach which Andromache is able to level against Hector: "Now, with his dear father gone, he [Astyanax] has much to suffer" (XXII.505).

Andromache's failure to take this possibility into account is not only a product of psychologically realistic despair, but a revelation that the resolution of Book VI was a false one. Hector's heroic ideal — his insistence on his pursuit of *kleos* and simultaneous use of the scale of affections — was a false resolution because it was achieved not by truly merging the two spheres into one, but by subordinating one to the other. His affective ties, and his duties as a father and husband, he had asserted, were subsumed under his pursuit of *kleos*. Homer's use of parallels with Book VI in his depiction of Andromache's reaction to Hector's death serves to remind us of the claims made there and of the vision of harmony between opposing interests. Andromache's bleak and despairing vision in XXII, which is coupled with an acknowledgement that Hector has indeed achieved the *kleos* among the Trojans and the Trojan women (XXII.514) for which he had longed earlier (VI.442), reaffirms the essential incompatibility of the masculine and feminine spheres, and returns us to the world of the first five books of the *Iliad*. There, as in XXII, the warrior strives for glory at any cost, including that of his own life and the bereavement of his wife and child. Hector in his pride, and especially under the exhilarating influence of his *aristeia* in VIII and his triumph over Patroclus in XVI, gradually dissociates himself from the community of Troy which had earlier formed the basis for his heroic enterprise. In XXII, when he refuses the appeal of his parents to re-enter the walls of the city, he closes his deliberative speech with a line in which he affirms the priority of the quest for glory:

> Better to bring on the fight with him [Achilles] as soon as it may be.
> We shall see to which one the Olympian grants the glory.
>
> XXII.129-130[38]

The woman, for her part, either suffers helplessly or seduces her husband away from the battlefield to the bedroom.

A true resolution of the competing claims of *kleos* on the one hand, and *philia* ("love") and *eleos* on the other, is only achieved when the drama is played out entirely in the male domain, as it is after Book VI. Thus, Achilles' love for Patroclus[39] brings him back to the battlefield, and ensures victory for the Greeks, even though Achilles fights for purely personal reasons and refuses to enter whole-heartedly into the community of the Greeks by sharing a meal with them (in XIX). And Achilles' pity for Priam, who reminds him of his own father, induces him to accept Priam's supplication and so to acknowledge the common bond of humanity which unites all men.[40]

In Book VIII of the *Ethics* Aristotle explores the nature of *philia* ("friendship," "love"[41]) and its relationship to *koinōnia* ("community"[42]). As in many other areas, so in this one Aristotle has codified principles which are inherent in Greek thinking from the earliest period. Here Aristotle explains that the *philia* which binds husband and wife, and parent and child, is implanted in us by nature,[43] but that the highest and most perfect form of friendship is that between equals:[44]

Philia is present to the extent that men share something in common, for that is also the extent to which they share a view of what is just. And the proverb 'friends hold in common what they have' is correct, for friendship consists in community. Brothers and bosom companions (*hetairoi*) hold everything in common, while all others only hold certain definite things in common . . .[45]

Although it was not his intention so to do, Aristotle's formulations in *Ethics* VIII might be understood as a statement of the ethical rules which underlie the themes of the *Iliad* which explore the dynamic between male and female, hero and community, and the city and the battlefield.

Notes

A preliminary version of this paper was presented at the annual meeting of the American Philological Association (Chicago, Ill.) in December, 1974.

1.   This is described most fully by Pierre Bourdieu, in *Outline of a Theory*

of Practice [1972], transl. Richard Nice (Cambridge, 1977), esp. Ch. 2, "Structures and the Habitus," and Ch. 3, "Generative Schemes and Practical Logic: Invention Within Limits." See also Bourdieu's statement, "It is not hard to imagine the weight that must be brought to bear on the construction of self-image and world-image by the opposition between masculinity and femininity when it constitutes the fundamental principle of division of the social and symbolic world" (93). Other major works in anthropology which describe the dual classification system are A.M. Hocart, *Kings and Councillors* [1936], ed. and intro. Rodney Needham (Chicago and London, 1970), esp. Ch. 20, "Heaven and Earth," and Rodney Needham, ed., *Right and Left: Essays on Dual Symbolic Classification* (Chicago and London, 1973).

2. Such societies are studied by anthropologists who work in the modern Mediterranean, including modern Greece, e.g. J.K. Campbell, *Honour, Family, and Patronage: A Study of Institutions and Moral Values in a Greek Mountain Community* (New York and Oxford, 1964), Julian Pitt-Rivers, ed., *Mediterranean Countrymen: Essays in the Social Anthropology of the Mediterranean* (Paris and La Haye, 1963), and J.G. Peristiany, ed., *Mediterranean Family Structures* (Cambridge, 1976).

3. See, *inter alia*, my "Origins of the Western Attitude Toward Women," *Arethusa* VI (1973) 7-58, and esp. 47-48 on the "[assimilation] . . . of the social roles of male and female to the polarities whose opposition defined the world order." For tragedy, the reader should consult Froma Zeitlin, "The Dynamics of Misogyny: Myth and Mythmaking in the *Oresteia*," *Arethusa* XI (1978) 149-184, and esp. 171-172 where Zeitlin sets out a tabulation of a "series of antitheses [which] form about the polarization of male and female roles." For comedy, see Helene Foley, " 'The Female Intruder' Reconsidered: Women in Aristophanes' *Lysistrata* and *Ecclesiazusae*," *Classical Philology* (forthcoming). And on history, consult Michèle Rosellini and Suzanne Saïd, "Usages de Femmes et Autres Nomoi chez les 'Sauvages' d'Hérodote: Essai de Lecture Structurale," *Annali della Scuola Normale Superiore di Pisa* VIII (1978) 949-1005.

4. Jean-Pierre Vernant, "Hestia-Hermès: sur l'expression religieuse de l'espace et du mouvement chez les Grecs," in *Mythe et Pensée chez les Grecs* I (Paris, 1971) 124-170.

5. See my "Origins" (*op. cit.*, note 3) 10-19, and Helene Foley, " 'Reverse Similes' and Sex Roles in the Odyssey," *Arethusa* XI (1978) 7-26. And although I shall have occasion to cite passages from C.R. Beye, "Male and Female in the Homeric Poems," *Ramus* 3 (1974) 87-101, it will be evident throughout that I do not agree with the idea that "the conception of women [which appears] in the *Iliad*" is "the notion of woman as an object and possession" (87).

6. See S.C. Humphreys, "Public and Private Interests in Classical Athens," *The Classical Journal* 73 (1977/78) 97-104, and the same author's "Introduction" to *La Donna Antica*, ed. Lanza and Vegetti (Turin, forthcoming).

7. Foley (*op. cit.*, note 5), esp. 24-25, note 19.

8. This aspect of the *Iliad* will not be the subject of sustained discussion in this paper. For a full treatment, see G.K. Whitfield, " 'The Restored Relation': A Study of Supplication in the *Iliad*," (diss., Columbia University, 1967) and James Redfield, *Nature and Culture in the ILIAD: The Tragedy of Hector* (Chicago, 1975).

9. Critical attention has not been focused on this book since the time when "Hektors Abschied" and the whole scene in Troy was a favorite target of the analysts. Wilamowitz, in *Die Ilias und Homer* (Berlin, 1916; 302-316); Bethe, *Homer* I (Leipzig, 1914; 245f.); and E. Schwartz, *Zur Entstehung der Ilias* (Schr. d. Strassb. wiss. Ges. 34, 1918; 17ff.) treated the section as an *Einzellied* which had simply been inserted into the poem. These scholars paid particular attention to the theme of Paris' anger (VI.326), and suggested that it may have occupied the central position in a short epic. Robert, *Studien zur Ilias* (Berlin, 1901; 194ff.) proposed that a council of the elders of Troy (cf. VI.86ff.) was the primary theme, and that it followed Hector's meeting with Paris. The most recent work in the "Separatist" tradition is G. Jachmann, *Homerische Einzellieder* (Cologne, 1949), who returns to the "lays" theory of Karl Lachmann and details the outlines of an original lay which had the story of the hero Hector at its center. According to Jachmann, the "Schöpfer" ("der nicht Homer hiess") originally designed a tale which united the events which in our *Iliad* are separated into Books VI and XXII, and which climaxed in the tragic death of Hector. One of the last major works on Book VI, that of W. Schadewaldt, "Hektor und Andromache," [1935] in *Von Homers Welt und Werk* (Stuttgart, 1965, 207ff.), takes up a very different line of inquiry. Schadewaldt defends the unity of the *Iliad* and the structural integrity of VI within the poem as a whole; his essay also analyses the structure of the book as an "Akt," which he calls "Hektor in Troja," and divides into three major sections, corresponding to the three principal stages of the "ascending scale of affections" as defined by Kakridis (see below, note 21). My debt to Schadewaldt's essay will be evident throughout, although it will also be clear that I am not content to allow Homer's delineation of "die grosse Grundpolarität" to stand as the central meaning of the book. My analysis also has certain points in common with Alfred Schmitz, "La Polarité des Contraires dans la Rencontre d'Hector et Andromaque: *Iliade* VI, 369-502)," *Les Etudes Classiques* XXI (1963), 129-158, although I do not treat the scene, as he does, from the point of view of Hector's "psychology," which is determined by an overriding opposition between the "Je social" and the "Je personnel" (154ff.).

10. Quotations from the *Iliad* and *Odyssey* are cited in the translations of Richmond Lattimore; citations from the *Iliad* employ Roman numerals for book numbers; those from the *Odyssey* use Arabic numerals to designate books.

11. Her departure from the battlefield at the end of Book V marks the termination of the period during which Diomedes is under her special

protection. See J.H. Gaisser, "The Glaucus-Diomedes Episode," *TAPA* 100 (1969) 166-167.

12. See Carroll Moulton, "Similes in the *Iliad*," *Hermes* 102 (1974) 381-397, and esp. 392-393, where he treats the simile under discussion.

13. This is, as J.H. Gaisser (*op. cit.*, note 11) points out, the "message" behind the opposition of two "Weltanschauungen" in the exchange of speeches between Diomedes and Glaucus in VI: "In the sorty of Lycurgus [Diomedes] makes the point that the gods punish mortals who dare to oppose them; by implication, the man who does not oppose the gods will be safe from their wrath . . . On the other hand . . . the story of Bellerophon, as [Glaucus] tells it, shows mortals as the victims of the gods" (175).

14. "Then, though he be very strong indeed, let the son of Tydeus [Diomedes] take care lest someone even better than he might fight with him, lest for a long time Aigialeia, wise child of Adrastos, mourning wake out of sleep her household's beloved companions, longing for the best of the Achaians, her lord by marriage, she, the strong wife of Diomedes, breaker of horses."

15. "Son of Priam, do not leave me lying for the Danaans to prey upon, but protect me, since otherwise in your city my life must come to an end, since I could return no longer back to my own house and the land of my fathers, bringing joy to my own beloved wife and my son, still a baby."
V.684-688

16. The nurse (or servant-girl, as in *Lysias* I) figures in this way often in tragedy (e.g., *Medea, Hippolytus*) and, although Eurynome seems to be Penelope's special servant in the *Odyssey*, in 23 Eurycleia takes over this function. On her special status, see E.A.S. Butterworth, *Some Traces of the Pre-Olympian World in Greek Literature and Myth* (Berlin, 1966) 106ff.

17. On the possible sexual overtones to the horse-simile applied to Paris at the end of VI (VI.506-511), see C.R. Beye, *The Iliad, the Odyssey and the Epic Tradition* (Garden City, New Jersey, 1966), 27.

18. Leaf's comment *(ad loc.)* that the variant *dameien* for *migein* "looks like the prudery of a more fastidious age" is apropos. On *dameien*, see below, notes 19 and 20.

19. Note that when Hera is finally able to subdue Zeus and work her own will in the war, she resorts to the charms of Aphrodite and Zeus admits that she has "conquered" him:
"For never before has love for any goddess or woman so melted about the heart inside me, broken it to submission [*edamassen*].
XIV.315-316
Δαμάζω and the related δάμνημι are the terms regularly used to mean subjection of two kinds: (a) that of a woman to a man in marriage (XVIII.432; III.301) and (b) that of one man to another in battle (III.432; VIII.244; XV.376).

20. Note that in Book III, when Helen and Paris go up into the "bed of love," a spat precedes their lovemaking, in which Helen goes so far as to wish that Paris had been killed in the duel: "Oh, how I wish you had died there / beaten down [dameis] by the stronger man, who was once my husband" (III.428-429).

21. Homeric Researches (Lund, 1949), esp. "Meleagrea" and p. 20.

22. As Kakridis (above) points out, each of the women makes a suggestion (258, 354, 431); in all three cases Hector refuses their appeal (264, 360, 441 — this last request he rejects more gently); and to each woman he gives an order and explains his own intentions. The passages are cited and discussed in the chapter "Hektorea," 50-52. See also the discussion in Schmitz (op. cit., note 9) 147.

23. Margaret Alexiou, in The Ritual Lament in Greek Tradition (Cambridge, 1974), discusses women's role as mourners when a city is destroyed. She distinguishes between "the thrēnos of the professional mourners . . . and the goos of the kinswomen" (12), and devotes a chapter (5) to "The historical lament for the fall or destruction of cities."

24. The word also means "chariot", which ordinarily carries the hero and his henchman or companion (e.g. III.261-262). Although Cunliffe (A Lexicon of the Homeric Dialect [1924] [Norman, Oklahoma, 1963] s.v.) says that, when the word means "seat", "the notion of 'two' [is] apparently lost," neither the Iliadic usage (as discussed here) nor that of the Odyssey (e.g. the fact that diphros is the kind of seat that is drawn up for Odysseus in Book 19, when the interview with Penelope takes place) suggests that the etymology of the word (from di = two and pherō = carry) was in every case irrelevant.

25. Long before Freud, these were recognized as the two primary instinctual urges. See, for example, Plato's discussion of the irrational part of the soul in Republic 439d, where it is described as that part "with which it [the soul] loves, hungers, thirsts, and feels the flutter and titillation of other desires, the irrational and appetitive — companion of various repletions and pleasures" (transl. Shorey).

26. It is disputed whether mainadi in XXII.460 means "maenad" or just "mad woman." See the discussion of this question by C.P. Segal, in "Andromache's Anagnorisis," HSCP 75 (1971) 47, n. 31.

27. Pentheus, in Euripides' Bacchae, complains about Dionysus' influence as follows:
   "I happened to be away, out of the city,
   but reports reached me of some strange mischief here,
   stories of our women leaving home to frisk
   in mock ecstasies among the thickets on the mountain . . ."
   215-218 (transl. Arrowsmith)

28. Mainomai can mean "martial rage" (e.g. VI.101) and hence any condition of heightened emotionality, but as the participle mainomenoio is used of Dionysus in VI.138, it may have had a specialized meaning as well.

29. Lines 116, 263, 342, 359, 369, 440, 520. The epithet is more frequent

in this book than any other, although Hector appears more often in other books of the *Iliad*. On this question see William Whallon, "The Homeric Epithets," *YCS* XVII (1961) 95-142, esp. "A Group of Epithets for Hector," 110-114.

30. The "type" is Alcestis; see Kakridis (*op. cit.*, note 21) 20.

31. On Hector's pursuit of *kleos*, see Gregory Nagy, *The Best of the Achaeans: Concepts of the Hero in Archaic Greek Poetry* (Baltimore and London, 1979) 28-29, 148-149, and compare Andromache's reference, in XXII.457, to Hector's "bitter pride of courage."

32. Schadewaldt (*op. cit.*, note 9) is particularly eloquent in this point: "Man sieht von selber, wie beide Reden in Gedanke wie Form durch Entsprechung und Gegensatz bis ins einselne hinein aneinander gebunden sind. Jede der beiden Gestalten hängt in schmerzlicher Sorge am Schicksal des andern. Aber verbunden in ihrem Schmerz und ihrer Liebe, sind sie in ihrem Sein doch tief voneinander geschieden — wie eben Glück und Grösse sich nich aufeinander reimen" (221).

33. A.W. Gouldner, *The Hellenic World* (New York, 1969) is one of the few scholars who have systematically studied this feature of Greek society. See especially his chapter, "The Greek Contest System: Patterns of Culture."

34. "Still, I [Penelope] will go to see my son, so that I can look on these men who courted me lying dead, and the man who killed them."
23.83-84

35. Segal (*op. cit.*, note 26) 55.

36. Segal (*op. cit.*, note 26) 43.

37. On this point see K. Reinhardt, *Sophokles* (Frankfurt, 1935) 31.

38. The word which is here translated "glory" is not *kleos*, but *euchos* ("boast"). On the relationship between the two concepts see Nagy (*op. cit.*, note 31) 44-45. It will be evident that I do not entirely agree with Redfield's interpretation of this scene, when he argues that "Hector's isolation here is . . . not a lack of relation to his community but a negative relation with it; he is sure that his community . . . rejects him" (*op. cit.*, note 8) 158. Although here and elsewhere (esp. 113-127) Redfield successfully highlights the role of *aidōs* ("shame") in Hector's sense of self, he does not altogether take into account the relationship between honor and shame, which in the *Iliad* and in "shame cultures" in general, form a natural pair. See Pierre Bourdieu, "The Sentiment of Honour in Kabyle Society," in J.G. Peristiany, ed., *Honour and Shame: The Values of Mediterranean Society* (Chicago and London, 1966) 191-241.

39. On this subject see Nagy (*op. cit.*, note 31) 105ff., and Beye (*op. cit.*, note 5): "The erotic nature of their [Achilles' and Patroclus'] relationship is unclear and unimportant. What the poet shows is a non-competitive relationship, something unusual in the competitive society of Homer. It is something secure, something valuable; perhaps it seems so much like the male-female tie because the poet had only the model of the male-female relationship for something empathetic and accepting between men" (89).

40. See Redfield's (*op. cit.*, note 8) revealing discussion of "The Ransoming of Hector" (210-218) and his statement that "the final purification of the *Iliad* [is] achieved not by the reconstruction of the human community but by the separation of the hero from the community" (210-211).

41. On the meaning of this term in the *Ethics*, see Martin Ostwald, ed., transl., comm., *Aristotle, Nichomachean Ethics* (Indianapolis and New York, 1962) 214.

42. On the meaning of this term in the *Ethics*, see Ostwald (above) 231.

43. "It seems that nature implants friendship in a parent for its offspring and in offspring for its parent, not only among men, but also among birds and most animals" (transl. Ostwald [*op. cit.*, note 41] 215 [1155a 17-18]; all subsequent citations from Aristotle's *Ethics* are from this translation). "The friendship between man and wife seems to be inherent in us by nature. For man is by nature more inclined to live in couples than to live as a social and political being . . ." (239 [1162a 17-19]).

44. "The perfect form of friendship is that between good men who are alike in excellence or virtue" (219 [1156b 6-7]). "The highest form of friendship, then, is that between good men, as we have stated repeatedly" (223-224 [1157b 25-26]). Also cf. Aristotle on "friendship between unequals": "There exists another kind of friendship, which involves the superiority of one of the partners over the other, as in the friendship between father and son, and in general, between an older and a younger person, between husband and wife, and between any kind of ruler and his subject . . . In all friendships which involve the superiority of one of the partners, the affection, too, must be proportionate: the better and more useful partner should receive more affection than he gives, and similarly for the superior partner in each case" (227 [1158b 11-13; 1158b 24-27]).

45. P. 231 (1159b 30-34).

Sappho's private world

EVA STEHLE STIGERS

Wheaton College, Norton, MA.

OF ALL THE LYRIC POETS writing love poetry in Greek between about 700 and 500 BC, Sappho is the most intense, the most immediate. "The isles of Greece, the isles of Greece! Where burning Sappho loved and sung," wrote Byron.[1] Other readers, less passionate themselves perhaps, have emphasized rather the atmosphere of magic and incantation in her poems, or the exotic settings, the Lydian head-dress and slippers, soft robes, flowers, everything rich, delicate, and lovely.[2] All these elements flow together to form the unique quality of Sappho's poetry, which I shall call her romanticism.[3] To suggest the source and nature of that romanticism is the purpose of this paper.

Sappho wrote within a tradition of love poetry in archaic Greece. Her poetry had roots; it was surely in its craft and themes a familiar form of expression. Hymns, poems of praise and blame, re-tellings of myth with culturally normative motives, and love poems are all traditional types found in Sappho's work. Yet the theme of love itself forced on Sappho a different structure of narrative from that of any other extant lyric poetry. The difference might be defined in two stages. The formal problem facing Sappho was to find a way of presenting the female persona as an erotic subject. Culturally acceptable models presumably did not include woman's pursuing man. Sappho's solution, to direct the erotic impulse toward other women, was perhaps a traditional one. On the social plane quite possibly girls before marriage were encouraged to cultivate female poetry, friendships, liaisons, and among them Sappho may have found her audience.[4]

But Sappho's confining of her poetic love-objects to other women did not in itself determine that she would write love poetry different from that of the male lyric poets. Sappho is fundamentally different because she explores what a woman might desire and might offer erotically and how these interact. Her romanticization of erotic life is based on woman's understanding of experience in a totally feminine context.[5] This paper, then, must first distinguish the patterns of erotic relations used by the male poets and by Sappho before describing how Sappho exploited the romantic possibilities of the lesbian patterns. Sappho's actual, personal experience in sexual relationships is not in question here; I am interested in Sappho's imaginative projection of emotional life into aesthetically pleasing, abstract shapes.

Fragments of love poems from the male lyric poets are scrappy, but a pattern of expression can be observed. The man is helpless, prostrate, stricken by the power of Eros or Aphrodite, but toward the particular boy or girl who attracts him the man is confident and prepared to seduce. For Eros or Aphrodite is the universal, eternal sexual longing which can never be mastered, while the individual provoking it is only a temporary focus of the longing, the prey or prize which loses its allure once the man has captured it. A short poem of Ibycus, a poet writing about sixty years later than Sappho, expresses the pattern very neatly (6 P):[6]

> Ἔρος αὖτέ με κυανέοισιν ὑπὸ
>   βλεφάροις τακέρ' ὄμμασι δερκόμενος
> κηλήμασι παντοδαποῖς ἐς ἄπει-
>   ρα δίκτυα Κύπριδος ἐσβάλλει·
> ἦ μὰν τρομέω νιν ἐπερχόμεον,
> ὥστε φερέζυγος ἵππος ἀεθλοφόρος ποτὶ γήραι
> ἀέκων σὺν ὄχεσφι θοοῖς ἐς|ἄμιλλαν ἔβα.

> Eros, again looking at me meltingly with his
> eyes under dark eyelids, flips me with manifold
> charms into the inescapable nets of Aphrodite.
> In truth I tremble at his coming as a yoke-
> bearing, prize-winning horse, nearing old age,
> unwillingly goes with his quick chariot into
> the fray.

The two rather disparate images reflect the poet's two responses, the one toward sexual longing in the abstract, the other toward the object. Eros has driven the narrator into the nets of Aphrodite; he is like a trapped and helpless wild animal.[7] But toward the object of his love the narrator is like an old prize-winning horse who returns again to the contest. Now he is active, competitive, and the boy will be his prize (if he wins).[8] There is a boast implicit in the epithet "prize-winning" for the horse: the narrator hints that he has won the individual boy before — but previous victories have secured him no respite from the power of Aphrodite. The reason is implied in the poem. Eros is said to look at him bewitchingly, to use charms as his snare. Surely it is the boy's eyes and charms that have captivated the narrator, but they are treated as the momentary location of Eros. When the narrator has won this boy for himself, Eros will laughingly skip off elsewhere. Anacreon too thought that the contest was with Eros (53 P):

> ἀστραγάλαι δ' Ἔρωτός εἰσιν
> μανίαι τε καὶ κυδοιμοί
>
> The dice of Eros are madnesses and uproars.

Other poets express the same dichotomy, though not so succinctly. Several fragments of Archilochus proclaim that the narrator is being overwhelmed by desire, for instance:[9]

> δύστηνος ἔγκειμαι πόθωι
> ἄψυχος, χαλεπῆισι θεῶν ὀδύνηισιν ἕκητι
> πεπαρμένος δι' ὀστέων
>
> Miserable I lie wrapped in longing, soulless,
> pierced through the bones by harsh griefs
> from the gods.

But in a long fragment, the Cologne Epode, Archilochus describes the seduction of a virgin girl. As the fragment takes up the girl is trying to dissuade the narrator from action, suggesting that he pay court to another girl, Neoboule, instead. The narrator, promising to go along with the girl's wish, promising to decide something with her (marriage?) later on, expends most of his eloquence in abuse of Neoboule. Then, putting an end to the dialogue, the narrator lays the girl among the flowers, gently caresses her, and "lets go his force," probably without deflowering her.[10] The narrator acts, despite his admitted haste, with a graceful, gentle masterfulness that bespeaks control, experience, self-assurance. The implied impotence of the first fragment is not imagined as impeding action where opportunity presents itself.

The same pattern can be demonstrated from Anacreon. In a fragment (68 P) the narrator complains that Eros like a bronze-smith again hit him with a hammer and dipped him in a wintry river. But elsewhere he has the speaker boast to a skittish girl (72 P):[11]

> πῶλε Θρηικίη, τί δή με
>   λοξὸν ὄμμασι βλέπουσα
> νηλέως φεύγεις, δοκεῖς δέ
>   μ' οὐδὲν εἰδέναι σοφόν;
> ἴσθι τοι, καλῶς μὲν ἄν τοι
>   τὸν χαλινὸν ἐμβάλοιμι,
> ἡνίας δ' ἔχων στρέφοιμί
>   σ' ἀμφὶ τέρματα δρόμου
> νῦν δὲ λειμῶνάς τε βόσκεαι
>   κοῦφά τε σκιρτῶσα παίζεις,
> δεξιὸν γὰρ ἱπποπείρην
>   οὐκ ἔχεις ἐπεμβάτην.

> Thracian filly, why do you glance at me askance
> and flee pitilessly? Do you think I have no art?
> Know, then, neatly could I throw on the bridle and
> holding the reins steer you around the course.
> At the moment you pasture in meadows and play,
> lightly prancing, for you do not have an adroit
> experienced rider.

The girl is pitiless as the incarnation of the pitiless pressure of Eros; as a particular girl she is tameable. The narrator's assurance of dominating the girl if he chooses is as complete as his helpless observation of her suspicious rejection of him.[12]

It is essential to the male lyric poet that the object of his passion be vulnerable to seduction, but unseduced. So the seducer in Archilochus's Cologne Epode, mentioned above, rejects the girl named Neoboule because she is too lusty. Neoboule is no longer virgin, innocent, sexually unaware, so she does not attract the erotic impulse. It is significant that Archilochus does not consider Neoboule, unlike himself, to be justified in her eagerness through her subjection to Aphrodite's power. Her drives are simply not brought into relationship with Aphrodite at all. Neoboule is in the poem to point up by contrast the pattern of ever-pursuing male lover and innocent beloved, whose innocence makes his or her allure almost abstract, suprapersonal.

Anacreon gives lovely expression to the allure of innocence in a brief poem (15 P):[13]

ὦ παῖ παρθένιον βλέπων
δίζημαί σε, σὺ δ᾽ οὐ κλύεις,
οὐκ εἰδὼς ὅτι τῆς ἐμῆς
ψυχῆς ἡνιοχεύεις.

Oh child, virgin-glancing, I seek you, but you
do not hear, not knowing that you are the
charioteer of my soul.

The child as a figure of Eros is charioteer, but the child in himself is passive, unaware, while Anacreon actively pursues him and must ultimately, in terms of the poetic pattern, seduce him.[14]

This pattern of longing for the ever uncapturable essence of Eros and excitement at discovering its momentary embodiment in a vulnerable, innocent figure, is the poetic rhythm of the male lyric poets. It allows the male to exalt passionate anguish and justify his loss of autonomy while maintaining a claim of potency. Both desire and the sweetness of potential triumph are raised to the highest pitch without the complexities and inhibitions of more prolonged interaction between two people. And the pattern remains the same whether girl or boy is the object of desire.

This pattern Sappho could not use. Had Sappho portrayed herself as an active seeker after the virginity of a succession of girls, even, she might have presented a figure too close to Neoboule for cultural acceptance or aesthetic appreciation among her contemporaries. But the poetic reason for the inappropriateness of the male pattern to Sappho is that the implicit metaphors of recurrent prostration, domination, and release are based on male sexual psychology, the man's sense of his action in sexual encounter. In order to make aesthetically integrated, convincing love poetry Sappho had to find (or make use of) patterns based on metaphors of female biology and psychology. The patterns had to allow her to express romantic longing, fulfillment, and struggle with the mystery of sexuality, with truth to her emotional and bodily sense of them.

Sappho's poetry is also in frustrating tatters. But the pattern that Sappho did use is revealed by two of her poems. The first, LP 1, the only definitely complete poem we have, goes in translation thus:[15]

> Richly-throned immortal Aphrodite, daughter of Zeus,
>   weaver of wiles, I pray to you: break not my
>   spirit, Lady, with heartache or anguish;
>
> But hither come, if ever in the past you heard my cry
>   from afar, and marked it, and came, leaving your
>   father's house,
>
> Your golden chariot yoked: sparrows beautiful and
>   swift conveyed you, with rapid wings a-flutter, above
>   the dark earth from heaven through the mid-air;
>
> And soon they were come, and you, Fortunate, with a
>   smile on your immortal face, asked what ails me now,
>   and why I am calling now,
>
> And what in my heart's madness I most desire to have:
>   Whom now must I persuade to join your friendship's
>   ranks? Who wrongs you, Sappho?
>
> For if she flees, she shall soon pursue; and if she
>   receives not gifts, yet shall she give; and if she
>   loves not, she shall soon love even against her will.
>
> Come to me now also, and deliver me from cruel anxieties;
>   fulfil all that my heart desires to fulfil, and be
>   yourself my comrade-in-arms.

This is the only poem of Sappho's in which the narrator expresses an adversary relationship with the love-object.[16] The attitude is the same as that of the male poets quoted, but the components are related in a different fashion. Sappho's narrator (identified with

Sappho by Aphrodite's use of her name) is on good terms with Aphrodite but helpless in the face of the love-object, the opposite of the male pattern. Comparison with the Ibycus poem quoted above (p. 48) makes the contrast clear. Sappho does not portray herself as a woman skilled in seduction, nor does she claim the potential to master the other or to "win." On the other hand, Aphrodite is not the capricious, impersonal force that she and Eros are for the male poets. She does not play games of challenge with Sappho. Far from trembling at her approach, Sappho calls her for help.[17] Aphrodite here is a cosmic affirmation of Sappho's own eroticism, the source of terrible pain but also of loveliness and joy, of contact with the divine, of heightened self-awareness, as the vivid sensuousness of the poem bears witness.[18] Sappho's address, consequently, is not to the girl she loves but to Aphrodite: her orientation in her helpless state is different from that of the male poets.[19]

But though Aphrodite may be her ally Sappho does not ask her to make the other girl submit, and Aphrodite offers only to have the other girl suffer too. Connection with Aphrodite does not lend Sappho any new power to impose herself on the other girl. It grants her rather a way of making manifest her own eroticism, which will perhaps, via the epiphany itself, draw the other girl closer to her. Aphrodite's spectacular arrival, in other words, will not only comfort Sappho with evidence of the goddess's affection but also give the other girl a potent new sense of Sappho's attractiveness.

Only in this fashion can the other girl be won. The other girl's response to Sappho must be spontaneous, for Sappho can find consummation of love only if it is offered; she cannot achieve her desire by "taking" the other girl. Thus unlike the innocent beloved of the male poets, the other girl's envisioned role here is to turn to Sappho out of her own longing. She must come independently to want Sappho before either woman can find intimacy satisfying.[20] But, again in contrast with the male poets, Sappho imagines that either woman might initiate the relationship, for the two women must be equals, each understanding the other from insight into herself.[21]

In a fragment (LP 49) Sappho says:[22]

ἠράμαν μὲν ἔγω τέθεν, Ἄτθι, πάλαι ποτά....
σμίκρα μοι πάις ἔμμεν᾽ ἐφαίνεο κἄχαρις.

I loved you, Atthis, long ago. . . . You seemed to
me to be a small and graceless child.

The name Atthis recurs in other of Sappho's poems (e.g. LP 96, 131) as a companion, so one can imagine the narrator telling Atthis about her previous attraction only after the two have become intimate, when Atthis is in a position to appreciate it. The second line also implies that Atthis's potential attractiveness was intuited by the narrator's insight before it became visible. The tone is very different from that of Anacreon's little poem about the boy who rules his soul (above, p. 51).

Sappho's poem LP 94 confirms the pattern I have been extrapolating from LP 1 and 49. The poem is damaged and incomplete, but the first twenty-six lines can be made out. The legible portion goes, in translation:[23]

> Honestly I wish I were dead. Weeping she left me
> With many tears, and said 'Oh what unhappiness is ours;
>   Sappho, I vow, against my will I leave you.'
> And this answer I made to her: 'Go, and fare well, and
>   remember me; you know how we cared for you.
> If not, yet I would remind you . . . of our past happiness.
> Many wreaths of violets and roses and . . . you put
>   around you at my side,
> And many woven garlands, fashioned of flowers, . . .
>   round your soft neck,
> And . . . with perfume of flowers, fit for a queen, you
>   anointed . . .
> And on soft beds . . . you would satisfy your longing . . .
> And no . . . holy, no . . . was there, from which we were
>   away

In this poem are found the mutual understanding and mutual desire that were absent from LP 1. The narrator (again named Sappho) recalls a whole range of shared experience, including but not limited to the erotic. The intimacy, she suggests, engages two complete personalities.[24]

The poem makes an interesting contrast with the Cologne Epode of Archilochus (described above, p. 49), for both poems involve conversations meant to define the erotic relationship between two people. In Archilochus's poem the girl presses for a verbal statement, perhaps an offer of marriage, rather than sexual contact, and the seducer must cut off the conversation in order to further the seduction. Sexual intimacy and verbal understanding here inhibit one another. In Sappho's poem the conversation is a continuation and confirmation of erotic intimacy, an attempt to perpetuate it. In Archilochus the conversation is manipulative, she negotiating, he trying to disarm her. The tension, directly reflected in dialogue, is between man and girl over who will get his or her way. As the narrator usurps control of the dialogue to bring it to a halt, so he gains ascendency over the girl. In LP 94 Sappho, the persona, also takes over the dialogue, but uses it to banish impending separation between herself and the other woman. Sappho's method of recreating the intimacy verbally to the girl whom she comforts is to reflect the girl's past happiness back to her: the verbs of the description are all second person (so far as can be told, given the broken text), and Sappho's only mention of herself is the "at my side." Thus Sappho dramatizes her absorption with the other woman, the lapse of her separate self-consciousness as she is caught up in the other's sensuousness. The other woman's happiness is in turn a reflection of her closeness to Sappho, since memory of it serves as the token of warmth that Sappho would have the girl carry away with her. The tension in Sappho's poem, then, is between the friends and the outside forces that are requiring them to separate. The aim of the dialogue is to obliterate the tension; it becomes monologue in order to insist on the unity of the two participants.

As a result of these differences the sense of space in the two poems is very different. Although the beginning of the Cologne Epode is lost, the extant portion implies that the narrator and the girl are alone somewhere in an open, undefined space, a flowery meadow, with nothing interposed between them and the cosmos. The girl herself is assimilated to this uncivilized world by the use of metaphors to describe her anatomy – "under beetling crags" and "grassy gardens."[25] She is trembling like a fawn with fear. In this natural world, where sex is a cosmic, inhuman force, conversation and plans have no place.

Sappho's poem presupposes a protected place containing the two women in perfect understanding. No problems of jealousy, no social pressures penetrate, yet it is not the natural world either, for art and luxury enclose it. I will return to this dimension of the poem later.

Sappho's poetic problem was to find a pattern consistent with female experience of love within which to express her romantic sensibility. The pattern of love I have been tracing in her poetry, of mutuality rather than domination and subjection, of intimacy based on comprehending the other out of the self, is the ideal characteristic of lesbian love, as Simone de Beauvoir asserts in *The Second Sex*:

> Between women love is contemplative; caresses are intended less to gain possession of the other than gradually to re-create the self through her; separateness is abolished, there is no struggle, no victory, no defeat; in exact reciprocity each is at once subject and object, sovereign and slave; duality becomes mutuality.[26]

De Beauvoir also speaks of seeing the self in the other, which she calls mirroring.[27] As de Beauvoir confirms, Sappho's sense of eroticism is based on feminine biology, on the fact that sexual response is felt within as an urge to receive and that a woman cannot aggressively "take" another in the absence of reciprocal interest. She confirms, too, a felt identity of two lovers which erases the distinction between "self" and "other," at least ideally, so that Sappho's concentration on the other woman in LP 94 can be seen as a poetic equivalent of erotic fulfillment.

So far, I have concentrated on the differences between Sappho's patterns of erotic imagination and those of the male lyric poets. But if Sappho was to create a romantic posture, she had to intensify and idealize the patterns of love and pain as a woman experiences them. Her method was to pick three aspects, or moments, of love to dramatize. The first I have already discussed:

it is the appeal to Aphrodite, who displaces the desired girl in Sappho's attention in LP 1 (quoted above, p. 52). In that poem Aphrodite becomes an affirmation of Sappho's own eroticism as a value in itself. Sappho is implicitly claiming that erotic desire, if cherished above release or calm, opens a path to divinity and absolute beauty, that through intensity of longing comes transcendence.[28]

So, too, in LP 2 Aphrodite is called to come to a lovely, protected sanctuary and pour out nectar. Ritual, celebratory terms are used this time to describe the same wish for the goddess's acknowledgement, the same claim on it, as in LP 1. In this poem apparently no second woman is present.[29] The one who prays here wishes for contact with sensuousness not as a directed feeling but as an embracing atmosphere.

But Aphrodite's coming is not pictured as bringing rest or resolution with it. As Sappho calls Aphrodite in LP 1 she recalls previous occasions when Aphrodite has responded. Those moments of glory occurred, but left in time a woman as limited and vulnerable and thwarted as before (so the poem implies). For the erotic impulse as Sappho projected it is less a matter of loving another individual than of finding in love a form of intensification and grandeur which must be ever renewed. As the male lyric poet stands in the throes of desire, contemplating the possibility of possessing the desired object, but knowing that no permanent peace will result, so Sappho in the grip of love calls on Aphrodite but knows she will find in Aphrodite's coming no enduring solution to her griefs. Whichever way it is envisioned, the rhythm is romantic, for it leads the individual on in a never-ending quest to escape the confines of the self.

The second aspect of love which Sappho romanticizes is the loss of the beloved by parting. Like the summons to Aphrodite, the poems of longing for one absent imply that bliss would come with the numinous presence of that individual. But the happiness theoretically attainable depends always on an impossible rearrangement of reality, so one must forever mourn its elusiveness. In LP 94 (quoted above, p. 54), Sappho uses the moment of parting as the frame for the picture of intimacy, for intimacy seems most precious, union most complete in the face of imminent loneliness. By viewing the relationship through the lens of idealization provided by the moment of parting, Sappho exacerbates present pain, while the earlier time together seems blissful and perfect, without complexity. Consequently, previous closeness and present desire can both be viewed as absolutes.[30]

In LP 96 Sappho recalls a beautiful woman now in Lydia with the certainty that she is longing for Atthis. The emotional dynamic of the poem is impossible to recover in full, though longing for a lost intimacy is at the heart of it. The poem is addressed to someone, perhaps Atthis. And in the broken section beyond line twenty-four someone, probably Aphrodite, is said to have poured nectar once. The poem must have juxtaposed the transcendence of a time in Aphrodite's presence with the subsequent absence of a lovely woman. Fragmentary LP 95, addressed to Gongyla, has verbs in the past tense narrating some event, followed by the wish to die. The two themes, Aphrodite and the pain of loss, are again connected, now in ritualized form, in LP 140. The two-line fragment comes from a lament for Adonis addressed to Aphrodite. The lamenters participate in Aphrodite's grief, and perhaps the instructions, "beat your breasts, maidens, and tear your clothes," were actually carried out in ceremony. In these poems the extremes of emotional life, presence of Aphrodite and mortal pain of loss, come together. Sappho here romanticizes what is in fact the dominant experience of women in love-making and in child-birth — intimacy followed by withdrawal.

The final way in which Sappho shapes her pattern to romanticism is in the creation of a private world. In this she depends specifically on the homosexual relationship, that is, on the fact that two women can mirror one another. For to come together each woman must spontaneously wish to be close to the other; the act of love requires communication between the two, since it has no other outward manifestation. Then each woman can imagine the other by reference to herself. The dynamic of mutual erotic attraction, the interplay between two women, becomes an invisible bond, or in Sappho's formulation a single enclosure, impenetrable by others, in which the two are so open to one another that they feel united. It is the poetic equivalent of Simone de Beauvoir's phrase, "duality becomes mutuality."

The private space is a metaphor for emotional openness in a psychological setting apart from the normal, separate from marriage, home, social life, from everything experienced by a woman in the ordinary course of life.[31] In LP 2 this private space is given form as a shrine to which Aphrodite is to come. The sacred spot, set apart from the rest of the world, is not accessible to non-worshippers, that is, those who do not participate in this intimacy with Aphrodite.

In LP 94, Sappho creates the private world in subtler fashion. This is the poem whose use of space was contrasted with the Cologne Epode. Sappho implies that the two women have been alone together in soft and sensuous surroundings, somehow cut off from the rest of the world. But once they have parted their private intimacy can be found only in memory. The poem preserves the moment when Sappho transmutes the old physical closeness into a new purely emotional connection. So the poem becomes the container of the shared memories, hence itself the private space, the common world into which either can enter and find the other imaginatively.

In LP 96, the poem recalling a woman in Lydia, the private space is created by evoking the moon. The woman in Lydia is lovelier than those about her as the moon outshines the stars when the sun has set, the moon which shines on fields and sea, while dew falls and flowers bloom. The moon's light forms an analogy for the girl's beauty, defines a non-daylight world in which it is to be found, and unites the speaker with the girl, since the speaker is a privileged observer of the radiance spreading over an otherwise empty world. Having entered the world of moonlight the speaker can "see" the woman in Lydia and know that she in turn is longing for someone. A kind of communication defies the separation even while it sharpens it. And as with LP 94, the poem itself is the entry into this world by revealing the analogy between moon and girl. Thus the auditor of the poem has the key to entry into a special state of mind in which she can feel connected with an absent or fictional lover while intensifying the clarity of her longing and loneliness.

The beautiful robes and ornaments and flowers with which Sappho decorates her poems are the furnishings of this poetically-created private space. And the charm and enchantment of her poetry in themselves recreate the experience of being rapt out of ordinary preoccupations into a special, lovely, divinely-inspired world. For the private space exists, in fact, only in the poem.

The existence of a private space, created by the poem, counterbalances the focus on loss in Sappho's poetry. Indeed, the continuation of the private space is asserted in the face of the loss of the loved woman. Thus the private space is the most important metaphor for love in the poetry of Sappho. Itself based on a contradiction, that the inward can become outward, that solitude can be replaced by perfect intimacy, the claim of a private world can mediate the contradictions of Sappho's romanticism. Powerful erotic drive can coexist with a biological role as non-aggressor, Sappho's self-involvement can coexist with intimacy with another, and lament for the loss of another can coexist with the certainty that the unity of the two still exists. So Sappho's romanticism devolves on the creation of a poetic metaphor that both affirms and transcends the inward, self-contained nature of woman's love.

Even within Sappho's poetry the private world has only fictional existence. That is, she never presents herself or her speakers as being within it, but only as looking forward or back to it. But for Sappho's audience the poetry itself was a private imaginative world within whose bounds they might open themselves to rich and sensuous self-expression.

Notes

An earlier version of this paper was given at the Fourth Berkshire Conference on Women's History, Mount Holyoke College, August, 1978.

1. *Don Juan*, Canto III, stanza 86.
2. E.g. D. Page, *Sappho and Alcaeus* (Oxford 1955) 141, quoting J.A. Symonds; C. Segal, "Eros and Incantation: Sappho and Oral Poetry," *Arethusa* 7 (1974) 139-60; G. Lanata, "Sul linguaggio amoroso di

Saffo," *QUCC* 2 (1966) 63-79.

3. Romanticism is a tricky term to use since it is so ill-defined. I mean to evoke literary, not popular associations, essentially yearning for escape from the isolation of the self and affirmation of the yearning in the face of knowledge that escape is impossible. It is a self-conscious, aesthetic attitude that paradoxically distances the individual from that into which he would lose himself. For nineteenth-century romanticism see R. Wellek, "Romanticism Re-examined," in N. Frye, ed., *Romanticism Reconsidered* (New York 1963), 107-33, who characterizes it as "the implication of imagination, symbol, myth, and organic nature . . . as part of the great endeavor to overcome the split between subject and object, the self and the world, the conscious and the unconscious," (132). If for "world," one substitutes "other," the definition fits Sappho. On the other hand the nineteenth-century view of the lyric poet as communing with himself (for which see M.H. Abrams, *The Mirror and the Lamp* [New York 1958] 21-26 and *passim*) does not apply to Sappho.

4. G. Nagy, *Comparative Studies in Greek and Indic Meter* (Cambridge, Mass. 1974) 118-39, concludes that Sappho's meters are more archaic than the hexameter of epic. He suggests that Sappho, like epic, had inherited a traditional language and traditional subject matter adapted to the meters she uses. C. Calame, *Les choeurs de jeunes filles en Grèce archaïque* I (Rome 1977) collects extensive evidence for an established practice of grouping young girls under the leadership of one who is both choral leader and educator. Sappho may have fulfilled some such function. On the question of Sappho's audience see J. Russo, "Reading the Greek Lyric Poets," *Arion* n.s. 1 (1973-74) 707-30; also J. Hallett, "Sappho and Her Social Context: Sense and Sensuality," *Signs* 4 (1979) 447-64, and my response, 465-71.

5. The psychological reality and romantic treatment of it may also have been an inherited part of women's poetry. But at the very least Sappho exploited the possibilities of such poetry with great personal sensitivity. Calame (above) 430-31, sees Sappho's poetry as escaping from its institutional context into accents of compelling individual emotion. P. Friedrich, *The Meaning of Aphrodite* (Chicago 1978) 112-23, is emphatic about Sappho's distinctiveness, both from male poets and, implicitly, from all earlier poets.

6. The texts of the poems by Ibycus and Anacreon are taken from the edition of D. Page, *Poetae Melici Graeci* (Oxford 1962). The translations, unless otherwise stated, are my own.

7. By use of the term "narrator" I mean to distinguish the first-person of the poem from the poet.

8. The figure implied by the poem is presumably a boy if the poem was written for the court of Polycrates on Samos. See D. Campbell, *Greek Lyric Poetry: A Selection* (Glasgow 1967) 305-307 (notes on Ibycus).

9. Archilochus 104, E. Diehl, ed., *Anthologia Lyrica Graeca* (rev. R. Beutler, Leipzig 1952). Cf. Archilochus 112 and 118. Archilochus is not strictly speaking a lyric poet but for my purposes can be included

under that rubric.
10. For text, translation, and discussions see J. Van Sickle, ed., *The New Archilochus, Arethusa* 9 (1976). On the lyric voice of Archilochus see see K.J. Dover, "The Poetry of Archilochus," *Archiloque, Entretiens sur l'Antiquité Classique* X (Geneva 1964), 181-222.
11. According to Heracleitus, who quotes the poem, it was addressed as a reproach to a woman of meretricious mind and haughty disposition. See Campbell (*op. cit.*, note 7) 328.
12. On the playful and ironic tone of Anacreon's poetry see G.M. Kirkwood, *Early Greek Monody* (Ithaca 1974) 161-63.
13. See Kirkwood (above) 164, for a slightly different text and for the bibliography cited there.
14. Anacreon's poetry does not always portray suffering over an innocent figure. In 13 P the narrator says that Eros invited him to play with a girl, but she is from Lesbos, disdains his grey hair, and gapes at another (girl or set of hair). In 1 P, fr. 4, Anacreon's narrator claims to have fought Eros and won.
15. The translation is that of D. Page, *Sappho and Alcaeus* 4. The text is given in Page and in E. Lobel and D. Page, *Poetarum Lesbiorum Fragmenta* (Oxford 1955), hereafter LP.
16. On the recast epic tone of this poem see J. Marry, "Sappho and the Heroic Ideal: ἔρωτος αρετή," *Arethusa* 12 (1979) 71-92. He does not consider the difference in tone between this poem and Sappho's other extant poetry.
17. See H. Saake, *Zur Kunst Sapphos* (Paderborn 1971) 41f., for the surprise of Sappho's asking Aphrodite to come (rather than simply release her from pain).
18. The question of the tone of this poem has occasioned much controversy. For an interesting analysis see K. Stanley, "The Role of Aphrodite in Sappho Fr. 1," *GRBS* 17 (1976) 305-21. For the controversy cf. his bibliography.
19. Sappho treats Eros somewhat differently. Cf. LP 47 and 130.
20. Page's contention (*Sappho and Alcaeus* 14-15) that Sappho implies that the other girl's suit will not be met with favor because Sappho will have lost interest in her is disputed by others (bibliography in Kirkwood [*op. cit.*, note 12] 249, note 23). But certainly some effort on the girl's part is indicated. She will behave like an active suitor for favor, giving gifts, rather than simply fall into waiting arms.
21. See W. Schadewaldt, *Sappho: Welt und Dichtung: Dasein in der Liebe* (Potsdam 1950) 138-45, for emphasis on Aphrodite as the one who calms and joins together.
22. The lines are paraphrased by Terentius Maurus, implying that they were consecutive originally. Modern editors place dots between them because the train of thought appears very abrupt. Campbell (*op cit.*, note 7) 276, in his notes to the poem remarks that ἄχαρις probably has the additional sense of "immature" attributed to it by Plutarch, *Amat.* 5.
23. The translation is by Page, *Sappho and Alcaeus* 76. The first line of the poem is missing. In the stanza following the last one I quoted the word

"grove" is preserved.

24. For an analysis of this poem along similar lines see T. McEvilley, "Sappho, Fragment Ninety-Four," *Phoenix* 25 (1971) 1-11.

25. Lines 14-16 of the text given in *Arethusa* (*op. cit.*, note 10).

26. *The Second Sex* (tr. H.M. Parshley, New York 1974) 465.

27. *The Second Sex* 465.

28. See B. Gentili, "La Veneranda Saffo," *QUCC* 2 (1966) 37-40, for discussion of Alcaeus's phrase, "awesome Sappho."

29. For an analysis of the formal aspects of the poem see T. McEvilley, "Sappho, fragment 2," *Phoenix* 26 (1972) 323-33.

30. On the "love and death" motif in Sappho's poetry, including this poem, see Lanata (*op. cit.*, note 2) 72-73. For the recalled happiness as imaginary see McEvilley (*op. cit.*, note 25) 8ff.

31. On the psychology of a private erotic world see my article, "Retreat from the Male: Catullus 62 and Sappho's Erotic Flowers," *Ramus* 6 (1977) 92-93.

Gardens of nymphs: Public and private in Sappho's lyrics

JACK WINKLER

Stanford University

MONIQUE WITTIG and Sande Zeig in their *Lesbian Peoples: Material for a Dictionary* devote a full page to Sappho.[1] The page is blank. Their silence is one quite appropriate response to Sappho's lyrics, particularly refreshing in comparison to the relentless trivialization, the homophobic anxieties and the sheer misogyny that have infected so many ancient and modern responses to her work.[2] This anxiety itself requires some analysis. Part of the explanation is the fact that her poetry is continuously focussed on women and sexuality, subjects which provoke many readers to excess.[3] But the centering on women and sexuality is not quite enough to explain the mutilated and violent discourse which keeps cropping up around her. After all, Anacreon speaks of the same subjects. A deeper explanation refers to the *subject* more than the object of her lyrics — the fact that it is a *woman* speaking about women and sexuality. To some audiences this would have been a double violation of the ancient rules which dictated that a proper woman was to be silent in the public world (defined as men's sphere) and that a proper woman accepted the administration and definition of her sexuality by her father and her husband. I will set aside here the question of how women at various times and places actually conducted their lives in terms of private and public activity, appearance and authority. If we were in a position to know more of the actual texture of ancient life and not merely the maxims and rules uttered by men, we could fairly expect to find that many women abided by these social rules or were forced to, and that they sometimes enforced obedience on other women; but, since all social codes can be manipulated and subverted as well as obeyed, we would also expect to find that many women had effective strategies of resistance and false compliance by which they attained a working degree of freedom for their lives.[4] Leaving aside all these questions, however, I simply begin my analysis with the fact that there was available a common understanding that proper women ought to be publicly submissive to male definitions, and that a very great pressure of propriety could at any time be invoked to shame a woman who acted on her own sexuality.

This is at least the public ethic and the male norm. It cannot have been entirely absent from the society of Lesbos in Sappho's time. What I want to recover in this paper are the traces of Sappho's own consciousness in the face of these norms, her attitude to the public ethic and her allusions to private reality. My way of "reading what is there"[5] focuses on the politics of space — the role of women as excluded from public male domains and enclosed in private female areas — and on Sappho's consciousness[6] of this ideology. My analysis avowedly begins with an interest in sexual politics — the relations of power between women and men as two classes in the same society. My premise is that gender-consciousness is at least as fundamental a way of identifying oneself and interpreting the world as any other class-membership or category. In some sense the choice of a method will predetermine the kind and range of results which may emerge: a photo-camera will not record sounds, a non-political observer will not notice facts of political significance. Thus my readings of Sappho are in principle not meant to displace other readings but to add to the store of perceptions of "what is there."

There are various "publics" and "privates" which might be contrasted. What I have in mind for this paper by "public" is quite specifically the recitation of Homer at civic festivals considered as an expression of common cultural traditions. Samuel Butler notwithstanding, Homer and the singers of his tradition were certainly men and the Homeric epics cannot be conceived as women's songs.[7] Women are integral to the social and poetic structure of both *Iliad* and *Odyssey,* and the *notion* of a woman's consciousness is particularly vital to the *Odyssey.*[8] But Nausikaa and Penelope live in a male-prominent world, coping with problems of honor and enclosure which were differentially assigned to women,[9] and their "subjectivity" in the epic must ultimately be analyzed as an expression of a male consciousness. Insofar as Homer presents a set of conventional social and literary formulas, he inescapably embodies and represents the definition of public culture as male territory.[10]

Archaic lyric, such as that composed by Sappho, was also not composed for private reading but for performance to an audience.[11] Sappho often seems to be searching her soul in a very intimate way but this intimacy is in some measure formulaic[12] and is certainly shared with some group of listeners. And yet, maintaining this thesis of the public character of lyric, we can still propose three senses in which such song may be "private": composed in the person of a woman (whose consciousness was socially defined as outside the public world of men), shared only with women (that is, other "private" persons; τάδε νῦν ἐταίραις ταῖς ἔμαις τέρπνα κάλως ἀείσω, "and now I shall sing this beautiful song to delight the women who are my companions," frag. 160 L-P[13]), and sung on informal occasions, what we would simply call poetry readings, rather than on specific ceremonial occasions (sacrifice, festival, leave-taking, initiation).[14] The lyric tradition, G. Nagy argues,[15] may be older that the epic, and if older perhaps equally honored as an achievement of beauty in its own right. The view of lyric as a subordinate element in celebrations and formal occasions is no more compelling than the view, which I prefer, of song as honored and celebrated at least sometimes in itself. Therefore I doubt that Sappho always needed a sacrifice or dance or wedding *for which* to compose a song; the institution of lyric composition was strong enough to occasion her songs *as songs.* Certainly Sappho speaks of goddesses and religious festivities, but it is by no means certain that her own poems are either for a cult-performance or that her circle of women friends (*hetairai*) is identical in extension with the celebrants in a festival she mentions.[16] It is possible that neither of these latter two senses of "private" were historically valid for Sappho's performances. Yet her lyrics, as compositions which had some publicity, bear some quality of being in principle from another world than Homer's, not just from a different tradition, and they embody a consciousness both of her "private," woman-centered world and the other, "public" world. This essay is an experiment in using these categories to unfold some aspects of Sappho's many-sided meaning.

Poem 1 is one of the passages in Sappho which has been best illuminated in recent criticism. Several analyses have developed the idea that Sappho is speaking in an imagined scene which represents that of Diomedes on the battlefield in *Iliad* 5.[17] Sappho uses a traditional prayer formula, of which Diomedes' appeal to Athena at *Iliad* 5.115-117 is an example ("Hear me, Atrytone, child of aegis-bearing Zeus; if ever you stood beside my father supporting his cause in bitter battle, now again support me, Athena"), and she models Aphrodite's descent to earth in a chariot on the descent of Athena and Hera (5.719-772), who are coming to help the wounded Diomedes (5.781). Sappho asks Aphrodite to be her ally, literally her companion in battle, *symmachos*.

> Intricate, undying Aphrodite, snare-weaver, child of Zeus, I pray thee,
> do not tame my spirit, great lady, with pain and sorrow. But come to me
> now if ever before you heard my voice from afar and leaving your father's
> house, yoked golden chariot and came. Beautiful sparrows swiftly brought you
> to the murky ground with a quick flutter of wings from the sky's height
> through clean air. They were quick in coming. You, blessed goddess,
> a smile on your divine face, asked what did I suffer, this time again,
> and why did I call, this time again, and what did I in my frenzied heart
> most want to happen. Whom am I to persuade, this time again . . .
> to lead to your affection? Who, O Sappho, does you wrong? For one who flees will
> soon pursue, one who rejects gifts will soon be making offers, and one who
> does not love will soon be loving, even against her will. Come to me even

now, release me from these mean anxieties, and do what my heart
   wants done,
you yourself be my ally.[18]

One way of interpreting the correspondences which have been
noticed is to say that Sappho presents herself as a kind of Diomedes
on the field of love, that she is articulating her own experience in
traditional (male) terms and showing that women too have *aretê*.[19]
But this view that the poem is mainly about *erôs* and *aretê*, and
uses Diomedes merely as a background model, falls short.
Sappho's use of Homeric passages is a way of allowing us, even
encouraging us, to approach her consciousness as a woman and
poet reading Homer. The Homeric hero is not just a starting point
for Sappho's discourse about her own love, rather Diomedes as he
exists in the *Iliad* is central to what Sappho is saying about the
distance between Homer's world and her own. A woman listening
to the *Iliad* must cross over a gap which separates her experience
from the subject of the poem, a gap which does not exist in quite
the same way for male listeners. How can Sappho murmur along
with the rhapsode the speeches of Diomedes, uttering and im-
personating his appeal for help? Sappho's answer to this aesthetic
problem is that she can only do so by substituting her concerns
for those of the hero while maintaining the same structure of
plight/prayer/intervention. Poem 1 says, among other things,
"This is how I, a woman and poet, become able to appreciate a
typical scene from the *Iliad*."
   Though the Diomedeia is a typical passage, Sappho's choice of
it is not random, for it is a kind of test case for the issue of
women's consciousness as participants without a poetic voice of
their own at the public recitations of traditional Greek heroism. In
Iliad 5, between Diomedes' appeal to the goddess and the descent
of Athena and Hera, Aphrodite herself is driven from the battlefield after Diomedes stabs her in the hand. The poet identifies
Aphrodite as a "feminine" goddess, weak (*analkis*), unsuited to
take part in male warfare (331f., 428ff.). Her appropriate sphere,
says Diomedes exulting in his victory over her, is to seduce weak
(*analkides*) women (348ff.). By implication, if "feminine" women

(and all mortal women are "feminine" by definition and prescription) try to participate in men's affairs — warfare or war poetry — they will, like Aphrodite, be driven out at spear point.

Poem 1 employs not only a metaphorical use of the *Iliad* (transfering the language for the experience of soldiers to the experience of women in love) and a familiarization of the alien poem (so that it now makes better sense to women readers), but a *multiple identification* with its characters. Sappho is acting out the parts both of Diomedes and of Aphrodite as they are characterized in *Iliad* 5. Aphrodite, like Sappho, suffers pain (ὀδύνῃσι, 354), and is consoled by a powerful goddess who asks "Who has done this to you?" (373) Aphrodite borrows Ares' chariot to escape from the battle and ride to heaven (358-367), the reverse of her action in Sappho's poem.[20] Sappho therefore is in a sense presenting herself both as a desperate Diomedes needing the help of a goddess (Athena → Aphrodite) and as a wounded and expelled female (Aphrodite → Sappho) seeking a goddess' consolation (Dione → Aphrodite).

This multiple identification with several actors in an Iliadic scene represents on another level an admired feature of Sappho's poetics — her adoption of multiple points of view in a single poem. This is especially noteworthy in poem 1 where she sketches a scene of encounter between a victim and a controlling deity. The intensification of pathos and mastery in the encounter is due largely to the ironic *double consciousness* of the poet-Sappho speaking in turn the parts of suffering "Sappho" and impassive goddess. Such many-mindedness is intrinsic to the situation of Greek women understanding men's culture, as it is to any silenced group within a culture which acknowledges its presence but not its authentic voice and right to self-determination. This leads to an interesting reversal of the standard (and oppressive) stricture on women's literature that it represents only a small and limited area of the larger world.[21] Such a view portrays women's consciousness according to the *social* contrast of public/private, as if women's literature occupied but a small circle somewhere inside the larger circle of men's literature, just as women are restricted to a domestic sanctuary. But insofar as men's public culture is truly public, displayed as the governing norm of social interaction "in the streets," it is accessible to women as well as men. Because men define and exhibit their language and manners as *the* culture and segregate women's language and manners as a subculture, inaccessible to and protected from extra-familial men, women are in the position of knowing two cultures where men know only one. From the point of view of consciousness, we must diagram the circle of women's literature as a larger one which includes men's literature as one phase or compartment of women's cultural knowledge. Women in a male-prominent society are thus like a linguistic minority in a culture whose public actions are all conducted in the majority language. To participate even passively in the public arena the minority must be bilingual; the majority feels no such need to learn the minority's language. Sappho's consciousness therefore is necessarily a double-consciousness, her participation in the public literary tradition always contains an inevitable alienation.

Poem 1 contains a statement of how important it is to have a double consciousness. Aphrodite reminds "Sappho" of the ebb and flow of conflicting emotions, of sorrow succeeded by joy, of apprehensiveness followed by relief, of loss turning into victory. This reminder not to be single-mindedly absorbed in one moment of experience can be related to the pattern of the *Iliad* in general, where the tides of battle flow back and forth, flight alternating with pursuit. This is well illustrated in *Iliad* 5, which is also the Homeric locus for the specific form of alternation in fortunes which consists of wounding and miraculous healing. Two gods (Aphrodite and Ares) and one hero (Aeneas) are injured and saved. Recuperative alternation is the theme of poem 1, as it is of *Iliad* 5. But because of Sappho's "private" point of view and double consciousness it becomes not only the theme but the *process* of the poem, in the following sense: Sappho appropriates an alien text, the very one which states the exclusion of "weak" women from men's territory; she implicitly reveals the inadequacy of that denigration; and she restores the fullness of Homer's text by isolating and alienating its very pretense to a justified exclusion of the feminine and the erotic.

Sappho's poetic strategy finally leads to a re-reading of *Iliad* 5 in the light of her poem 1. When we have absorbed Sappho's complex re-impersonation of the Homeric roles (male and female) and learned to see what was marginal as encompassing, we notice that there is a strain of anxious self-alienation in Diomedes' expulsion of Aphrodite. The overriding need of a battling warrior is to be strong and unyielding; hence the ever-present temptation (which is also a desire) is to be weak. This is most fully expressed at *Iliad* 22.111-130, where Hector views laying down his weapons to parley with Achilles as effeminate and erotic. Diomedes' hostility to Aphrodite (= the effeminate and erotic) is a kind of scapegoating, his affirmation of an ideal of masculine strength against his *own* possible "weakness." For, in other contexts outside the press of battle, the Homeric heroes have intense emotional lives and their vulnerability there is much like Sappho's: they are as deeply committed to friendship networks as Sappho ("He gave the horses to Deipylos, his dear comrade, whom he valued more than all his other age-mates," 325f.); they give and receive gifts as Sappho does; they wrong each other and re-establish friendships with as much feeling as Sappho and her beloved. In a "Sapphic" reading, the emotional isolation of the Iliadic heroes from their domestic happiness stands out more strongly ("no longer will his children run up to his lap and say 'Papa'," 408). We can reverse the thesis that Sappho uses Homer to heroize her world and say that insofar as her poems are a reading of Homer (and so lead us back to read Homer again), they set up a feminine perspective on male activity which shows more clearly the inner structure and motivation of the exclusion of the feminine from male arenas.

I return to the image of the double circle — Sappho's consciousness is a larger circle enclosing the smaller one of Homer. Reading the *Iliad* is for her an experience of double consciousness. The movement thus created is threefold: by temporarily restricting herself to that smaller circle she can understand full well what Homer is saying; when she brings her total experience to bear she sees the limitation of his world; by offering her version of this experience in a poem she shows the strengths of her world, the apparent incompleteness of Homer's, and finally the easily-overlooked subtlety of Homer's. This threefold movement of appropriation from the "enemy," exposure of his weakness and recognition of his worth is like the actions of Homeric heroes who vanquish, despoil and sometimes forgive. Underlying the relations of Sappho's persona to the characters of Diomedes and Aphrodite are the relations of Sappho the author to Homer, a struggle of reader and text (audience and tradition), of woman listening and man reciting.

A sense of what we now call the sexual politics of literature seems nearly explicit in poem 16:

> Some assert that a troup of horsemen, some of foot-soldiers, some a fleet of ships is the most beautiful thing on the dark earth; but I assert that it is whatever anyone loves. It is quite simple to make this intelligible to all, for she who was far and away preeminent in beauty of all humanity, Helen, abandoning her husband, the . . .,
>   went
> sailing to Troy and took no thought for child or dear parents, but beguiled . . . herself . . ., for . . . lightly . . . reminds me now of
>   Anaktoria
> absent: whose lovely step and shining glance of face I would prefer to see than Lydians' chariots and fighting men in arms . . . cannot be . . . human . . . to wish to share . . . unexpectedly. (This is a poem of eight stanzas, of which the first, second, third and fifth are almost intact, the rest lost or very fragmentary.)

It is easy to read this as a comment on the system of values in heroic poetry. Against the panoply of men's opinions on beauty (all of which focus on military organizations, regimented masses of anonymous fighters), Sappho sets herself — "but I" — and a very abstract proposition about desire. The stanza first opposes one woman to a mass of men and then transcends that opposition when Sappho announces that "the most beautiful" is "whatever you or I or anyone may long for." This amounts to a re-interpretation of the kind of meaning the previous claims had, rather than a mere contest of claimants for supremacy in a category whose meaning is agreed upon.[22] According to Sappho, what men mean when they claim that a troup of cavalrymen is very beautiful is that they intensely desire such a troup. Sappho speaks as a woman opponent entering the lists with men, but her proposition is not that men value military forces whereas she values desire, but rather that all valuation is an act of desire. Men are perhaps unwilling to see their values as erotic in nature, their ambitions for victory and strength as a kind of choice. But it is clear enough to Sappho that men are in love with masculinity and that epic poets are in love with military prowess.

Continuing the experiment of reading this poem as about poetry, we might next try to identify Helen as the Iliadic character. But Homer's Helen cursed herself for abandoning her husband and coming to Troy; Sappho's Helen, on the contrary, is held up as proof that it is right to desire one thing above all others, and to follow the beauty perceived no matter where it leads. There is a charming parody of logical argumentation in these stanzas; the underlying, real argument I would re-construct as follows, speaking for the moment in Sappho's voice. "Male poets have talked of military beauty in positive terms, but of women's beauty (especially Helen's) as baneful and destructive. They will probably never see the lineaments of their own desires as I do, but let me try to use some of their testimony against them, at least to expose the paradoxes of their own system. I shall select the woman whom men both desire and despise in the highest degree. What they have damned her for was, in one light, an act of the highest courage and commitment, and *their own poetry* at one point makes grudging admission that she surpasses all the moral censures levelled against her — the Teichoskopia (*Iliad* 3.121-244). Helen's abandonment of her husband and child and parents is mentioned there (139, 174), and by a divine manipulation she feels a change of heart, now desiring her former husband and city and parents (139) and calling herself a bitch (180). But these are the poet's sentiments, not hers; he makes her a puppet of his feeling, not a woman with a mind of her own. The real Helen was powerful enough to leave a husband, parents and child whom she valued less than the one she fell in love with. (I needn't and won't mention her lover's name: the person — male or female — is not relevant to my argument.) Indeed she was so powerful that she beguiled Troy itself at that moment when, in the midst of its worst suffering, the senior counsellors watched her walk along the city wall and said, in their chirpy old men's voices, 'There is no blame for Trojans or armored Achaians to suffer pains so long a time for such a woman.' (156f.)"

So far I have been speaking Sappho's mind as I see it behind this poem. There is an interesting problem in lines 12ff., where most modern editors of Sappho's text have filled the gaps with anti-Helen sentiments, on the order of "but (Aphrodite) beguiled her . . ., for (women are easily manipulated,) light(-minded . . .)." We do not know what is missing, but it is more consistent with Sappho's perspective, as I read it, to keep the subject of παράγαγ', "beguiled," the same as in the preceding clause — Helen. "Helen beguiled . . . itself (or, herself)," some feminine noun, such as "city," "blame" (nemesis), or the like. What is easily manipulated and light-minded (kouphōs) are the senior staff of Troy, who astonishingly dismiss years of suffering as they breathe a romantic sigh when Helen passes.

Perhaps Sappho's most impressive fragment is poem 31:

> That one seems to me to be like the gods, the man whosoever sits facing you and listens nearby to your sweet speech and desirable laughter — which surely terrifies the heart in my chest; for as I look briefly at you, so can I no longer speak at all, my tongue is silent, broken, a silken fire suddenly has spread beneath my skin, with my eyes I see nothing, my hearing hums, a cold sweat grips me, a trembling seizes me entire, more pale than grass am I, I seem to myself to be little short
> of dead. But everything is to be endured, since even a pauper . . .

The first stanza is a makarismos, a traditional formula of praise and well-wishing, "happy the man who . . .," and is often used to celebrate the prospect of a happy marriage.[23] For instance, "That man is far and away blessed beyond all others who plies you with dowry and leads you to his house; for I have never seen with my eyes a mortal person like you, neither man nor woman. A holy dread grips me as I gaze at you." (Odyssey 6.158-161) In fact this passage from Odysseus' speech to Nausikaa is so close in structure (makarismos followed by a statement of deep personal dread) to poem 31 that I should like to try the experiment of reading the beginning of Sappho's poem as a re-creation of that scene from the Odyssey.

If Sappho is speaking to a young woman ("you") as Nausikaa, with herself in the role of an Odysseus, then there are only two persons present in the imagined scene.[24] This is certainly true to the emotional charge of the poem, in which the power and tension flow between Sappho and the woman she sees and speaks to, between "you" and "I." The essential statement of the poem is, like the speech of Odysseus to Nausikaa, a lauding of the addressee and an abasement of the speaker which together have the effect of establishing a working relationship between two people of real power. The rhetoric of praise and of submission are necessary because the poet and the shipwrecked man are in fact very threatening. Most readers feel the paradox of poem 31's eloquent statement of speechlessness, its powerful declaration of helplessness; as in poem 1, the poet is masterfully in control of herself as victim. The underlying relation of power then is the opposite of its superficial form: the addressee is of a delicacy and fragility which would be shattered by the powerful presence of the poet unless she makes elaborate obeisance, designed to disarm and, by a careful planting of hints, to seduce.

The anonymous "that man whosoever" (κῆνος ὤνηρ ὄττις in Sappho, κεῖνος ὅς κε in Homer) is a rhetorical cliché, not an actor in the imagined scene. Interpretations which *focus* on "that someone (male)" as a bridegroom (or suitor or friend) who is actually present and occupying the attention of the addressee miss the strategy of persuasion which informs the poem and in doing so reveal their own androcentric premises. In depicting "the man" as a concrete person central to the scene and godlike in power, such interpretations misread a figure of speech as a literal statement and thus add the weight of their own pro-male values to Sappho's woman-centered consciousness. "That man" in poem 31 is like the military armament in poem 16, an introductory set-up to be dismissed: we do not imagine that the speaker of poem 16 is actually watching a fleet or infantry; no more need we think that Sappho is watching a man sitting next to her beloved. To whom, in that case, would Sappho be addressing herself? Such a reading makes poem 31 a modern lyric of totally internal speech, rather than a rhetorically-structured public utterance which imitates other well known occasions for public speaking (prayer, supplication, exhortation, congratulation).

My reading of poem 31 explains why "that man" has assumed a grotesque prominence in discussions of it. Androcentric habits of thought are part of the reason, but even more important is Sappho's intention to hint obliquely at the notion of a bridegroom just as Odysseus does to Nausikaa. Odysseus the stranger designs his speech to the princess around the roles which she and her family will find acceptable — helpless suppliant, valorous adventurer, and potential husband.[25] The ordinary protocols of marital brokerage in ancient society are a system of discreet offers and counter-offers which must maintain at all times the possibility for saving face, for declining with honor and respect to all parties. Odysseus' speech to Nausikaa contains these delicate approaches to the offer of marriage which every reader would appreciate, just as Alkinoos understands Nausikaa's thoughts of marriage in her request to go wash her brothers' dancing clothes: "So she spoke, for she modestly avoided mentioning the word 'marriage' in the presence of her father; but he understood her perfectly." (*Odyssey* 6.66f.) Such skill at innuendo and respectful obliquity is one of the ordinary-language bases for the refined art of lyric speech. Sappho's hint that "someone" enjoys a certain happiness is, like Odysseus' identical statement, a polite self-reference and an invitation to take the next step. Sappho plays with the role of Odysseus as suitor extraordinary, an unheard of stranger who might fulfill Nausikaa's dreams of marriage contrary to all the ordinary expectations of her society. She plays too with the humble formalities of self-denigration and obeisance, all an expansion of σέβας μ' ἔχει εἰσορόωντα, "holy dread grips me as I gaze on you." (*Odyssey* 161).

"That man is equal to the gods": this phrase has another meaning too. Sappho as reader of the *Odyssey* participates by turn in all the characters; this alternation of attention is the ordinary experience of every reader of the epic and is the basis for Sappho's multiple identification with both Aphrodite and Diomedes in *Iliad* 5. In reading *Odyssey* 6 Sappho takes on the roles of both Odysseus and Nausikaa, as well as standing outside them both. I suggest that "that man is equal to the gods," among its many meanings, is a reformulation of Homer's description of the sea-beaten Odysseus whom Athena transforms into a god-like man: νῦν δὲ θεοῖσιν ἔοικε τοὶ οὐρανὸν εὐρὺν ἔχουσιν, "but now he is like the gods who control the expanse of heaven." (6.243) This is Nausikaa's comment to her maids as she watches Odysseus sit on the shore after emerging from his bath, and she goes on to wish that her husband might be such.[26] The point of view from which Sappho speaks as one struck to the heart is that of a mortal visited by divine power and beauty, and this is located in the *Odyssey* in the personae of Odysseus (struck by Nausikaa, or so he says), of Nausikaa (impressed by Odysseus), and of the Homeric audience, for Sappho speaks not only as the strange suitor and the beautiful princess but as the *Odyssey* reader who watches "that man" (Odysseus) face to face with the gently laughing girl.

In performing this experiment of reading Sappho's poems as expressing, in part, her thoughts while reading Homer, her consciousness of men's public world, I think of her being naturally drawn to the character of Nausikaa, whose romantic anticipation (6.27) and delicate sensitivity to the unattainability of the powerful stranger (244f., 276-284) are among the most successful presentations of a woman's mind in male Greek literature.[27] Sappho sees herself both as Odysseus admiring the nymph-like maiden and as Nausikaa cherishing her own complex emotions. The moment of their separation (*Odyssey* 8.461f.) has what is in hindsight, by the normal process of re-reading literature in the light of its own reformulations, a "Sapphic" touch: μνῆσῃι ἐμεῖ', "Farewell, guest, and when you are in your homeland remember me who saved you — you owe me this." These are at home as Sappho's words in poem 94.6-8: "And I made this reply to her, 'Farewell on your journey, and remember me, for you know how I stood by you.'"[28]

The idyllic beauty of Phaiakia is luxuriously expressed in the rich garden of Alkinoos, whose continuously fertile fruits and blossoms are like the gardens which Sappho describes (esp. poems 2, 81b, 94, 96), and it reminds us of Demetrios' words, "Virtually the whole of Sappho's poetry deals with nymphs' gardens, wedding songs, eroticism." The other side of the public/private contrast in Sappho is a design hidden in the lush foliage and flower cups of these gardens. There are two sides to double-consciousness: Sappho both re-enacts scenes from public culture infused with her private perspective as the enclosed woman and she speaks publicly of the most private, woman-centred experiences from which men are strictly excluded. They are not equal projects, the latter is much more delicate and risky. The very formulation of women-only secrets, female *arrhêta*, runs the risk not only of impropriety (unveiling the bride) but of betrayal by misstatement. Hence the hesitation in Sappho's most explicit delineation of double-consciousness: οὐκ οἶδ᾽ ὄττι θέω· δίχα μοι τὰ νοήμματα, "I am not sure what to set down, my thoughts are double," could mean "I am not sure which things to set down and which to keep among ourselves, my mind is divided." (51)

Among the thoughts which Sappho has woven into her poetry, in a way which both conceals and reveals without betraying, are sexual images. These are in part private to women, whose awareness of their own bodies is not shared with men, and in part publicly shared, especially in wedding songs and rites, which are a rich store of symbolic images bespeaking sexuality.[29] The ordinary ancient concern with fertility, health and bodily function generated a large family of natural metaphors for human sexuality and, conversely, sexual metaphors for plants and body parts. A high degree of personal modesty and decorum is in no way compromised by a daily language which names the world according to genital analogies or by marriage customs whose function is to encourage fertility and harmony in a cooperative sexual relationship. The three words which I will use to illustrate this are *nymphê*, *pteryges*, and *mêlon*. The evidence for their usage will be drawn from various centuries and kinds of writing up to a thousand years after Sappho; but the terms in each case seem to be of a technical and traditional nature rather than neologisms. They would constitute then scattered fragments of a locally variegated, tenacious symbolic system which was operative in Sappho's time and which is still recognizable in modern Greece.

Nymphê has many meanings: at the center of this extended

family are "clitoris" and "bride." *Nymphê* names a young woman at the moment of her transition from maiden (*parthenos*) to wife (or "woman," *gynê*); the underlying idea is that just as the house encloses the wife and as veil and carriage[30] keep the bride apart from the wedding celebrants, so the woman herself encloses a sexual secret. "The outer part of the female genital system which is visible has the name "wings" (*pteryges*), which are, so to speak, the lips of the womb. They are thick and fleshy, stretching away on the lower side to either thigh, as it were parting from each other, and on the upper side terminating in what is called the *nymphê*. This is the starting point (*archê*) of the wings (labia), by nature a little fleshy thing and somewhat muscular (or, mouse-like)."[31] The same technical use of *nymphê* to mean clitoris is found in other medical writers[32] and lexicographers,[33] and by a natural extension is applied to many analogous phenomena: the hollow between lip and chin,[34] a depression on the shoulder of horses,[35] a mollusc,[36] a niche,[37] an opening rosebud,[38] the point of a plow[39] — this last an interesting reversal based on the image of the plowshare penetrating the earth. The relation of *nymphê*, clitoris, to *pteryges*, wings/labia, is shown by the name of a kind of bracken, the *nymphaia pteris*, "nymph's-wing," also known as *thelypteris*, "female wing," by the name of the loose lapels on a seductively opening gown,[40] and by the use of *nymphê* as the name for bees in the larva stage just when they begin to open up and sprout wings.[41]

This family of images extends broadly across many levels of Greek culture and serves to reconstruct for us one important aspect of the meaning of "bride," *nymphê*, as the ancients felt it.[42] Hence the virtual identity of Demetrios' three terms for Sappho's poetry: nymphs' gardens, wedding songs, eroticism. Several of Sappho's surviving fragments and poems make sense as a woman-centered celebration and revision of this public but discreet vocabulary for women's sexuality. The consciousness of these poems ranges over a wide field of attitudes. The first can be seen as Sappho's version of male genital joking (which she illustrates in 110 and 111),[43] but when applied to the *nymphê* Sappho's female ribaldry is pointedly different in tone.

> Like the sweet-apple ripening to red on the topmost branch,
> on the very tip of the topmost branch, and the apple-pickers have
>   overlooked it —
> no, they haven't overlooked it but they could not reach it. (105a)

Mêlon, conventionally translated "apple," is really a general word for fleshy fruit — apricots, peaches, apples, citron, quinces, pomegranates. In wedding customs it probably most often means quinces and pomegranates, but for convenience' sake I will abide by the traditional translation "apple." Like *nymphê* and *pteryges*, *mêlon* has a wider extension of meanings, and from this we can rediscover why "apples" were a prominent symbol in courtship and marriage rites.[44] *Mêlon* signifies various "clitoral" objects: the seed vessel of the rose,[45] the tonsil or uvula,[46] a bulge or sty on the lower eyelid,[47] and a swelling on the cornea.[48] The sensitivity of these objects to pressure is one of the bases for the analogy; I will quote just one. "And what is called a *mêlon* is a form of fleshy bump (*staphylôma*, grape-like or uvular swelling), big enough to raise the eyelids, and when it is rubbed it bothers the entire lid-surface."[48]

Fragment 105a, spoken of a bride in the course of a wedding song, is a sexual image. We can gather this sense not only from the general erotic meaning of "apples" but from the location of the solitary apple high up on the bare branches of a tree,[49] and from its sweetness and color. The verb ἐρεύθω, "grow red," and its cognates are used of blood or other red liquid appearing on the surface of an object which is painted or stained or when the skin suffuses with blood.[50] The vocabulary and phrasing of this fragment reveal much more than a sexual metaphor, however; they contain a delicate and reverential attitude to the elusive presence-and-absence of women in the world of men. Demetrios elsewhere (148) speaks of the graceful naivete of Sappho's self-correction, as if it were no more than a charming touch of folk speech when twice in these lines she changes her mind, varying a statement she has already made. But self-correction is Sappho's playful format for saying much more than her simile would otherwise mean. The words are inadequate — how can I say? — not inadequate, but they encircle an area of meaning for which there have not been faithful words in the phallocentric tradition. The real secret of this simile is not the image of the bride's "private" parts but of women's sexuality and consciousness in general, which men do not know as women know. Sappho knows this secret in herself and in other women whom she loves, and celebrates it in her poetry. Where men's paraphernalia are awkwardly flaunted (bumping into the lintel, 111, inconveniently large like a rustic's feet, 110), women's are protected and secure. The amazing feature of these lines is that the apple is not "ripe for plucking" but unattainable, as if even after marriage the *nymphê* would remain secure from the husband's appropriation.[51]

Revision of myth is combined with a sexual image in fragment 166: φαῖσι δή ποτα Λήδαν ὐακίνθωι πεπυκάδμενον / εὔρην ὤιον, "They do say that once upon a time Leda found an egg hidden in the hyacinth." As the traditional denigration of Helen was revised in poem 16, so the traditional story of Helen's mother is told anew. Leda was not the victim of Zeus' rape who afterwards laid Helen in an egg, rather she discovered a mysterious egg hidden inside the frilly blossoms of a hyacinth stem, or (better) in a bed of hyacinths when she parted the petals and looked under the leaves. The egg discovered there is

(1) a clitoris hidden under labia
(2) the supremely beautiful woman, a tiny Helen, and
(3) a story, object and person hidden from male culture.[52]

The metaphor of feeling one's way through the undergrowth until one discovers a special object of desire is contained in the word μαίομαι, "I feel for," "I search out by feeling." It is used of Odysseus feeling the flesh of Polyphemos' stomach for a vital spot to thrust in his sword (*Od.* 9.302), of animals searching through dense thickets for warm hiding places (Hesiod *Erga* 529-533), of enemy soldiers searching through the luxurious thicket for the hidden Odysseus (*Od.* 14.356), of Demeter searching high and low for her daughter (Hom. Hymn 2.44), of people searching for Poseidon's lover Pelops (Pi. *Ol.* 1.46). The contexts of this verb are not just similar by accident: *maiomai* means more than "search for," it means "ferret out," especially in dense thickets where an animal or person might be lurking. In view of the consistency of connotations for this verb there is no reason to posit a shifted usage in Sappho 36, as Liddell-Scott does. As those lexicographers read it, Sappho's words καὶ ποθήω καὶ μάομαι are redundant — "I desire you and I desire you." Rather they mean "I desire and I search out." I would like to include the physical sense of feeling carefully for hidden things or hiding places.[53] In the poetic verb *maiomai* there is a physical dimension to the expression of mutual passion and exploration. Desire and touching occur together as two aspects of the same experience: touching is touching-with-desire, desire is desire-with-touching.

The same dictionary which decrees a special meaning for *maiomai* when Sappho uses it invents an Aeolic word μάτημι (B) = πατέω, "I walk," to reduce the erotic meaning of a Lesbian fragment of uncertain authorship, Incert. 16: "The women of Krete once danced thus — rhythmically with soft feet around the desirable altar exploring the tender, pliant flower of the lawn." μάτημι is a recognized Aeolic equivalent of ματεύω, akin to μαίομαι. The meanings "ferret out," "search through undergrowth," "beat the thickets looking for game," "feel carefully" seem to me quite in place. Appealing to a long tradition, Sappho (whom I take to be the author) remarks that the sexual dancing of women, the sensuous circling of moving hands and feet around the erotic altar and combing through the tender valleys, is not only current practice but was known long ago in Krete.

I have been able to find no *simple* sexual imagery in Sappho's poems. For her the sexual is always something else as well. Her sacred landscape of the body is at the same time a statement about a more complete consciousness, whether of myth, poetry, ritual or personal relationships. In the following fragment, 94, which contains a fairly explicit sexual statement in line 23,[54] we find Sappho correcting her friend's view of their relation.

> . . . Without guile I wish to die. She left me weeping copiously and said, "Alas, what fearful things we have undergone, Sappho; truly I leave you against my will." But I replied to her, "Farewell, be happy as you go and remember me, for you know how we have stood by you. Perhaps you don't — so I will remind you . . . and we have

> undergone beautiful
> things. With many garlands of violets and roses . . . together, and
>   . . . you
> put around yourself, at my side, and flowers wreathed around your
>   soft
> neck with rising fragrance, and . . . you stroked the oil distilled from
> royal cherry blossoms and on tender bedding you reached the end
>   of longing
> . . . of soft . . . and there was no . . . nor sacred . . . from which we
>   held back,
> nor grove . . . sound . . .

As usual the full situation is unclear, but we can make out a contrast of Sappho's view with her friend's. The departing woman says δεῖνα πεπόνθαμεν, "fearful things we have suffered," and Sappho corrects her, κάλ᾽ ἐπάσχομεν, "beautiful things we continuously experienced." Her reminder of these beautiful experiences (which Page calls a "list of girlish pleasures"[55]) is a loving progression of intimacy, moving in space — down along the body — and in time — to increasing sexual closeness: from flowers wreathed on the head to flowers wound around the neck to stroking the body with oil to soft bed-clothes and the full satisfaction of desire. I would like to read the meager fragments of the succeeding stanza as a further physical landscape: we explored every sacred place of the body. To paraphrase the argument, "When she said we had endured an awful experience, the ending of our love together, I corrected her and said it was a beautiful experience, an undying memory of sensual happiness that knew no limit, luxurious and fully sexual. Her focus on the termination was misplaced; I told her to think instead of our mutual pleasure which itself had no term, no stopping-point, no unexplored grove."

Poem 2 uses sacral language to describe a paradisal place[56] which Aphrodite visits:

> Hither to me from Krete, unto this holy temple, a place where
>   there
> is a lovely grove of apples and an altar where the incense burns,
> and here is water which ripples cold through apple branches, and all
> the place is shadowed with roses, and as the leaves quiver a profound
> quiet ensues. And here is a meadow where horses graze, spring flowers
> bloom, the honeyed whisper of winds . . . This is the very place where

you, Kypris . . ., drawing into golden cups the nectar gorgeously
   blended
for our celebration, then pour it forth.

The grove, Page comments, is "lovely," "elsewhere in the
Lesbians only of *personal* charm."[57] But this place is, among other
things, a personal place, an extended and multi-perspectived metaphor for women's sexuality. Virtually every word suggests a
sensuous ecstacy in the service of Kyprian Aphrodite (apples,
roses, quivering followed by repose, meadow for grazing, spring
flowers, honey, nectar flowing). Inasmuch as the language is both
religious and erotic, I would say that Sappho is not describing a
public ceremony for its own sake but is providing a way to experience such ceremonies, to infuse the celebrants' participation with
memories of lesbian sexuality. The twin beauties of burning
incense on an altar and of burning sexual passion can be held
together in the mind, so that the experience of either is the richer.
The accumulation of topographic and sensuous detail leads us to
think of the interconnection of all the parts of the body in a long
and diffuse act of love, rather than the genital-centered and more
relentlessly goal-oriented pattern of love-making which men have
been known to employ.

I have tried to sketch two areas of Sappho's consciousness as
she has registered it in her poetry: her reaction to Homer, emblematic of the male-centered world of public Greek culture, and her
complex sexual relations with women in a world apart from men.
Sappho seems always to speak in many voices — her friends',
Homer's, Aphrodite's — conscious of more than a single perspective and ready to detect the fuller truth of many-sided desire. But
she speaks as a woman to women: her eroticism is both subjectively
and objectively woman-centered. Too often modern critics have
tried to restrict Sappho's *erôs* to the strait-jacket of spiritual
friendship. A good deal of the sexual richness which I detect in
Sappho's lyrics is compatible with interpretations such as those of
Lasserre and Hallett,[58] but what requires explanation is their
insistent denial that the emotional lesbianism of Sappho's work
has any physical component. We must distinguish between the

physical component as a putative fact about Sappho in her own life and as a meaning central to her poems. Obviously Sappho as poet is not an historian documenting her own life but rather a creative participant in the erotic-lyric tradition.[59] My argument is that this tradition includes pervasive allusions to physical *erôs* and that in Sappho's poems both subject and object of shared physical love are women. We now call this lesbian.[60] To admit that Sappho's discourse is lesbian but insist that she herself was not seems quixotic. Would anyone take such pains to insist that Anacreon in real life might not have felt any physical attraction to either youths or women? It seems clear to me that Sappho's consciousness included a personal and subjective commitment to the holy, physical contemplation of the body of Woman, as metaphor and reality, in all parts of life. Reading her poems in this way is a challenge to think both in and out of our time, both in and out of a phallocentric framework, a reading which can enhance our own sense of this womanly beauty *as subject and as object* by helping us to un-learn our denials of it.

Acknowledgements

I would like to thank generous readers who have offered thoughtful criticisms of earlier drafts of this paper, especially Helene Foley, Cathy Winkler, Carolyn Dewald, Susan Stephens, Carey Perloff, Carol Dougherty, Barbara Kosacz, Catharine MacKinnon, Anne Simon, Page DuBois, Anne Mellor, Aleine Ridge, Bruce Rosenstock, and the anonymous readers of this journal.

Notes

1.   (English translation of *Brouillon pour un dictionnaire des amantes* (Avon Books, New York 1976)). There are some uncritical myths in Wittig's own account of Sappho in her essay "Paradigm" in *Homosexualities and French Literature*, G. Stambolian and E. Marks, eds., (Ithaca and London 1979) 116f.
2.   M.F. Lefkowitz, "Critical Stereotypes and the Poetry of Sappho," *GRBS* 14 (1973) 113-123, and J. Hallett, "Sappho and her Social Context," *Signs* 4 (1979) 447-464, have good analyses of the bias and distortions found in critical comments, ancient and modern, on Sappho.

3. My statement that this is Sappho's central topic throughout her nine
    books is based not merely on the few fragments (obviously), but on the
    ancient testimonies, especially that of Demetrios, who provides my
    title: " . . . nymphs' gardens, wedding songs, eroticism — in short the
    whole of Sappho's poetry" (περὶ ἑρμηνείας 132 — νυμφαῖοι κῆποι,
    ὑμέναιοι, ἔρωτες, ὅλη ἡ Σαπφοῦς ποίησις). Testimonies are collected in
    C. Gallavotti, *Saffo e Alceo: Testimonianze e frammenti* (Napoli 1947).
4. There was also the category of heroic, exceptional woman, e.g. Hero-
    dotos' version of Artemisia, who is used to "prove the rule" every time
    he mentions her (7.99, 8.68, 8.87f., 8.101), and the stories collected by
    Plutarch *de virtutibus mulierum.* The stated purpose of this collection is
    to show that *aretê*, "virtue" or "excellence," is the same in men and
    women, but the stories actually show that merely some women in times
    of crisis have stepped out of their regular anonymity and performed
    male roles when men were not available.
5. "A feminist theory of poetry would begin to take into account the
    context in history of these poems and their political connections and
    implications. It would deal with the fact that women's poetry conveys
    . . . a special kind of consciousness . . . Concentrating on consciousness
    and the politics of women's poetry, such a theory would evolve new
    ways of reading what is there." L. Bernikow, *The World Split Open*
    (New York 1974) 10f.
6. Consciousness of course is not a solid object which can be discovered
    intact like an easter egg lying somewhere in the garden (as in the
    Sapphic fragment 166 Leda is said to have found an egg hidden under
    the hyacinths). Sappho's lyrics are many-layered constructions of
    melodic words, images, ideas and arguments in a formulaic system of
    sharable points of view (personas). I take it for granted that the usual
    distinctions between "the real Sappho" as author and speaker(s) of the
    poems will apply when I speak here of Sappho's consciousness.
7. S. Butler, *The Authoress of the Odyssey* (London 1897).
8. H. Foley, " 'Reverse Similes' and Sex Roles in the *Odyssey" Arethusa*
    11 (1978) 7-26; M. Domingo *The Role of the Female in Ancient Epic*
    (Ph.D. diss., Princeton 1980), chapter 2.
9. As Kalypso complains, *Od.* 5.118ff. Perhaps the poet means this to be a
    short-sighted criticism, illustrating *Od.* 1.32.
10. In this territory and at these recitations women are present — Homer is
    not a forbidden text to women, not an arcane *arrhêton* of the male
    mysteries. In the *Odyssey* (1, 325-329) Penelope hears and reacts to the
    epic poetry of a bard singing in her home, but her objections to his
    theme, the homecoming from Troy, are silenced by Telemachus.
    Arete's decision to give more gifts to Odysseus (*Od.* 11, 335-341) after
    he has sung of the women he saw in the underworld may be an implicit
    sign of her approval of his poetry. Helen in *Iliad* 6 delights in the fact
    that she is a theme of epic poetry (357-358) and weaves the stories of
    the battles fought for her into her web (125-128).
11. R. Merkelbach, "Sappho und ihr Kreis" *Philologus* 101 (1957) 1-29;
    J. Russo, "Reading the Greek Lyric Poets (Monodists)" *Arion* n.s. 1

(1973-74) 707-730.

12. G. Lanata, "Sul linguaggio amoroso di Saffo" *QUCC* 2 (1966) 63-79.

13. The text used in this essay is that E. Lobel and D. Page (L-P) *Poetarum Lesbiorum Fragmenta* (Oxford 1955).

14. Homer seems to include this possibility in the range of performing *klea andrôn* when he presents Achilles singing to his own *thymos*, while Patroklos sits in silence, not listening as an audience but waiting for Achilles to stop (*Il.* 9.186-191).

15. *Comparative Studies in Greek and Indic Meter* (Cambridge, Mass. 1974).

16. Sappho is only one individual, and may have been quite untypical in her power to achieve a literary life. Claims that society in her time and place allowed greater scope for women to attain a measure of public esteem are based almost entirely on Sappho's poems (including probably Plutarch *Lykourgos* 18.4, *Theseus* 19.3, Philostratos *VA* 1.30 — the invention of early women poets is taken to extremes by Tatian *adv. Graecos* and Ptolemy Hephaistion, who relates that Helen was a poet who composed the narrative of the Trojan war before Homer, that she was the daughter of the Athenian Musaeus and that Homer took his plot-outline from her [Photius *Bibl. cod.* 190. 149b22] ; and that Phantasia of Memphis composed the narrative of the Trojan war before Homer also, and the *Odyssey* as well; she deposited the books in Memphis and Homer managed to obtain copies of them from Phanitis the sacred scribe of the temple [151a38]). The multiplication of women who like Sappho were the centers of literary groups is merely one interpretation of the character of Sappho's "rivals."

17. A. Cameron, "Sappho's Prayer to Aphrodite," *HTR* 32 (1949) 1-17; D. Page, *Sappho and Alcaeus* (Oxford 1955) 7; J. Svenbro, "Sappho and Diomedes," *Musuem Philologum Londiniense* 1 (1975) 37-49; K. Stanley, "The Role of Aphrodite in Sappho Fr. 1," *GRBS* 17 (1976) 305-321; L. Rissman, *Homeric Allusion in the Poetry of Sappho* (Diss. U. of Michigan 1980).

18. Translations in this essay are my own; ellipses indicate that the Greek is incomplete.

19. G. Bolling, "Restoration of Sappho, 98a 1-7," *AJP* 80 (1959) 276-287; J.D. Marry, "Sappho and the Heroic Ideal," *Arethusa* 12 (1979) 271-292.

20. V. di Benedetto, "Il volo di Afrodite in Omero e in Saffo," *QUCC* 16 (1973) 121-123: he refers to the poem as "Aphrodite's revenge" (122).

21. E.g. J.B. Bury, ". . . while Sappho confined her muse within a narrower circle of feminine interests" (*CAH* IV, 1953, 494f.) and similarly W. Jaeger, *Paideia* (English translation, B. Blackwell, Oxford 1965) vol. 1, p. 132.

22. G. Wills, "The Sapphic 'Umwertung aller Werte'," *AJP* 88 (1967) 434-442; P. Dubois, "Sappho and Helen," *Arethusa* 11 (1978) 88-99.

23. B. Snell, "Sappho's Gedicht φαίνεταί μοι κῆνος," *Hermes* 66 (1931) 71-90; G. Koniaris, "On Sappho fr. 31 (L-P)," *Philologus* 112 (1968) 173-186; H. Saake, *Zur Kunst Sapphos* (Verlag F. Schöningh, München-

Paderborn-Wien 1971) 17-38.

24.   C. Del Grande, "Saffo, Ode φαίνεταί μοι κῆνος ἴσος," *Euphrosyne* 2 (1959) 181-188.

25.   N. Austin, *Archery at the Dark of the Moon* (Univ. California Press, Berkeley-Los Angles-London 1975) 191-200.

26.   The comparison to gods runs throughout the Phaiakian scenes: Nausikaa (16, 105-109), her maids (18), the Phaiakians (241), Nausikaa's brothers, ἀθανάτοις ἐναλίγκιοι (7.5).

27.   Apollonius of Rhodes' Medea is conscious of love in terms drawn from Sappho: G.A. Privitera, "Ambiguità antitesi analogia nel fr. 31 L-P di Saffo," *QUCC* 8 (1969) 71f., and note especially the characteristic presentation of Medea's mental after-images and imaginings (3.453-458, 811-816, 948-955), which is the technique of Sappho 1, 16, 96.

28.   W. Schadewaldt, "Zu Sappho" *Hermes* 71 (1936) 367.

29.   P. Bourdieu, *Algeria 1960* (Cambridge, England 1979) 105; G.F. Abbott, *Macedonian Folklore* (Cambridge University Presss 1903) chap. 11.

30.   "One of the men in Chios, apparently a prominent figure of some sort, was taking a wife and, as the bride was being conducted to his home in a chariot, Hippoklos the king, a close friend of the bridegroom, mingling with the rest during the drinking and laughter, jumped up into the chariot, not intending any insult but merely being playful according to the common custom. The friends of the groom killed him." Plutarch *virt. mul.* 244E.

31.   Soranos *Gynaecology* 1.18.

32.   Rufinus ap. Oribasius III.391.1, Galen II. 370E, Paulus Aigin. 6.70 (description of clitoridectomy for lesbians).

33.   Photius *Lex. s.v.*, Pollux 2.174, with the anagram σκαῖρον σαρκίον, "throbbing little piece of flesh."

34.   Rufus *Onom.* 42, Pollux 2.90, Hesychios.

35.   *Hippiatr.* 26.

36.   Speusippos ap. Athen. 3.105B.

37.   Kallixinos 2 (Müller *FHG* III, p. 55).

38.   Photius *Lex. s.v.* νύμφαι· ... καὶ τὸ ἀνὰ μέσον τῶν γυναικείων αἰδοίων νύμφην καλοῦσιν. καὶ τῶν ῥόδων αἱ κάλυκες αἱ μεμυκυῖαι νύμφαι. καὶ αἱ νεόγαμοι κόραι νύμφαι. The equation of flowers and female genitals is ancient (Krinagoras *AP* 6.345, Achilles Tatius 2.1) and modern (art: L. Lippard, "Quite contrary: Body, Nature, Ritual in Women's Art," *Chrysalis* 2 [1977] 30-47; Betty Dodson *Liberating Masturbation* [B. Dodson, Box 1933, New York 10001]; Judy Chicago *The Dinner Party* [Garden City N.Y. 1979], *Through the Flower* [Garden City N.Y. 1975]. Poetry: A. Lorde "Love Poem" in E. Bulkin and J. Larkin, eds., *Amazon Poetry* [Out & Out Books, Brooklyn, N.Y. 1975]). Sappho appears to have made the equation of bride and roses explicit, according to P. Wirth, "Neue Spuren eines Sapphobruchstücks" *Hermes* 91 (1963) 115-117. I would not reject the suggestion that Sappho's feelings for Kleis, as imagined in fragment 132 were given a consciously lesbian coloring: "I have a beautiful child, her shape is like

that of golden *flowers*, beloved Kleis; in her place I would not . . . all Lydia nor lovely . . ." Indeed, taking it a step further, this "child" (*pais*) may be simply another metaphor for clitoris (*kleis* → *kleitoris*). The biographical tradition which regards Kleis as the name of Sappho's daughter and mother may be (as so often) based on nothing more than a fact-hungry reading of her poems. (The same name occurs at 98b1.) On flowers and fruit see E.S. Stigers, "Retreat from the Male: Catullus 62 and Sappho's Erotic Flowers," *Ramus* 6 (1977) 83-102.

39. Pollux, 1.25.2, Proklos *ad* Hesiod *Erga* 425.

40. Pollux 755, 62, 66 (= Aristophanes *Thesm. Deut.* frag. 325 OCT).

41. Aristotle *HA* 551b2-4; Photius *Lex. s.v. nymphai*; Pliny *NH* 11.48.

42. For the connection of Nymphs to marriage and birth, see F.G. Ballentine "Some Phases of the Cult of the Nymphs," *HSCP* 15 (1904) 97-110.

43. G.S. Kirk, "A Fragment of Sappho Reinterpreted," *CQ* 13 (1963) 51f.; Killeen, "Sappho Fr. 111," *CQ* 23 (1973) 197; Fragment 121 may be "una variazione scherzosa nel nota fr. 105," G. Lanata (*op. cit.*, note 12) 66.

44. B.O. Foster, "Notes on the Symbolism of the Apple in Classical Antiquity," *HSCP* 10 (1899) 39-55; E.S. McCartney, "How the Apple Became the Token of Love," *TAPA* 56 (1925) 70-81; J. Trumpf, "Kydonische Apfel," *Hermes* 88 (1960) 14-22; M. Lugauer, *Untersuchungen zur Symbolik des Apfels in der Antike* (diss. Erlangen-Nürnberg 1967); A.R. Littlewood, "The Symbolism of the Apple in Greek and Roman Literature," *HSCP* 72 (1968) 147-181; Ph. I. Kakridis, "Une Pomme mordue," *Hellenica* 25 (1972) 189-192; P. Oxy, 2637, frag. 25.6; Abbott (*op. cit.*, note 29) 147f., 170, 177.

45. Theophr. *HP* 6.6.6.

46. Rufus *Onom.* 64; Galen *de usu partium* 15.3: "The part called *nympha* gives the same sort of protection to the uteri that the uvula gives to the pharynx, for it covers the orifice of their neck by coming down into the female pudendum and keeps it from being chilled." Fragment 42, on the warmth afforded by enfolding wings (*ptera*), may be read of labia as well as of birds.

47. Hesych. *s.v. κύλα.*

48. Alexander Tralles περὶ ὀφθαλμῶν, Puschmann, ed., p. 152.

49. "In other parts (of Macedonia) . . ., especially among the Wallachs, a pole with an apple on top and a white kerchief streaming from it . . . is carried by a kilted youth in front of the wedding procession." Abbott (*op. cit.*, note 29) 172.

50. Hippocrates *Epid.* 2.3.1, *Morb. Sacr.* 15, *Morb.* 4.38 (of a blush).

51. This sense of *nymphê* gives further meaning to a fragment of Praxilla, 754 *PMG*. "Looking in beautifully through the windows, your head that of a maiden, but you are a *nymphê* underneath." ὦ διὰ τῶν θυρίδων καλὸν ἐμβλέποισα / παρθένε τὰν κεφαλὰν τὰ δ᾽ ἔνερθε νύμφα. Praxilla is, according to Aly's fine interpretation (*RE* XXII [1954] 176), addressing the moon shining through her windows (cp. 747 *PMG*, σεληναίης τε πρόσωπον); its mystery and elusive attraction are expressed

by the image of a woman with a youthful, innocent face and a look
that bespeaks deeper experience and knowledge. The physical comparison is to a woman whose face alone is visible: wrapped up under all
those clothes, says Praxilla, is the body of a sexually mature woman.
Page at the opposite extreme envisions a woman peeping into the
windows of houses in order to attract other women's husbands (*quae
more meretricio vagabunda per fenestras intueri soles, scilicet ut virum
foras unde unde elicias, PMG* 747 *app. crit.*). This level of significance
may also be relevant to Ibykos 286 *PMG* and anonymous 929 e-g *PMG*.

52. The verb πυκάζω refers not to just any kind of "hiding" but to covering an object with clothes, flower garlands, or hair, either as an adornment or for protection. "Thick" flowers (ὑάκινθον / πυκνὸν καὶ μαλακόν)
cover the earth to cushion the love-making of Zeus and Hera (*Il.* 14.
347-350).

53. Fragment 48 may be read in a similar sense: ἦλθες καί μ' ἐπόθησας,
ἔγω δέ σ' ἐμαιόμην· / ὂν δ' ἔφλεξας ἔμαν φρένα καιομέναν πόθωι,
"You came and you desired me; I searched you carefully; you stirred
the fires of my feeling, smoldering with desire." (ἔφλεξας is Wesseling's
conjecture for φύλαξας; μ' ἐπόθησας is my conjecture for ἐπόησας. I
would support this conjecture by reference back to fragment 36,
which joins *poth/* and *mai/*, and by the symmetry achieved: you
desired me — I felt you — you stirred me — I desired you, which we
might call Sapphic reciprocity. cf. G. Lanata (*op. cit.*, note 12) 79.

54. M.L. West "Burning Sappho," *Maia* 22 (1970) 322.

55. Page (*op. cit.*, note 17) 83.

56. A. Turyn, "The Sapphic Ostracon," *TAPA* 73 (1942) 308-318.

57. Page (*op. cit.*, note 17) 36.

58. F. Lasserre, "Ornements érotiques dans la pòesie lyrique archaïque," in
Serta Turyniana, J.L. Heller, ed., (Urbana, Illinois 1974); J.P. Hallett
(*op. cit.*, note 2). "Sarebbe augurabile che nelle allusioni all'amore
saffico cadesse in disuso la sgradita definizione di 'turpe amore' in-
ventata da un moralismo se non altro anacronistico." (B. Gentili, "La
veneranda Saffo," *QUCC* 2 (1966) 48 n. 55). "It is a favorite occupation
of scholars to pass laws and regulations for the conduct of ancient
Greeks, . . . for the proper behaviour of young ladies . . ." (A. Gomme,
"Interpretation of Some Poems of Alkaios and Sappho," *JHS* 78 (1957)
255). E.S. Stigers, "Romantic Sensuality, Poetic Sense: A Response to
Hallett on Sappho," *Signs* 4 (1979) 464-471, is excellent.

59. Late Greek rhetoric maintains the tradition of praising a public official
at a ceremonial event by a declaration of love. Himerius (48) and
Themistius (13) tell their audiences that the honoured official is their
boyfriend.

60. "Women who love women, who choose women to nurture and support
and create a living environment in which to work creatively and independently, are lesbians." B.W. Cook, " 'Women Alone Stir my Imagination:' Lesbianism and the Cultural Tradition," *Signs* 4 (1979) 738.

Women and culture in Herodotus' *Histories*

CAROLYN DEWALD

University of Southern California

HERODOTUS' PURPOSE, as his proem describes it, is to narrate and explain the great war between the Persians and the Greeks. In the process he displays a rich panorama of sixth- and fifth-century society, both Greek and barbarian, in which women play a prominent role. Many are members of the great families, Greek and barbarian, that form the backbone of the narrative, but a variety of others appears as well — concubines, nurses, bakers, priestesses, and even an occasional oddity like the Egyptian lady sodomist in 2.46.

This essay investigates Herodotus' portrait of women, in the belief that he is an important and generally neglected witness to fifth-century assumptions and attitudes about women in society. In the first place, Herodotus himself was born in Asia Minor and lived at some point in his life both in Athens and in western Greece; many of his sources were oral, and they seem to have been drawn from the whole of the Greek-speaking Mediterranean world. Thus his portrait of women reflects not the narrow anxieties or controversies of a particular state at a given moment, but a composite oral tradition with some claim to representing underlying and broadly Greek beliefs. Furthermore, as the first historian, Herodotus is the first extant Greek author whose stated purpose is to record *ta genomena*, that is, facts and events. As much as he can, he presents his narration stripped of the elements of myth and special pleading. The women who appear in his account are not depicted according to the prior conventions of a genre — as, for instance, they are in Attic tragedy with its organizing polarities, in which women often signify disruption and disorder, or as in oratory, whose conventional typologies require that women appear as docile homebodies if they belong to the speaker, ubiquitous harridans or worse if they belong to the speaker's opponents.[1] A real effort is made instead to describe women as they were, or at least as Herodotus thinks they must have been. Finally, because Herodotus virtually invented the genre in which he was writing, his narrative structure is a great deal freer than that of his successors, and it is frequently shaped by loose associations of ideas. In the paratactic progression of accounts that winds through the *Histories*, women are not his chief focus of attention. He does not write the *Histories* in order to prove a thesis about them as social actors (as, for instance, Xenophon does in the *Oeconomicus*); they tend instead to occur incidentally, as part of the background of his main narrative themes. His portrait is for that reason likely to reveal aspects of feminine behavior and social values that more aggressively argumentative accounts neglect.

Herodotus mentions women in the *Histories* 375 times. For the main arguments of this essay I have tried to depend principally on the weight and shape of the full range of this data, since I believe it is the accumulation of evidence, and not one or two or ten striking examples, that will reveal Herodotus' habitual assumptions about women.[2] Moreover, as we shall see in discussing several queens whose behavior has often been assimilated to that of the violent and vengeful queens of Attic tragedy, a sense of the dominant lines of Herodotus' interpretation can help us see complex stories in a new light, and women who disrupt their husbands' plans not as wild or irrational forces, but as representatives themselves of social norms their husbands have flouted.

This essay argues that Herodotus' portrait of women emphasizes their full partnership with men in establishing and maintaining social order. When he mentions clichés about women or femininity in the abstract (thirty-five times, or about a tenth of the total), it is usually in order to undercut them.[3] When he portrays women as passive figures in the context of family politics (128 times, or about a third of the total), they indicate the several kinds of danger that the family confronts: aggression from without, natural causes and political strife from within. When he portrays women as actors who themselves determine the outcome of events (212 times, or well over half the total), they articulate and transmit the conventions of their societies to others and work creatively within the constraints of their individual situations in order to accomplish their goals.

I WOMEN WHO DO NOT ACT (128)

Most of the women who do not act are mentioned in a narrative context of fear or danger.[4] Women in groups are depicted as victims of political or military aggression, or their sufferings indicate some disturbance in the society at large, or they are manipulated or victimized by the men of their own culture. Individual passive women, too, are the victims of outside aggression, or they represent in their function as childbearers some of the natural threats the family faces, or, finally, they are involuntary participants in family political crises. When we consider the whole range of passive women in the *Histories*, a twofold conclusion emerges. On the one hand, by continuously juxtaposing the presence of women with a number of threats, internal and external, confronting their societies, Herodotus allows passive women to become a motif repeatedly emphasizing the thin line that in ancient societies separated cultural survival from cultural extinction. On the other hand, it is equally important to recognize that for Herodotus women in this role are not themselves dangerous; they rather mark the importance of the family as a political and social institution.[5]

Acts of external aggression account for a third of the mentions of passive women in the *Histories*. Herodotus uses women in groups to show the vulnerability of a culture as a whole to outside attack; most commonly, someone either threatens or mistreats enemy women and children, or a group anticipates attack and removes its own women and children to safety. Individuals within the family also suffer from enemy men. They either share in a disaster that has befallen the whole family, or they are abducted from the family unit by outsiders intending them for forcible marriage or concubinage. The persistent possibility of unexpected disaster falling on the family is also illustrated by the passages in which Herodotus mentions a supposedly stable marriage in neutral or positive terms. In all but one, the immediate narrative context includes crisis and danger: impending defeat in war, a mad heir, murder (twice), guileful plots, and the enemy capture of a son.[6]

As this list suggests, danger did not only confront ancient society at the hands of enemy men. All property in a Greek state was passed through the male line; civic and tribal identities (and thus also a city's fighting force) were based on the assumption of family stability and the production of legitimate male descendants in each new generation. Herodotus uses women to describe a number of natural difficulties that affect a family's ability to reproduce itself over time. In groups, women fail to perform their function as childbearers when they are struck with madness or with sterility (9.34, 6.139.1). As individuals, Herodotus mentions women when they have failed to bear the necessary male heir, or when they bear children who will grow up to disappoint the expectations of their families and societies. A number of children in the *Histories* die, or are physically disabled, or grow up themselves to initiate family or civic conflict. Twice, for instance, the infertility of a Spartan queen forces the king to resort to bigamy or polygamy; the consequence, Herodotus makes clear, is fraternal and civic strife in the next generation (5.39, 6.61).[7]

Disasters principally centering on problems of generation, however, are less important than a third set of family-oriented crises in which passive women appear: political crises within the family itself, most often between family members. Thirteen times Herodotus mentions women in the context of successful dynastic politics; more than twice that often the politics of the family, however necessary for its survival or prosperity, explicitly embroils it in new kinds of difficulty and danger. The woman is only twice the victim of familial conflict; most often she is the involuntary spectator or innocent cause of strife between brothers, between relatives by marriage, or within some other more complex domestic political tragedy.

Herodotus' picture of marriage as a political institution in which women form the underlying basis for conflict, without themselves participating in it, is represented particularly clearly in accounts of conflict between relations by marriage. Several accounts describe stress between in-laws from the narrative viewpoint of the husband. When the tyrant of Corinth, Periander, kills his wife, he loses his share in the offspring of his marriage also, because his wife's father, the tyrant of Epidaurus, deliberately turns his adolescent son against him (3.50). A number of other accounts of heiresses or daughters of famous men suggest the anxieties that a powerful marriage connection can pose for a man.[8] The most poignant (and poignantly funny) of these describes the year-long test that the tyrant Cleisthenes of Sicyon imposes on his daughter's suitors (6.126 ff.). One of the front runners, Hippocleides of Athens, cracks under the strain and loses both the noble bride and the lofty alliance by doing a headstand and waving his feet about in time to the music, one evening after supper. "Son of Tisandros, you have certainly danced away your marriage," Cleisthenes remarks; Hippocleides' response, *ou phrontis Hippokleidēi*, "Hippocleides doesn't care," became a Greek byword from that time on for cheerful insouciance in the face of social disapproval.

Several stories relate the anxieties implicit in a marriage connection from the viewpoint of the wife's family. Two explicitly sexual dreams warn Astyages, king of Media, that he will lose his kingdom to his daughter's offspring. He dreams first that his daughter urinates so copiously that all Asia is flooded, and then that a vine growing from her genitals covers all Asia (1.107, 1.108). Despite Astyages' efforts to avert the danger by killing the child, Cyrus does indeed grow up to depose him. The story of the infant Cypselus represents a similar set of anxieties (5.92). Cypselus too grows up to destroy the power of his mother's aristocratic clan, despite their efforts to kill him as a baby. The chest in which Labda hides her child from his would-be murderers is a suggestive equivalent of the uterine imagery in the Cyrus story. Both indicate the mother's involuntary role as the destroyer of her own family heritage.

The fullest statement of the threat to the family that marriage can pose occurs in book five, and its consequences are traced in the later books of the *Histories*. A group of Persian grandees visiting the Macedonian court drunkenly propose to enjoy the women of the Macedonians as part of the lord/vassal relationship they have come to establish (5.18). Alexander of Macedon, the heir apparent, resists the attempted rape of "our mothers and sisters" by disguising Macedonian youths as women and murdering the Persian visitors. A casual sexual transgression against the family is thus defeated, but the continuation of the narrative makes it clear that the ultimate cost to Alexander is a much deeper political bondage to Persia, in the form of marriage. Alexander must marry his own sister to the Persian investigator who comes to inquire about the disappearance of the earlier ambassadors, in order to avoid further investigation about the incident. Mardonius, commander-in-chief of the Persian army in Greece, later uses Alexander as the mouthpiece of his promises and threats to Athens during the war, in large part because of this connection by marriage (8.136). Alexander's sense of his own oppression is made clear in his last appearance in the *Histories*. On the eve of the battle of Plataea, he betrays his Persian overlords by warning the Greek army of an impending attack (9.45); he begs them to remember to free him also from slavery. Herodotus does not imply that Alexander should have ignored the initial affront. 5.18 and its sequels do, however, suggest one sense in which rape is less threatening to the family than marriage. It is marriage that binds the unwilling Alexander to the Persian court; Herodotus ironically implies that Alexander becomes so deeply embroiled in his servitude precisely because he has refused to abandon his female relatives to a night of drunken revelry.

II   WOMEN WHO ACT (212)

Despite all the social tensions connected with family, marriage, and procreation that Herodotus describes in the context of passive family women, he pointedly does not allow this sense of vulnerability and danger to affect his portrait of women who act. Active women do not exacerbate the strains implicit in the way marriage and society work but rather are depicted working themselves to guarantee the stability of both family and culture. They are almost without exception passionately loyal to the family into which they have married. Perhaps most important for our understanding of their social role as Herodotus portrays it, women in the *Histories* are shown not only teaching the conventions of their cultures to their children but reminding male peers as well of the rules within which the whole society is supposed to act.

Five types of active women are portrayed in the *Histories*: groups of women who act within the context of a *polis*; women described as part of an ethnography; individual women defined by the role they play within the family; women who act in the public sphere; and, finally, priestesses. We shall begin with the women who act in groups, since these sketch the most general outlines of the balance between men and women that Herodotus thinks essential for creating and maintaining a healthy society. When we turn to individual women, we shall see the more innovative and idiosyncratic ways in which women work to maintain social order even when they protest and thwart the objectives of their menfolk.

A.   Groups of women within a *polis* (12)

Herodotus occasionally depicts groups of women acting together with men, but more frequently they band together to achieve some goal of their own, as women. Herodotus almost always emphasizes their positive and protective social role.

Several accounts show them in a narrow sense acting to preserve human life or to protest its destruction. Lacedaemonian women rescue their Lemnian husbands from death by playing a clever trick on the murderers, their own Lacedaemonian brothers and fathers (4.146). When Scythian women have children by their slaves while their men are gone on campaign, the emphasis of the account falls on the twenty-eight-year absence of the army. The motives of the women are not immoral (the slaves, after all, are domesticated and blind) but deeply conservative; they are trying to guaranteee the survival of their culture by continuing to produce children despite the long absence of their husbands (4.1).

Once, after a disastrous Athenian raid on Aegina from which one Athenian man returns home alive, the new-made widows take out their brooches and stab the survivor to death, each woman asking, as she stabs, where her own husband is. The Athenians, more upset at the murder than at the raid itself, change their women's style of dress so that in future they will have no brooches (5.87). This account springs from a complex of misogynous folk motifs, including the Pentheus motif, groups of maddened women attacking a defenseless male. In the form in which Herodotus tells it, however, the women are not mad but grief-stricken; their response is a political one against the destructive effects of war. The account is grimly humorous, but some of the humor lies in the contrast between the seriousness of the women's position and the triviality of the fearful and repressive reaction of the men. The women's action also suggests the extent to which Herodotus sees men and women alike reflecting a single set of social values; the violence of war here infects a whole culture and not just its male sector. The same point is made much later in the *Histories* too. When Athenian men stone to death the one councillor advocating submission to Persia, Athenian women on Salamis run to his house in order to stone to death his wife and children (9.5). In each account, Herodotus presents female violence as the complement and mirror of male violence, not as its antithesis. When violence pervades a culture, both men and women reflect its presence.

Women do not only passively reflect the values of their cultures; in Herodotus' eyes, they are actively responsible both for creating social conventions and for maintaining them over time. In 1.146, Ionian men abduct Carian women after killing their Carian menfolk in battle. The captive women, Herodotus tells us, make a *nomos*, a custom, which they themselves observe under oath *and which they hand down to their daughters after them*, to maintain a state of passive unresponsiveness toward their new Ionian husbands. Herodotus tells the story principally to mock Ionian racial pretensions. Contemporary Ionians pride themselves, he sarcastically remarks, on being true-blooded Athenians, but the briefest look at their traditions shows them to be half-Carian. He implies that the custom handed down from mother to daughter still exists in his own time; in any case, it testifies to the power of women to change the conventions of the society into which they have been forcibly integrated, despite their own loss of home, family, and culture, and their subject status. The same point is made more darkly in another abduction account, in which Lemnian men abduct Attic women to be their concubines and proceed to have children by them (6.138). Although, again, the women do not overtly resist their captors, they bring their sons up "in the Attic manner" — so much so that the Lemnian men take counsel and decide to kill both mothers and children, to avoid the threat to their own culture that the half-Attic children pose.

Herodotus' resistance to traditional fantasies of gynocracy, groups of women banding together in order to assert control over men, is particularly evident here, as well as his sense of symmetry between male and female activity within a given culture. A "Lemnian deed" popularly indicated any unspeakable atrocity committed by women against men, taking its name from an episode in Greek myth in which the women of Lemnos kill their husbands. Herodotus narrates instead an account of Lemnian men murdering women and children and adds in conclusion that this story "as well as the earlier one in which women killed their husbands . . ." forms the source of the traditional saying. In other words, he pointedly isolates murder of blood kin as a "Lemnian" tendency, not a male or female one.[9] The most important point both of this account and of the account of the Carian women in 1.146, however, remains the persistent loyalty that the women display to the culture of their birth, and their ability to transmit the sense of that culture to their children, although they are now in a foreign land and their children also the children of their captors. In both 6.138 and 1.146 it is the mothers and their *nomoi* to which the children give their loyalty.[10]

Women do not create culture by themselves, but they are depicted as its representatives. They reflect its values even in the face of male opposition, and they transmit it to their children. The fullest statement of the kind of cultural reciprocity that exists, in Herodotus' eyes, between women and men occurs in the foundation account of the Sauromatae in 4.110-117; it can almost be used, because of the fullness of the detail included, as a model that sets out Herodotus' idea of how societies begin and are enabled to endure over time.[11] Some Amazons are captured by the Greeks after the battle of Thermidon and are put on board ship as prisoners of war. The Amazons overpower and kill the Greek crew but, since they do not themselves know the art of sailing, they are forced to put ashore wherever the winds and currents have taken them. As chance has it, they come ashore in the country of the Scythians and are met and courted by Scythian young men. Together the Amazon women and Scythian men remove to a near-by uninhabited area to found a new people that will exhibit a blend of Scythian and Amazonian qualities; Herodotus implicitly accepts the account as a historical one since he derives some current Sauromatian peculiarities from details narrated in the romantic story.

The courtship is structured as a comedy of mutual response and adaptation between the sexes. The women accept the advances of the men partly because the men (the youngest of their own tribe) have already changed their ways to do everything as the Amazons do. The Amazons learn Scythian (with an accent and some peculiar idioms) but draw the line at becoming ordinary Scythian women. What is particularly interesting is that neither the women nor the men dominate the process of assimilation. Herodotus describes it first as a matter of Scythian policy (the Scythians admire the women and want to gain such fine specimens for their own people), then as one of sexual attraction, and finally as one of reasoned discussion, with the Amazons, it is true, doing most of the talking. Throughout the account the actors, male and female alike, avoid acts of defiance or enmity toward each other. Instead there is continuous responsiveness on both sides and an emphasis on the gradual adjustments that will allow men and women from such culturally different backgrounds to live together satisfactorily.[12]

The foundation account of the Sauromatae can be read in two ways, either as a true story from the past, or as a mythic account that cloaks in a temporal mode truths Herodotus understands as timeless. In either case, it presents some useful generalizations about the nature of the social reciprocity, stripped to its essentials, that exists in the *Histories* between men and women. For one thing, the Sauromatian account implicitly rejects the notion that any particular social role played by women (or by men) is a natural rather than a cultural phenomenon. It does not isolate a particular set of activities as male or female but, instead, isolates as truly natural the requirement of a mutually satisfactory division of function between the sexes. Herodotus implies that this alone will assure the cultural stability sufficient for providing food, raising children, and resisting external aggression. The Sauromatian pattern, as the Amazons and Scythians work it out, is an unusual one, but Herodotus gives no sign that the resulting culture is inadequate. As a story of origins, it shows in an extreme form what is implied in the other accounts in which groups of women play an active role: culture is, and must be, a construct of both men and women. Both reflect its values; both contribute to the creation of those values.

B.   Groups of women in ethnographic accounts (76)

When we go on to look at groups of women who are not presented in a historical context but as part of a timeless description of the manners and customs of exotic peoples, we see this same set of assumptions repeated in almost every context. In the first four books of the *Histories*, Herodotus inserts into the historical account of the various peoples the Persians encounter a number of more or less lengthy descriptions of native customs. These serve several purposes; most obviously, they are part of the unusual and remarkable, the *thōmata*, whose record Herodotus considers it his responsibility to preserve. He is rarely interested, however, in wonders that are simply bizarre. He almost always attempts to report habits that seem odd to Greek eyes in a large cultural context that makes sense of them.[13]

One of his most consistent ethnographic interests is the relation between the sexes and the variety of relationships that different cultures offer. He mentions details of feminine dress or appearance only six times, while fifteen times he discusses family customs (courtship, marriage, children); twenty-three times he describes

sexual adaptations; twenty-one times he describes the participation
of women in religious cult; and, finally, eleven times he describes
women as part of the public or social sphere that in Greece was
usually reserved for men. A brief overview of several of these categories reveals the extent to which, stripped of diachronic details,
Herodotus perceives culture in its timeless essentials to be an intri-
cate set of complementary institutions. No particular pattern is
necessarily better than another; in each, however, men and women
together provide for the essential requirements of a stable society.
For instance, in discussing family organization, Herodotus principally emphasizes how customs of courtship and marriage are
integrated into larger structures of behavior and belief, either
within a single culture or in comparison with Greek custom. Thus
three observations about Lycian matrilineality all explore the legal
ramifications of a system where legitimacy is transferred through
the female line (1.173); a prohibition against marrying one's
daughter to a swineherd is set in the context of a society that
abominates pigs (2.47). The ethnographic description of contemporary Sauromatian customs includes the provision that girls
must kill an enemy before they can marry (4.117), a comment
that the preceding historical narrative of the courtship of the
Amazons is partly designed to introduce and explain.

When he describes sexual customs, Herodotus' attention is
chiefly directed to sexual customs that combine aspects of culture
kept separate in Greece and, in general, that contrast with Greek
sexual norms. Four times he describes a degree of sexual propriety
that exceeds normal Greek standards. He also describes cultures in
which sexual intercourse is combined with religious cult, or with
the production of the dowry, or with the marriage ceremony itself
— habits that would have seemed odd indeed to a Greek reader.
Finally, he reports some customs because they virtually reverse
Greek categories of thought. The Thracians, he says, keep their
married women carefully guarded but allow complete freedom to
unmarried girls.[14]

As Pembroke indicates, ethnography is an ideal medium in
which to convey the hidden fears and fantasies of one's own
culture.[15] In reports of exotic sexual customs, if anywhere, one

would expect some of the darker aspects of Greek folk culture to assert themselves. Here, however, Herodotus once more pointedly avoids the theme of gynocracy, female domination of the male. Although some of the habits reported are strange and even shocking in the context of Greek custom, in Herodotus' ethnographies women never threaten the men of their own society or arrogate to themselves a power not rightfully theirs. In every culture except for the two that are nearly bestial at the edges of the world, sexual customs are presented as a set of limits and controls, with an emphasis placed on the boundaries that integrate sex into other aspects of society. In societies that are virtually promiscuous but have marriage (1.216, 4.172), access to the woman is regulated to guarantee privacy. Where there is complete promiscuity, Herodotus in one culture describes it as a choice the men have made in order to encourage communal cohesiveness (4.104); in another, he describes how one of its major drawbacks in Greek eyes is overcome: the men gather to decide the paternity of the child when it is old enough to resemble its father (4.180).[16]

Finally, when Herodotus describes women as part of the public life of their societies, he repeatedly displays a set of assumptions we have already noted in the context of women in the *polis*. When women participate in the public and political life of the community, their behavior parallels that of their menfolk. The women of the Zauekes participate in warfare by driving their husbands' chariots for them (4.193); both men and women in Asia plead with the Persian king for irrigation water (3.117); men, women, and children together among the Caunians hold drinking parties, choosing their companions on the basis of age and friendship (1.172). Although these customs too must have seemed strange to a Greek, in no instance does Herodotus use them to suggest the spectre of women seizing power from men or in combat with men over the distribution of power. The emphasis throughout lies on mutual adaptation and reciprocity between the sexes. Herodotus seems chiefly concerned to show the enormous variety of such adaptations that work to guarantee cultural stability.

Feminist anthropologists have recently argued that societal and sexual conflict seem least pronounced among peoples who have managed to maintain similar functions and similar spheres of work for women and men alike.[17] Herodotus twice explicitly assimilates women and men. Among the Argippeans, women resemble men physically, since both sexes are bald, snub-nosed, and bearded from birth (4.23). Among the Issedones, women presumably perform similar functions in society, since he calls them *isokrateis*, equal in power (4.26). These two cultures, Herodotus takes special pains to emphasize, are renowned among their neighbors for their justice and for their skill in solving disputes and protecting exiles fairly. No causal connection is overtly drawn between their reputation and the roles their women play; clearly, however, Herodotus does emphasize the possibility that societies in which the roles of men and women are virtually symmetrical can meet basic cultural requirements in a fully satisfactory fashion.

Herodotus marvels at the divine *pronoiē*, forethought and planning, exhibited in the fact that timid animals, who are naturally the prey of others, give birth to great numbers of offspring, while fierce and predatory animals bear few young (3.108). Similarly, in geography, while he mocks cartographers who insist on an absolute and rigid symmetry between the lands north and south of the Mediterranean, he accepts as reasonable a certain balance and correspondence, both between the north and south and between the qualities found at the ends of the earth and those found at its center (2.33, 3.106, 4.36). In his schematic descriptions of the customs of exotic peoples, or unusual customs among the Greeks themselves, he again emphasizes elements illustrating the principles of balance and complementarity, both within the individual culture and between the culture as a whole and those that surround it.[18] It is in the light of this general principle that we are to interpret Herodotus' descriptions of women in society. Women in the *polis* guarantee the survival of their cultures both by preserving life and by transmitting the *nomoi* of the culture to the next generation. The ethnographic descriptions show that Herodotus does not consider any particular distribution of social function between the sexes to be the right one, but tries instead to show that each viable culture embodies a balance of its own.

C.   Individual women who act in a family context (40)

The first part of this essay described the tensions created by family politics. Nevertheless, when individual women act in a family context, Herodotus lays emphasis on their positive and protective motives. Mothers shape the views of their sons or defend the lives and honor of their children; daughters act as their fathers' agents in the public sphere and defend family interests when they are threatened; wives generally support the political objectives of their husbands and work to maintain family stability and status.[19]

Especially striking in Herodotus' portrait of active family women is the clear connection between their role as prudent defenders of family status and authority and the resistance they display to the wishes of their menfolk. When a woman comes in conflict with a male relative, her role is to remind her son, father, brother, or husband of prudential considerations or of social norms that he is in danger of ignoring. The mother of the Egyptian thief threatens to betray her son to the king if he does not regain and provide a decent burial for his brother's body (2.121g); Polycrates' daughter warns her father that a political enemy will kill him (3.124); two sisters chastize their brothers for outrageous or immoral behavior (2.135.6, 3.32); eight-year-old Gorgo tells her father, the king of Lacedaemon, that if he listens to Aristagoras the crafty Ionian he will be corrupted (5.51).

Herodotus develops the implications of the social role of family women most sharply, however, in the context of crisis between husband and wife; here occur the most pointed examples of women working to resist male aggression and check male excess. In most accounts of marital crisis, the wife does not directly confront her husband but manipulates her situation in order both to protect herself and placate her husband at the same time.[20] Twice, however, the conflict is overt. Candaules at the very beginning of the *Histories* and Xerxes at its very end abuse their position as husbands by considering their queens' honor and status negligible in the face of their own sexual desires. In each account, the wife gains the upper hand because she does not act according to her husband's vision of reality but takes steps independently to defend her own honor and social status. It is the blindness of both monarchs to the possibility of such independence that brings them down.

The story of Candaules' wife is the first episode in the *Histories* that Herodotus narrates in detail; in it, the queen of Lydia is displayed naked, at her husband's command, to his favorite bodyguard (1.8 ff.). The queen hides her knowledge of the outrage and waits until she can confront the guard, Gyges, privately. She then gives Gyges the choice of killing Candaules, who plotted the deed (*ton tauta bouleusanta*), or of dying himself as its executor (*poiēsanta ou nomizomena*). The line she founds with her new husband lasts five generations and rises to real greatness in Croesus, its final heir. In the other account of marital conflict in the *Histories*, Xerxes' head wife, Amestris, is openly humiliated by her daughter-in-law, whom Xerxes has taken as mistress (9.108 ff.). Biding her time, Amestris waits until Xerxes' birthday when, by Persian convention, the king must grant any request made of him. Amestris asks and receives complete power over the girl's mother and tortures the woman brutally before releasing her back to her husband, an act resulting ultimately in the death of the girl's whole family.

Herodotus abstains from overt moral judgment upon either Amestris or Candaules' wife. The reflection sometimes cited as his, that what Amestris proposed to do was a "perverse and terrible deed" (9.110), is in fact Xerxes' reported thought as he abandons Masistes' wife to the savage mutilation Amestris intends to inflict on her.[21] Neither account, to be sure, is structured so that we entirely approve of the wife's vengeful action. Reacting to male abuses of cultural convention, Amestris and Candaules' wife exhibit the same kinds of shortcomings as their royal husbands. Yet, because they are aware of the limits within which they must act and the nature of the conventions their husbands have flouted, they are more lethally efficient in obtaining their goals.

Thus, although Herodotus does not present Amestris and the wife of Candaules as innocent and outraged heroines, he does depict them as serious social actors and their actions as serious responses to issues of social authority and status. The fact that the whole narrative of the *Histories* is sandwiched between the two accounts gives them a programmatic weight at odds with the domestic and frivolous light in which they are often read. Moreover, one of the basic motifs in the *Histories* is the divine retribution that attends wrongdoing. Both Amestris and Candaules' wife survive to a vigorous and authority-filled old age; this in itself suggests that Herodotus is not here concerned principally with stories of wifely misbehavior or Clytemnestra-like revenge. On the contrary, the emphasis in both accounts falls on a causal sequence that shows what happens when royal husbands forget that wifely obedience is a voluntary and contingent affair, one based on the premise of certain standards of husbandly behavior.[22]

Herodotus does not advance these stories, or others in which wives ward off husbandly aggression, as an argument for a more symmetrical sharing of political power between men and women. "Custom is king of all," Pindar says, and Herodotus agrees with him (3.38). What he does implicitly argue, here as in the ethnographies and portraits of women in the *polis*, is that any society functions because of the reciprocity that exists between women and men. When a wife is ignored as an independent and responsible member of her society, she acts on her own behalf to rectify the imbalance. Unless we read it in from tragedy, even in these extreme accounts we do not find a portrait of women in revolt, overturning the conventions of their cultures, behaving in short as wild and irrational forces that need to be contained. In Herodotus, the family women who scheme do so to protect their own position and authority in response to male outrage. Because of their sensitivity to convention and its limits, they are more successful than men in achieving their objectives.

D.   Individual women in the public sphere (22)

This fourth category represents women in extreme situations, that is, unconstrained by the opinions and wishes of male family members. Nonetheless, they continue, like the other women we have examined, to defend human life and conserve and articulate the values of their societies.[23] The mother of Sataspes requests her nephew, the king, to commute the death sentence of her son into a command to circumnavigate Africa (4.43). Two queens are great builders to cities; three more use their royal power to avenge the murders of brother, husband, and son.[24]

Women in the public sphere continue frequently to articulate the social values that underlie their actions. Cyno, a slave herself and married to a cowherd, saves the life of the infant Cyrus and thus sets in motion the events that will destroy Astyages' kingdom (1.110 ff.). The whole account of the birth of Cyrus is structured to emphasize an improper devolution of authority: Astyages, when he has decided to murder his daughter's child, entrusts the execution to his vizier, Harpagus; Harpagus in turn entrusts it to the cowherd; the cowherd, finally, allows his wife to have the deciding voice in the child's fate. Cyno is the only actor in the entire account who is willing both to give voice to the full range of practical and moral considerations that, in her opinion, govern the situation and to accept responsibility for acting on them. She substitutes her own dead child for the baby her husband is to murder, telling him: "for thus neither will you be caught outraging the overlords nor will we have committed acts evilly conceived. For the dead child will gain a kingly burial and the survivor will not lose his life" (1.112).

Cyno represents a form of behavior characteristic both of family women and of women in the public sphere. As we have seen, feminine activity in the *Histories* is usually depicted as a creative manipulation of the constraints of the situation in which the woman finds herself, while males frequently ignore such limitations and are brought low in consequence by some factor they have not anticipated.[25] Women in Herodotus are often shown choosing carefully between difficult courses of action. Among family women, Polycrates' daughter would choose to remain unmarried if she could thereby save her father (3.124); Sesostris' wife chooses to sacrifice two sons to the flames to save the rest of the family (2.107); Intaphrenes' wife, allowed to save one male relative, saves her own brother rather than a husband or son (3.119). Sometimes the woman cleverly obviates the necessity for choice: a queen of Sparta gains the throne for both her sons by refusing to choose between them (6.52); Candaules' wife, seen naked by Gyges, forces the choice of vengeance upon Gyges himself (1.8 ff.). This element of clear-sighted choice, choice made by considering the constraints of the situation and the rules that the society lives by, is what gives women, Herodotus implies, their unusual success in attaining their goals.

Tomyris and Artemisia are the female rulers described in most detail in the *Histories*. They are particularly striking examples of a number of the themes we have developed here. Tomyris presides over the death of Cyrus in book one (1.205 ff.), and Artemisia presides over Xerxes' defeat in the last books of the *Histories*. Both of these queens, like other women we have noted, take pains to articulate the moral and political basis for their actions. Both see, as their Persian and male counterparts do not, that human power has its limitations; both predict defeat for the Persian if he oversteps these bounds.

Tomyris is a noble savage; she conducts her military campaign in a Homerically irreproachable fashion. Herodotus emphasizes the odd disjunction between her speech and actions at the end of the account, as Tomyris proclaims her noble, almost Achillean, scorn of Cyrus' deviousness while pushing his severed head into a skin filled with human blood (1.214). Appearances here are deceptive; Tomyris, the rude savage, is not only more civilized but more manly than her enemies. Cyrus' advisor in the ignoble stratagem that undoes him is Croesus, a man who himself lost his former kingdom and deliberately unmanned his former subjects (1.155). Another set of deliberate inversions of traditional sex roles occurs in the account of Artemisia in books seven and eight. Herodotus singles out Artemisia as the only commander in Xerxes' fleet attending through *andreia*, manly courage, rather than compulsion (7.99). She alone of Xerxes' advisors gives advice with an eye to the military situation rather than to her own standing at court (8.68). Unlike Tomyris, she saves herself and her ship by extremely unconventional military behavior; she sinks an allied ship so that the Athenians pursuing her turn their attention elsewhere, thinking that she is on their side (8.87).[26]

Artemisia and Tomyris are successful military leaders, as generals unusual in the extent to which they articulate the moral and political basis of their actions and in their correct perception of Persian ambition overreaching itself. These portraits set the capstone on the interpretation of women as actors I am advancing here. Women in Herodotus act to preserve themselves and those in their care; they also act as responsible members of the societies in which they live. They reflect the same social values as the men of their cultures but they differ from most men in their willingness to analyze these values within a given context. Cyno, eight-year-old Gorgo, the mother of the Egyptian thief, Demaratus' mother, Cambyses' sister, Polycrates' daughter, Intaphrenes' wife, and a number of other women as well share with the great queens this capacity. They generally see society for what it is, a series of moral conventions and constraints within which everyone must act.

E.   Priestesses and founders of religious cults (62)

Four accounts describe women as the heroines of religious foundation stories, as part of the aetiology of a cult. Like the Athenian and Carian women taken from their homelands by enemy men, women who found cults in the *Histories* involuntarily must renounce their own cultures, but they nonetheless manage to bring with them their conventions, and to establish new religious rites in a new land, among new people. Thus two Egyptian women abducted from Egyptian Thebes found oracles in Libya and Dodona (2.54). Like the Amazons who become Sauromatian, moreover, they exhibit considerable ingenuity in learning a new language and integrating themselves into their new circumstances while preserving the essence of their former cultural role. The daughters of Danaus bring the festival of Demeter to Greece (2.171) and found a temple of Athena in Lindus (2.182); two pairs of Hyperborean girls, finally, enrich the rites of Apollo in Delos (4.33-35). The emphasis is on great distances of time and space: women in the distant past travelling great voyages to transmit religious belief and ritual from one culture to another.[27]

Priestesses in a more contemporary context also resemble other active women. If we were to count number of appearances as the principal criterion, the Pythia would be the most important woman in the *Histories*; she appears in every book but the second and on forty-five occasions advises kings, tyrants, aristocrats, and commoners, both Greek and barbarian.[28] She predicts the outcome of war and directs the foundation of colonies, sometimes extremely persistently (4.150 ff.). The Pythia represents the intersection of politics and morality for those who consult her. She seeks to resolve conflict and correct misbehavior; as the representative of one of the few Greek institutions open to all Greek cities alike, she works for the benefit of the society as a whole rather than in the narrow self-interest of an individual *polis*. In all these ways, the Pythia can be viewed as a stunning and extreme example of the nomothetic woman, setting out the cultural limits and controls within which Greek society will thrive, beyond which it will perish.[29]

In a most important respect, however, the Pythia resembles not the other active women in the *Histories* but the passive women in a family context with which this essay began. The advice she gives is not her own but, in Herodotus' eyes, the god's: she is Apollo's intermediary. Like passive family women, she represents limits, but while passive family women represent the mortal and finite nature of family security, and the family's vulnerability to human strife and natural disaster, the Pythia at the other end of the spectrum of human experience represents the limits that divine order places on mankind. Herodotus makes it clear, by the extensive use he makes of the Pythia and other oracles in the *Histories*, that he sees human experience as a continuum, an unbroken spectrum comprised first of nature, then of culture, and finally, at its upper limit, of the moral and causal patterns imposed by divinity. When men and women act in the *Histories*, they do so in the middle range of experience represented by society and culture: the nexus of rules and common assumptions that allows people to live together in human communities. Passive women on one end of the spectrum and priestesses on the other, however, represent natural and religious aspects of human life that are, in the *Histories*, as real and as important as the cultural sphere. It is because we cannot as men and women fully understand them that we do not experience them rationally but instead suffer them as a series of inexplicable constraints.

The Pythia represents the relationship between humanity and the cosmic order that controls and patterns the world: events do have a shape and a meaning that can be defined in moral and causal terms. These terms the god conveys through the Pythia but, because of our own limited perception of the sphere of reality she stands for, we understand her only faintly and through the distractions of our own desires. Thus we perceive her advice as a series of injunctions rather than as indication of the pattern that reality takes. Herodotus shows in the Solon-Croesus episode (1.30-33) that the problem lies partly in the fact that we must live through time ourselves and are thus subject to its limitations. We cannot begin to understand what the Pythia darkly and ambiguously conveys to us until, like the historian himself, we look back upon it later.[30]

In 1913 Jacoby demonstrated that a relatively straightforward, sequential account of Persian military aggression provides the overall narrative structure of the *Histories*.[31] Herodotus describes each new culture at that point in the narrative when it must confront the advance of the Persian army. Within the theme of Persian expansionism, women are rarely the principal actors, although the women who do enter the political and military spheres — Nitocris, Artemisia, Tomyris, even, until her moral downfall, Pheretime — acquit themselves well. Instead, as we have seen, women in the *Histories*, presented in an astonishing number of settings and often depicted as idiosyncratic and creative social actors, generally occur in the context of a subtler motif that acts as a counterpoint to the record of Persian military success. In hundreds of brief passages throughout the *Histories* Herodotus' women, active and passive, build up a picture of the kinds of balance, control, and limits that define Herodotus' understanding of culture itself. Passively, women represent the mortal threats that family and society face and the constraints that the gods impose on humankind; actively, they observe the conventions of their cultures, transmit them to the next generation, and remind their menfolk of them as well.

Throughout the *Histories*, Persians habitually violate the limits that women stand for. In more than a score of passages, they demonstrate their inability to distinguish between sex and politics, and they abuse women in consequence.[32] Herodotus depicts this as one aspect of a larger Persian inability to accept diversity and balance as principles governing culture and society: they deny the notion of balance and reciprocity between the sexes, the separation of the marital and the political spheres, and, finally, the distinction between one's own territory and the territory that belongs to others. Their very military progress shows them intent upon subordinating everything, male and female, foreign and Persian, to a single structure of absolute royal authority. It is the quality of Herodotus' vision of society and culture, with women as essential elements of both, that makes us understand why the Persians ultimately meet defeat.

Herodotus was almost certainly an exceptional witness to his world. He travelled more widely than most Greeks, and his freedom from narrow ethnocentrism is reflected on almost every page. Moreover, the breadth and originality of his literary achievement alone would suggest that the portrait of women he has given us is not a naive reflection of his culture's clichés but a distillation that reflects his own passionate intellectual achievement. On the other hand, Herodotus' picture of women forms part of the first extant Greek attempt to look seriously at human culture for its own sake and on its own terms. It deserves incorporation into our larger picture of Greek society and the relations of women and men within it.

Acknowledgements

I would like to thank J. Appleby, J. Dewald, J. Ginsburg, D. Lateiner, P. Manning, M. Ostwald, L. Pearson, S. Stephens, R. Stroud, J. Winkler, the editor and two anonymous referees of this issue of *Women's Studies* for their helpful comments on earlier drafts of this essay.

Notes

1. For women in tragedy, see M. Shaw, "The Female Intruder: Women in Fifth-Century Drama," *CP* 70 (1975) 255-266 and F. Zeitlin, "The Dynamics of Misogyny: Myth and Mythmaking in the *Oresteia*," *Arethusa* 11 (1978) 166-169. For women in oratory, see W.K. Lacey, *The Family in Classical Greece* (Ithaca 1968) 158-162.

2. An Appendix at the end of this essay sets out the evidence topically arranged. The present discussion loosely follows the order of the outline given in the Appendix, and the reader is encouraged to consult it for examples beyond those given in the text and notes. Recent studies considering individual aspects of Herodotus' views of women include A. Tourraix, "La femme et le pouvoir chez Hérodote," *DHA* 2 (1976) 369-386; J. Annequin's critique of Tourraix in the same volume, 378-390; M. Rosellini and S. Saïd, "Usages de femmes et autres *nomoi* chez les 'sauvages' d'Hérodote: essai de lecture structurale," *Annali della Scuola Normale di Pisa* 8 (1978) 949-1005; R. Weil, "Artémise ou le monde à l'envers" in *Recueil Plassart* (Paris 1976) 215-224; and a forthcoming article in *Hermes* by M. Cain, kindly sent me in xerox by the author.

3. This essay does not consider the passages where femininity is used as an abstraction or a metaphor. Seventeen such passages concern a geographical phenomenon that is either named after a woman or is named metaphorically as the mother, wife, sister, or daughter of something else. Herodotus generally ignores the myth and once, in 4.45, explicitly questions the whole habit, declaring that he accepts it only because convention makes it convenient to do so. Another eighteen times Herodotus either uses the concept of the feminine neutrally (1.17, a treble flute is "feminine") or, if female is contrasted unfavorably to male, the context makes it clear that he is reporting a character's thoughts (often in the context of military insult: 1.189, 2.102, 9.20, 9.107). If Herodotus uses antonymous clichés himself, he generally uses the context to undercut them. In 7.153 he emphasizes that Telines, the founder of a great Sicilian dynasty and obviously a resourceful and ambitious man, was also soft and effeminate by nature. For the complete list of such passages, see the Appendix, Section III.

4. Ninety-three of 128, or 73%, reflect a direct threat or danger. Most of the remaining thirty-five reflect another, subtler kind of threat. Herodotus does not use female lineage to describe family accumulation of power; instead, he mentions female genealogies either to indicate the inappropriate confusion of family and political power practiced in the Persian royal family, or to indicate the inappropriate confusion of history and myth at the point in stories about the past where women begin marrying gods and heroes.

5. Many passages that do not mention women convey the same theme, of course: the Lampsacenes are terrified when they learn what Croesus' threat to destroy them like a pine tree means — a pine leaves no shoots behind to spring up after it has been cut (6.37); Egyptian soldiers, kept

on border duty too long, revolt and declare with a somewhat desperate bravado that wherever their genitals are, there will also be wives and children. The point is their absolute need for women and children, family structures, even if they have to found a new nation to get them (2.30). The theme of the family's importance to society is found throughout Greek literature, from the *Iliad* through Aristotle's *Politics* (1252 b9). To our eyes, Herodotus is perhaps unusual in the extent to which he discusses family affairs as part of a larger overtly political context — to the Greeks, Thucydides' inclination to consider only the superstructure of the *polis* and decisions reached by civic deliberation probably seemed much more radical, severe, and strange.

6. 1.51.5b, 2.1, 2.110, 2.111.4, 3.130, 6.41.2. Only 7.69, Darius' fondness for Artystone, is not mentioned in the context of threatening change.

7. Passages only concerned with difficulties of generation are listed in Section I.A.2 in the Appendix. A number of them are set in Sparta, since the kingship there was hereditary. The account of Demaratus (6.61) is the most striking of these, since it is Demaratus' doubtful paternity that ultimately loses him the kingship and exiles him to Persia, where he becomes Xerxes' chief advisor on things Greek (7.101 ff., 7.234 ff.). Many other passages with more complex aspects as well could be added here, such as the accounts concerning heiresses (Section I.A.3.b.3), and a number of births of great men (not only 1.59 and 5.67, but also 6.131.1, 1.107, and 5.92g). Children who are disabled are mentioned in 1.34, 5.92b, 3.51 and 53, 3.145, 4.161, 4.155, 3.33, and 6.75. Cf. also Dorieus' disappointed assumption in 5.42 that his physical and mental superiority over Cleomenes would win him in Spartan kingship.

8. Atossa as the daughter of Cyrus (7.2-3) and perhaps Pheretime as the daughter of Battus (4.205) show the kinds of power available to a woman because of a powerful father. Herodotus, however, does not depict women wielding the power of their own lineages over their husbands; see below, p. 107 and note 19. An *epiklēros*, or heiress, creates additional kinds of tension. In herself, she represents the failure of her father to produce a male heir; Herodotus twice uses the word *apais*, childless, to mean "left with only female issue" (5.48, 5.67). She also represents the inversion of normal marriage patterns, and a consequent dislocation of family structure. See Lacey (*op. cit.*, note 1) 139-, 145 and J.-P. Vernant, "Hestia-Hermès. Sur l'expression religieuse de l'espace et du mouvement chez les Grecs," *Mythe et pensée chez les Grecs* I (Paris 1971) 144-147. The anxieties of a powerful female lineage are well summed up by Lycophron's sister in 3.53: "Many men prefer the reasonable to the just, and many before now seeking their maternal inheritance have thrown away their paternal one."

9. For the traditional portrait of the "Lemnian deed," see, for instance, Aeschylus, *Libation Bearers* (631-634). For the Greek concept of *gynaikokratia*, see Aristotle, *Politics* 1313 b33-34 and 1269 b40, where he defines it as women "getting out of hand," *anesis* (the translation of

S. Pembroke, "Women in Charge: the Function of Alternatives in Early Greek Tradition and the Ancient Idea of Matriarchy," *Journal of the Warburg and Courtault Institute* 30 [1967] 20). The fear of female insubordination and resulting loss of control by men is visible in Greek thought from the Homeric Hymns and Hesiod onward. M.B. Arthur, "Early Greece: The Origins of the Western Attitude toward Women," *Arethusa* 6 (1973) 24-26 and 48-50 relates the fear of female domination to more complex questions of developing political ideologies; P. Vidal-Naquet, "Esclavage et gynécocratie dans la tradition, le mythe, l'utopie" in C. Nicolet, ed., *Recherches sur les structures sociales dans l'antiquité classique* (Paris 1970) 63-80 relates it to the structures of Greek marriage and inheritance patterns and the continuous possibility that women might provide descent without the aid of "citizen" males (cf., in Herodotus, 6.83 and 4.1).

10.   Both abduction accounts show that a whole society suffers when men ignore the part played by women in the establishment and maintenance of cultural conventions. Herodotus makes the same point ironically in 3.159, where he implies that the Babylonians effectively destroy their own culture by killing most of their women, in their zeal to win independence from Persia. (Babylonians in the *Histories* seem habitually to misjudge the relationship of means and ends; cf. 1.191, 3.157, and 1.196. In every case the innovation undercuts the purpose for which it was intended.)

11.   See W.K.C. Guthrie, *The Sophists* (Cambridge 1971) 60 ff. for the prevalence of such rationalized "myths of origin" among Herodotus' contemporaries and the role of such myths in developing theories of nature and society. Another foundation story in which men and women play complementary roles, Herodotus explicitly introduces as myth (4.8-10).

12.   It is interesting that commentators often seize on a straightforward description of linguistic adaptation in 4.114 and 4.117 in order somewhere in the account to find evidence of latent contrast or opposition between the sexes. I do not find, with R.W. Macan, the Scythian men displaying "their characteristic stupidity" (*Herodotus. The Fourth, Fifth, and Sixth Books* [1895; rpt. New York 1973] 82 note 115.4) or, with W.W. How and J. Wells, that "[t]he greater aptness of the Amazons is a delightful touch of nature; but they were inaccurate . . . as lady linguists often are" (*Commentary on Herodotus* [1912; rpt. Oxford 1936] I, 341 note 114). It is true that the account begins with the etymology of the Scythian word for Amazon as "man-killer," and with a battle between the Amazons and their new neighbors, but that only underlines the absence of hostility from the rest of the story.

13.   The articles by Rosellini and Saïd (*op. cit.*, note 2) and Pembroke (*op. cit.*, note 9) have especially helped my thinking in this section.

14.   Propriety: 1.198 (twice), 2.41, 2.64; sex and religion: 1.181, 1.182 (twice), 1.199 (twice); sex and the dowry: 1.93, 1.196; sex and the wedding ceremony: 4.168, 4.172; reversal: 5.6.

15.   Pembroke (*op. cit.*, note 9) 34-35.

16.   As these passages indicate, Herodotus continues to assume male control
of sexuality, even in exotic contexts. A vivid illustration of this assumption occurs in 4.176, where the number of a woman's anklets testifies
to her sexual prowess; if the point of the passage had been the woman's
control over her sexual activity (as, for instance, Aristophanes fanta-
sizes at the end of the *Ecclesiazusae* [1000 ff.]), the anklets would not
have indicated excellence but merely appetite.

17.   M.Z. Rosaldo, "Woman, Culture, and Society: A Theoretical Overview,"
in Rosaldo and L. Lamphere, eds., *Woman, Culture, and Society*
(Stanford 1974) 41.

18.   See G.E.R. Lloyd, *Polarity and Analogy. Two Types of Argumentation
in Early Greek Thought* (Cambridge 1966) 341-344 for Herodotus' use
of balance and symmetry in geographical description. See J.L. Myres,
Herodotus, Father of History (Oxford 1953) 49-50 for lists of other
passages that translate this idea of balance and order into the human
and moral sphere, especially 1.32: "now it is impossible for one who is
human to have all these blessings, just as no land is self-sufficient,
producing everything for itself, but one thing it has, and another it
lacks."

19.   The section on passive family women above describes a number of
tensions that surround marriage as a social institution. Given such
tensions, the strength of the marriage bond in the portrait of active
women in the *Histories* is quite striking. Three women alone betray the
marriage connection, and for all of them Herodotus presents extenuat-
ing circumstances. In 1.61 and 3.119 the husband will not or cannot
behave like a husband; for 1.8, see below, pp. 108-109. (In two others,
the wife implicitly contests her husband's will; for 9.108 ff., see below,
pp. 108-109, while in 4.154, Herodotus remarks that a woman behaves
like "a true stepmother" in wishing to murder her husband's daughter.)

20.   The wife of Amasis, blamed for her husband's temporary impotence,
saves herself from death and relieves her husband from his condition by
dedicating a statue to Aphrodite in Cyrene (2.181); Melissa, murdered
by her husband, nonetheless agrees to help him with his necromancy
if he will rectify her improper burial rites (5.92); Isagoras' wife wins
Spartan support for her husband's political ambitions by granting her
favors to the Spartan king (5.70); Atossa supports Darius' political
ambitions and at the same time fulfills the oath she has privately sworn
to her physician (3.134).

21.   Amestris is seen again in 7.114, burying Persian children alive as a
grateful tribute to the god of the underworld. There Herodotus explicitly cites her behavior not as a personal aberration but as proof that
live burial was a Persian custom, *Persikon de to zōontas katorussein*. In
9.108 ff. also, her behavior can be interpreted as nasty but clever politics. She holds the mother *aitiēn*, responsible, as in a very indirect and
innocent way she was. Had Amestris merely tortured or humiliated the
girl, she would have left intact and hostile to her the second most
powerful family in Persia. By immediately destroying Masistes' wife,
she throws the whole family into confusion and forces them to react

while disorganized and unprepared for conflict.

22.   E. Wolff, "Das Weib des Masistes," *Hermes* 92 (1964) 51-58 also considers the programmatic placement of the two "Harems-Liebesgeschichten" at the beginning and end of the *Histories*. Both he sets in the context of a larger Persian royal tragedy, one that culminates many years after the final episode narrated in the *Histories* in the death of Xerxes himself at the hands of the son to whom he had married Masistes' daughter.

23.   Eight women in the public sphere are mentioned principally because they occur in the context of some unusual event: 1.51.5a, 1.60, 2.2, 2.46, 2.131.2b, 2.134, 2.135.5, and 6.61.3a. They are servants, or courtesans, and usually perform an individual striking action.

24.   1.184, 1.185, 2.100, 4.160, 4.202. One of these, Pheretime (4.202), oversteps conventional limits, and the gods punish her for it with a horrible death — not, however, because she has adopted a role inappropriate for a woman, but because she has transgressed the limits set by the gods on *human* vengeance (*hōs ara anthrōpoisi hai liēn ischurai timōriai pros theōn epiphthonoi ginontai*, 4.205). Once more, she is part of an account full of acts of cruelty and excess. Her son incinerates his political enemies, despite the warning of the Pythia (4.164); her Persian general captures Barca through an act of brutal treachery (4.201).

25.   H. Bischoff, *Der Warner bei Herodot* (Marburg 1932) discusses the number of times in the *Histories* that actors, almost all male, ignore good advice — advice, that is, that correctly points out the limitations of their circumstances. (Selections are reprinted in W. Marg, *Herodotus* [Darmstadt 1962] 302-319.) See also H.-P. Stahl, "Learning through suffering? Croesus' conversations in the history of Herodotus," *YCS* 24 (1975) 1-36.

26.   The reversals and ironies in the account of Artemisia are well developed by R. Weil (*op. cit.*, note 2). I argue that she is depicted successfully manipulating an extremely difficult situation; she emerges personally victorious, despite Xerxes' blindness and vanity and despite the fact that she is on the losing side of the war. Herodotus emphasizes her prudence and intelligence at a number of points; she is last seen counselling retreat for Xerxes and escorting his bastard children to safety (8.102-103). In 8.103, Herodotus sarcastically distinguishes between Artemisia's merit in giving the advice to retreat and Xerxes' cowardice in taking it.

27.   Thematically, the women who found religious cults remind us also of the four mythic rapes that begin the *Histories*. Although the tone of 1.1-1.5 is amused and skeptical (myths, whether Greek or barbarian, are not for Herodotus history), the cumulation of stories suggests on a plane deeper than that of historical fact one sense in which culture is defined by the dislocation and exchange of women. It is through myth, after all, that cultures define their own past, and each of the myths told at the beginning of the *Histories* involves a foreign woman who is brought in and helps thereafter to identify the culture to which she is brought.

Io in Greek myth becomes an Egyptian goddess and mother of a god; Medea names the Medes; Europe has a continent named after her; and, finally, Helen is the mythic cause of the first open military split between East and West. In Herodotus' carefully indirect account, it is the act of exchanging women back and forth that causes East and West to define themselves, and to define their differences with each other. This is, perhaps, the essence of exogamy itself as the Greeks understood it, but practiced on a cultural rather than a narrowly familial scale.

28. Herodotus does not imply that the Pythia spoke unintelligibly or through male intermediaries (5.92b). See J. Fontenrose, *The Delphic Oracle* (Berkeley 1978) ch. 7 for a complete evaluation of the evidence. For the general independence of women serving their religious functions, see 6.16.2 and the interpretation of the sacerdotal functions of the women in the *Lysistrata* of Aristophanes by H. Foley, " 'The Female Intruder' Reconsidered: Women in Aristophanes' *Lysistrata* and *Ecclesiazusae*," to appear in *CP*.

29. The Pythia is not perfect; twice she is suborned (5.63, 6.66), and once some Athenian ambassadors argue with her and receive a more hopeful response (7.141). See also the openly political engagement of other priestesses in 5.72 and 6.134.

30. J. Kirchberg, *Die Funktion der Orakel im Werke Herodots* (Göttingen 1965) 116-120 points out several parallels between the function of oracles in the text and the role of the historian himself, arranging and interpreting his material. For a more general understanding of Herodotus' sense of religion and history, see W. Schadewaldt, "Das Religiös-Humane als Grundlage der geschichtlichen Objektivität bei Herodot," in Marg, ed. (*op. cit.*, note 25), 185-200. Two women have been added to the list of priestesses in the Appendix because, like religious women, they represent aspects both of Herodotus' portrait of passive women and of his active women. The mother of Cleobis and Biton in 1.31 symbolizes at once the mysterious functions of nature and divinity (she brings her sons life; she brings them, by her prayers, death) and, in her actions, an entirely proper sphere of social activity. The snake-lady of 4.8 ff. represents both the chthonic and natural component to which Heracles beings culture and, in her actions, a reasonable human being. She bargains, stands by her bargain, and it is she who actually brings the sons up according to the rules Heracles gives her.

31. F. Jacoby, "Herodotus," in *RE*, Supplementband 2 (Stuttgart 1913) 347 ff., rpt. in *Griechische Historiker* (Stuttgart 1956) 78 ff.

32. See, for instance, Cambyses' incest in 3.32, Artayctes' use of the temple of Protesilaus for sexual intercourse in 9.116, the problems of Darius' succession and jealousy between sons of different wives in 7.3; Darius' overpersuasion by Atossa in 3.134; the Persian assumption that the women of the Macedonians are at their disposal in 5.18, and, of course, the scene of domestic and political chaos at Sardis in 9.108 ff. with which Herodotus' account of Persian royal politics ends.

33. Good studies of other, more military, aspects of "Persian expansionism" occur in H.R. Immerwahr, "Historical Action in Herodotus," *TAPA* 85

(1954) 14-45, and "Aspects of Historical Causation in Herodotus," *TAPA* 87 (1956) 241-280. D. Lateiner's unpublished study, *Herodotus' Histories. An Invention in History* contains excellent observations on the broader, non-Persian implications of boundary transgression in Herodotus.

Appendix

I. PASSIVE WOMEN (128)

A. Individual passive women presented in a family context (97)

1. External aggression (25)
   a. Against whole family: 3.14, 3.68, 7.107.2a, 7.107.2b, 8.106.
   b. Abduction: 1.1, 1.2a, 1.2b, 1.3, 2.112 ff., 4.43.2, 5.18.3, 5.21, 5.94.2, 6.62, 6.65, 8.136, 9.73.
   c. Instability of marriage: 1.51.5b, 2.1, 2.110, 2.111.4, 3.130, 6.41.2 (7.69).
2. Family and difficulties of generation (9): 1.34, 1.59, 5.39, 5.40, 5.67.1, 6.61a, 6.61b, 6.71a, 6.71b. (cross ref: 1.107, 5.92b, 6.52, 6.131 and section I.A.3.b.3 below [heiresses].)
3. Family politics (39)
   a. Successful dynastic marriage: 1.74, 3.88a, 3.88b, 3.88c, 3.88d, 5.67.3, 5.94.1, 6.38, 6.39, 6.41.4, 7.165. (cross ref: 3.137, 6.126.)
   b. Family crisis
      1. Between brothers: 1.92.3a, 1.92.3b, 1.173.2, 3.30, 7.2.2a, 7.2.2b.
      2. Between in-laws: 1.75, 1.107 ff., 3.50 ff., 4.147, 5.30.
      3. Daughters of famous men and heiresses: 3.137, 5.48, 5.67.4, 6.126, 7.205, 7.224. (cross ref: 4.205, 7.2.)
      4. Other: *2.111*, 3.31.6, 3.118, 4.78.2, 4.78.5, 4.80.1, *4.154.1*, 4.164, 5.32, 5.47, 9.111. (italics = woman victim.)
4. Genealogies (24)
   a. Persian: 5.116a, 5.116b, 5.116c, 6.43, 7.5, 7.61.2, 7.64,

7.73, 7.78, 7.82, 7.97a, 7.97b.
b. Mythological: 1.7, 1.84, 2.98.2, 2.145.4a, 2.145.4b, 2.145.4c, 6.53, 7.61.3a, 7.61.3b.
c. Other: 5.118, 6.103, 7.166.

B. Passive women in groups (31)

1. Political or military aggression: 1.164, 3.45, 3.97, 4.121, 4.145.2, 4.202, 5.15, 5.98, 6.16, 6.19, 6.32, 6.137, 7.114.1, 8.33, 8.36, 8.40, 8.142.
2. Indication of disturbance in society: 3.159, 6.139.1, 7.33, 7.83, 7.187, 9.34, 9.81, 9.116.
3. Coerced by men of own society: 1.176, 3.150, 4.145.5, 5.87.3, 5.88, 5.92ē.1.

II. ACTIVE WOMEN (212)

A. Groups of women within a *polis* (12)

1. Activities complementary to male activities: 1.31.3, 3.48, 5.83.3a, 5.83.3b, 9.5.
2. Independent of male control: 1.146.3a, 4.1, 4.110 ff., 4.146, 5.87.2, 6.138.2, 6.138.4.

B. Groups of women within ethnographic accounts (76)

1. Dress and appearance: 1.82, 2.35.3b, 2.36, 4.23, 4.168.1, 4.189.1.
2. Family: 1.135, 1.136, 1.137, 1.146.3b, 1.173.4, 1.173.5a, 1.173.5b, 1.196.1a, 1.196.1b, 2.35.4b, 2.47, 2.92, 4.117b, 5.16, 6.57.
3. Sex: 1.93, 1.181.5, 1.182.2a, 1.182.2b, 1.196.5, 1.198a, 1.198b, 1.199.1, 1.199.5, 1.203, 1.216.1a, 1.216.1b, 2.41, 2.64, 3.101, 4.104, 4.168.2, 4.172.2a, 4.172.2b, 4.172.2c, 4.176, 4.180.5, 5.6.
4. Religion: 2.35.4a, 2.48, 2.60, 2.61, 2.65.3, 2.65.4, 2.85, 2.89, 3.99, 4.33.5, 4.34, 4.35.3, 4.71, 4.180.2, 4.186.2a, 4.186.2b, 4.189.3, 5.5.1a, 5.5.1b, 6.58.1, 6.58.3.
5. Society: 1.172, 2.35.2, 2.35.3a, 2.98.1, 3.117, 4.26, 4.69, 4.75, 4.191, 4.193, 4.195.

C. Individual women who act in a family context (40)

1. Daughters: 1.5, 1.61.1, 2.121e, 2.126, 2.129, 3.1, 3.53, 3.69, 3.119, 3.124, 5.51, 9.76.
2. Mothers: 2.91, 2.121g, 3.3, 4.78.1, 4.162, 4.165, 5.92d, 6.52.2, 6.68.
3. Wives: 1.8, 1.61.2, 1.109, 2.107, 2.131.2a, 2.181, 3.133, 4.154.2, 5.70, 5.92ē.2, 6.131, 7.3, 8.137, 9.108.1a, 9.108.1b, 9.109.
4. Sisters: 2.135.6, 3.32, 5.12.

D. Individual women in the public sphere (22):
1.51.5a, 1.60, 1.110, 1.184, 1.185, 1.205 ff., 2.2, 2.46, 2.100, 2.131.2b, 2.134, 2.135.5, 4.43.1, 4.160, 4.202, 6.61.3a, 7.99, 7.114.2, 8.68, 8.87, 8.101, 8.103b.

E. Priestesses (62)

1. Founders of cults: 2.54a, 2.54b, 2.171, 2.182, 4.33.3a, 4.33.3b, 4.35.1a, 4.35.1b.
2. Pythia: 1.13, 1.19, 1.47, 1.55, 1.65, 1.66, 1.67, 1.85, 1.91, 1.167, 1.174, 3.57, 4.15, 4.150, 4.151, 4.155, 4.156, 4.157, 4.159, 4.161, 4.163, 5.43, 5.63, 5.66, 5.67.2, 5.79, 5.82, 5.90, 5.92b, 6.34, 6.36, 6.52.5, 6.66, 6.75, 6.77, 6.86, 6.123, 6.135, 6.139.2, 7.140, 7.148, 7.169, 7.220, 8.51, 9.33.
3. Other priestesses: 1.175, 2.55.3a, 2.55.3b, 2.55.3c, 5.72, 6.134, 7.111.
4. Women in mixed structures: 1.31.2, 4.8 ff.

III. THE FEMININE AS AN ABSTRACTION (35)

A. Geographical phenomena:
2.29, 4.5, 4.45.1, 4.45.3a, 4.45.3b, 4.52, 4.86, 4.180.5, 5.80, 6.61.3b, 7.58, 7.62, 7.178, 7.189, 8.31, 8.53, 9.51.

B. Distinction into male and female:
1.17, 1.105, 1.189, 2.30, 2.102, 3.66, 3.84, 4.67, 5.13, 5.18.2, 7.120, 7.153, 8.103a, 9.20, 9.107.

C. Female dreams or visions:
6.61.4, 6.107, 8.84.

Notes to Appendix

In this study, I have been concerned chiefly to measure the degree to which Herodotus presents women as independent actors, with initiative of their own and an opportunity to influence events. The categories adopted here reflect this interest; in investigating other kinds of concern, other criteria of organization might be more valid.

Each separate mention of a woman or a group of women, or the concept of the feminine is counted. A woman is categorized according to the greatest degree of independent activity she achieves within a single continuous narrative. Thus, for instance, Candaules' wife is not first counted as a passive object of attention (1.8) and then as an actor (1.10). Rather, the whole narrative account in which she eventually acts is considered under the heading of II.C.3, "wife," since her greatest degree of independent action occurs in response to an act of her husband's.

If a single woman (or group) appears within several different narrative accounts, she is counted in each according to the degree of independent activity she there displays. Thus Demaratus' mother is counted once in 6.62 as a woman abducted from her husband (I.A.1.b), and once in 6.68 as a mother explaining events to her son (II.C.2). Apart from the Pythia, the extreme case of a single woman appearing in multiple accounts is Artemisia. She appears in 7.99, 8.68, 8.87, 8.101, and 8.103b. (The Pythia, we should note, is an institution rather than an individual person; she is not named unless something odd diverts her from her priestly function [6.66].)

No effort is made here to distinguish between narrative accounts Herodotus expressly accepts and those he narrates with reservation (e.g., 2.131, 3.3). First, it is often difficult to determine the degree of belief Herodotus intends us to feel; Herodotus is an extremely ironic author and it is difficult to know what he believes about many things he reports. See L. Pearson, "Credulity and Scepticism in Herodotus," *TAPA* 72 (1941) 335-355. More importantly, the point of this study is not the historicity of Herodotus' account, whether women really did the things he reports, but the range of activities he is willing to report for them — his assumptions about the kinds of things they might do. For this reason I have also not distinguished between women who figure within long speeches that virtually continue the narrative (2.121, 5.92) and women whom Herodotus himself describes.

In family contexts, it is sometimes difficult to determine whether a woman is actually mentioned or not. Family situations, or other situations implicitly involving women, do not figure here unless the woman's presence is expressly indicated. 6.83 must have involved Argive women (cf. 4.2 ff.) but, because Herodotus does not say so, it is not counted. Similarly, conflicts between brothers are ignored unless a woman (wife or mother) is explicitly mentioned in the account. I have, however, perhaps erred on the side of completeness by including in discussions of family politics all words like *gambros* (son- or brother-in-law), *mētrōs* (maternal uncle), *thugatrideos* (daughter's son), and *mētropatōr* (mother's father) since they signify relationships established only through women.

Women mentioned within reported speech are generally not considered in this study unless the comment directly affects the action in the surrounding narrative. Thus, Masistes' insult in 9.107 almost leads to murder and is included, but many picturesque comments made by a number of characters, female and male, are not. Some of the more striking examples of the mention of women or the concept of the feminine in reported speech in the *Histories* include: 1.35, 1.91a, 1.91b, 1.155, 3.53, 3.65, 3.80, 3.134, 4.80, 4.114, 6.19, 6.77, 7.11, 7.39, 7.51, 7.52, 7.141, 7.150, 7.169, 8.60, 8.68-69, 8.88, 8.96, 9.27.

Female animals and divinities (e.g., 2.66, 4.180.5a, 8.65) are not included in this study unless they occur incidentally in the context of geography or quasi-mythic genealogies (Sections III.A and I.A.4.b). They would be relevant to a larger study, but they raise issues of natural science and the constraints imposed by traditional myth that are not directly relevant to Herodotus' views about human women.

6.122, 7.239, and 8.104 are not counted largely because the consensus of most editors omits them (6.122 and 7.239 as interpolations, 8.104 as a repetition of 1.175). It is worth noting that 6.122 and 7.239 contain kinds of women not found elsewhere in Herodotus — Greek girls allowed to choose their own husbands, the wife as wise woman, solving the mystery of the blank tablet. The implicit ideas are not inherently un-Herodotean — the interest in the unusual, the interest in intelligent women — but the tone is unusual. Wise women in Herodotus, as we have noted, generally reflect on matters of ethical or political choice; they do not solve tricks. 8.104 is a more difficult case. The bearded priestess of Pedasa is relevant in a suggestive way to the story of Hermotimus the eunuch that she introduces. She is one of three characters from the area just around Halicarnassus whose actions display some degree of sexual inversion or, at least, of unexpected sexual characteristics. The priestess of Pedasa grows a beard in times of trouble; Artemisia the queen of Halicarnassus is more "manly" than Xerxes' male commanders and repeatedly displays her intelligent *andreia*; Hermotimus the eunuch in 8.104 ff. takes what Herodotus characterizes as the most complete revenge known to him, by playing on his enemy's assumptions about eunuchs. All three, in other words, disappoint normal sexual expectations; all three are presented in a neutral or positive light. What this says about Herodotus' sense of Halicarnassus I do not know. As we have seen, in a number of accounts he undercuts sexual assumptions or sexually oriented clichés; the appearance in one brief stretch of book eight of three characters from the area of Halicarnassus who embody this theme may be coincidental.

The conception of women in Athenian drama

HELENE P. FOLEY

Barnard College

THE POSITION AND CONCEPTION OF WOMEN IN CLASSICAL ATHENS

THE POSITION of women in classical Athens has been much debated by scholars for some years. The nature of the evidence is fragmentary and contradictory. All our sources are male, and therefore represent a limited view of a complex reality.[1] While the contradictory evidence does not break precisely along the lines of genre, prose texts tend to give us one picture of women's lives and personalities, and poetic texts another.[2] Each source — the physical evidence unearthed by archeologists (including inscriptions), the prose texts written by historians, orators, philosophers, popular moralists, and medical writers, the fine arts and poetic texts — represents a distorted or partial conception of Athenian women and their lives.

The historians' views are shaped by their conception of what events are worthy to be recorded as history and what causes historical events to take the form that they have. Hence the historian Thucydides, who confined himself primarily to political history, barely mentions women, while Herodotus, whose history includes both public and private life and is more anthropologically oriented, includes women frequently (for an evaluation of his perspective on women see Dewald in this volume). The philosophers' testimony subordinates fact to argument and logical system, the

127

medical writings are shaped by their "scientific" conceptions of the female body and its purposes, while the rhetoricians select and color their testimony concerning women to convince an audience of their cause. The fine arts idealize or romanticize, and it is frequently difficult to draw the line between depictions of life and representations of myth. Drama often represents women as far more powerful and prominent than in the prose texts; while the prose texts emphasize women's confinement to the private sphere, drama frequently gives them an important role in public social crises. As A.W. Gomme said in 1925: "There is, in fact, no literature, no art of any country, in which women are more prominent, more carefully studied and with more interest, than in the tragedy, sculpture, and painting of fifth-century Athens."[3]

All of this diverse and contradictory evidence must, of course, be included in our final fragmentary picture of women in classical Athens. For, as one scholar has recently argued, woman is a "cultural product" and an "ideological formation" which we must "situate . . . within the semantic field formed by Athenian society."[4] Our aim must be to clarify the relations between systems of thought, representations, institutions and practices, and to discover how the concept of woman is articulated throughout.

Recent articles have brought a new methodological sophistication to the problem of women in classical Athens and its articulation in the minds of Athenian writers, and have eliminated many previous misconceptions.[5] These articles reach a convincing consensus on the major if tentative conclusions to be drawn from the prose evidence (although they do not not include the medical texts) concerning the social and legal status of women in Athens and the effect that this social status may have had on the conception of women in these texts. When they turn to the question of poetic texts or "myth," they offer preliminary insights only. My purpose here, then, is to summarize briefly the evaluation of the evidence drawn from physical remains and the prose texts concerning the social and legal status of women in Athens made by previous scholars, and then go on to treat at some length the conception of women in the poetic texts, and specifically in Greek drama. I do this with the conviction that considerably more progress has been made in formulating and exploring these issues than much recent work on the position and conception of women in Athens allows. My own effort will be to summarize and evaluate the state of the research on the conception of women in Athenian literature at this time, to deal specifically with the methodological problems involved, to consider the strengths and weaknesses of the major approaches that have been employed up to this time, and to offer a number of suggestions of my own which develop these lines of research and propose directions for future research. The evaluation of the evidence from the fine arts has not reached the stage where it can be used with precision to complement or modify the interpretations of myth by drama, and it is in any case too large a topic for this brief study.

II EVIDENCE FROM THE PHYSICAL REMAINS AND PROSE TEXTS FOR THE LEGAL AND SOCIAL POSITION OF WOMEN; THE CONCEPTION OF WOMEN IN THE PROSE TEXTS

In so far as women's legal status gives us an indication of her social status, our sources give us some basis upon which to understand women's place in Athenian society.[6] Women in Athens were lifelong legal minors, who exercised no positive political and financial rights. The female Athenian citizen was legally excluded from participation in the political (legislative, judicial, and military) life of the city, and this exclusion was of particular importance in a radical democracy which placed great importance on the participation of the male citizen in public life.

In the private sphere, women spent their lives acting under the authority of a male guardian (*kurios*). Women could not choose their husbands, who were often much older than themselves (the bride was 12 to 18, the groom usually over 30), manage their dowries, divorce without the support of a male relative willing to be their guardian, or conduct financial transactions over the value of one *medimnos* of barley (enough to sustain the average family for several days). A woman's consent to the way her property was managed was not only not required, but the law court cases indicate that the guardian sometimes abused his privileges in this respect.[7] The dowry, which had to be returned to her natal family with her if she left the marriage, offered the women financial security if not freedom, and every effort was made to dower even the poorest of respectable women. If her father's household was left without a male heir, the daughter, as an *epikleros*, "inherited" her father's property. This meant that she acquired the right to transfer the ownership of the family property to a male member of the immediate family; she was legally obligated to marry the next of kin on her father's side — even if she was already married to another man — in order to produce a male heir for her father's *oikos* (household). Because a woman was in essence lent (*ekdosis*) in marriage by her natal household, a father often retained some influence in the life of a married daughter. In sum, the Athenian citizen woman's status was derived entirely from kinship with males, and her primary function was to produce a male heir for the *oikos* of her husband, or, as an *epikleros*, for the *oikos* of her father. Adultery was for this reason a severe offense; the adulterous woman was divorced and banned from participation in religious festivals. While respectable women were expected to be chaste above all things, men sought sexual gratification from both sexes primarily outside the household (Peudo-Dem. 59. 118–22). Woman's social status also affected her health and life span. Girl children ate less and less well than their brothers, and many female children were exposed at birth.

Respectable women were, ideally at least, confined as much as possible to the interior of the house and to the women's quarters within it. Men, by contrast, spent relatively little time indoors. In the house women wove, cooked, and supervised the running of the household and the rearing of children with the help of female slaves. Poorer women may have participated in agriculture, and certainly sold goods at markets. Respectable women left the house only to visit neighbors, to aid in childbirth, or to attend religious rituals — marriages, funerals, and festivals. As Pericles stressed in his Funeral Oration, respectable women should have no public reputation, whether for good or bad (Thuc. 2. 46). Orators praise the modesty of female relatives who were embarassed even to dine with male kinsmen (respectable women did not attend male dinner parties and symposia even in their own households);[8] in some law court cases witnesses had to be produced to certify the existence of a respectable wife, a woman who was referred to only by the name of her husband or father. In fact, the names of living women were rarely mentioned in the courts, unless the orator intended to cast suspicion on the woman.[9]

Women did, however, have an active religious life. They were the primary mourners at funerals, central actors at weddings, and participated in an enormous range of rituals and festivals, both public and private. Young women were initiated into religious life by participation in the cult of Artemis at Brauron, by serving as basket bearers, water carriers and corn grinders in religious processions. A group of chosen girls, the *arrhephoroi*, began the weaving of the *peplos* for Athena Polias and performed secret rituals for Athena on the acropolis. Married women participated in exclusively female fertility rituals like the Thesmophoria, and in numerous public festivals throughout the year. It seems likely that this included attendance at the dramatic festivals. Women gave the ritual cry (*ololugê*) at sacrifices, and received their share of the sacrificial meat. All women, slave and free, could be initiated into the Elusinian Mysteries. Women acted as priestesses in the cults of goddesses; the Basilinna, the wife of the Archon Basileus, performed an annual sacred marriage with the god Dionysus. Women also participated in ecstatic cults which were not part of the state religion, such as those for Dionysus.

The exclusion of women from political life did not, of course, preclude them from influencing family life, or even, through their husbands, public life. Pseudo-Demosthenes' *Against Neaira* (59. 110–11) refers to a possible adverse female reaction to the acquittal of the notorious Neaira, who had committed a number of crimes by pretending illegitimately to Athenian citizenship. The education of Athenian women was probably limited, and most were probably illiterate (see Cole in this volume). Yet court cases refer to women who mediated between kin through their knowledge of matters of finance and inheritance, and took considerable initiative in family affairs.[10] If they attended the dramatic festivals, their level of oral education in literature may have been quite sophisticated. Again, arranged marriages and the considerable age difference between husband and

wife did not preclude in some cases affectionate relationships between spouses.[11] Most women had at least one slave to assist them
in domestic work, which would have offered them some leisure and
an opportunity in wealthy households to manage a complex household economy. I have deliberately not examined here our fragmentary evidence concerning non-citizen women, slaves, courtesans
(*hetairai*) and prostitutes because our knowledge of non-citizen
women is not particularly relevant to our comparison between the
evidence of prose sources and drama.

The major picture that emerges from prose texts is of a sharp division between political and domestic life, with respectable women
confined to domestic spaces, and men dominating exterior space except during religious occasions, and of a concept of female virtue and
of male honor which depended on the respectability, public silence
and invisibility of the Athenian wife. The legal minority of women
was justified in the literature by allegations that women were naturally lacking in the self control, emotional stability, rationality and
personal authority required for exercising virtue in a manner appropriate to a free citizen. Socrates seems to have been virtually alone
in arguing that the virtue of men and women was the same (*Meno*
72d–73b). The medical writers too found woman's instability in her
physical nature.[12] Women were subject to "hysteria" — a disease
in which women's womb wandered to various parts of her body to
cause physical and emotional disturbances. Such diseases could
only be cured by recurrence of menstruation, intercourse and pregnancy. Women's physical and mental health was thus dependent
on her reproductive system, and her reproductive function justified
her exclusion from public life. Theories of conception, which in all
cases represented the woman's contribution to the child as inferior
to the male's, also justified patrilineal inheritance.

III THE CONCEPTION OF WOMEN IN ATHENIAN LITERATURE

The conception of women in Athenian literature poses special problems. How is one to deal with a literary and artistic tradition which
borrows from and is shaped by earlier Greek literature and myth,

a tradition which does not seem to reflect directly our fragmented and tentative picture of the social life and status of women in classical Athens drawn from physical evidence and the prose texts? While women in daily life appear to have been confined to the internal spaces of the household, to public silence, and to non-participation in the political life of Athens, women play an exceptionally prominent role in drama. They speak for themselves, lay claim to a wide-ranging intelligence, criticize their lot, and influence men with their rhetoric. They leave the household and even take action in the political sphere denied to them in life.

Some of these anomalies are to be expected in a literature based on a mythological tradition whose inherited plots emphasize intrafamilial crises. The informal power that women exercise within the domestic sphere should not come as a surprise in any culture. But the continued popularity and privileged public place in democratic Athens of these mythical stories of aristocratic families and intrafamilial conflicts still demand further explanation, particularly since the role of women in these stories is often expanded, radically transformed and accentuated in comparison to the pre-classical versions available to us.

We have only to compare, for example, the titanic Clytemnestra of Aeschylus' *Agamemnon*, who takes full responsibility for the murder of her husband, to her Odyssean counterpart, who obeys the will of her seducer Aegisthus, or to consider the difference in the treatment of the adulterous Helen in the *Iliad* and in Greek tragedy. The Helen of the *Iliad* is a victim of Aphrodite (*Iliad* 3. 165), a creature of such divine beauty that the old men of Troy feel inclined to agree that a war fought for such a woman is by no means worthy of blame (*Iliad* 3. 155); in tragedy, the various Helens are generally envisioned as morally responsible for a disastrous war. Furthermore, Greek drama, while it often deals with familial crises, calls attention to the public nature and significance of its actions in every possible way. Production — the use of masks, the rare staging of interior scenes — brought women into the outside world and de-emphasized (except in Euripides) the interior and private self. The presence of the chorus, representing various forms of communal reaction, and the formal rhetoric of the speeches reinforce the public tone of the drama.[13]

Most recent scholarship has agreed on the necessity to adopt an appropriately eclectic approach to the problem of women in Athenian literature. Many have used contemporary anthropology and in particular Levi-Strauss' dichotomy, female:nature as male:culture to provide analytical openings. Despite her confinement within the household in Athenian life, woman in Greek myth is associated with animals and the wild; the untamed female must submit to the civilizing effects of the marriage yoke before she can begin to be envisioned as cultured. Woman's association with nature is linked with the natural irrationality, lack of control and irresponsibility attributed to her in the entire range of our Athenian evidence. Hence women in Athenian literature and Greek myth are seen as naturally inimical to culture, a source of anarchy in the male-controlled *polis*. Their fearfulness may arise in part from their position as outsiders brought into a household primarily to produce legitimate children, and in part from the fear and dependence produced through the Athenian male's problematic infant psycho-sexual experience analyzed by Philip Slater or other psychoanalytic critics.[14] Analyses of individual plays have offered a wider range of specific and suggestive insights, but there has been no systematic attempt to confront the methodological problems involved in reaching a general understanding of the conception of women in Attic drama.[15]

Nevertheless, it seems to me that recent work on woman in classical Athenian literature, taken collectively, offers the possibility of establishing more specific methodological guidelines for approaching these problems than such useful preliminary insights suggest. First of all, we are not dealing simply with an unwieldy category, "myth." To be sure, Athenian poets use and re-use the same plots, a series of stories or "collective representations" handed down from their predecessors in epic, lyric, and the fine arts. Most of these myths are non-Athenian, and many are located in the homes of Athens' greatest enemies. In Athenian drama we are dealing with interpretations of these mythical stories made by poets who are composing in new genres — comedy and tragedy — and who are adapting their material to create a complex public dialogue between the interpretation of myth in earlier poetic genres and the contemporary Athenian democracy.[16] Drama, then, sets out to challenge, change and re-interpret past myths. It deliberately takes on the question of sex roles, and uses them to ask important public questions before an audience which includes the whole citizen population. We must not fall into the methodological trap of using non-Athenian literature to analyze the conception of women in Athenian drama.[17] The nature of drama as a genre, the way that this specifically Attic literary form treats myths, and the social and historical context in which these myths are interpreted must be central to our analysis.

Second, we cannot isolate the problem of women in drama from the general difficulties posed by the genres, or from a careful reading of individual texts as a whole. Zeitlin's contribution to this volume, for example, shows the importance of analyzing the problem of women in relation to the larger problems of genre and poetic imitation posed in a text from old comedy; the sexual dialectic of drama is always part of a larger one which concerns the contradictions posed by the social and philosophical systems of Athens as a whole.

Most scholars agree that the relationship of tragedy and comedy to daily life in Athens is distorted and oblique. The male tyrants of tragedy differ from contemporary democratic statesmen — a fact which has, with others, posed considerable difficulty to those who wish to evaluate possible political allusions in the texts. Nor did small farmers take over the world and regenerate themselves like the heroes of Aristophanes. Similarly, women step out of the household in drama and act and speak publicly in a manner apparently denied them in life. Many traces of the norm of Athenian life for women appear in the admonitions to female characters to stay in their proper place within, in the horror expressed by male characters when confronted with a female challenge, or in the categorization of unusual female behaviour as "masculine."[18]

Tragic women are certainly subject to limits in their actions, pay for their transgressions of those limits, and remain in the end subordinate to men, although the range and details of these limits may differ in degree from those we find in Athenian life. Hence we must begin by accepting all of the complex distortions of life which belong to the genre. Then we must go on to categorize the precise nature and range of these distortions in the context of the symbolic systems presented in Athenian literature, systems in which sex roles obviously play a central part. In short, we must investigate how the concept of woman operates in the symbolic systems of drama as a whole. At the same time we should not despair of uncovering comprehensible — if oblique — relations between life and literature. While attempts to use Sophocles' *Oedipus Rex* as a comment on the life and career of Pericles make very little sense, the Athenian audience certainly brought their experience of Pericles to their understanding of Oedipus.[19] Similarly, the Athenian audience must have brought to their experience of the remarkable women of drama a way of understanding these characters which grew out of their psychological, religious, political, and social lives and problems.

To summarize, then, the methodological points we have raised so far: an adequate analysis of the conception of women in Attic drama must account for the way Attic drama interprets Greek myth, for the nature of the comic and tragic genres and the ways in which each represents human action, character and reality, and for the relation between drama and the social context in which it is presented. Finally, we must establish a methodology which allows us to read sex role conflicts in tragedy in relation to the larger social and philosophical issues they are used to explore, and to put the insights gained to the test of a full reading of individual texts.

Recently, the attempt to pursue the analysis of women and their symbolic role in classical literature has proceeded primarily — if not exclusively — from two directions. One approach grows out of Freudian psychology and sociology, the other finds its theoretical basis in structuralist anthropology and linguistics. Each group assumes that drama reflects in its battle of the sexes a deeper and broader set of cultural tensions. I will deal briefly with the first and extensively with the second, which seems to me to offer a particularly promising line of research. Certainly the anthropological approach has been the dominant one in current research on women in Athenian literature and in my own work, and it is in this area that I can offer the most extensive insights and proposals for further research.

IV THE PSYCHO-SOCIOLOGICAL APPROACH

Psychoanalytic critics of classical literature have long been examining the role of characters of both sexes on Greek literature. But few have addressed the question of the relation between the sexes and the powerful women of Greek drama on as extensive and ambitious a scale as the sociologist Philip Slater.[20] His work has directly influenced all subsequent psychoanalytically-oriented papers on male–female conflicts in drama, and thus, although many of Slater's predecessors and followers offer readings of individual texts which avoid many of the weaknesses of Slater's analysis, it seems appropriate to concentrate in this brief review on his work alone.

Slater tries to explain the powerful females of Greek literature and myth as psychological projections which find their origins in the psychosexual experience of the Greek male child. "All a playwright requires for drama is a vivid memory for his own childhood and family — especially Greek drama, which is intensely concerned with intrafamilial conflict." (p. 10) For Slater the narcissism, pedophilia, obsessive competitiveness, and gynephobia of the classical Athenian male are a result of a problematic mother–son relationship. The Greek mother, due to her extreme social and political seclusion, was alternately hostile to her son because of his impending freedom, and seductive to him. The Greek father, who was rarely at home, was simultaneously idealized by his son because of his remoteness, and resented, through the mother's presentatation of him, as capricious and hostile. At seven the Athenian boy was initiated into the world of men and was eventually nursed to maturity by competition with his peers, or in many cases, by homosexual relations with older men. He remained, however, unsure of his identity and abnormally ambivalent towards mature women, whom he both wished to depend upon and feared. If correct, Slater's theory offers an attractive explanation for the unusual degree of authority and power vested in so many dramatic heroines, their prominence in drama, and the threatening nature of many of their actions.

This theory, as I have tried to show in some detail elsewhere, relies primarily on evidence from poetic rather than prose sources.[21] As a result, Slater ignores some contrary evidence which suggests that the estrangement of the father from early child-rearing in Athens may have been less extreme in practice than in the ideal. It entirely ignores the question of female psychosexual development.[22] By using as an implicit model the modern American suburban mother–son relationship and contemporary case studies of pedophilia, he is almost certainly failing to evaluate correctly similar practices in a different cultural context. Most important of all, Slater's decision to pay only cursory attention to the larger historical, political and social context in which Greek family life took place, and to abjure any attempt to analyze myths in the context of a particular literary work, leads to misreadings or narrow readings of the texts.

Attic dramas are concerned with something more than intrafamilial conflict, and Slater's theory fails to account, for example, for the action of women in drama in the political sphere denied to them in life. It does not provide an explanation for the precise ideological form in which male–female conflicts are presented — the symbolic equation between domestic, state and divine order such as we find at the close of Aeschylus' *Eumenides*. It does not explain why Aeschylus plays down the psychological conflicts between mother and son in the *Libation Bearers*, while Euripides emphasizes them in his *Orestes*. We can only suggest an explanation for these different treatments of the myth by examining the political world of the plays in which these familial crises take place and the point that each playwright wishes to make about them. Aeschylus must downplay the element of guilt in Orestes' matricide, since he will found the Athenian system of justice on Orestes' acquittal in the final play of the trilogy, while Euripides makes suggestive analogies between his Orestes' neuroses and the deteriorating political world of his play. Or, to use the analogy between contemporary and Greek experience preferred by Slater, both Portnoy and Orestes may suffer from an ambivalent mother–son relation; but we would be hard put to make any further meaningful comparisons between the two characters without considering the very different cultural contexts within which the two works were composed.

Nor does Slater's theory allow for the conscious manipulation of myth by Athenian playwrights to justify or deconstruct the nature of Greek family life and prevailing Athenian political ideology. By allowing Medea to make powerful speeches on the crippling confinement of women to childrearing and marriage, and by showing her inability to take action which does not also destroy herself, Euripides — who apparently invented Media's deliberate killing of her children — is not so much reflecting his unconscious fears of maternal hostility as using this plot to explore the contradictory nature of the Greek ethics of revenge which Medea adopts, and perhaps even the inherently problematic nature of the marital relationship. As in this play, it is the male characters in drama who consistently provoke the dangerous female to action by an act of hostility towards or neglect of his children.

Finally, conflicts in drama often seem to address similar political and social issues (we will examine the nature of these issues in Part V). Yet the family structures which give rise to these conflicts seem to be less consistent in their form than the recurring social issues which they are used to express. Antigone and Clytemnestra threaten the stability of the state and take public action to challenge abuses of family interests by male rulers. Both are defined in the language of the play as threatening, as usurping male prerogatives. Clytemnestra's actions and the threat she poses to Orestes could be analyzed as a projection of the Greek family tensions examined by Slater. But Antigone is a virgin. Her relations to her parents are apparently untroubled, while her brothers' deaths were the result of hostility between Oedipus and his sons (in Slater's theory the father is idealized by the son, except insofar as the mother distorts and taints the image of the father), not between these sons and their mother, or between Oedipus and Jocasta. In order for a Slaterian analysis of Greek drama to be effective, then, the critic would have to be armed with a more extensive theory which would show how the sex/gender system of Athenian society was reproduced not only by the family structure in isolation, but by the conscription of the individual psyche into the Athenian kinship system and into the social and economic system of the *polis* as a whole.

Space does not permit a detailed discussion of this complex point, but as Gayle Rubin has recently suggested in a general essay on women and society, a synthesis between the work of Claude Levi-Strauss and Jacques Lacan could provide the theoretical groundwork for making the connections between Freudian theory and anthropology necessary for a fuller analysis of the role of women in

Athenian thought and literature.[23] In other words, we need a theory which can explain the making of Athenian consciousness in terms which would allow us to understand the precise ideological terms in which familial conflicts are described in drama, and to identify with more confidence the relation between these intrafamilial conflicts and the larger social issues which these conflicts are used to explore. As Plato argued in the *Republic*, the nature of the soul and the state is reciprocal; the nature of the one can only be understood in relation to the other, and an examination of the soul can offer a beginning point for understanding the larger structure. Certainly the dramatists shared the philosophers' sense that man was in essence a political animal, that the exploration of the private aimed at an understanding of the public. Thus, while Freudian critics other than Slater may meet some of the criteria established in this paper for an adequate reading of the conception and role of women in Attic drama that he did not — a precise awareness of the limits of the evidence, a sophisticated sense of genre, and a careful reading of individual texts — a fully satisfactory reading must bridge the gap between the artist's consciousness and his unconscious, between the individual and his particular society.

V FEMALE:NATURE AS MALE:CULTURE

The second approach to women in classical literature has applied theoretical insights drawn from structural and symbolic anthropology to readings of individual literary texts.[27] Such readings see the conception of women in drama in relation to larger social questions posed through the structure of these texts and the symbolic systems of thought which shape them. Critics who adopt this approach tend to stress either the structuralist equation female:nature as male:culture or female:domestic and male:public. I will examine the application of these two equations in order, emphasizing the latter, which seems to me to offer a more promising, if problematic line of analysis.

Sherry Ortner has offered the most extensive defense and exploration of Levi–Strauss' nature/culture dichotomy in relation to the sexes.[25] She begins with the assumption that human cultures universally devalue women in relation to men and that women are nearly always excluded from that part of the society where its highest powers are felt to reside. Human consciousness is engaged in an attempt to separate itself from the world around it and thereby to control its environment; what is above culture is defined as divine, what is below it is defined as nature. Woman is identified with or becomes symbolic of those orders of existence which are external to culture, and especially with what is inferior to it. Hence she represents principles of transcendence on the one hand, or is linked to the world of beasts on the other. Through her relatively closer position to nature, woman also mediates for man between nature and culture. Woman's affinity with nature and hence her cultural inferiority derive from her greater identification with sexual reproduction, early child care and the unruly world of infancy that culture is designed to control and eventually to repress. Women's lives are dominated by intrafamilial ties and emotional relationships, while men are linked with interfamilial relations and abstract and integrative cultural systems. Qualities attributed to woman — irrationality and subjectivity — derive from her primary association with the family and reinforce her associations with "nature". Woman is conceptually both a part of culture and what culture is designed to tame or suppress. For our purposes, the origins of woman's greater association with "nature" and her mediating role between nature and culture are unimportant; we are primarily concerned with the questions of how such conceptual categories operate, consciously or unconsciously, in Greek thought.

A group of French classicists headed by J.-P. Vernant, Marcel Detienne and P. Vidal-Naquet have been engaged for some time in applying structuralist anthropology in a modified form to ancient Greek culture.[26] In their analysis, Greek texts locate man between God and beast, and systematically oppose those institutions which are particular to culture — marriage, agriculture, sacrifice, and life in the enclosed *oikos* — to the promiscuity, eating of raw meat, allelophagy and living in the open characteristic of nature. Woman is defined as cultured insofar as she accepts these institutions by consenting to marriage and chastity, remaining within the *oikos*, cooking and weaving, and as closer to nature when she aligns herself, as a maenad in the cult of Dionysus for example, with the wilds, eating raw meat, and escape from marriage and the *oikos*. The pervasive organization of Greek life and thought and sexual ideology by structural polarities is characterized with particular precision in the Pythagorean table of opposites, which aligns female with unlimited, even, plurality, left, curved, darkness, bad, and oblong, and male with limit, odd, one, resting, straight, light, good and square. As Froma Zeitlin has recently noted, the Greek woman in her role as maenad also embodied those characteristics attributed to her in the Pythagorean table, as she rushes, head thrown back, often at night, in a group trance which violates her normal cultural limits and responsibilities.[27]

The nature/culture dichotomy certainly provides us with a way of analyzing some aspects of Greek poetic texts. It corresponds to some degree with the difference between "good" and "bad" women in drama. The former align themselves with marriage, or, as virgins, sacrifice themselves for the preservation of family, state or nation, while the latter (e.g. Clytemnestra, Medea, the Theban women of the *Bacchae*) resist marriage and confinement to the *oikos*, behave irrationally, and uphold private interests. Indeed, women can even achieve *kleos* and heroic status — a reputation generally reserved for men — through the dedication of their lives to culture. Alcestis will win celebrations in festal song for her sacrifice of her life for her husband; Admetus regains a meaningful life through a symbolic remarriage with his wife. Iphigeneia at Aulis, as I have recently argued, comes to accept her sacrificial death for Greece through envisioning it in terms of the marriage she was expecting to make with Achilles.[28] Both women achieve heroism through enacting the myth central to Greek marriage — the symbolic death and rebirth of Persephone, who is raped by Hades, the god of the underworld. On the other hand, other "good" women who align themselves with the cultural status-quo like Ismene in Sophocles' *Antigone* and Chrysothemis in Sophocles' *Electra* receive an ambivalent and perhaps even a negative treatment in comparison with their iconoclastic sisters Antigone and Electra.

The nature/culture dichotomy also rationalizes woman's association, despite her actual confinement within the *oikos* in life, with animals and the wild in Greek myth. Here, however, we should be cautious. Men in Greek literature have no primary and stable association with Greek culture. Mythical warriors are often indistinguishable from beasts, and they are subject, like Ajax, Heracles, or Pentheus, to bouts of madness, erotic seizures and other anti-cultural outbursts. The partners of maenads in the wild are male pans and satyrs; Amazons are paired with Centaurs. From this perspective culture occupies a precarious position between nature and the divine, and its instabilities are located in the roles, actions, and psyches of both genders. One could still argue that women retain their role as relatively more anti-cultural, relatively closer to "nature" than men. But is Euripides' *Bacchae*, for example, primarily a play about the threat posed by the more "natural" female to culture? Certainly this is a cliché which Pentheus accepts. Certainly the women succumb to the lure of the Dionysiac more quickly than the men, and their alternative world on the mountains, although it is far from natural and includes elements of culture, could be viewed as simultaneously closer to beast and god than their world within culture, and offering an unstable mediation between nature and culture.

This world has its own order — the women divide themselves into three *thiasoi* with leaders and their activities have an uncanny unity and harmony. They play the roles of hunters and nurturers — they give their breasts to wild animals — simultaneously. They drink raw milk, and wine, Dionysus' gift to culture. But does Agave's fantasy that she has become a successful hunter pose a greater threat than Pentheus' partially willing transformation into a woman? Why is woman most dangerous when she becomes a man? Does this dangerous transformation reflect more on women than on men?[29] Are we to interpret this transformation as a reflection of women's repressed and undervalued status in Greek society, which results in a state of trance and in an absorption of the qualities of the dominant group?[30] Or is Euripides also consciously exploiting and subverting a set of cultural assumptions about sex roles and their place in the cultural system? That is, when Dionysus removes normal cultural limits, we confront the ways in which cultural norms warp and dangerously confine human beings of both sexes, and create cultural instabilities.

Certainly the play seems to be suggesting that the relation between nature and culture is dialectical (a suggestion incomprehensible to Pentheus) and that culture must absorb "nature" and the inversions of culture brought to it in the shape of Dionysus.[31] That is, as is the case with all polarities in Greek thought, the relation between nature and culture is simultaneously one of opposition and of complementarity. Culture separates itself from nature while simultaneously imitating it. Marriage is a symbolic ploughing or acculturizing of nature; but in the women's festival of the Thesmophoria the women ensure birth, as Plato says, not by imitating the earth, but by making the earth imitate them.[32] Women mediate between nature and culture as a part of culture; but culture as a whole is always accomplishing such mediations. The precepts of the chorus of barbarian women are not designed simply to expose the threat of female religious movements to culture, but also to strike the audience forcibly with the similarity of their ethics and actions to that of the contemporary Athenian male-dominated democracy.[33] It is difficult to be certain whether the play challenges or reinforces those distinctions which culture makes in establishing its differences from nature. Certainly we cannot read this self-conscious and iconoclastic text as an example of the Levi-Straussian precept that "myths think through men" and their *unconscious* minds. The nature/culture dichotomy certainly reveals something important about the way women are envisioned in the *Bacchae*. But by itself it only illuminates assumptions that the play seems to throw into question. It cannot offer us an adequate reading of the play, or of the way in which sexual polarities are used to investigate larger cultural issues for which Greek men were primarily responsible. It does not provide us with a way to shift from one level of the action and meaning of the play to another, but confines us to a literal reading which poses the problems of the play entirely in terms of sex roles.

The choral odes of the *Bacchae* take up the contemporary sophistic debate over *nomos* and *physis*, a debate which put the categories "nature" and "culture" into a deeply uncertain relation to each other. We would expect such shifts in the conceptual relation of nature and culture to destabilize as well the ideological relation between the sexes. In other words, women might retain their position as relatively closer to nature, or as mediators between nature and culture, but what this would mean in a specific context would obviously depend on what the categories nature and culture meant in that context. Hence, applying the nature/culture dichotomy to a specific text as if it were some easily defined universal will result in a simplistic analysis. In the *Odyssey* or Hesiod, the just kingship aligns itself with nature (*Od.* 19. 108–14 and Hesiod, *Erga* 225–47); the people of a good ruler flourish, while under an unjust ruler they wither and die. Penelope in the *Odyssey* is so thoroughly acculturated that she shares thoughts, goals, and even similes with her husband; it is she who is compared by Odysseus to the image of the good king described above.[13] There would be little point in trying to locate in the *Odyssey* the ways in which the text showed Penelope as relatively closer to nature than her husband, even though she is barred from a full public role by the limits of her sex. In contrast to the *Odyssey*, the Thebes of the *Bacchae*, which is not, of course, the Dionysus-worshipping Athens before whom the play was presented, walls itself off from nature, rather than aligning itself with it, and views its women as the central source of instability. The different views of the relation between nature and culture seems to reverberate in the relations between the sexes in these two texts, although we would need a much more complex social and historical analysis to explain fully the presence of these ideological divergences. One would expect (and I believe closer analysis of the sexual ideology of the period will bear out this assumption) a similar shift during the Hellenistic period, where mystery religions, Dionysus, and Aphrodite acquired a new cultural prestige, and the natural world was no longer viewed as antithetical to culture.[35] In Stoic philosophy, for example, a rational and moral life was lived in conformity with a nature which was animated by a supremely rational divine being.

Greek literature does offer examples which seem to resist, or at least to make extremely complex, the application of the nature/culture dichotomy. A non-Athenian example is Hesiod's myth of Pandora, the first woman.[34] In Hesiod, man's origin is not described. Apparently, prior to his fall into culture, he lived a golden age existence with the gods. Culture imposed upon man the institutions of sacrifice, agriculture and marriage, which emerged with the creation of the first woman. In this myth it is the female sex which has the primary association with culture (and even, if the analysis of P. Pucci is correct, with the origin of human language),[37] while men are originally outside it, victims who can only hope through a laborious struggle to return to a pale imitation of the earlier existence they shared with the gods. In so far as culture is a fall from a better state, women are more strongly aligned both with culture and what culture must control than men.

Hesiod's unwillingness to align men fully with "culture" reappears in a different form in Athenian literature. Here too men struggle simultaneously to uphold culture and to resist its limitations. On the one hand every Greek male is attracted by the *kleos* and the competition for *kleos* through which he can achieve immortality and a partial escape from the limits of human existence. But the fact that this *kleos* is primarily achieved through competition and war can threaten as well as defend culture, and especially a democratic culture.[38] If Clytemnestra in the *Agamemnon* is a female monster who slays her husband in a gesture which explicitly undermines and perverts marriage, sacrifice, and agriculture, the Greek army led by Agamemnon turns into a monstrous beast which destroys helpless animals (the image of the pregnant hare torn apart by the eagles and of the monstrous and bestial creature who leaps over the walls of Troy in lust for blood at *Ag.* 115–20 and 823–28) and the shrines of the gods. Agamemnon returns with a remnant of his army, and with few spoils to compensate for the sacrifice of his people in the name of the adulterous Helen except his mistress Cassandra. This last prize is viewed by Clytemnestra as an insult to her status as legitimate wife.

While Xenophon celebrates agriculture as the only work suitable for an Athenian citizen, since it promotes the qualities needed by the state (*Oec.* 11. 13ff.), Athenian political life celebrated and promoted the transcending of marriage and agriculture in the relation of the citizen to the state. Pay was introduced for many civic duties, and Aristophanes frequently makes a mockery of this new dependence on the state for a livelihood. Xenophon in his *Ways and Means* offers a plan by which no citizen will have to work, but all will be enabled to devote full time to public affairs through public funds derived from the working of the silver mines by slaves. The Athenian empire with its reliance on the navy also resulted in a new separation of the citizen from his land. Plato in the *Republic* is attracted to the Spartan model of the state and the community of women and children precisely because it transcends completely the need for the highest class of citizens to reproduce their individual households through marriage and agricultural labor. The demands of Athenian political life sometimes put the male citizen in opposition to "culture" as defined by the institutions of marriage, sacrifice, and agriculture. The result was a split (in actuality if not in the ideal) in the concept of "culture" itself, between the political and the private realm. Marriage and agriculture moved relatively closer to "nature", and the concept of women, who were excluded from politics, and the definition of *aretai* for both sexes shifted accordingly. In other words, while marriage, sacrifice and agriculture can be said roughly to define culture in the epic world, the world of the Athenian *polis* puts these institutions — and hence women — into a separate and subordinate position to the political world which both serves and transcends it.

Fantasies of cultural transcendence (of abandoning marriage and agriculture altogether in favor of the pursuit of non-biological immortality) and the tensions and contradictions produced by these fantasies beset male characters in Greek drama in a variety of forms. Euripides' Hippolytus wishes to withdraw from politics and marriage into a world of hunting and asexuality. Echoing the wish of other male characters in tragedy, he longs for a world in which women are unnecessary for reproduction. The Athenian myth of autochthonous birth from the earth, and their patron goddess Athena, a female born from the male, offered further opportunities to express these desires. As J.-P. Vernant points out, the cult of Hestia in the household perpetuates an ideal of asexual reproduction and endogamy, in which the male line is reproduced through the virgin goddess of the heart, and not through the female stranger who must in reality be imported to perform this task.[39] My point here, then, is that "nature" and "culture", as culturally defined rather than natural concepts, are unstable, historically relative assumptions.[40] The meaning of each term can shift in relation to the other; contradictions and divisions may occur within these concepts which we can see reflected in the sexual and other conflicts in drama, or in the intellectual debates concerning nature and convention in human law also reflected in dramatic debates. Each sex in drama can be responsible for anti-cultural gestures which bring them closer to "nature", and dramas do not simply reflect the nature/culture dichotomy in the relations of the sexes, but use this dichotomy as a cultural cliché to explore larger cultural questions, or to turn such clichés on their heads. The nature/culture dichotomy, however correct at one level of analysis, becomes a blunt and unilluminating tool for understanding the role of women in the poetic texts without a clear understanding of the dialectical relation between nature and culture in Athenian life and ideology. More important, it does not provide us with a precise way of understanding the way sex roles are used in drama to explore political, ethical and philosophical issues, or to bridge successfully the gap between the world of drama and that of the prose texts.

VI FEMALE:DOMESTIC AS MALE:PUBLIC

The second structuralist equation for reading the symbolic role played by women in culture assumes that women are primarily associated, because of their affiliation with children and with the economic reproduction of the household, with the domestic sphere and the expressive, affective and nurturant values appropriate to this sphere.[41] Women's extra-domestic contributions to the society are rarely made explicit, and their goals are shaped by a lack of access to political privilege, authority and esteem. Men, by contrast, are primarily linked with those activities, institutions and forms of organization that link, rank, organize or subsume mother-child groups. Their work is viewed as public, intellectual, rational, and instrumental, as belonging to a larger sphere of complex and carefully articulated social relations, which ultimately controls and demands compliance from the domestic sphere. This opposition does not determine sexual assymetry in a culture, but it underlies the general association of female with domestic, and male with public in most cultures. Women's status appears to be "lowest", however, in cultures where the division between the public and domestic sphere is most articulated, and where women are isolated from each other and placed under one man's authority. Nevertheless, as Michelle Rosaldo has recently argued in a re-evaluation of her initial articulation of the domestic/public question, while biological sex may be used to organize and articulate sexual roles, opportunities and kin networks and the ideology which grows out of these arrangements, the precise way in which the domestic/public dichotomy is expressed in any one particular social system depends on the specific ways in which such social roles, kin networks, or economic and political opportunities are organized and articulated by that society.[42] Hence, for example, the domestic/public dichotomy will be explicitly affected by shifts in the relations of the two realms such as we find emerging at the close of the fifth-century in Athens, where there was an increasing withdrawal into and revaluing of private life.

This second structuralist equation for reading the symbolic relations of the sexes in Greek drama, female:domestic as male:public, has the initial advantage of reflecting directly Greek conceptions of their own culture and its organization. The relation of *oikos* (household) to *polis* (city) was openly debated in the philosophical texts, and the life of the Athenian *polis* was clearly organized to create a sharp division between public and private space.[43] Xenophon's formulation in the *Oeconomicus* of the division of space and labor between the sexes in the household seems to have represented a cultural ideal, if not necessarily a reality. Respectable wives were in principle confined to the interior spaces of the household, where they wove, cooked, and supervised children and household, while men were active on the outside, performing agricultural labor and protecting the position of the household in the larger world of the *polis*. Women were not confined to the domestic sphere in their religious life, where they participated in public festivals; but J.-P. Vernant has shown how the sexualization of space within the domestic sphere pervades the organization of space in public religious and political life as well.[44] If the differentiation between domestic and public were shown to provide a useful reading of the battle of the sexes in Greek drama, then, we would be able to shift more easily from the evidence of the prose texts to a reading of the plays.

Second, given the historical developments which molded the relation between household and state in democratic Athens, and created various real tensions between these two spheres, it would not be surprising if the sexual conflicts of drama reflected these problems. As Marylin Arthur in particular has argued,[45] the Athenians saw their society as deliberately constructed to ensure the survival of the individual *oikos* and hence of an egalitarian society; at the same time the legal system separated the state from civil society, and the interests of the individual household were ultimately subsumed in those of the state. Once the aristocratic society of early Greece was overturned in Athens, the new "middle class" society held property in the form of small, inviolable household units, and the nuclear family became an economic and political as well as a biological and social unit. Laws protected the household as an economic unit through restrictions on the sale of family property, and as a social unit through marriage laws concerning the *epikleros*, which guaranteed a male heir to each *oikos* (Aristotle considered that female inheritance would lead to a consolidation of property not conducive to the perpetuation of a middle class society). Pericles' citizenship law of 450–451 restricted citizenship to children of two Athenian parents, thus transferring to the public arena the dream of endogamy reflected in private inheritance patterns.[46]

The function of women in this system was to produce legitimate male children for the *oikos*, and to guarantee its integrity by cooking, weaving, childrearing and the supervision of household goods. By contrast the aristocratic women of early Greece had some share in the political life of the community and the division between domestic and public spheres was considerably less radical. Arete in the *Odyssey* arbitrates quarrels outside the household (7. 73–74); women give gifts (19. 309–11), and the use of their dowries to support their new household was unrestricted. Clytemnestra is said by the chorus of Aeschylus' *Agamemnon* to have the authority to preside over Argos in the absence of her husband (259–60). Aristocratic men could produce heirs from concubines as well as wives. Hence the concern with adultery and controlling female sexuality is relatively less intense in the Homeric poems. The frequent references in all Athenian sources to fear of adultery, to justifications of or criticisms of the subordination of women in Athenian society, reflect a consciousness of these historical shifts in women's role and an uneasiness concerning this aspect of the new democraticv society. Because the single-family household had emerged relatively recently from a clan-based society, the *polis* only gradually gained the loyalty which had previously been paid to family and tribe. The radical separation of the domestic sphere from the political sphere, and the relatively greater subordination of household to state and of female to male undoubtedly posed more problems in reality than it did in the ideal. Too radical a privatization and cultural isolation of the female accompanied by extensive public demands on the male created a potential imbalance between the values, needs and interests of the two spheres.

When we come to try to analyze Greek drama in relation to the equation female:domestic as male:public, however, we confront multiple problems. Women in drama do not confine themselves to the domestic and religious spheres to which they were relegated in reality. They not only take action in the political sphere denied to them in life, but they rarely defend the household and its interests, or support affective, nurturant, non-competitive values. The rare exceptions — Alcestis, Megara, Macaria, and perhaps Antigone and Lysistrata — prove the rule. While Clytemnestra in the *Agamemnon*, for example, is initially propelled into action over the sacrifice of her daughter, her motives by the end of the Trojan war have become considerably more complex. She rejects her husband and chooses her own mate, and acts to secure political power for herself. She tempts her husband to trample upon the wealth of his household, a wealth which it is her duty as a wife to guard. Instead, as she herself says, she relies on this wealth to consolidate her power. Clytemnestra's rebellion masculinizes her and turns her against her own children; she is repeatedly described in the language of the play as playing a male to Aegisthus' female. Her thinly disguised relief at Orestes' "death" in the *Libation Bearers*, which is contrasted to the distress of the nurse, emphasizes her sacrifice of maternity.

This masculinization of the female, and her rebellious rejection of the interests of the *oikos* is not uncommon in those women who intrude into public life in Greek drama. Medea, openly declaring her lack of feminine *sophrosyne* in her uncontrolled passion for her husband, takes revenge in an explicitly male heroic style (with the exception of her weapon), makes political alliances for herself with Athens, and destroys her husband's *oikos* by killing her sons.[47] Like many other female characters she possesses rhetorical powers and a forceful intelligence feared by the men around her, and admired by the chorus of women, who lament the historical lack of a poetic voice for women. Medea describes the painful restrictions which marriage places on the woman, forced to buy a husband upon whom she may not be able to rely, confined to the interior of the household, a stranger in a lonely world in which she needs prophetic powers to survive (*Medea* 288–40); and she is not alone in explaining why women are unlikely to be the ideal representatives of the interests of an institution which is not designed primarily to serve her interests. Feminine rejection of marriage is not infrequent in Greek drama (e.g. Sophocles' *Tereus*, frag. 524 Nauck, or Aeschylus' *Suppliants*). The *Agamemnon* opens with Helen's and Clytemnestra's challenge to the institution; the disastrous results of this rejection are only rectified at the close of the *Eumenides*, where the Erinyes, who represent the female side, agree to accept marriage sacrifices and to use their powers of fertility for the state. In the *Oeconomicus* Xenophon plans to *educate* his young wife to think that both sexes will benefit from a common and active devotion to the *oikos* (7. 13). Frequently, in contrast to Herodotus, where wives' devotion to the interests of their husbands can often prove dangerous, female characters in drama are more likely to show an active devotion to their natal households (e.g. Antigone, Electra, Macaria).[48]

While women in drama frequently fail to perform the social duties assigned to them in the *oikos*, men in drama often initiate female rebellion, as Michael Shaw has pointed out,[49] by abusing their responsibilities to household and state. Creon in the *Phoenissae* abandons the interests of the state when he discovers he must sacrifice his son to preserve it (919). In the *Ecclesiazusae* men are criticized for making the legislature an organ to serve private rather than public interests (395ff.). Other male characters ignore the interests of the household in an over-eager pursuit of war (e.g. men in the *Lysistrata*, *Iphigeneia at Aulis*, or *Agamemnon*), ignore the welfare of their families (Jason), or violate the sanctity of the household by bringing home a mistress (Agamemnon with Cassandra, Heracles with Iole). Male over-interest in private concerns is often represented in the language of the text as feminine or feminizing. Blepyrus in the *Ecclesiazusae* must adopt female clothing and call on the goddess of childbirth to deliver a wild pear (369–71); Cinesias in the *Lysistrata* must play the nurse to his neglected child (and phallus, 880–81 and 956), while the magistrate is forced to experience womanhood as the women thrust the badges of the female and her tasks upon him — veils, baskets, girdles and wool (531–37); Aegisthus gives up authority to Clytemnestra, and Jason surrenders his heroism to Medea. She claims his deeds for herself, and mockingly prophesies for him an ignominious death from a piece of his old ship Argo.

Up to this point, we could see the sexual confrontations of drama as representing an inversion of the norm female:domestic as male:public, an inversion which indirectly confirms the importance of the ideal. Violators of the cultural norm are generally punished, and women are often returned to silence, death or suicide, and the domestic interior where they "belong". But women in drama also act for the *polis*. Euripides' Iphigeneia agrees to be sacrificed for Greece, and Praxithea in Euripides' *Erectheus* offers her daughter's life for the city (frag. 360N2). Lysistrata claims to be acting in the interests of both household and state. Jocasta in the *Phoenissae* defends the interests of the state against her sons, who are prepared to sacrifice their own city to acquire power for themselves (528–85). Antigone in the *Antigone* is an ambiguous case. Knox has argued that she acts for the *oikos* against Creon, who represents the *polis*.[50] Yet surely in defending the unwritten laws she is touching on an issue of public policy, the burial of traitors, while Creon's view of the state is shown to be inadequate. Teucer, a male character, makes a comparable defense of burial for Ajax, and Pericles in his Funeral Oration defends the importance of the unwritten laws to the public life of Athens. On the other side, characters like Heracles in the *Heracles* celebrate their retirement from public life to defend the interests of the household (575–6).

Perhaps what we need here is to emphasize the dialectical aspects of the relation between public and private, male and female in our initial set of equations. Clearly, both men and women share an interest in the *oikos* and in the values which help it to survive. But each sex performs for the *oikos* a different function, each requiring different virtues, and acts in separate spaces, one inside, one outside. Each sex also shares an interest in the *polis*, and performs different public functions which help to perpetuate the state, the male political and military functions, which exclude women, the female religious functions. In each sphere the male holds legal authority over the female. When men and women participate in state religious festivals, each sex supports the communal values necessary for the welfare of the state. *Oikos* and *polis* are organized on a comparable and complementary basis, although they differ in scale. As Aristotle says at the close of his discussion of the relation between family and state in *Politics* I, "For, inasmuch as every family is part of a state, and these relationships are part of a family, and the virtue of the part must have regard to the virtue of the whole, women and children must be trained by education with an eye to the constitution, if the virtues of either of them are supposed to make any difference in the virtues of the state. And they must make a difference; for the children grow up to be citizens, and half of the free persons in the state are women" (1260b, 10–20, trans. Jowett). What this means is that the simple equation female:*oikos* as male:*polis* does not hold fully even at the level of an ideal. Any situation in which the female alone defends the *oikos* is counter to the norm, while to assume that woman has no avenue for exercising her powers positively for the state is to dismiss her public religious function. Ideally, as Pericles' Funeral Oration demonstrates (Thuc. 2. 36ff.), women can be excluded from the political sphere because men bring a balanced sense of their private interests to bear on public policy. Men act as citizens and fathers simultaneously. They treat the unwritten laws with respect, and in their eagerness and opportunity to serve the state they treat their neighbors without jealousy. They conserve and expand public funds, just as the women of the *Ecclesiazusae* claim to practice thrift in the household (236–39; cf. also 600).

This dialectical relation between *oikos* and *polis*, in which each institution defines the other, puts household and state into a relation which is simultaneously antithetical and complementary. The political needs of the state can run counter to those of the household, and the household does not offer to men the chance of living a full human existence. This dilemma is particularly well demonstrated in the *Agamemnon*, in Agamemnon's choice concerning the sacrifice of Iphigeneia. The king's choice to kill his daughter is forced upon him by Zeus' injunction to defend the laws of hospitality and his own eagerness for glory in war, but the sacrifice redounds equally in its negative effects on the private and public spheres.

As economic institutions, however, *oikos* and *polis* are organized in a more complementary fashion.[51] Each aims at self-sufficiency, thrift, a pooling of common resources, and production for use rather than exchange. Xenophon's Socrates, for example, argues that the economic management of household and state differ mainly in scale (*Mem.* 3.4.12 and *Oec.* 8.22 and 9). When women in the *Lysistrata* and *Ecclesiaszusae* claim to be able to manage public affairs, because of their knowledge of household management, the poet plays on the complementarity of *oikos* and *polis* as economic institutions.[52] It should be emphasized that in neither play do the women actually take over the legislative, judicial and military functions of the city; the utopia of the *Ecclesiaszusae* will eliminate the need for a political sphere, slaves will run the farms, and the women will control a state which, as I argue in a forthcoming article, is primarily an enlarged *oikos*.[53]

Finally, women's role in public religion helps us distinguish between positive heroines in drama who act publicly to defend the *polis*, and those heroines who intrude into the public sphere to make a political challenge to male authority. Clytemnestra pays for her desire to usurp male power; Antigone is simultaneously condemned and celebrated. She dies for her challenge to the edict, but is acclaimed for her defense of the unwritten laws, which have a primary association with the religious sphere, and which are more "natural" than conventional. Jocasta in the *Phoenissae* also defends the state with an appeal to natural law (528–85). Lysistrata in the *Lysistrata*, a character whose name clearly identifies her with the contemporary priestess of Athena Polias Lysimache, can save household and state and create a positive compromise between the interests of the sexes through her legitimate religious authority.[54] Praxithea in Euripides' *Erectheus*, who argues the case for sacrificing her own daughter to save the state (frag. 360N2), was also the first

Athenian priestess of Athena. The chorus in the *Lysistrata* lay claim to symbolic "citizenship" not only through their payment of "taxes" to the state in the form of sons (65, 589–90), but through the state's demonstrated concern in their participation from girlhood on in public religious life (638–48). Euripides' captive Melanippe makes the most eloquent defense of women on these grounds:

> They manage the home, and guard within the house the sea-borne wares. No house is clean or prosperous if the wife is absent. And in religion — highest I judge this claim — we play the greatest part. In the oracles of Phoebus, women expound Apollo's will; and at the holy seat of Dodona, beside the sacred oak, woman conveys the will of Zeus to all Greeks who may desire it. As for holy rites performed for the Fates and the Nameless Goddesses — they are not holy in the hands of men; among women they flourish all. So righteous is woman's part in holy service. How then should her kind be fairly abused? Shall they not cease, the vain reproaches of men; and those who deem too soon that all women must be blamed alike, if one be found a sinner? Let me speak on, and distinguish them: nothing is worse than the base woman, and nothing far surpasses the good one. Only their natures differ . . .[33]

Ideally, then, *oikos* and *polis* are mutually defining institutions; order in one sphere is inextricably related to order in the other, and each sex has legitimate functions to perform in support of each. On the other hand, contradictions can arise within each part of the system and the interests of the one institution can conflict with that of the other. The political and religious aims of the state are not always in harmony, as the many debates in drama concerning conventional and natural law attest. Similarly, the *oikos* is ideally designed as to perpetuate the patrilineal line; but in order to do so, a female stranger must be introduced to reproduce children and to protect the material interests of the *oikos* in the absence of the male, a stranger who does not receive in exchange anything more than the pleasure of supervising and nourishing that which is not her own.

We do see in drama rare instances of an adherence to the ideal in characters like Alcestis, Lysistrata, Iphigeneia at Aulis, or Macaria. But the relation of drama to life and to cultural ideals tends to be obscured by its self-conscious and deliberate obsession with cultural contradictions and crises. Some dramas can be understood as explicit inversions of the ideal. Women commit adultery and sacrifice children and the material resources of the household to their own desires to rebel and attain power for themselves, and men sacrifice their households for fame, or divert public resources to private gain. The boundaries between household and state becomes spatially and ideologically blurred. Women take on masculine vices, and men female vices and limits. Men pervert their political authority to conflict with the survival of household and state. Women pervert their religious powers to serve anarchy and destruction.

The state of inversion produced is well characterized in the *Agamemnon*, where the masculinized Clytemnestra subverts all her functions in the household and "sacrifices" her husband and perverts prayer to destroy him, while Cassandra, who rejected Apollo, cannot use her prophetic powers to communicate the truth. Agamemnon, on the other hand, sacrifices the youth of the state and its resources, and piety towards the gods for victory in war; he falls victim to the will of a woman and his own desire for oriental and hence feminizing luxury. In the *Eumenides*, by contrast, the Erinyes accept for women an important role in cult which serves the state. Women will be removed from the political sphere and confined in the *oikos*, as the Erinyes are confined underground. The Erinyes accept for women their subordination in marriage, and their role as secondary parent. The male regains political authority with a new system of justice and distribution of wealth; wars will be fought only to counter external aggression, and the fear of the Erinyes will be remembered in the political sphere. The trilogy closes with an assertion of the norm in sexual and social relations expressed in the prose texts.

Many dramas, however, do not reflect the tensions between *oikos* and *polis* in the battle of the sexes by creating an outright inversion of the norm. Yet we can still read the male/female relationship in such plays as Sophocles' *Trachiniae*, Euripides' *Phoenissae*, or Aeschylus' *Seven Against Thebes* against the implicit ideal relation between *oikos* and *polis* suggested earlier. Sophocles' *Trachiniae* offers a poignant example of a failure of communication between the sexes which is reflected in a failed relation between the spheres in which each operates. Dejaneira, the ideal wife, is chaste to the point that she fails to understand the true nature of sexuality. The victim of a near marriage with a monster and an attempted rape by a centaur, she has closed off her mind from the implications of male lust altogether; she was unable experience the battle for her hand between Heracles and the river god Achelous objectively (21–25). Nor does she fully understand the implications of her own feelings of jealousy towards the young Iole. Her isolation in her confinement to the *oikos* is extreme. Heracles returns home only to sow children; she compares his behaviour to that of a farmer who occasionally visits an outlying field (32–33). She receives indirect information about her husband from messengers who do not always tell the truth, and is oppressed by her fears over the ambiguous oracles concerning Heracles' fate left behind by the hero. Given her isolation from both the outside world and her limited knowledge of human nature, it is not surprising that she disastrously misinterprets the motives of the Centaur in giving her a "love charm" through which he in fact intended to destroy Heracles. Full of explicitly constructive intentions to preserve the *oikos*, she falls victim to her wifely virtues and the limited vision imposed on her by her social role.

Heracles has spent his existence not only outside, but on the borders of civilized life. He has subjected his family to constant movement and life in foreign lands. His entrance into culture is explosive. He sacks a city to win the girl Iole, and then introduces her into his own household with no thought for convention and his wife's feelings. He was subject to a foreign queen for a treacherous killing, which violated host/guest relations. He forces his son to marry his own mistress at the end of the play. He catches fire while sacrificing to the gods, overturns the ritual, and murders his companion Lichas. This play carries to an extreme the division between the sexes, by showing the dangers of extreme masculinity and extreme feminity, and of the spatial and functional divisions in the lives of men and women. As Arthur's paper in this volume argues, Hector and Andromache in *Iliad* 6 can temporarily reach a state of full communication at a point in space which lies between the domestic and public worlds, a point at which the complex reciprocal relationship between male and female and their separate spheres can be fully revealed; then their social roles carry them off to permanent and tragic separation. But in the *Trachiniae* husband and wife never meet on stage, and neither enters the world of the other or shares in the value and perceptions belonging to their spheres. Reciprocity between the sexes and their worlds is severed. Heracles, remaining outside to the last, ignores Dejaneira and her suicide in his self-absorption during the final scenes, while Dejaneira remaining within the *oikos* she has never left, chooses a silent but strangely masculine death by the sword. In the final scene Heracles authoritatively restores the institutions of marriage and sacrifice disrupted by the action of the play.[56] He is sacrificed in propitious silence on the mountain, and extracts a promise from his son Hyllus that he will marry his mistress Iole. Hyllus is visibly torn between his feelings of allegiance to both parents, and shocked at Heracles' requests that he assist his father to destroy himself and marry Iole. We are left with a feeling that cultural order has been recreated at too high a price, and that the problems raised by the play have been only superficially resolved.

Euripides' *Phoenissae* stresses in a similar fashion the drastic pressures which history can put on the sexual divisions in Greek social life. At the opening of the play the young Antigone emerges from the cloistered seclusion appropriate to a young Athenian maiden to look at the battlefield from a wall. Chaperoned assiduously by her Pedagogue, she makes naive comments about the scene below, and romanticizes the incipient war. Eteocles, Polyneices and Creon abandon the city in favor of self-interest, while the defense of the public sphere comes to rest in the hands of Jocasta and Creon's young son Menoiceus, who sacrifices himself for the city. Finally, in the later part of the play, Jocasta, in an attempt to prevent her sons Eteocles and Polyneices from killing each other, drags Antigone roughly from her maiden seclusion (1264–69). From then on, Antigone, though unequipped to play the role of her powerful Sophoclean counterpart, nevertheless struggles bravely to do so, despite the protests of her uncle Creon and her father Oedipus, who want her to go back inside where she belongs (1636, 1747ff.). The result is simultaneously moving and monstrous. She threatens to kill Haimon on their wedding night like a Danaid (1675). In the concluding scenes she apparently fails to accomplish her traditional public role in burying her brother, but sacrifices her marriage and maiden seclusion to accompany her father into exile.

Aeschylus' *Seven Against Thebes* again plays on the sexual division of space and function in an ambiguous fashion.[57] Neither sex actually crosses the boundaries of cultural limits appropriate to their sex. At the opening of the play Eteocles initially shows himself to be the ideally efficient military leader, who is preparing to defend a ship of state which he imagines in his address as an exclusively male world (1–38). He then encounters a group of excited young virgins praying to the gods at the center of the city. He orders them back home, telling them that their presence is a dangerous disruption in the besieged city and that they should pray to the gods of the city in a more propitious fashion; he wishes that he could live entirely separate from women (187–88). The Greek audience would remember, however, that women's function in war was to pray to the gods on the acropolis. Hector returns to Troy in *Iliad* 6 to instruct his mother to do so. Furthermore, the women, as Seth Benardete has pointed out,[59] are praying, as they continue to do after Eteocles' departure, to a broader and older set of gods than those of the city to whom Eteocles' prays. Their gods, specified by name, are both male and female members of the family of Zeus, while Eteocles tells them to appeal to the anonymous gods of the city directly. Their prayers create a reciprocal relation between the separate worlds of *oikos* and *polis* ignored by Eteocles. When Eteocles departs, they do not follow his instructions precisely. No mention is made of the proptiatory *ololugmos*. Their meter is calmer, their gods are gods of the state. But in their song they bring within the city the war and strife which Eteocles is striving to keep outside. In so doing they implicitly remind the audience of the curse of Oedipus and the internal, familial tensions of the royal house of Thebes, of all that Eteocles regards as sub-political and unworthy of attention. Eteocles, by suppressing his own identity as a son of Oedipus until the fatal moment where he realizes he will meet his own brother at the seventh gate and eagerly goes out to destroy him, has forgotten his private self, and imagines himself as one with the autochthonous earthborn (rather than from human parents of both sexes) heroes whom he mobilizes against the enemy at the other gates. At the close of the shield scene, the roles reverse, and the women of the chorus now try to persuade the maddened Eteocles not to pollute the city with fraternal blood. Once again the tragic conflict is played out against a sexual division in which Eteocles has separated himself irrevocably from the domestic and religious spheres presided over by the women, whom the play leaves to mourn in traditional fashion over a leaderless if free city.[59] The problem here is not so much the failure of either sex to perform its proper social functions, as a crucial lack of communication and reciprocity between their two worlds.

To summarize my point then. The simple equation female:*oikos* as male:*polis* does not hold on the Greek stage. Yet occasionally we catch a glimpse of a more complex, reciprocal model of the relation between public and private, male and female, which helps us to define a norm against which to read the inversions and aberrations of drama. The end of the *Oresteia* is one. *Lysistrata* is another. Here the married women's sex strike puts women back into their homes and marriages and restores men to public dominance without a violation by the female of the social limits imposed upon her.[60] In general structural polarities present in dramatic texts are obscured precisely because drama deals with social crisis, with the exposure of contradictions in the social system. At the same time, the reciprocal relation between the two institutions, and the parallel ways in which each is organized, allows the dramatist to make complex symbolic links between these two apparently separate spheres. Hence domestic crises can be used to delineate public ones, and public crises can be signs of abuses to the domestic sphere.

The radical privatization of the female except in the religious sphere offers, as we can see from any one of the standpoints presented in this paper, the most central question and source of unease in drama. Slater's model of the ambivalent mother/son relation depends first and foremost on the woman's ambivalent reaction to her social confinement. Her role as outsider in the social system, both within marriage and in relation to the political sphere classifies her as a more "natural" being to be controlled by this system and potentially hostile to it, although this is a problem she sometimes shares with the men of her society. As a problematic social link between households (see for example, Hermione in Euripides' *Andromache*, whose father Menelaus remains an officious mediator in the sterile and tension-filled marriage of his daughter to Neoptolemus, while the concubine Andromache displays a wifely subservience to the interests of her master) and a stranger who threatens the household from within, she is nevertheless crucial, particularly in view of the frequent absence of the male, to the biological and economic survival of the household. In the public sphere the religious values associated with women must be kept separate from the political sphere to serve as a counterbalancing force; but women can use these religious powers in cultural or anti-cultural ways.

Finally, the democratic *polis* made extrardinary demands on the male citizen to subordinate private interests to public, while simultaneously encouraging ambition and competition. The result, drama seems to suggest, is a constant failure of the male to stay within cultural limits. Female characters often make a radical intrusion into the breach, either to expose and challenge this failure, or to heal it with transcendent sacrificial or other religious gestures. If the female uses religious powers to serve household or state, or to mediate between "nature" and "culture" as these two terms are defined by a specific text, the result can be positive. Otherwise the intrusion of a being ill-equipped for political life can be as dangerous as the disasters which provoked it, the female becomes the locus of oppositions between "nature" and "culture", household and state, and the dramas close with a punishment of the female intruder which implicitly reasserts the cultural norm. The relatively more limited and defined role in which the female is confined by Athenian culture can thus be used to define the more inclusive male role by contrast.

The preliminary suggestions made here about the symbolic role of women in classical drama, and the approaches which might be taken to illuminate this problem, do not begin to touch on a number of crucial aspects of the question. We have not considered any of these questions in relation to the ethical, philosophical and aesthetic issues which are central to drama; it would be interesting to discover, for example, what relation debates over *nomos* and *physis* have to confrontations between the sexes. We have ignored female characters who cannot be successfully analyzed by any of the means considered here. We have not made a sufficient distinction between the treatment of male–female relations in the comic and tragic genres, or between the three tragic playwrights, Aeschylus, Sophocles, and Euripides. We have not given an interpretation which puts these insights into the context of a full reading of a drama. We need to understand considerably more about the role of women in Greek religion or the Greek conception of honor in order to analyze women's role in drama.[61] We have not made any adequate theoretical alignment between the psychological and structuralist interpretations, or between the two difference structuralist polarities explored. Nevertheless, it seems to me that we have made a beginning, a beginning which locates the problems posed by a myth-based literature in a specific social and cultural context, and shows us that social theory can offer us some avenues to open up and illuminate these problems. As Levi-Strauss observes, women are like words which must be "communicated" and exchanged in a cultural system; yet they are also speakers as well as signs:

But women could never become just a sign and nothing more, since even in a man's world she is still a person, and insofar as she is defined as a sign she must be recognized as the generator of signs. In the matrimonial dialogue of men, woman is never purely spoken about; for if women in general represent a certain category of signs, destined to a certain kind of communication, each woman preserves a particular value arising from her talent, before and after marriage, for taking her part in a duet. In contrast to words, which become wholly signs, woman has remained at once a sign and a value. This explains why the relations between the sexes have preserved that affective richness, ardour and mystery which originally permeated the entire universe of human communications.[62]

Acknowledgements

I wish to thank Rachel Kitzinger and Duncan Foley for comments on a draft of this paper. Laura Slatkin, Richard Sacks, Cathy Eden, and Doug Frame gave helpful suggestions on an oral version.

Notes

1.   See E. Ardener, "Belief and the Problem of Women", in J.S. La Fontaine ed., *The Interpretation of Ritual* (London 1972) 135–158, for a thoughtful dis-

cussion of the unrepresented female point of view in anthropological studies of women.

2. Marylin Arthur points out in her review essay on women in the classics (*Signs* 2.2 (1976) 382–403) that the evidence concerning women in the prose and poetic texts often coincides. This is certainly true, but for the purposes of this paper the distinction will remain useful, since there are certain areas where the dramatic texts offer a consistently different picture

3. "The Position of Women in Athens in the Fifth and Fourth Centuries", *CP* 20 (1925) 4.

4. Roger Just, "The Conception of Women in Classical Athens", *Journal of the Anthropological Society of Oxford* 6.3 (1975) 157.

5. The two most recent are Just, note 4 above, 153–70, and John Gould, "Law, custom and myth: aspects of the social position of women in Classical Athens", *JHS* 100 (1980) 38–59. I deliberately ignore in this article previous misconceptions concerning the question of the status of women in classical Athens (the "optimists" versus the "pessimists"; culturally relative judgments on how the Greeks treated women) which have been well treated by Gould, Just, and Pomeroy. For other important essays on this topic see A.W. Gomme, note 3 above, H.D.F. Kitto, *The Greeks* (Harmondsworth, Middlesex 1950) 219–236, and D. Richter, "The Position of Women in Classical Athens", *CJ* 67.1 (1971) 1–8; Sarah Pomeroy treats both the literary and historical aspects of these questions in several chapters of *Goddesses, Whores, Wives*, and *Slaves: Women in Classical Antiquity* (New York 1975). On the historical side of the issue see also W.K. Lacey, *The Family in Classical Greece* (Ithaca, N.Y. 1968). Other helpful works are V. Ehrenberg, *The People of Aristophanes* (Oxford 1943), Marylin Arthur, "Early Greece: The Origins of the Western Attitude Towards Women", *Arethusa* 6 (1973) 7–58, "Liberated Women: The Classical Era", in R. Bridenthal and C. Koontz eds., *Becoming Visible: Women in European History* (Boston 1977) 60–89, and the *Signs* article cited in note 2, and P. Vellacott, *Ironic Drama: A Study in Euripides Method and Meaning* (Cambridge 1975).

6. On women's legal and social status in Athens see especially Lacey, note 5, A.R.W. Harrison, *The Law of Athens: The Family and Property* (Oxford 1968), D.M. McDowell, *The Law in Classical Athens* (Ithaca, N.Y. 1978), H.J. Wolff, "Marriage, Law and Family Organization in Ancient Athens", *Traditio* 2 (1944) 43–95, and D.M. Schaps, *Economic Rights of Women in Ancient Greece* (Edinburgh 1978).

7. For a guardian's abuse of property see Aeschines I 95–99; for a husband's mistreatment of his wife see Andocides' I 124–77. Concerned male relatives of such women could obviously bring cases into court in their interest, so that women did not necessarily go unprotected even if they could not exercise legal rights on their own behalf.

8. Lysias 3.6; for dining practices see Isaeus 3.13–14 and Lysias 1.22.

9. For court cases which question the existence of respectable women see Dem. 43.29–46 and Isaeus 8.9–10; for the naming of women in court see D.M. Schaps *CQ* 25 (1975) 53–57. For general discussions of the court evidence see especially Lacey, Gould and Just (note 5 above).

10. For female initiative in family affairs see esp. Lysias 32 and 13, and Dem. 36.14.
11. For affectionate relations between spouses see Gould (note 5 above) 50.
12. See especially the "Diseases of Virgins" in the Hippocratic corpus for hysteria; for a discussion see B. Simon, *Mind and Madness in Ancient Greece* (Ithaca, N.Y. 1978) 238–70. For ancient theories of conception see the section on "The Seed" in the Hippocratic writings, and Aristotle, *The Generation of Animals* esp. 727 a–b. For a discussion see James Hillman, *The Myth of Analysis* (Evanston, Ill. 1972) 215–246.
13. A recent article by John Gould, "Dramatic characters and 'human intelligibility' in Greek tragedy", *PCPS* N.S. 24 (1978) 43–67, stresses the consequences of the public nature of Greek drama for characterization, and emphasizes the distortions of "life" that it may bring.
14. *The Glory of Hera: Greek Mythology and the Greek Family* (Boston 1968).
15. In this paragraph I stress particularly the insights given in recent general articles on the conception of women in Athens such as those by Gould and Just cited in note 5 above. Pomeroy's chapter (note 5 above) treats the individual playwrights, and emphasizes the importance of women's representation of family and religious interests, and the masculinization of many tragic heroines to be discussed in section VI. The remaining sections of the article will develop these and other perspectives, and note some of the many other helpful contributions made in pieces on individual plays or playwrights to our understanding of the conception of women in Attic drama. Many articles emphasize the victimization of women in drama by war and the patriarchal system, and the capacity of women for noble suffering. In this paper I intend to concentrate on the anomalous aspects of women's role in drama (those which cannot be easily explained on the basis of the prose evidence), and how the conception of women is articulated in the action of drama on the broadest scale.
16. For an excellent treatment of this dialogue between past myth and the Attic present in drama see J.-P. Vernant, "Greek Tragedy" in *The Structuralist Controversy*, ed. R. Macksey and E. Donato (Baltimore and London 1970) esp. 283ff. On Greek myth in general and the problem of treating the sophisticated literature of Greece as myth see G.S. Kirk, *Myth: its Meaning and Function in Ancient and Other Cultures* (Berkeley 1970), B. Vickers, *Towards Greek Tragedy* (London 1973) 166ff. and 617ff., and J. Peradotto, "Classical Mythology: An Annotated Bibliographical Survey", *APA* (Urbana, Ill. 1973).
17. I stress the methodological importance of using Athenian literature as evidence for the Attic conception of women because J. Gould (note 5 above) and P. Slater (note 14 above), for example, use Athenian and non-Athenian texts indiscriminately.
18. For examples of commands to women to stay within see *Eur. Pho.* 88ff., 193ff. or *Electra* 341ff.; for male resistance to a female challenge see among many examples, Soph. *Ant.* 484–85. On the masculinity of tragic women see esp. Pomeroy (note 5 above) 98–101 and B.M.W. Knox, "The Medea of Euripides", *YCS* 25 (1977) 192–226.

19. This point was made by James Redfield in his Gildersleeve lecture of January 1981. On the relation between Pericles and Oedipus see B.M.W. Knox, *Oedipus at Thebes* (New Haven 1957).

20. See Slater, note 14 above. For a sophisticated Freudian interpretation of women in tragedy which uses Slater see, for example, R. Caldwell, "The Misogyny of Eteocles", *Arethusa* 6, 197–231.

21. H.P. Foley, "Sex and State in Ancient Greece", *Diacritics* 5.4 (1975) 31–36. See also Arthur (note 2 above) and Pomeroy (note 5 above).

22. For female psycho-sexual development see especially N. Chodorov, *The Reproduction of Mothering* (Berkeley and Los Angeles 1978).

23. Gayle Rubin, "The Traffic in Women: Notes on the 'Political Economy' of Sex", in R. Reiter ed., *Towards an Anthropology of Women* (New York and London 1975) 157–210. I borrow the term "sex-gender system" from her persuasive discussion.

24. For individual articles on women in Greek literature which make use of structuralist methodology see especially the articles by Foley, Sussman, Loraux, du Bois, Zeitlin and Segal in *Arethusa* 11 (1978), the paper by Arthur in this volume, the papers by Arthur, Foley and Zeitlin in the forthcoming issue of *Arethusa* in honor of J.-P. Vernant (1982), the papers by Rosellini, Said and Auger in "Aristophane, les femmes et la cité", *Les Cahiers de Fontenay* no. 17 (1979), and my paper, "The Female Intruder Reconsidered: Women in Aristophanes' *Lysistrata* and *Ecclesiazusae*", forthcoming in *Classical Philology*. For further background on this methodology see the ensuing discussion in this paper.

25. Sherry Ortner, "Is Female to Male as Nature is to Culture?", in M. Rosaldo and L. Lamphere, eds., *Woman, Culture, and Society* (Stanford 1974) 67–88.

26. For particularly useful examples of the work of this group which state their general theses and refer specifically to the problem of women see esp., M. Detienne, *The Gardens of Adonis*, trans. J. Lloyd (Brighton 1977), with an important introduction by J.-P. Vernant, and "Violentes 'Eugénies' " in *La cuisine du sacrifice en pays grec*, ed. Detienne and Vernant (Paris 1979); J.-P. Vernant, *Mythe et société en Grèce ancienne* (Paris 1974) and "Hestia-Hermès: sur l'expression religieuse de l'espace et du movement chez les Grecs", in *Mythe et pensée chez les Grecs* (Paris 1969) 97–158; P. Vidal-Naquet, "Esclavage et gynecocratie dans la tradition, le mythe, l'utopie", in *Recherche sur les structures sociales dans l'antiquité classique* (Paris 1970) 63–70, and "Valeurs religieuses et mythiques de la terre et du sacrifice dans l'Odyssée", in M.I. Finley, ed., *Problemes de la terre en Grèce ancienne* (Paris 1973) 269–92.

27. F.I. Zeitlin, "Cultic Models of the Female: Rites of Dionysus and Demeter", forthcoming in *Arethusa* 1982.

28. Foley, "Marriage and Death in Euripides' *Iphigeneia in Aulis*", forthcoming in *Arethusa* 1982.

29. On this point see R. Girard, *Violence and the Sacred* (Baltimore 1972) 139–42. For Girard the myth attributes male violence to women as part of a mythical strategy which conceals the true nature of the religious violence lying at the heart of the drama.

30. On women in Dionysiac and ecstatic religion see Zeitlin (note 27 above), R.

Kraemer, "Ecstasy and Possession: the Attraction of Women to the Cult of Dionysus", *HThR* 72 (1979) 55–80, B. Simon (note 12 above), and I. Lewis, *Ecstatic Religion* (Middlesex and Baltimore 1971).

31. On the nature/culture dichotomy in the *Bacchae* see C.P. Segal, "The Menace of Dionysus: Sex Roles and Reversals in Euripides' *Bacchae*", *Arethusa* 11 (1978) 185–202.

32. On this passage in Plato's *Menexenus* see E.D. Dodds, *The Ancient Concept of Progress and Other Essays on Greek Literature* (Oxford 1973) 146–47.

33. On this aspect of the odes see especially M. Arthur, "The Choral Odes of the *Bacchae* of Euripides", *YCS* 22 (1972) 145–181.

34. See my discussion in "'Reverse Similes' and Sex Roles in the *Odyssey*", *Arethusa* 11 (1978) 7–26.

35. On this point see Arthur, "Liberated Women" (note 5 above) 73–78.

36. On Pandora see esp. J.-P. Vernant, "Le mythe prométhéen chez Hesiode", *Mythe et société en Grèce ancienne* (Paris 1974) 177–194, and P. Pucci, *Hesiod and the Language of Poetry* (Baltimore and London 1977) 82–126.

37. Ibid., Pucci 100–101.

38. On the incompatibility of competition and democracy in the Athenian system see A. Gouldner, *Enter Plato: Classical Greece and the Origins of Social Theory*, Part I (New York 1966).

39. "Hestia-Hermès" (note 26 above).

40. I understand that Ortner is arguing on another level than I am here myself. Nevertheless, many have tried to apply this dichotomy without a recognition of the difficulty of using the concept in a particular cultural context. I was unable to acquire a recent book of critical essays on the nature/culture question (C. MacCormack and M. Strathern, *Nature, Culture and Gender* (Cambridge 1980)) by the time this paper went to press.

41. For a general expression of the domestic/public theory see Michelle Rosaldo, "A Theoretical Overview", in Rosaldo and Lamphere, eds., *Woman, Culture and Society* (Stanford 1974) 17–42. In classics this view has been expressed most explicitly, although by no means exclusively, by Michael Shaw, "The Female Intruder: Women in Fifth-Century Drama", *CP* (1975) 255–66; see also my forthcoming response in *CP* to this article, "The Female Intruder Reconsidered: Women in Aristophanes' *Lysistrata* and *Ecclesiazusae*". My argument here borrows some theoretical points from that article. The general position was traditional long before structuralism. S. Freud, for example, remarked that "women represent the interests of the family and sexual life; the work of civilization has become more and more men's business." (*Civilization and its Discontents* (London 1957) 73.)

42. Rosaldo, "The Use and Abuse of Anthropology: Reflections on Feminism and Cross-cultural Understanding", *Signs* 5.3 (1980) 389–417.

43. On the relation between domestic and public space in Greek culture see Xenophon's *Oeconomicus*, and Vernant, "Hestia-Hermès", note 26 above. For an important modern treatment of the issue see P. Bourdieu, *Outline of a Theory of Practice*, trans. R. Nice (Cambridge 1977).

44. See note 39 above.

45. See Arthur, note 5 above, both "Liberated Women" and "Early Greece".

46. For a discussion of the dream of endogamy and its contradictions see Vernant, "Hestia-Hermès" (note 26 above), and J. Pitt-Rivers, *The Fate of Shechem or the Politics of Sex* (Cambridge 1971) esp. 71–93.

47. On *Medea* see especially Knox (note 18 above) and P. Pucci, *The Violence of Pity in Euripides' Medea* (Ithaca and London 1980).

48. For a discussion of such passages (esp. IV. 145, VI. 137–140) see Dewald in thi\ volume and Gould (note 5 above) 54–55.

49. Shaw, note 41 above.

50. B.M.W. Knox, *The Heroic Temper* (Berkeley and Los Angeles 1964) 76–90.

51. For a more detailed discussion see my forthcoming paper, note 41 above. The polarity *oikos/polis* does not necessarily correspond precisely with the more general distinction domestic/public. I have chosen to explore the issue in terms of the former polarity because it is the one made by Attic authors. The larger distinction is more complex and would require a thorough exploration of prose texts and non-literary evidence as well as a broader study of the limits between public and private (/idios and /koinos) in Attic literature. As Pauline Schmidt has emphasized to me, the major and pervasive role of women in cult makes their supposed confinement to the /oikos more theoretical than actual.

52. *Ibid.*

53. *Ibid.*

54. *Ibid.* On the identity of Lysistrata see D.M. Lewis, "Notes on Attic Inscriptions II, XXIII. Who Was lysistrata?", *ABSA* 1 (1965) 1–13. See now also Jeffrey Henderson, "Lysistrate: the Play and its Themes", *YCS* 26 (1980) 153–218.

55. Translated by Denys Page, *Select Papyri* III (Cambridge, Mass. 1962) 113–114.

56. For this interpretation of the end of the play see C.P. Segal, "Mariage et sacrifice dans les *Trachiniennes* de Sophocle", *AC* 44 (1975) 30–53.

57. On male–female relations in the *Seven* see especially H. Bacon, "The Shield of Eteocles", *Arion* 3 (1964) 27–38, Caldwell (note 20 above), S. Benardete, "Two Notes on Aeschylus' *Septem*", Part I *WS* 80 (1967) 22–30, and F.I. Zeitlin, "Language, Structure, and the Son of Oedipus in Aeschylus' *Seven Against Thebes*. A Semiotic Study of the Shield Scene", forthcoming in *Filologia e Critica*, Editione di Ateneo e Bizarri (Roma).

58. Benardete, note 56 above.

59. The end of the *Seven* may not be genuine. I end my interpretation with the mourning by the chorus of the death of the brothers.

60. See Foley, note 41 above.

61. For modern Greek and Mediterranean concepts of honor see Pitt-Rivers, note 46 above, Bourdieu, note 43 above, and J. Peristiany, ed., *Honor and Shame: the Values of Mediterranean Society* (Chicago 1965).

62. C. Levi-Strauss, *The Elementary Structures of Kinship* (Boston 1969) 496.

Travesties of gender and genre in Aristophanes' *Thesmophoriazousae*

FROMA I. ZEITLIN

Princeton University

Equal of opposites, evolved by a onesame power of nature or of spirit ... as the sole condition and means of its himundher manifestation and polarized for reunion by the symphysis of their antipathies.

James Joyce

The sexes were not two as they are now, but originally three in number; there was man, woman, and the union of the two, having a name corresponding to this double nature, which had once a real existence but is now lost, and the word "Androgynous" is only preserved as a term of reproach.

Aristophanes in Plato's *Symposium*

Three of Aristophanes' eleven extant comedies use the typical comic device of role inversion to imagine worlds of topsy-turvydom in which women are "on top".[1] Freed from the social constraints which keep them enclosed within the house and silent in the public realms of discourse and action, women are given a field and context on the comic stage. They issue forth to lay their plans, concoct their plots, and exercise their power over men.

169

The *Lysistrata* and the *Ecclesiazousae* stage the intrusion of women into the public spaces of Athens — the Acropolis and Agora, respectively — as an intrusion into the political and economic life of the city. The *Thesmophoriaszousae*, however, resituates the battle of the sexes in another domain — that of aesthetics, and more specifically, that of the theater itself. Instead of the collective confrontation of men and women, the play directs the women's actions against a single male target — the tragic poet, Euripides. Like the better known *Lysistrata*, performed the same year (411 B.C.), the *Thesmophoriazousae* (or the *Women at the Festival of the Thesmophoria*) is set on the Acropolis; this time it is not appropriated by the women as the crucial and outrageous strategy to further their plans, but is granted to them in accordance with the rules of their annual festival, which reserved this sacred space for the exclusive use of women in their fertility rites, dedicated to Demeter and Persephone.

Criticism has not been generous to this play. Studies of role inversion, even in more recent feminist perspectives, have focused on the other two plays because of their implications for the political and economic problems which are the city's dominant interests.[2] The *Frogs* has claimed almost exclusive attention with regard to literary questions, both because of the formal structure of the contest between Aeschylus and Euripides in the play and because of the emphasis on the role of the poet as teacher and 'savior" of the city in its time of need.[3] Judgments on the *Thesmophoriazousae*, on the other hand, while admiring its ingenuity and wit, generally dismiss it as a "parody play", a trifling interlude in the comic poet's more significant and enduring dialogue with the city and its institutions. Some critics look for simplistic equivalences between transvestism, effeminacy, and Euripides' newer forms of tragedy, and all find difficulties with the plot, especially with Euripides' apparently sudden reconciliation with the women at the end.[4]

But the *Thesmophoriazousae* is a far more complex and more integrated play. It is located at the intersection of a number of relations: between male and female; between tragedy and comedy; between theater (tragedy and comedy) and festival (ritual and myth); between festival (the Thesmophoria) and festival (the Dionysiac, which provides the occasion for its performance and determines its comic essence); and finally, between bounded forms (myth, ritual, and drama) and the more fluid "realities" of everyday life. All these relations are unstable and reversible; they cross boundaries and invade each others' territories, erase and reinstate hierarchical distances, ironically reflecting upon each other and themselves.

I intend to take another look at this play from the joint perspectives of the theme of "women on top" and that of the self-reflectiveness of art concerned with the status of its own mimetic representation. However satirically the play may represent Euripides' "unnatural" and "unmanly" concern with *eros* and with women, with female sexuality and female psyche, it poses a more necessary and intrinsic connection between the ambiguities of the feminine and those of art, linked together in various ways in Greek notions of poetics from their earliest formulations. The setting of the play and the progress of the plot are constructed not only to make the most of the perennial comic value of female impersonation, but also to use the notions of gender in posing questions of genre and to draw attention to the problematics of imitation and representation which connects transvestism of costume with mimetic parody of texts. Transvestism works on the visual level; parody, on the verbal level. Together they expose the interrelationship of the crossing of genres and the crossing of genders; together they exemplify the equivalence of intertextuality and intersexuality.

My plan is to examine these different issues under the rubric of mimesis — the plot, transvestism, parody, myth and ritual — to uncover the "secret" logic of the text which illuminates a play that works through the fusion of festival, theater, and gender, and finally, to offer some speculations on the relation of the feminine itself with the principles of imitation.

I MIMESIS: GENDER AND GENRE

There are those who want a text (an art, a painting) without a shadow, without the "dominant ideology" but this is to want a text without fecundity, without productivity, a sterile text.

                                                    Roland Barthes

In this brilliant and ingenious play, the contest between the genders must share the spotlight with the contest between the genres, comedy and tragedy. Along with the parody of other serious forms of discourse within the city (judicial, ritual, political, poetic), *paratragodia*, or the parody of tragedy, is a consistent feature of Aristophanic comedy.[5] Figures of poets and philosophers and other intellectuals are often found too on the comic stage, along with politicians and other prominent figures which comedy, in its license for abuse, delights in demoting from high to low. But the effect of placing a tragic poet as the comic protagonist in a comic plot and of elevating parody to the dominant discourse of the play modulates the contest between the sexes into another key, one that reflects not only the tensions between the social roles of men and women, but also focuses on their theatrical representation as tragic and comic personae on the stage.

In the privacy of their ritual enclosure, the women have determined to act in their own defense — to exact vengeance from the tragic poet, Euripides, whom they charge with the offenses of misogyny and slander in his dramatic representation of women. He has made their lives intolerable, they complain, for they can no longer have the freedom at home which they once enjoyed. Their husbands come home from the theater all fired up with suspicion at every gesture, every movement the women make, and keep them locked up in the house. Euripides himself appears at the opening of the play to devise his counter-plot and to rescue himself from this clear and present danger which will determine his fate this day, whether he will live or die.

Euripides tries and fails to persuade the effeminate tragic poet, Agathon, to go in woman's dress to infiltrate the women's rites and to argue in the poet's defense, and must finally send his old kinsman instead. Dressed as a woman with costumes from Agathon's own wardrobe, shaved and depilated on stage, the kinsman, Mnesilochus, makes his way to the Acropolis to mingle unnoticed with the other women and to carry out the mandates of the master plotter. He is ultimately unmasked and his true sex revealed both by the nature of his defense of Euripides and by the information of Cleisthenes, the effeminate politician, and friend of woman, who comes to warn them of the interloper in their midst. While Cleisthenes goes off to bring back the Scythian policeman to remove the malefactor, the poor kinsman has recourse to elaborate parodies of Euripidean drama. In his increasing desperation, he tries now one tragic role then another in his efforts to save himself, bringing Euripides finally on stage, not once but twice, to impersonate the characters in his own plays who might rescue the kinsman. When this strategy fails, Euripides at last reconciles himself with the women and, dressed now as an old procuress, he succeeds in diverting the Scythian policeman with a comic, not a tragic, ploy — the perennial dancing girl — so that he and the kinsman can make their escape.

The meeting of the poet and the women complicates both the typical *topos* of "women in charge" and the role and stance of the comic hero himself. The launching of the great comic idea, which is the heart and soul of the comic plot, is divided between the women whose decision to prosecute Euripides is taken before the play actually begins, and the poet hero, who cannot initiate action in the free exercise of his own imaginative vision of the world. Instead, as comic protagonist, he must employ all his professional techniques to extricate himself from a situation in which he is not only hero, but potential victim.

Similarly, the device of staging the women's presence on the Acropolis has a double edge. On one level, their occupation of civic space maintains the transgression which their exhibition upon the public stage implies, and the ritual regulations which put women in charge offer, as in the other cases, the rich comic possibilities for women's use and misuse of male language in their imitation of the typical male institutions of tribunal and assembly. Moreover, the *topos* of role inversion gives the women, as always, an opportunity to redress the social imbalances between male and female in an open comic competition with men for superior status, here especially in the *parabasis*.[6] But on another level, their legitimate presence at their own private ritual also reverses the direction of the transgression; now men are forced to trespass on forbidden space and they penetrate the secret world of women for the purpose of spying upon them and disclosing their secrets to open view.

Another paradox is evident as a result of the confrontation of the poet and the women. To the women the scandal of Euripides' theater lies in his exhibition of erotic heroines upon the tragic stage who openly solicit men, like the unhappy Phaedra with her Hippolytus and the wanton Sthenoboia, who, like Potiphar's wife, shamelessly tempted the young Bellerophon. The kinsman's defense, however, claims that Euripides exercises restraint: he could have told other stories, worse than these (473–75).[7] His charge of misdoing leveled against all women incurs the women's anger at their supposed betrayal by one of their own within their very midst, a betrayal that will serve, in part, to unmask the female impersonator. Yet the anecdotes he tells of adultery and supposititious babies come straight out of the typical male discourse of the comic theater and the women he depicts as overly fond of wine and sex conform to the portrait of the comic woman, who displays her unruly Dionysiac self (even in this play) in the spirit of carnival and misrule. As the comic male character in the comic play, the kinsman then is only playing true to form. And if he defends the tragic poet in the comic way, he makes "unspeakable" what comedy has always claimed as its right to speak. Is tragedy taking the fall for comedy? Is the kinsman's defense, in fact, the defense mounted by comedy against the trespass on its ground by Euripidean tragedy?

The speech in which the kinsman corroborates Euripides' intimate familiarity with women's secrets, repeats and replicates Euripides' transgression of tragic decorum, a transgression which is also spatialized in dramatic form as the violation itself of the sacred enclosure reserved for women at their ritual. Having penetrated earlier into a world which he was forbidden to enter, he now penetrates it again through the kinsman's infiltration of the Thesmophoria, an act which profanes the pieties again, now on two accounts. In comedy, these revelations of women's "nature" cause no indignation among the spectators, but rather laughter. It is in the tragic theater that the mimetic effects of representation work with such realism and such persuasiveness that drama overtakes and invades the real world, sending the husbands away, wild with anxiety, to look to their womenfolk at home.

At the heart of this repeated violation is the transgression of the distance which normally maintains the fiction of theater with relation to the "real" world to which it refers and in which it registers its effects of pity and fear. Tragedy is "the imitation of a serious action", as Aristotle tells us. Designated as the genre which holds up a more heroic and more mythic mirror to the society of its spectators, who come to learn its lessons and to participate in its imaginative *mise en scène*, tragedy must depend upon the integrity of its fictions within its own theatrical conventions and generic norms. The violation of that integrity is focused on the issue which for the society of men bears the greatest psychological charge — namely, the integrity of their households, and above all, of their women.[8] The violation of women's sexual secrets therefore can stand not only as the actual subject for complaint, but as the metaphorical representation in social terms of the poet's trespass of aesthetic modes.

At stake in this theatrical tug of war between tragedy and comedy is the nature of mimesis itself. The *Thesmophoriazousae* wants it all ways — dramatizing and exploiting up to their furthest extremes the confusions which the notion of imitation suggests — as to whether art is a mimesis of *reality* or a *mimesis* of reality, whether it conceals its art by its verisimilitude or exposes its fictions in the staging and testing of its own illusions.

Consider the complications of the mimetic process when character and poet are conflated in the personage of Euripides, when the comic character (the kinsman) is designated as the actor who is to carry out the plot which Euripides has devised within the comic play. Then, once his "true" identity is revealed, the kinsman must transform himself into the theatrical actor of the Euripidean parodies whose lines he now self-consciously and incongruously renders with reference to his comic role.

Moreover, the play as a whole takes its cue from and sets as the condition of its plot the offense of Euripides in having tilted his dramas too far in the direction of a mimesis which exceeds the boundaries of the theater. For, given the comic stage as the ground of "reality" in the play, the "real" women, who resent being "characters" in his drama, put him in a "real" situation in which he himself must live out for himself the mimetic consequences of his own mimetic plots. As others have noticed, Euripides is not a character in a typical comic scenario; rather he plays the hero/victim in a parodic version of his favorite type of tragic drama — the intrigue-rescue play which often includes a recognition of a lost loved one. From the beginning the hero/heroine faces overwhelming danger and only reaches the desired salvation (often after that recognition with another has taken place) through a series of clever intrigues.[9] What better comic version of tragic justice than to turn the tables on Euripides? Yet what better stage than this for Euripides, the man of a thousand plots (927), a stage upon which to display all his *mēchanai* and to turn at last from victim to savior of himself and the kinsman? He plays first in the tragic mode, at the end, in the comic mode, when Aristophanes, cleverer than he, puts him squarely on the "real" ground of the comic play.

From the beginning, Euripides must act the part of the playwright within the play to devise his own plot, to direct the actor to play his appointed part, next, to furnish him with the texts from which to read, and eventually, to intervene as actor in the parodies of two plays which he has already composed. The comedy can never, therefore, escape the metatheatrical implications of play within play and all the variations and permutations of the device. As the comedy progresses, as the kinsman's own improvisations founder and he is "unmasked", the temple and the altar of the Thesmophorion conveniently serve as the "theatrical" space within the play on which to stage those parodies of Euripidean theater.[10] By the last paratragic scene, the comedy draws upon all its theatrical resources, from within and from without. The Scythian policeman's cruel fastening of the kinsman to the punishment plank suggests the cast, the setting, and the prop for Euripides' poor Andromeda, bound to the rock in far off Ethiopia, awaiting her fate from the sea monster who is to devour her. But then Euripides himself as Perseus flies by on the "real" theatrical device of the *mēchanē* and cues the kinsman as to the role he intends to play. Thus, as the play moves on to the end, as Euripides, in fact, assumes not only one but two parts in the *Andromeda*, the *Thesmophoriazousae* exposes more and more the obvious inconcinnities between theater and "reality", to the apparent detriment of the former, even as it implicitly conspires, as we shall see, to validate those same dramatic fictions.

II MIMESIS: TRANSVESTISM

Everyday, precious, . . . m'm'ry's leaves are falling deeply on my Jungfraud's Messongebook . . .

James Joyce

The feat is to sustain the mimesis of language (language imitating itself), the source of immense pleasures, in a fashion so radically ambiguous (ambiguous to the root) that the text never succumbs to the good conscience (and bad faith) of parody (of castrating laughter, of the "comical that makes us laugh").

Roland Barthes

The theme of mimesis is specifically set, in fact, in the prologue of the play, the first attested technical use of the word, mimesis, and the first demonstration, albeit ludicrous, of the mimetic theory of art which will later figure so largely in Plato's and Aristotle's aesthetic theories.[11] Agathon, the tragic poet, for whom Euripides is searching, is wheeled out the house on the *ekkyklēma*, the stage device used in the theater to bring an interior scene outside, singing sensual hymns that send the kinsman into an erotic swoon (130–33). Androgynous in appearance, Agathon wears women's clothing and an incongruous assortment of accessories (134–40). In reply to the kinsman's questions as to his identity and his gender, Agathon now replies:

> I wear my garb according to my thought.
> The poet, you see, must shape his ways
> In accordance with the plays to be composed.
> If someone is composing women's plays,
> His body must needs share in women's ways
> If plays of men, he has already what it takes.
> Whatever we don't have, we must capture by mimesis.

(146–52) (tr. Hansen)

So far, so good. The poet is a versatile fellow who must dress the dramatic roles he creates. But Agathon then declares that a beautiful poet wears beautiful clothes and writes beautiful dramas — and vice versa for the ugly poet. One must compose in accordance with one's nature (159–72). The clue to this apparent confusion between mimesis as impersonation, as investiture, and mimesis as a harmony of body, soul, and poetry, lies in the comic fact that Agathon is indeed by nature an effeminate man, just the type whom Aristophanes always love to mock.[12] Hence, what Agathon imitates (female appearance) is indeed harmonious with his nature and his ways. And this is precisely the reason why he must refuse to go as a spy among the women — because he fits the role too well. As a poet, he is second only to Euripides (187); as a "woman", he passes so well that he claims the women at the Thesmophoria would resent him for unfair competition in stealing away their nocturnal lovers (204–05); the sample of his poesy, the choral hymns he sings, beginning with an invocation to the two goddesses, Demeter and Persephone, and ending with an appeal to Leto, the mother of Apollo and Artemis, are all too much in tune. In short, he is the unnatural "natural" for the part, the pathic well adapted for tragic pathos, as the kinsman wryly observes (199–201). How could Agathon defend Euripides against the charges which are leveled against his fellow poet? He is as much or more a friend to women, "mad for women" (*gynaikomanēs*), their kindred spirit, as the effeminate Cleisthenes declares of himself when he enters into the women's festival to denounce the male imposter in their midst (574–76).

No, Mnesilochus, the bushy kinsman, all male, must go instead; he must be dressed on stage in a woman's costume; he must be shaved of his beard and raise his rump in full view of the audience to have it singed with a flame, as women do, in accordance with Greek standards of female beauty, when they depilate their genitals. With this prologue scene, in the interchange between Agathon and Mnesilochus, Aristophanes has accomplished a real *coup de théâtre*. For he has managed with artful economy to introduce his *topos* of "women on top" in a way which exposes its implications to the naked eye. Making Mnesilochus into a woman exactly reproduces in advance the inevitable result of the inversion of gender roles — when women are in a position to rule men, men must become women.[13] In the miniature reversal played out between Agathon and Mnesilochus, Mnesilochus, as the comic character, first indulges in all the witty obscenities to which he is entitled at the expense of the effeminate poet. But the transfer of Agathon's persona to him returns against the kinsman the full measure of that social shame which the breach of gender norms poses to identity, manhood, and power. Comedy's scandalous privilege to expose those parts and functions of the body which decorum keeps hidden — physically, in the padded leather phallos which the comic actor wears, verbally, in the obscenities and sexual jokes which are licensed by the Dionysiac festival — takes on a double twist here. For in exposing Mnesilochus, the lusty comic male, only in the process of becoming a woman, the comedy is playing with the extreme limit of its own promiscuous premises where all can converge in the ambiguities of intersexuality.

But transvestism in the theater, and especially in this scene, has yet another function in addition to exposing the natural facts of the body which the social conventions keep off stage[14] and away from public notice, namely, the exposing of the secret artifices which theatrical conventions keep off stage to maintain the fictions of its mimesis. Mnesilochus is, after all, dressing as a woman because he is to play the part of a woman, carrying out the clever stratagem of Euripides.

In this theatrical perspective, taking the role of the opposite sex invests the wearer with the power of appropriation, of supplement, not only loss. Androgynous myths and transvestite rites speak to this increased charge in symbolic terms even as androgyny and transvestism incur the shame of deviance within the social code. Thus the depilation of Mnesilochus is balanced by the putting on of women's clothing, for in this ambivalent game of genders, the female is not only a "not", but also an "other".[15] When the women in the *parabasis* examine the comic contradictions of misogyny and put the superiority of men to the test, they joke in terms of attributes common to each: we women have still kept safe at home our weaving rod (*kanōn*) and our sunshade (*skiadeion*), while you men have lost your spear shaft (*kanōn*) and your shield (*skiadeion*) (821–29). The play with castration is appropriate enough to the inversion of roles, but the ambiguities of role playing involve both this and that, even for Mnesilochus who plays so ill, and by his misplaying, exposes, when the women expose him, the limits of mimesis.

Since all female roles in the Greek theater were played by men, the exhibitionist donning of female costume focuses the problem of mimesis at its most ambiguous and most sensitive spot, where social and artistic rules are most in conflict with each other: impersonation affects the whole creative process from the poet to the actor and determines its aesthetic success, but feminization attracts to itself all the scorn and abuse which the culture — and comedy — can muster. To reverse the terms, in fact, it first unmans those whom the culture would scorn and abuse, those it would lay open to aggressive violence, and finds the point of entry through which to master the other. Just so in this play, Aristophanes makes mock of Euripides at the end by finally putting a female dress on him, but yet grants him the stage on which to display with ultimate impunity the repertory of his mimetic range.

The contradictions inherent in the mimetic process, as adumbrated by Agathon, between what you play and what you are, are tested again and again from within the play itself, as it uncovers the dissonances between the fictive theatrical device and the comic ground of "reality". Twice Mnesilochus is put up against a "true" effeminate, once with Agathon and once with Cleisthenes, as if to pose a theatrical distance between one actor in women's clothes and another, and let us not forget that the women of the Thesmophoria are, of course, played by men. Mnesilochus himself, in the instability of his dual roles, in his male discomfort with his female role, is best suited to reflect ironically upon his position during the course of the play. Still disguised, he indignantly asks Cleisthenes, the "true" impersonator, "what man would be such a fool as to allow himself to be depilated?" (592–94). Yet when his first two theatrical parodies of Euripides fail, parodies in which he plays male roles in female costume (another inversion), he has a new and happy idea: "Why, I'll play Helen, the new version — I've got the female dress I need." (850–51). In the next stage, when the magistrate whom Cleisthenes has summoned comes and orders the poor Mnesilochus to be bound to the punishment plank for breaking the city's laws and invading the secret rites of women, he begs: "At least, undress me and bind me naked to the plank; I'm an old man, sir; please don't leave me dressed up in feminine fripperies! I don't want to give the crows a good laugh as well as a good dinner." (939–42). Now that the masculine world of authority has intruded into the play, Mnesilochus expresses well the full reversal from mastery to subjugation his position as a male has taken. When the magistrate reports the council's decree that it is precisely in woman's costume that he is to be bound to the plank in order to exhibit his villainy to all as an imposter, here is the point that he most fits the role of the pitiful Andromeda which he now will play. Yet at the same time he offers the last and best incongruity between himself, an old man, and his persona of the beautiful maiden.

III MIMESIS: PARODY

Parodic writing can be defined as triangular desire — the desire of a subject (parodist) only projected into a text (parodying) by the detour of another text (parodied).

Claude Leroy

Just as the comic actor's discrepancies between character and costume threaten his mimetic integrity, so does parody, in more complex and more extended fashion, address the critical questions of mimesis in the service of a fictive reality. The transvestite actor might succeed in concealing the tell-tale sign that marks him as an imitation with a difference, but parody, by its nature and its definition, is the literary device which openly declares its status as an imitation with a difference. In the rhetorical logic of the play, the exposure of the kinsman's intersexual game appropriately brings parody fully out of hiding to play its intertextual game with comedy and tragedy. Given the thematic logic of the play, the first defense of Euripides, misconducted by the kinsman in the comic mode, is properly transferred to the parodies of the plays that will eventually bring Euripides on stage to play the tragic roles he has composed. It is also consonant with the narrative logic of the plot that the kinsman have recourse to Euripidean parodies. For with the *peripeteia* in his comic situation, he is now truly imitating the typical Euripidean plot of danger-recognition-intrigue-rescue. The sequence of the four plays might read as a chronological survey of Euripidean drama —

the *Telephus* of 438, already parodied in Aristophanes' *Acharnians*(425), the *Palamedes* of 415, and the *Helen* and the *Andromeda*, both presented the year before in 412.

The parodies themselves then function as the new intrigues of the kinsman (and later of Euripides), invoked in suitable response to each new exigency of his plight. But these are also intrigues now carried out fully on the theatrical plane, whose comic success depends upon their ability as specimens of tragic art to deceive the comic audience within the play with their mimetic credibility. Read as successive intrusions into the text, the parodies function like metatheatrical variants of the series of different imposters who come to threaten the comic hero's imaginative world and which, like those figures, must be deflated and driven out. If we read the parodies as a sequence, however, we see that the kinsman most move further and further into the high art of mimesis with increasing complications and confusions as the comic spectators on stage, whom he would entice into performing in his plays, move further and further down the scale of comprehension, ending with the barbarian Scythian policeman, who speaks only a pidgin Greek. In the course of their development, the parodies play again with notions of gender and genre, with costume and character, with comic and tragic, and orchestrate a medley of variations on the theme of mimesis itself.

Some have judged these parodies as opportunistic displays of Aristophanic skill, which take over the play and resign the conflict of the women and Euripides to the sidelines. Others respond to the discontinuous leaps from one text to another as signs of the failure of Euripidean tragedy in each case to maintain the necessary mimetic illusion which would effect the rescue of the kinsman. And the success, in turn, of Euripides' last plot, a comic not a tragic strategy, only confirms the opinion that Aristophanic parody is remaining true to its usual vocation as aesthetic critique of another's work. Certainly, Euripides' scandalous novelties in the theater lend themselves as ideal targets for the satirist's broad brush. It is also true that, on the surface level, comedy seems to be indulging its license for dispensing with strict dramatic coherence. But such judgments overlook the fundamental ambiguities which arise from "the taking in and taking over"[16] of another's text to generate what has been called "a poetics of contradiction"[17] (at what price imitation?). And they do not perceive that comedy can deliberately call upon its looser forms of structure to work through paratactic arrangements which imply rather than state. In the artful composition of the second part of the play, the parodies, I suggest, serve double and discrepant purposes — as framed disruptions of its narrative continuity and as integral and integrating elements of the entire plot. The outer and inner surfaces of the texts play off each other, with and against each other, as sequence and/or juxtaposition. Furthermore, each parody has a double allegiance — the comic context in which it now is situated and the tragic context of the play from which it is drawn. Thus each parodic scene conveys multiple messages, including each time some reflection of its status as a theatrical artifact.

A. *Telephus*

In the *Telephus* of Euripides, Telephus, the Mysian king, who has been wounded by Achilles on a Greek expedition which went to Mysia instead of Troy, and advised by an oracle that only the one who wounded him could cure him, dresses as a beggar and comes to Agamemnon's court. In the safety of his disguise, he argues in his own defense, but fails to persuade all the Greeks. Then identified by Achilles, who makes a late entry upon the scene, he snatches up the baby Orestes and takes refuge at an altar, threatening to slay the infant if he does not attain his cure, and the play ultimately reaches a satisfactory conclusion.[18]

In the comic parody, the kinsman, once unmasked by Cleisthenes, who departs to fetch the magistrate and the policeman, snatches up the baby of a woman nearby and threatens it with Orestes' fate. The woman and the kinsman play the paratragic scene up to the hilt — with a difference. For the child is named as a daughter, not a son, and once undressed by the kinsman, turns out to be a wineskin, four or five pints old, conceived at the last Dionysiac festival, whom the "mother" will go to any lengths to save. And the kinsman, unlike Telephus, makes good his threat and slays the Dionysiac "child" with a sacrificial bowl to catch every last drop, accompanied by the mother's lament that she has lost her "*korē*" (maiden/maidenhead) (689–761).

The kinsman, we should remember, is playing a male role in female costume. Given the earlier coincidences of the comic scene between the kinsman and the women with the dramatic details of the *Telephus* (disguise, infiltration, speech of defense), we realize retrospectively that the kinsman has indeed been playing a specific male role in woman's garb from the beginning of the scene whose underlying plot the open parody has now at last explicitly exposed.[19] Now his identity has been revealed, the verbal insults with which he had assailed the women turn into an open masculine show of force against them, although this scene with its wine-happy women would seem to confirm everything he has already said about them in his earlier defense of Euripides. But it should also be noted that the exposure of the male is exactly matched by the exposure of the "female child", and the mimesis of the transvestite male is exactly symmetrical with the mimesis of the "transvestite female". The genders of the roles are reversed between the comic and tragic versions, but comic character and tragic role turn out to be fully consonant with each other.

B. The *Palamedes*

The *Palamedes*, which is set in the Greek camp at Troy, has as its plot the treachery of Odysseus against Palamedes, the wisest of the Greeks, the man who invented writing and many other skills beside. Odysseus, the wiliest of the Greeks, probably envious of the higher prestige of Palamedes, contrives the conviction of Palamedes on a charge of treason with fabricated evidence — a forged letter from King Priam and Trojan gold planted in his tent. In the trial which intervenes between the letter and the search for the gold, the innocent Palamedes gives a strong and eloquent defense of himself, the noble man unjustly accused, but he is condemned on the false evidence and put to death. In the aftermath, Oiax sends news of the death of his brother, Palamedes, to their father Nauplius in a novel way, and this is the scene which is parodied here. For the kinsman, in despair at the comic-tragic end of his tragic "Telephic" scheme, resolves in his isolation to send a message to Euripides, but how?

"I'll find a way from the *Palamedes*", he claims, and determines, like Oiax, to transmit word of his fate by writing his message on oars and casting them into the sea. No oars, of course, are to be found, but wooden votive tablets from the altar will do and he carves out the letters of Euripides' name to the accompaniment of a lyric apostrophe to his hands which are tracing the furrows of the letters with slow and painful toil (765–84). In rewriting this text in parodic form, the kinsman is playing the proper role from the proper play with the right gender, but still the wrong costume.[20]

C. *Parabasis*

This section of the play is closed by the *parabasis*, the formal convention of comedy, which allows the chorus to step forward and speak directly to the audience. In their tripartite appeal, they defend themselves against the slanders heaped upon women and prove their worth, this time in public and political terms. They speak first to the illogic of misogyny· (if we are such a bane, why lock us up and not let us out of your sight? If we are such an evil, why do those of you outside always try to get a peep at us? (785–99)) and move on to the verbal play with the semantics of male and female discourse (*Kanon/skiadeion*: 821–29). This last is an addendum to their version of the theme of mimesis which rules the play. In reduced and absurd form, they introduce the theory of imitation which Cratylus will make famous in Plato's dialogue, according to which names imitate the natures of those who bear them, are the true marks of their being. The women intend to meet the men on their own ground of war and politics and go one better: "No man can compete with Nausimache (battle at sea), Aristomache (best in battle), Stratonike (victory of the army), and Euboule (good counsel), or with Salabaccho", they add, forgetting etymology and tossing in the name of a famous courtesan. And, in pointed contrast to this comic literalism, they end with vaunting their role as mothers of useful citizens, officials and generals, mothers whom they reward at their own festivals by giving them the seats of honor, in contrast to the usurious mother of Hyperbolos, who is equally at fault with her two products — the interest (*tokos*) she begets and her son (*tokos*) (830–45).

I will return to this claim of theirs again, but would point out here that the *parabasis* serves as a specific closure to the theme of defense which has dominated the play from its beginning. It was extended, at length, of course, in the comic confrontation between the disguised kinsman and the women, with its latent parody of the *Telephus*, and continued in yet another key in the *Palamedes*. For while this last play is represented on stage in Oiax's ingenious graphic stratagem, its reference, I would suggest, also evokes the most famous and most dramatic aspect of the play — the trial and defense by Palamedes himself of his innocence — Palamedes, the wisest of men, the inventor of writing.

On the other hand, the women's defense of femininity opens up the play to its next developments. Here marks the turning point from male roles in the tragic theater to those of women — Helen and Andromeda, from the kinsman's solo performance to the duet with Euripides. Here marks too the shift, as I will argue, from a position of explicit to implicit defense now that the kinsman in the theatrical costume which he donned so long ago must fully enter into his female role to gain his rescue, must, in fact, "live through" the female experience.

D. *Helen*

The *Helen* holds the center of the play; it is carefully framed on one side by the *parabasis* and, on the other, by the brief removal of the transvestite imposter from the stage for the first time in the play, an event which leads the women to reinaugurate their festive dance and song. The parody of the *Helen* is the last direct appeal to the women of the Thesmophoria, for the *Andromeda*, the final parody scene in the series, is addressed now to a new audience — the barbarian Scythian archer.

The new Helen whom the kinsman will play refers not only to the recent production of the play the year before, but to the new representation of Helen in a new role as the chaste and virtuous wife. In this version (which has precedents in the mythological tradition), the true Helen never went to Troy, but was transported to Egypt, and an *eidolon*, a cloud-like imitation of herself was sent in her stead to Troy. She has remained for ten years in isolation, faithful to her husband and her ideas of purity, while the "phantom" Helen remained at the center of hostilities at Troy where Greeks and Trojans fought with each other and fell in battle — for her sake. In Euripides' play, the old king Proteus who had protected her has died, and his impious son Theoclymenus, equally smitten by her beauty, determined to impose a forcible marriage upon her. Theoclymenus has, in fact, vowed to slay all Greeks who come to his shores in order to keep Helen safe for himself.

Menelaus, now that the war is over, is returning home with his crew and with the phantom Helen he imagines is his real wife whom he has rescued from Troy. Storm and shipwreck drive him to Egypt where he confronts the "real" Helen. Once their complicated recognition is accomplished, the reunited couple plan their escape with a false story of Menelaus' death and a false promise by Helen to marry Theoclymenus if she can first perform funeral rites by the sea for her "dead" husband. The success of their fictions depends upon the cooperation of the prophetess Theonoe, the virgin sister of the king, whose purity of intellect and spirit stands in radical opposition to her violent brother. No synopsis can do justice to the brilliant energy of this romantic play which combines the themes of *eros* and *thanatos* with a philosophical testing of the categories of illusion and reality, of name (*onoma*) and fact (*pragma*), name (*onoma*) and body (*soma*), mind and body, truth and falsehood.[21] For our purposes, however, Aristophanes' parody is significant in two respects.

First, the audience in the comic parody is Critylla, the woman guarding Mnesilochus, whom they would convince with the dramatic fiction of their happy reunion as husband and wife so that Euripides can indeed rescue Mnesilochus from his/her plight. But Critylla doesn't know how to play, either as spectator or as Theonoe, the daughter of Proteus whose part the kinsman finally assigns to her ("By the gods, if I am not Critylla, the daughter of Antitheos from Gargettos and you are an evil wretch", 897–99). She knows where she is, not in Egypt, but in the Thesmophorion (877–80). This can't be the house of Proteus, for the man Proteus whom she knew has been dead for ten years (874–76; 881–84). As for the kinsman's insistence that his name is Helen, she rightly replies: "Have you become a woman again, before you have paid the penalty for that other "womanization" (*gynaikesis*) of yours?" (863–64). And when the kinsman claims to Euripides/Menelaus that he is being forced into a marriage with Proteus' son, she scolds the kinsman for deceiving the poor stranger with this and other lies (890–94).[22]

To Critylla, whose comic realism insists on literal readings, there is no Helen, only the scoundrel kinsman, and the stranger who has entered the scene is the innocent outsider whom she must enlighten until she recognizes their Egyptian intrigue for what it is and identifies the stranger/Menelaus as a co-conspirator, who must be driven off. Only once does she a make a concession to the theatrical mimesis — a wrong one. For correcting the kinsman's tale of forced marriage, she replies that he has come in truth to steal the women's gold (893–94) — clearly, a conflation of the comic situation at the Thesmophoria and the parody of the *Palamedes* which has just been played.

On the level of the comic plot, the parody of the *Helen* functions explicitly as the kinsman's lure to bring Euripides on stage to save him (846–51), and all its effects seem to be directed to this pragmatic end. But in this brief and absurd scene, all the issues which characterized the novelty of the original play are present, but wonderfully deflected through the comic travesty as a dissonance between the two levels of reference — the comic fiction of the play and the paratragic rendition. In the counterpoint of the text which sets the recognition scene from the *Helen* against Critylla's misrecognition of the identity of the parody, the questions of illusion and reality, of truth and falsehood, of mimesis and deception, are reframed in metatheatrical terms.

In this new key, the problem of the name as a guide to identity is transposed exactly in reverse to its Euripidean model. For in the *Helen*, the epistemological confusion lies in the possibility that the same name may be distributed to more than one (e.g., two Helens), but in the parody, the theatrical confusion lies in the refusal to allow the same character/actor to bear more than one name, to say nothing of more than one gender. The costume can never conceal what the naked truth has exposed and serves here as the focal point at which to test the mimetic premises of the theater in general, and the premises of this romantic play, in particular. The *eidolon* of Helen, not seen and not mentioned in the parody, nevertheless, as the personification of illusion itself, hovers over the scene.[23]

In the split perspective in which the incongruities of the comic and tragic fictions are made most evident, the failure of the tragic parody to persuade lies as much with the comic spectator, who entertains no illusions, as it does with those characters who are trying to create them. And in the relation of the parody to its larger comic matrix, we can note another set of reversals which come to play through the silent juxtaposition of different texts, reversals which are both thematic and theatrical. We may remember that the original basis of the women's complaint was the hyperrealism of Euripidean drama, its failure to create the proper distance between fiction and life. Now we see the opposite — a play, whose plot places it directly in the mode of the fabulous, the magical, and the exotic — in short, a mimesis in the service of the theater itself. And instead of the "bad" women whom Euripides has shamelessly put upon the stage, he has shown us a woman, who, against all odds (and credence), has never betrayed her husband, but has waited for him with true and faithful trust. When the women asked the kinsmen earlier why Euripides had never put any Penelopes upon the stage, he replied that Penelopes were nowhere to be found any more (547–50). Yet here he stages the myth of another Penelope, like her, besieged with importunate suitor(s). Best of all, Helen is not Penelope, but in the normative tradition, her exact opposite, the woman who ran off with another man, the woman whose beauty caused the Trojan war. Helen, in fact, is the "baddest" of women, who through the poet's art, is recreated as the best of them.

By reversing the myth of Helen, Euripides has indeed reversed the terms, and in playing the part of Menelaus, he has turned from the maligner of women to their potential redeemer, a role which he will play once again, in even better form, as Perseus to the kinsman's Andromeda.

E. Andromeda

The *Helen* and the *Andromeda* are doublets of each other, both presented by Euripides at the City Dionysia in the preceding year. Both imagine similar situations — an exotic locale (Egypt/Ethiopia), a woman in captivity and in danger, a dramatic rescue. But in the *Andromeda*, the situation is more extreme. Andromeda is immobilized, bound to a rock. She does not have to outwit a lustful suitor, but can only await death from a monster of the deep. No reunions or recognitions for her, but rather a handsome stranger, Perseus, who, flying by with the Gorgon's head tucked in his pouch, falls in love with her — irrevocably — at first sight. This play, unfortunately lost to us except for fragments, was famous in antiquity for the seductiveness of its erotic fantasy.[24] In the *Frogs*, Dionysus, who is in the Underworld to bring Euripides back to Athens, claims as the reason for his mission the sudden desire (*pothos*), the overwhelming passion (*himeros*) which struck at his heart while he was reading the *Andromeda*, a passion not for a woman but for a clever (*dexios*) poet, Euripides (51–56, 59). Euripides' Helen, rehabilitated and "revirginized", stands as the middle term between the whores that were his Phaedras and his Sthenoboias, and this purest of all pure virgins, Andromeda. If the *Thesmophoriazousae*, in a sense, traces out the career of Euripides as it moves from one extreme to another, from hyperrealism to seductive fantasy, the woman in her two faces — carnal sexuality and romantic eroticism — serves not only as the subject, but also as the essential metaphor for the art of mimesis as it is represented in two modes.

The parody of the *Andromeda* is addressed to two different audiences and provokes two different reactions. On the theatrical level, the *Andromeda* is not a critical success. The policeman spectator, far from being enraptured by its performance, can hardly understand a word of what's going on, and therefore unwittingly and fittingly plays the role of the sea monster. But the parody might well have been a thematic success with the women. The ensuing choral song that begins with the invocation to the virgin unyoked maiden Pallas Athena of the city and ends with the two goddesses of the Thesmophoria (1136–59), might only refer to the chorus' joy at the triumph of the policeman over the violator of their ritual, and this is a point to which I will return. But it cannot be a coincidence that immediately after, Euripides offers terms of peace to the women: "Never again will I slander women, this I promise" (1160–64), and adds: "If I can take away this kinsman of mine who is bound to the plank, never again will I speak ill of you. If you don't give in, I'll reveal everything you do at home to your husbands when they come back from the army" (1166–69). The women accept the offer, but the male world has taken matters out of their hands; Euripides must persuade the barbarian too (1170–71).

The appearance of the Scythian policeman who ties the kinsman to the punishment plank sets the stage for the performance of the *Andromeda*, but, at the same time, his entry creates the maximum distance between the romantic nature of the play itself and the one who is meant to fall under its spell. For the Scythian policeman belongs fully to the conventions of the comic theater, as do all barbarians and others whose outlandish language, gestures, and costumes offer, it would seem, a dependable source of laughter. The first scene of the *Telephus*, played between the kinsman and the mother of the "child", was played "straight", according to paratragic rules, which encourage comic characters in dire comic circumstances to resort to mock-tragic expressions of their plight. In the *Helen*, the comic already intrudes more directly in the intervention of Critylla, but in the *Andromeda* the parody takes on a double focus by playing both to the tragic and the comic: it exploits the props and scenery for its tragic setting and the intrinsic comic properties of the Scythian archer.

"Double exposure" rules this last and grandest finale and the perplexities of gender and genre reach their furthest extremes. Once Euripides, flying by on the machine, has given him the cue, the kinsman plays two roles (himself and Andromeda) and in two modes (as solo and duet), both with increasing skill and independence. His opening monody of lament is a wonderful mixture of the details of his own comic situation with those tragic ones of Andromeda, and now he shifts from one voice to the other, now he merges them together (1015–55). Euripides himself plays two roles, one, female — Echo, and one, male — Perseus. What is more, as Echo, Euripides plays a double role, first tormenting the kinsman with his abusive repetitions and then the Scythian policeman.

Echo itself is the doubling of another's voice; it is also the purest representation of mimesis itself as the imitation of another's words. Retrospectively, the two preceding parodies each bear this metatheatrical charge — the *Palamedes*, in the art of writing which imitates speech; the *Helen*, in its intimations of the *eidolon* which imitates the human form, and now Echo as the mimesis of the voice. And let us now also include the *parabasis* with its names whose etymologies mimetically represent the inner quality of the women who bear them.

What distinguishes Echo from the others is its paradoxical status as both nature and artifice. As the one example of a mimesis in nature itself, the mimetic reproduction of echo itself on the stage translates the imitation of nature into an artificial theatrical effect. In turning his parodic skills on Echo, Aristophanes has, in fact, singled out the most radical innovation in Euripidean art. By giving it a run in all its possibilities, he succeeds in exposing it as the highest example of conscious mimetic illusion. But it is also significant for the theme of mimesis in general that Echo, its mythic figuration, is not an "it", but a "she". She is the voice that imitates in both her myths, one that relates her to Narcissus (Ovid, *Met*.3. 356–401) and the other to Pan (e.g., Longus, 3.23). Euripides, the male, must dress as a female in order to imitate Echo who herself is the principle of imitation. Echo as the embodiment (more properly, disembodiment) of mimesis is also the focal point for the concept of the feminine which can never be grasped as primary and original, but only as the one who is imitated or the one who imitates and yet as such, is therefore also empowered as the mistress of imitation.

I will want to return to this connection between the feminine and mimesis later (in part VI). Here it is important to note that the exposure of Echo as played by Euripides who brings her out from behind the scenes, turns the tragic to comic, or better, mixes the tragic with the comic. Echo, in fact, might stand as the mediating figure between tragedy and comedy, divided between them and yet bringing the genres together, as the artful device of the original model and the slapstick cliché of the comic theater. If this is no longer a true contest between the women and Euripides, it is now fully a contest between the comic poet and his rival whom the comic poet imitates.[25] Imitation retains to the end its ambiguous status, its "poetics of contradiction". For in his last theatrical act, Euripides turns finally and fully to the comic stage. Dressed as an old procuress, he offers the Scythian policeman a dancing girl to distract him while he hustles the kinsman and himself off stage.

The play began with a tragic poet in drag and ends the same way, or does it? Is Euripides brought down to the comic level, his affinity for comedy revealed at last? Or is Euripides, with this plot — the expert ending to a comic play — led to imitate his imitator, but, by that imitation, allowed to take over the comic stage? This is a comedy, after all, and comedy ends with signs of unimpeded libido, most typically with a lusty man and a dancing girl. But on the grounds of the comic plot, the end, abbreviated as it is, means that the play of "women on top" has brought the female back to her normal place.

Yet the motif of "women on top" has not altogether disappeared; it is distilled and defused in the name Euripides adopts for his role as the old procuress — Artemisia, the Carian queen, who "manned" a ship during the Persian Wars and put up a brilliant fight, to the Greeks' undying shame, as they note again and again, that they had to do battle with a woman who was an equal of a man. In his accommodation to a comic ending, one that brings about his own salvation and that of the kinsman, Euripides has reverted back to the purely sexual mode. Already the barbarian has dispelled the erotic enchantment of the *Andromeda* with his crude and obscene interruptions, and Euripides meets him on his own terms. But he has kept his promise to the women — displacing as far as possible from the world of the married women of the Thesmophoria the open sexuality which the comic world demands as its program. Yet the Thesmophoria too is a festival, a sacred event, and it too has as its program a renewal of fertility. Thus, when the play draws to a close, comedy, tragedy, and festival have all converged together for a common purpose.

Euripides, by his cunning inventions and his myriad schemes for salvation, has rescued the kinsman and has redeemed himself of his impiety, more directly, I will argue, than we have recognized. For Euripides, despite his innovations on this stage and on his own, has not invented everything himself. He has perhaps reinvented, realigned his plots with more traditional paradigms. There are two "secrets" which lie at the heart of the text, secrets which integrate the ritual and aesthetic elements of the play, and which explain still more cogently, I will suggest, the women's willingness to accept Euripides' tender of peace. If, at one level, the parodies display their status as "mere" fiction which pretends to represent "reality" and to cause an effect in the real world, on another level, these fictions are essential to the mystifying properties of myth and poetry which are necessary for the revitalization of the ritual world and for the effect of the comic and tragic alike. The sottish Scythian policeman mistakes the name of the Gorgon which Perseus/Euripides carries, as that of Gorgias, the fifth century Sophist, for whom the power of tragedy resides precisely in its deception (DK fr. 23):[26] "Tragedy deceives by myths and the display of various passions; and whereas the tragic poet who deceives is juster than he who does not, the deceived is also the wiser than the one who is not deceived".

IV MIMESIS: FESTIVAL — DIONYSUS/DEMETER

It is not the earth that imitates the woman in the matter of conception and birth, but it is the woman who imitates the earth.

Plato

Myth is speech stolen and restored. Only, speech which is restored is no longer quite that which was stolen; when it was brought back, it was not put exactly in its place . . .

Roland Barthes

The *Thesmophoriazousae*, organized as a dialogue between comedy and tragedy, draws attention to and explores the inconstant relations between the realities of everyday life and the fictive arrangements of the theater. But there is a third term to be considered — that of the cultic dimension, which is integrated into the play as its scene and its context, but yet stands outside the fictional structures by its marked form as ritual.

At one level, the ritual center of the play serves as the intermediate and mediating borderland between the events of everyday life and those of the theater. The ritual space of the Thesmophorion, as suggested earlier, is analogous to the domestic space of the women at home so that the kinsman's intrusion into their ritual enclosure replicates the impious intrusion of Euripides' theater into that forbidden female domain.[27]

But on another level, the literal fact of that ritual identity invites us to reverse these terms to consider the import of the underlying mythos of the Thesmophoria and its dialectical relation with that other mythos which always and everywhere presides over the theater. More generally still, the focus on cult reminds us that the theater, after all, is an imitation with a difference of mythic and ritual forms. These provide the latent structuring patterns over which and with which drama plays out its variations and deviations in new and different keys.

Rereading the play in cultic terms brings to center stage a dialogue between Demeter and Dionysus, each representing a mode which defines the feminine and each furnishing a mythic mode which can be related to both genres of comedy and tragedy. The ritual space sacred to women invokes Dionysiac as well as Demetrian associations. Its trespass by men therefore also recalls the founding plot of the theater itself, best known from Euripides' late play, the *Bacchae*. The Dionysiac has a tragic and comic side: tragic, as the serious consequences of violating ritual taboos, when the male, who comes to spy on women's secrets, arouses their Bacchant madness and suffers *sparagmos* at their hands. The other, the comic side, has, as its carnivalesque license, even duty, to refuse all taboos. It therefore delights in sacrilege and in violating ritual solemnity and thus deflects a potential Dionysiac tragedy into comic farce.

On social grounds, the occasion of the Thesmophoria legitimates the women's intrusion into public space. But in ritual terms, the festival is, in a sense, an intrusion on to the comic stage, for this is its most solemn day, the Nesteia, when the women abstain from food in imitation of Demeter's mourning for her lost daughter. The Thesmophoria then answers to the role of anti-festival, as Lent is opposed to Carnival, for fast rules instead of feast and chastity replaces sexual indulgence. The women's intention which generates the comic plot

is then entirely consonant with the spirit of this ritual day — the trial
and punishment of one who has inappropriately exposed their sexual selves in a serious art form. The kinsman, therefore, performs
a double function: as the representative of Euripides, he goes to defend tragic art, but as the comic character, he rightly disrupts the
solemn proceedings by the terms of his defense — the further exposure of women's sexual secrets. This ambiguity also means that
the women must, in turn, play a double role, as followers of Demeter
and as Bacchants of Dionysus.

Theater encompasses both modes of drama and both modes of
cult. It can use one to test the other, as it already does in the prologue
scene with Agathon. For Agathon is more than tragic poet. His
mimetic theory which attributes his transvestite dress both to art
(mimesis) and to nature (effeminacy) is itself a mixture of manner
and modes. His ritual entrance, which sacralizes the calling of his
art by its invocations and prayers, also offers in advance a private
version of the Thesmophoria.[28] Yet his costume evokes from the
kinsman a quotation from Aeschylus' *Edonians* that describes
Dionysus himself, which suggests that this man-woman (*gynnis*) is
indeed the god of the theater (or a mimesis of him, which, according
to Agathon's theories, amounts to the same thing).

In the dramatic plot, Agathon refuses to infiltrate the Thesmophoria because he would play his part too well. In the Dionysiac
scenario, he refuses to go, for as the sacral figure in transvestite garb,
he stands outside the action as the spirit of theater itself. The one
who "plays at playing and visibly reduplicates the act of acting"[29]
has the power instead to transform others — to provide them with
their costumes and their roles for the play that is about to begin.

The robing of the kinsman on stage with articles from Agathon's
wardrobe functions within the mythic plot exactly like the robing of
Pentheus in the *Bacchae* — for precisely the same purpose — the infiltration of women's mysteries — and with precisely the same attitude — misogyny. What the kinsman, in fact, brings out of hiding, once his own
identity has been exposed, is the Dionysiac which lurks beneath the
Demetrian façade of the women — the wineskin that masquerades
as a baby and which was "conceived" at the last Dionysia, the baby
whose "mother", Mika, calls upon another woman, Mania (Mad-

ness) for help (728, 739).

By slaying the wineskin, the kinsman indeed turns tragedy into farce, but he also puts an end, so to speak, to the Bacchic plot. The situation now no longer conforms to the Dionysiac pattern in which the women would themselves overpower the male and do him violence. Instead, he becomes again the violator of women and, given the nature of his act, he makes the transition to the Demetrian plot.[30] While the abduction of the baby follows the plot of the *Telephus* where the king, disguised as a beggar, takes Orestes hostage among the men at Agamemnon's court, we note that the scene fits, but the genders are reversed. The "baby" whom the kinsman abducts from the women and consigns to "death" is a "female" baby, whose abduction and violation have deprived the "mother" both of her *Korē* (virginity) and her *Korē* (daughter) (760–61). These acts, I suggest, reactivate the scenario of the Thesmophoria which begins with the abduction of the maiden Korē-Persephone that takes her down to the Underworld. The Nesteia is located temporally at the midpoint of the Thesmophoria and at the midpoint of the myth, in the liminal time after the loss of Korē and before her salvation and return. Now that the kinsman himself will require rescue and salvation, he begins to reenact stages of Euripides' rescue dramas which can and should be correlated with the ruling mythos of salvation in the story of Persephone. In broadest terms, the mythos of Dionysus gives the pattern for transgression, but the Demetrian the pattern for redemption, both linked, of course, in their own way, to the larger theme of liberation.

The Dionysiac impulse is synchronic, divided in the same action between tragic and comic moods, like Dionysus Lysios himself, who destroys or redeems. But the Demetrian mode is diachronic: its scenario always passes through the spectrum from tragedy to comedy, from death, captivity, and mourning to return, recovery, and joy. The Demetrian plot exemplifies, in fact, the salvational motif, not only for the Themophoria in its invocation of fertility but, above all, in the Eleusinian mysteries. In this play, the Thesmophoria provides the ritual background for Euripides' rescue dramas, but in the *Frogs*, where Dionysus descends into Hades to rescue the poet who will save the city, his quest is properly accompanied by the songs of mystic initiates from Eleusis. The Demetrian plot mixing with the Dionysiac can bring together the genres of tragedy and comedy and can join the comic theater in a mutual celebration.

Once the kinsman is made captive, the parodies seem to meet with failure in their immediate reception. But, at the same time, they are increasingly invested with the unspoken power of mimesis, which "insists on the reality of the moment, even while practicing its own form of 'deceit' ".[31] This mimesis exposes theater as "mere" illusion, but reinstates it under the name of a higher mimesis. The kinsman thus moves *down* the scale of male potency to his last humiliating role as a woman. But the theatrical experience itself moves *upward* through the mythic plot as it converts the male who has abducted the Korē into the Korē herself whose story promises that she will be redeemed.

In this double perspective, the parodies stand out in high relief against the choral background of ritual songs, a contrast which places ritual and theater at opposite ends of the spectrum. In one sense, the increasing validation of the festival mood (which combines the fast with celebration), can be correlated with the deteriorating situation of the male intruder — first, after his temporary removal from the stage by the policeman, and then after the parody of the *Andromeda* scene which leaves the Scythian still in charge of his captive. But a closer look at the content of these songs shows a subtle series of responses on the part of the chorus to the underlying mythic tenor of the parody scenes.

The *Helen* scene, framed in its context, as already observed, by the *parabasis* on one side and the choral song on the other, is the focal point for this conversion both of the kinsman and the chorus. The last part of the *parabasis* which extols for the first time, although in comic terms, their roles as worthy mothers in the city rather than errant wives, introduces this turning from their Dionysiac to their Demetrian personae. The *Helen* scene, itself, with its conversion of Helen from the adulterous wife into the faithful spouse, in larger terms, from the whore to the virgin, is followed by a choral dance which turns around in a circle and then around again (*kuklos, tropos, ana-strepho, torneuo*, etc. in 959–1000). For the first time, the motif of legitimate marriage connected with Hera Teleia appears in their song (973–76), as if in response to the evocation of marriage in the parody of the *Helen*. In this festive mood, the chorus proclaims the sanctity of their rites at which it would now be inappropriate to slander men (962–64), and they offer a long invocation to the gods — to the Olympians, to Artemis, Apollo, Hera, Pan, and the Nymphs — inviting them all to dance. Now the chorus includes Dionysus himself in his idyllic setting on the mountain as he sports in lovely song and dance among his nymphs (987–1000).

That the *Helen* earns this response is consonant with Euripides' general treatment of Helen, but the connection with his play is still more intrinsic. For in the drama itself, the motif of Persephone is evoked over and over again and shapes the mythic frame of the play.[32] Helen, in fact, several times even likens herself to Persephone (E. *Hel.* 175, 244 ff.). Egypt is envisioned as the underworld, the place that threatens death to Greek sailors who touch upon its shores, while the lustful king who keeps Helen captive in anticipation of a forced marriage easily fills the role of Hades. At the critical moment of the play, when Helen and Menelaus have devised their rescue plot, the chorus sings an elaborate ode to the Great Mother, as she turns from grief at the loss of her daughter to laughter and joy through the consolation of dance and song (E. *Hel.* 1301–68). In the mythic plot, the laughter of Demeter marks the restoration of the mourning mother to life, laughter that echoes in this choral song of the *Thesmophoriazousae* (979).

But only the pure virgin Andromeda can properly evoke at last the theme of the maiden. The chorus first calls upon the city's Pallas Athena, the "unyoked virgin maiden" (*parthenon azuga kourēn*, 1139) to bring the peace that loves festivals (*phileorton*, 1147). In the previous chorus, Hera Teleia was invoked as she who holds the keys of marriage (976); now the virgin Athena is summoned as the holder of power, the keeper of the keys of the city (1141–42).[33] And appropriately in this choral song that now addresses only female deities, the women end by inviting the two goddesses to come with kindness to these sacred rites, forbidden for men to see, so that with their torches they might make manifest an immortal vision (*ambroton opsin* 1136–59). The women themselves whom "Andromeda" now addresses as her maiden chorus (1015) are virgins again, and "An-

dromeda" herself, repeatedly called *korē* and *parthenos*, laments the
fate that binds her to death instead of her marriage couch (1034–36;
cf. 1122).

In the division of the actors' roles between the kinsman and
Euripides, the kinsman stands in for the poet and speaks in his name.
But Mnesilochus assumes the transgressive role in both Dionysiac
and Demetrian plots until he takes on the opposite role of the maiden
who needs to be saved. Euripides himself, however, is reserved for
the role of potential rescuer, introduced on stage to bring liberation
to the Dionysiac figure of comedy and salvation to the "Korē"
heroine of his plays. At the comic end, Euripides assumes at last the
female role himself, and with it finally the role of redeemer. This time
he is the old woman who brings relief with laughter, thereby bringing Demeter and Dionysus together in incongruous harmony.

But this harmony is not, in fact, incongruous. The Nesteia, the
day of the fast at which the women imitated the mourning of Demeter, ended with *aischrologia*, obscene ritual banter, in commemoration
of the woman, Iambe, who met Demeter at the crossroads and with
her scurrilous jokes made Demeter laugh and so turned the world
around. Thus in the Thesmophoric ritual, *aischrologia* has its place
as it does in the cult of Dionysus, elsewhere and in the comic theater.[34] The *Andromeda* parody, played out as a mixture of erotic lyrical
pathos and obscene sexual jests, belongs then as much to the cult
of Demeter as it does to that of Dionysus. Within this ritual frame,
Euripides at last redeems himself — now of the *two* charges which
the women had earlier brought against him — his slander of femininity (which has been discussed in detail) and his general impiety
in creating characters who claimed that the gods do not exist (450–
51). (See note 27.)

V MIMESIS: ART AND THE LITERARY TRADITION

My language is the universal whore whom I have to make into a virgin.

Karl Kraus

The *Helen* is the ritual "secret" within the text; the *Helen* is also the
stage for the discovery of another "secret", one that belongs to the

domain of art and literary tradition. The kinsman's impersonation of the "new" Helen, I have suggested, introduces a new role for women in Euripides' plays which serves implicitly to counteract the charges of slander which the women of the Thesmophoria have brought against the poet. A new positive version of the feminine is offered in place of the old, and its representation forecasts the renunciation Euripides is to make of his earlier errant ways. In this respect, the *Helen* functions within the thematic terms of the play as Euripides' *palinode*, the song that reverses its former position, the song that "takes everything back" (palin-ode). More precisely still, that reversal is located within the *Helen* itself, since the play offers a revised version of the traditional Helen. In this, Euripides is not the inventor of the "new" plot of the *Helen*, but follows another earlier poet of the sixth century, Stesichorus, who was the first to compose a palinode. The subject of Stesichorus' palinode was, in fact, Helen herself and it introduced the original motif of the *eidolon*. The story goes that Stesichorus, having slandered Helen, was blinded for his blasphemy. But being a wise poet, he recognized the cause of his blindness and composed another song which began: "That story was not true; you did not go within the well-oared ships, nor did you come to the walls of Troy", and as a result he regained his sight (Plato, *Phaedrus* 243b).

The story has been interpreted as a reflection on the double and contradictory role of Helen — as goddess, daughter of Zeus, and as woman, the adulterous wife of Menelaus. The case of Stesichorus has been referred to the violation of the cultic norms of Sparta where Helen was indeed worshipped in a cult role as a goddess. The palinode, in its creation of the *eidolon*, therefore unequivocally confirmed her divine status. Generally, in the mythic tradition, the *eidolon*, the cloud-image, is appropriately the creation of Zeus, the cloud-gatherer, most often used as a substitute for a goddess whom a mortal man has attempted to ravish, as in the myth of Ixion who grasped at Hera, but found Nephele (cloud) instead.[35]

The *Thesmophorizousae*, in terms of its development, suggests a model of the female who veers between the profane ("bad woman") and the sacred ("pure virgin"), but Stesichorus' diptych of ode and palinode seems to propose a more radical division between the two categories of the female, separated by the fine but firm line which divides mortal and immortal. But if we look back at Stesichorus now in the light of the *Thesmophoriazousae*, the question of the two Helens might be posed differently. The fault for Stesichorus may not lie with the received mythos of Helen itself (i.e., that Helen went to Troy), but in its mode of poetic representation which violated Helen by violating the norms of poetic decorum.

Having revealed too much of the mortal Helen, i.e., her sexuality,[36] Stesichorus turns in repentance to the other extreme — untainted erotic beauty, which is preserved through the figure of the pure Helen who never went to Troy and her imitation, who played her traditional part. With his palinode, Stesichorus now avoids altogether the problem of the woman as morally "good" (respectable) or "bad" (shameless), but rather raises another question with regard to the feminine. This new eros that Helen incarnates divides itself from within to establish another set of opposites — the false illusory *eidolon* and the true figure of the divine — opposites which, however, are now both equally unattainable. One is a false imitation of the other, which itself (as divine) can never be grasped by mortals in a "real" state, but only in the empty form which is inevitably substituted for the original. Helen, as the darling of Aphrodite in any form and for all time, embodies in herself the irresistible principle of the erotic, perpetually desirable and desired by all. But Stesichorus' story also suggests that eros is not divided from poetics. The poet slandered Helen and to atone, he fabricated a fictive *eidolon* in her place and openly declared the original version as a fiction (*ouk etumos*). Helen, whose "true" (i.e., traditional mythos) may be denied as a fiction, therefore may also personify poetics even as she embodies eros. For as fictive *eidolon*, Stesichorus' Helen acquires the capacity to impersonate herself and to draw attention to the notion of imitation as a conscious poetic creation.

Stesichorus uses Helen, as it were, to assert his role as a poet. Working within a received tradition which he alters in two different ways (the "blasphemy" in the first version and the recantation in the second), he raises the notion of fictionality as a possible attribute of mythic texts in order to account for his own innovations, and in the process, he invents a new generic form — the palinode. In the process, he inaugurates a new tradition, establishes a new paradigm upon which Aristophanes can draw in the construction of his own piece by which the Helen of Euripides can serve to exonerate the poet from the charge of blaspheming against women. And this paradigm, reproduced in the Euripidean play itself, can serve at the same time to raise these questions of fictionality and imitation. Others have noted that Euripides' play itself shows a consciousness of its status as a piece of the theater, that Helen and Menelaus, when they contrive their fictions for escape, also strive *not* to imitate the clichés of other tragic plots. In satirizing Euripides' theatrical innovations in the *Helen* and in presenting a parody with metatheatrical dimensions, Aristophanes reaffirms, as it were, through the tradition that goes back to Stesichorus, the perennial utility of Helen as the figure upon whom can be focused the poetic problems of imitation itself.

One might call Stesichorus' *eidolon* a proto-theatrical and proto-mimetic representation insofar as the poet precedes the fifth-century developments of the theater and of theories of mimesis. Yet although Stesichorus invented the *eidolon* of Helen, he is not the first to associate Helen with questions of imitation. A longer tradition stands behind her that begins with her first appearance in Greek epic which is worth exploring briefly here in order to understand better the paradigmatic value of Helen for the particular aesthetic problems which are posed in the time of Aristophanes and Euripides. This exploration will serve in turn to shift the discussion now to my final area of concern, that is, the categories of Greek thought which associate the feminine with mimesis, whether figural or poetic.

VI MIMESIS: EROS AND ART

In dreams, a writing tablet signifies a woman, since it receives the imprint of all kinds of letters.

Artemidorus, Oneirocritica.

Already in the *Iliad*, Helen, as the erotic center of the poem, is connected with the art of poetry when she weaves a tapestry of double fold, depicting on it "many contests of horse-taming Trojans and

bronze-mailed Achaeans, which they suffered on account of her" (*Il.*
3. 125–28), as if she was "weaving the very fabric of heroic epic".[37]
Better still, in the fourth book of the *Odyssey*, when Telemachus visits
Sparta and finds Helen and Menelaus reunited as a married pair,
they each tell a tale of Helen and Odysseus from the days when she
was still at Troy. In her story, Odysseus, disguised as a beggar,
comes secretly into the city as a spy. She alone recognizes him and
does not betray him, but cares for him and rejoices that her homecoming will soon be at hand (*Od.* 4. 240–64). Menelaus, on the other
hand, tells another story of Helen, one that puts her in a very different light: on the night in which the Trojan horse stood within the
gates of the city, Helen, now the wife of Deiphobus, the brother of
Paris, came down, and by imitating all the different voices of their
wives, tempted the Greeks who were hidden inside to betray their
presence, a ruse which would have succeeded had it not been for
Odysseus' discerning prudence (*Od.* 4. 266–89). Two stories are juxtaposed, each the same characterization of Odysseus, but each a different version of Helen. She is the mistress of many voices, the mistress of mimesis, linked in both stories to secrecy, disguise, and deception.[38]
 Even more, Helen is the mistress of ceremonies, who stages the
mood and setting of the tales, when to counteract the grief which
their sad memories of Odysseus had stirred up, she casts a drug into
their wine, a *pharmakon* (from Egypt) which takes away pain and
brings forgetfulness of sorrows. And she bids them to delight themselves with stories (*mythoi*), which she herself will begin, narrating
a plausible (appropriate) tale (*Od.* 4. 220–39). These *pharmaka* belong to the poetics of enchantment, which seduce the hearer with
tales of deception, tales of impersonation in costume and speech,
which summon up the best memories of Odysseus for an evening's
recollection. As tales of Helen, they are told without comment, as
tales from a past that seems to have been forgiven, transmuted into
a play of symmetrical reversals that charm instead of dismay.[39]
 Yet the ordering of the two stories also makes clear that the second
story, as a story of Helen, is indeed an implicit comment on the first
story, a second version, which like a proto-palinode (but in reverse)
revises the first. Menelaus' tale operates on two levels: on the first,

it undermines the fidelity of Helen's earlier version, a version which represents her fidelity to the Greeks, in favor of a version which shows she can imitate many different voices, each time with the intention to seduce and betray. On the second level, within this setting ruled by the enchantment of the *pharmakon*, the story functions as a self-reflective comment on the nature of fiction and mimesis which Helen embodies. Menelaus' story thus intimates the status of Helen's earlier story as fiction and suggests in the process that Helen and story telling might be one and the same thing — the imitation of many voices in the service of seduction and enchantment. Helen is the figure, who by her imitation of the different voices of different men's wives, links *eros* and poetics together under the rubric of mimesis. This mimesis, it is worth noting, is appropriately divined as a fiction from within this story of Menelaus by the master story teller himself, Odysseus — the man of many turns.

Menelaus' story can only hint at the difference between fiction and truth. But another story is more precise in this regard, the one which Menelaus recalls the next day, that of his experience with Proteus, the old man of the sea, after he left Troy and came with Helen to Egypt. Proteus is the master of lies and truth; better still, he is the figure of the shifting nature of truth, which Menelaus can grasp as one and true, only if he grasps Proteus himself, who will change his shape from one creature to another, until, under Menelaus' unremitting grip, he will return to his single original form. Menelaus' success depends upon the advice of a female, Proteus' daughter, and note how she fulfills her feminine role. She betrays the existence of Proteus, the secrets of his powers, and the means of overcoming him — a mimetic disguise and a secret ambush (*Od.* 4. 351–570). The story of mimesis practiced by Helen can never escape the ambiguities of its telling, but the mimetic repertory of Proteus has a limit which will result in the revelation of an absolute truth. Here that truth is the future of Menelaus — his homecoming and his ultimate fate — not death, but eternal sojourn in the Elysian Fields, the paradisiac islands to the West, "because Helen is yours and you are son-in-law therefore to Zeus" (4. 561–70). Helen in the end rules both tales of mimesis — as divinity, connected through her genealogy to truth (and immortality), beyond the reaches of fiction (or perhaps the supreme fiction) and earlier, as mortal, skilled in the arts of mimesis and seduction.

For the *Odyssey*, this ultimate "truth", whether the translation of Menelaus to the permanence of the Elysian Fields, or the "truth" of the recognition between Odysseus and Penelope, grounded on the fact that Penelope has truly been "true" to him, suggests the alternatives to the ambiguities of poetics and erotics which the two stories of Helen and Menelaus propose. In the light of this reunion on Ithaca, these ambiguities are not only recollections of a past which belong to Helen and Menelaus, but potential forecasts for Penelope. This future depends upon Penelope's choice of one of the two possible roles which the two stories offer her — that of the faithful woman who receives the beggar in disguise and welcomes him, or that of the woman who, surrounded by men (read suitors for Greeks), practices the wiles of seduction, although another man's wife. Penelope is no teller of stories; quite the contrary. She is worn out with hearing the false tales of Odysseus which travellers have brought to her over the years and with meeting the false imposters of Odysseus himself. She has become skilled at testing the fictions of another's words which have no power to seduce her with a false truth. Yet she is the mistress of one fiction — and that to preserve her "true" self for Odysseus — one "story" which she tells again and again and never finishes, weaving and unweaving the fabric of Laertes' shroud, until Helen's story of herself, not that of Menelaus, becomes her very own.

The *Odyssey*, by virtue of its Penelope, can afford its Circes, Calypsos, Sirens, and Helens, whom Odysseus encounters in various ways. But the *Odyssey*, as the repertory of all stories, all fictions, adumbrates, even in the ambiguities of Odysseus himself, the ambivalence which Greek thought will manifest with increasing articulation towards the mimetic powers of the verbal and visual arts to persuade with the truths of their fictions. This ambivalence is not incongruent, at some level, with the increasing ambivalence with which the city's male ideology views its other gender, an attitude which serves to connect the feminine still more closely with art and artifice.[40] Thus the two Helens, the daughter of Zeus and the fictive *eidolon*, might exemplify in the erotic sphere the hesitation in the aesthetic domain between an art that is divinely inspired and a craft that makes counterfeits of the real.[41] But while the *eidolon* can be separated from the real Helen as an insubstantial likeness of herself, as no more than a figment of the imagination, the *eidolon* as a seductive *objet d'art* cannot be separated from the generic image of the feminine. For the "real" woman could be defined as a "real" *eidolon*, created as such from the beginning in the person of the first woman, Pandora.

Instead of the ambiguity maintained in the dual genealogy of Helen as mortal and divine, Pandora is from the outset, in Hesiod's text of the *Theogony*, a fictive object, a copy, not an original. Fashioned at the orders of Zeus as punishment for Prometheus' deceptive theft of celestial fire for men, the female is the first imitation and the counterpart to the first deception. She is endowed by the gods with the divine traits of beauty and adornment which conceal the bestial and thievish nature of her interior. Artefact and artifice herself, Pandora installs the woman as *eidolon* in the frame of human culture, equipped by her "unnatural" nature to seduce and enchant, to delight and deceive. More specifically, as has been argued, the origin of Pandora coincides in the text with the origin of language:

Because of her symbolic function and, literally, because of her ornaments and flowers, her glamor and her scheming mind, Pandora emblematizes the beginning of rhetoric; but at the same time she also stands for the rhetoric of the beginning. For she is both the 'figure' of the origin and the origin of the 'figure' — the first being invested with symbolic, referential elements. The text implies both the human dawn unmarked by imitation and rhetoric and a turning point that initiates the beautiful, imitative rhetorical process. In this way, the text reproduces the split between a language identical to reality and a language imitative of reality.[42]

This reading of Pandora is suggested by the implicit terms of the text, for rhetoric in Hesiod's time (c. 700 B.C.) has not yet been invented. But his negative view of Pandora, which arises naturally from his peasant's instrumental view of nature and culture, can still serve as a preview of the later philosophical thought which, in testing the world of physical appearances, finds it deceptive precisely in the spheres of physical eros and of artistic mimesis, and very specifically in the art of rhetoric itself.

It should therefore not surprise us that Gorgias, the historical figure most closely identified with the development of rhetorical theory in fifth-century Athens, should, in fact, have composed an encomium on Helen which is as much a defense of his art of the *logos* as it is a defense of Helen. I invoke this last example to return, after this long detour, to the text and context of Aristophanes, since Gorgias is very much present, I suspect, in the *Thesmophoriazousae*, and not only as the possible garbled reference to him by the barbarian policeman who confuses Gorgon with Gorgias. For the *Palamedes* and the *Helen*, while they serve, of course, as parodies of Euripides' plays, are also titles of the two specimens of Gorgias' epideictic oratory in which the rhetorician himself speaks for Helen and Palamedes speaks in his own defense. More broadly, Gorgias' theories owe much to the theater — to the psychological effects which it produces in the spectators and in the aesthetic effects which it employs.

Gorgias, having accepted the premise that the phenomenal world cannot be grasped as real, is free to embrace the shifting world of appearances, of *doxa* (opinion), in its deceptions and its fictions, and hence is also in a position to embrace Helen. The mastery of that world can only come about through the installation of the *logos* as its master, which, through the techniques of persuasion, manipulates the sense impressions and emotions of its auditors. For Plato, who is to stand directly on the other side of the divide, Gorgias (as the other sophists) will, like a painter, "make imitations which have the same names as the real things and which can deceive . . . at a distance". The sophists, who practice not the plastic arts, but those of the *logos*, can exhibit "spoken images (*eidola*) of all things, so as to make it seem that they are true and that the speaker is the wisest of all men in all things." (Pl. *Sophist* 234b–c).

For Gorgias, the *logos* is real, akin to a physical substance and possessing the magico-medical quality of the *pharmakon*. Hence its power (*dynamis*), like that "of the incantation, mingles together with the *doxa* (opinion) of the *psyche* and charms it and persuades it and changes it by enchantment". The force of persuasion, when added to the *psyche*, can make an impression, can stamp (*typos*) the *psyche* which responds, in turn, to its manipulation with the appropriate emotions. Persuasion of the *logos* affects the *psyche* of the one who hears; similarly, sight (*opsis*) affects the *psyche* of the one who sees, "stamping (*typos*) it with its sensations of objects", "engraving in the mind the images of the things one sees", if fearful causing fear, if beautiful, bringing pleasure, "like the sculpting of statues and production of images which afford the eyes divine delight; thus some things naturally please or pain the sight, and many things produce in many men love and desire for many actions or bodies".[43]

Gorgias' defense of Helen reverses the image of the seductive and deceptive woman by portraying a Helen overmastered by irresistible forces whether by the gods, by physical violence, by the persuasion of the *logos*, or by the power of *eros*. It is here that *opsis* (sight) enters into the discourse in order to propose a theory of *eros* and Gorgias can therefore query: "If Helen's eye was so entranced by Alexander's (Paris') body, and she delivered up her soul to an eager contest of love, what is so strange in that?" Since the entire discourse is a *logos* which is meant to persuade, the demonstration within the piece of the persuasive power of the *logos* gives the *logos* the dominant position in the piece. As the *megas dynastes*, the *logos* even proves to overmaster the other categories whose indisputable claims to power it appropriates for itself.

Stesichorus' and Euripides' excuse of the *eidolon* has, of course, no place in Gorgias' argument. But the aesthetics of the image remain, now interiorized within the body as the *psyche* which *logos* or *opsis* molds, as an artist shapes and molds his product. The *psyche*, in turn, responds to the physical body whose visual impressions it receives as a spectator who gazes upon an object of art. By treating the *psyche* as a corporeal entity and in endowing *opsis* and *logos* with physical properties, Gorgias introduces a set of tactile relations that somatizes psychology as it psychologizes aesthetics. *Opsis* is already invoked in the cause of *eros*, but *logos* behaves like *eros*, which takes possession of another's body to penetrate its interior and to work its effects. The relation between rhetor and auditor, therefore, is not unlike that between a man and a woman, even as the writing tablet, as Artemidorus tells us, signifies a woman to the dreamer, "since it receives the imprints (*typoi*) of all kinds of letters." (*Oneirocritica* 2. 45). Thus if Helen is the subject of the discourse, she is also the object within it. She is the auditor, who, seduced and persuaded by the deceptive rhetoric of Paris, is re-seduced (and therefore exonerated) by the rhetoric of Gorgias who claims as the *truth* of his discourse the demonstration of the power of rhetoric to *seduce* and *deceive*. For the outside auditor, the artful beauty of the text, with its persuasive *logos* about persuasion, operates as the rhetorical equivalent of the godlike beauty of Helen, which Gorgias mentions at the beginning of the text, to describe its irresistible erotic effect upon the suitors who came to her from all parts of Greece.

Moreover, the seduction of this *logos* works a double pleasure of the text — for the auditors it masters within and without the discourse — and for Gorgias himself, which he acknowledges when he concludes: "This speech is a plaything (*paignion*) for me, but an encomium for Helen", who, in his terms, is worthy not only of defense but also of praise. This ending explains perhaps best of all the choice of Helen for his discourse, beyond that of an unpopular case which he wishes to win by his rhetorical skill. Helen, as the paradigm of the feminine, is the ideal subject/object of the discourse; first, in sexual terms, as the passive partner to be mastered by masculine rhetorical persuasion, and second, in aesthetic terms. Helen, as the mistress of mimesis and the object of mimesis, is a fitting participant in the world of make-believe, the anti-world which reverses the terms in mimetic display and reserves the right under the name of play to take everything back. Seduction, like rhetoric, is a game, a *paignion*, and both *eros* and *logos* are now invested with a new power that is precisely the power of play, a delight in the aesthetic capacity to seduce and deceive. This point of view, I would submit, must inevitably invoke and rehabilitate the feminine whom Greek thought represents as the subject/object of eros (nature) and artifice (culture). In her corporeal essence, she functions both as the psychological subject and as the aesthetic object, and the artist needs her to substantiate his own conception of his art.

Thus for both Gorgias and Euripides, the woman has a place, a place that the end of the fifth century makes for her more and more to Aristophanes' comic chagrin: and this, from two points of view First, in the domain of art itself which is discovering a sense of its capacities for mimesis as an explicit category of the fictive, of the make-believe. This discovery takes place in the various verbal arts which, in turn, are influenced by the earlier advances in illusionist painting. In this development which includes the other plastic arts, theater too played no small role, as Aristophanes' play itself attests. Second, in the social world, as the war dragged on to its unhappy close, attention began to shift away from masculine values of politics to the private sphere — to the domestic milieu at home, to the internal workings of the psyche, and to a new validation of eros, all of which the feminine as a cultural category best exemplifies. This new focus will receive further emphasis in the next century with the emergence in sculpture of the female nude as an art form and in the literary genres of New Comedy, mime, romance, and pastoral. It is worth remarking here that Old Comedy comes to an end with Aristophanes whose last productions already make the transition to Middle Comedy, while Euripides, who scandalized his Athenian audiences again and again, winning only four first prizes in his lifetime, will become the theatrical favorite of the next era and thereafter.

In this "feminization" of Greek cultuure, Euripides was, above all, a pioneer, and so Aristophanes perhaps correctly perceived that Euripides' place was indeed with the women (as that of Socrates in the *Clouds* was with the men). In a second *Thesmophoriazousae*, which is lost to us except for a few fragments and testimonia, the same cast of characters (more or less) seem to have been involved (Agathon, Euripides, Mnesilochus). This time, our information (from an ancient life of Euripides, which seems to refer to this piece) states explicitly that the women because of the censures he passed on them in his plays, attacked him at the Thesmophoria with murderous intent; but they spared him, first because of the (his) Muses, and next, on his undertaking never to abuse them again. These Muses are perhaps still to be found in the play we have, hidden behind the noisy laughter of Aristophanic parody.

Notes

1. For this term, see Natalie Davis' "Women on Top" in *Society and Culture in Early Modern France* (Stanford 1975) 124–51. More generally, I am indebted to the members of the Aristophanes seminar at Princeton University, Spring 1980, who contributed more to this essay than I can acknowledge here.

2. Excellent work is now being produced on the *Lysistrata* and the *Ecclesiazousae*. See the studies of Michèle Rosellini, Suzanne Saïd, and

Danièle Auger in *Les Cahiers de Fontenay* (*Aristophane: Les femmes et la cité*) 17 (December 1979): 11–32, 33–70, 71–102, respectively. See also Nicole Loraux, "L'Acropole comique" in *Les enfants d'Athéna. Idées athéniennes sur la citoyenneté et la division des sexes*, in press (Paris 1981), and Helene Foley, "The Female Intruder Reconsidered: Women in Aristophanes' *Lysistrata* and *Ecclesiazousae*", forthcoming in *Classical Philology* (1982). For a historian's view, see E. Lévy, "Les femmes chez Aristophane", *Ktema* 1 (1976) 99–112.

3. For example, Rosemary Harriott, *Poetry and Criticism Before Plato* (London 1969) devotes half a page to one passage from the *Thesmophoriazousae* and Bruno Snell makes no mention of the play at all in his chapter, "Aristophanes and Aesthetic Criticism", in *The Discovery of the Mind: The Greek Origins of European Thought*, tr. T. Rosenmeyer (Cambridge, Mass. 1953), 113–35.

4. There is virtually no extended treatment of this play as a play. Cedric Whitman comes the closest with half a chapter in *Aristophanes and the Comic Hero* (Cambridge, Mass. 1964) 216–27, which generally takes a negative view of the play: "the parody here is without venom, and the plot, or fantasy, is without reference to very much beyond its own inconsequential proposition . . . The art of tragedy is shown to be on the wane, but any deeper implications that might have been involved in that fact are saved for the *Frogs*." 217. For him the play has "little of the theme of fertility or life", 216, and, continuing in this vein, he says: "Somehow . . . femininity, whether real or assumed, is under a somewhat morbid cloud; by contrast, there is something genuinely refreshing about the masculinity of Mnesilochus, however coarse, and of the Scythian archer, whose main male attribute plays an unblushing role in the solution of the play." 224. Hardy Hansen, "Aristophanes' *Thesmophoriazousae*: Theme, Structure, and Production", *Philologus* 120 (1976) 165–85, follows Whitman's interpretation, but pays attention to matters of theatrical presentation. He is the only critic, as far as I know, who sees the importance of the Thesmophoria as a setting in the play, but, unfortunately, does not seem aware of the structures and functions of ancient cult.

5. On paratragodia, see R. Rau, *Paratragodia. Untersuchung einer kömischen Form des Aristophanes* (Munich 1967) with appropriate bibliography. For other forms of parody, see, W. Horn, *Gebet und Gebetsparodie in den Komödien des Aristophane* (Nurnberg 1970), and A.M. Komornicka, "Quelques remarques sur la parodie dans les comédies d'Aristophane", *Quaderni Urbinati di Cultura Classica* 3 (1967) 51–74.

6. The parabasis is a peculiar and distinctive feature of Old Comedy, a section of about 100 lines (when complete), in which the chorus can break the dramatic illusion and address the audience directly on topical matters of the day. In the *Thesmophoriazousae*, the parabasis is actually integrated into the action insofar as the chorus remains the women at the festival and responds to the themes of the play. The parabasis will be discussed in more detail below. For a brief summary of the complex formal structure of the parabasis, see K.J. Dover, *Aristophanic Comedy* (Berkeley and Los Angeles 1972) 49–53.

7. All line numbers of the *Thesmophoriazousae* will be cited from the Budé text, *Aristophane*, vol. 4, ed. Victor Coulon (Paris 1954).

8. Cf. the interchange between Aeschylus and Euripides in the *Frogs*, where

Aeschylus reproaches the other for having put on stage Phaedras and Sthenoboias who behaved like whores (*pornai*, 1043). "And how did my Sthenoboias harm the city?" inquires Euripides. "By persuading noble wives of noble men to drink hemlock because they were so ashamed by your Bellerophons", replies Aeschylus. "But", asks Euripides, "didn't I tell a true story about Phaedra?" "Yes, indeed, but the poet must conceal what is wicked and not introduce or teach/produce (*didaskein*) such things . . . but only the good" (1049–56).

9.   On connections of the comic plot with Euripidean patterns, see C. Russo, *Aristofane, autore di teatro* (Florence 1962), 297, Rau, *Paratragodia*, 50, and "Das Tragödienspiel in den 'Thesmophoriazusen' " in *Aristophanes und die alte Komödie, Wege der Forschung*, vol. 265, ed. H.-J. Newiger (Darmstadt 1975) 349. On the importance of the motif of salvation in Euripidean drama, see Antonio Garzya, *Pensiero e tecnical drammatica in Euripide: Saggio sul motivo della salvazione* (Naples 1962).

10.   See Russo, 297.

11.   For a discussion of mimesis in antiquity with bibliography, see G. Sörböm, *Mimesis and Art* (Uppsala 1966). See also J.-P. Vernant, "Image et apparence dans la théorie platonicienne de la *mimésis*", *Journal de Psychologie* 2 (1975) 133–60. (= *Religions, histoires, raisons*, "Naissances d'images", 105–37, Paris 1979.) For useful surveys of aesthetic theory and criticism before Plato, see Herriott and also T.B.L. Webster, "Greek Theories of Art and Literature Down to 400 B.C.", *Classical Quarterly* 33 (1939) 166–79.

12.   Critics miss the point of this confusion, especially R. Cantarella, "Agatone e il prologo della 'Tesmoforiazuse' ", in *Komoidotragemata* (Amsterdam 1967) 7–15, who is most often cited on this prologue, and who imagines that since Agathon is effeminate, he is somehow no longer a male.

It should be noted that poets, beginning with Thespis, did, in fact, act in their own plays in the earlier years of the Greek theater before acting became a more professional specialty. Aeschylus most probably did so and Sophocles also in the beginning of his career. See Sir Arthur Pickard-Cambridge, *The Dramatic Festivals of Athens*, 2d ed., rev. J. Gould and D.M. Lewis (Oxford 1968) 93–94.

13.   "Feminine power is by nature abnormal . . . but this abnormality can take two forms which are rigorously opposed to each other and involve either a *virilization of women*, if women are adapting themselves to the nature of power, or, on the contrary, a *feminization of power*, if the women adapt power to their own nature and put the domestic domain over the political one." Saïd, 36.

14.   We may remember that obscene, *ob-scaenum*, in its usual etymology, means "off stage", i.e., off the "serious" stage.

15.   See now the excellent distinctions made by Sandra M. Gilbert, "Costumes of the Mind: Transvestism as Metaphor in Modern Literature", *Critical Inquiry* 7 (1980) 391–418.

16.   For this formulation I am indebted to Susan Stewart, *Nonsense: Aspects of Intertextuality in Folklore and Literature* (Baltimore and London 1979) 20. I have profited from her work more than I can indicate in this essay.

17.   I have borrowed this definition of parody from Margaret A. Rose, *Parody//*

Metafiction (London 1979) 185. In addition to Rose and Stewart, a very useful treatment of parody can be found in Claude Abastado, "Situation de la parodie", *Cahiers du 20ᵉ Siècle* 6 (1976) 9–37.

18.   The *Telephus* has not survived except in fragments. For an extensive treatment see E.W. Handley and J. Rea, *The Telephus of Euripides, Bulletin of the Institute of Classical Studies Supplement* no. 5 (London 1957) and see also T.B.L. Webster, *The Tragedies of Euripides* (London 1967) 43–48.

19.   On the *Telephus* in this play, see H.W. Miller, "Euripides' *Telephus* and the *Thesmophoriazousae* of Aristophanes", *Classical Philology* 43 (1948) 174–83 and Rau, *Paratragodia*, 42–50, and *Tragödienspiel*, 344–46.

20.   For a reconstruction and interpretation of the *Palamedes*, which, like the *Telephos*, is known to us from fragments and other testimonia, see now Ruth Scodel, *The Trojan Trilogy of Euripides, Hypomnemata* vol. 60 (Göttingen 1980). For the parodic treatment of Aristophanes, see Rau, *Paratragodia*, 51–53, and *Tragödienspiel*, 347–48.

21.   On Euripides' Helen, see the excellent articles of Friedrich Solmsen, "*Onoma* and *Pragma* in Euripides' *Helen*", *Classical Review* 48 (1934) 119–21, Ann Pippin (Burnett), "Euripides' *Helen*: A Comedy of Ideas", *Classical Philology* 55 (1960) 151–63, Günther Zuntz, "On Euripides' *Helena*: Theology and Irony", in *Euripide, Entretiens sur l'antiquité classique* 6 (Geneva 1960) 201-27, Richard Kannicht, Introduction to *Euripides, Helena* (Heidelberg 1969) 2 vols. (edition and commentary), Christian Wolff, "On Euripides' *Helen*", *Harvard Studies in Classical Philology* 77 (1973) 61–84, and Charles Segal, "The Two Worlds of Euripides' *Helen*", *Transactions of the American Philological Association* 102 (1971) 553–614.

22.   On the parody of the *Helen* in Aristophanes, see the technical analysis of Rau, *Paratragodia*, 53–65, and *Tragödienspiel*, 348–50. See also the useful discussion in Frances Muecke, "Playing with the Play: Theatrical Self-Consciousness in Aristophanes", *Antichthon* 11 (1977) 64–67.

23.   Rau assumes in both of his analyses that all these significant motifs have dropped out of the parody, and concludes that Aristophanes is just playing for laughs at the lowest level of humor.

24.   On Euripides' *Andromeda*, see Webster, 192–99, and the references in Rau, *Paratragodia*, 66, n. 111. For the parody itself, see Rau, *Paratragodia*, 66–89, and *Tragödienspiel*, 353–56. Rau sees this parody as redundant of the *Helen*, motivated solely by comic opportunism, not by dramaturgical need.

25.   This rivalry is, in fact, attested in ancient texts. A fragment of Aristophanes' older contemporary, Kratinos, reads: " 'And who are you?', some clever theater goer may ask: 'some subtle quibbler, an idea-chaser, a euripidaristophanizer?' " (K fr. 307) and the scholiast to Plato's *Apology*, who quotes these lines, observes: "Aristophanes was satirized for imitating Euripides through his mockery of him". That same scholiast continues with a quotation from Aristophanes himself: "I use his rounded elegance of style, but make the thoughts less vulgar than his" (K fr. 471/ schol. *Plat.* Clark. 330 Bekker).

26.   It should be mentioned that the reference to "Gorgo the scribe" may refer to another contemporary and not to the famous sophist, but Aristophanes

mentions Gorgias several times in his comedies and Plato's *Symposium*, 198c, contains a word play between Gorgias and Gorgon. See further B.B. Rogers, *The Thesmophoriazousae of Aristophanes* (London 1904) 119, commentary on 1. 1102.

27.   This link between invasion of domestic privacy and trespass against ritual piety can be supported from the text itself in still another way, so as to allow the women to make both charges when they complain of the negative effects which Euripides' plays have had upon their lives. Two women speak against Euripides, each with a different story. The first describes what has already been discussed in detail — suspicious husbands and curtailment of women's freedom. The second woman, however, asserts that she has lost her livelihood, that of selling garlands to the faithful, because Euripides has made characters who claim that gods do not exist (443–58).

28.   On this point, see H. Kleinknecht, *Die Gebetsparodie in der Antike* (Stuttgart and Berlin 1937) 101 and Horn, 101–02.

29.   Leo Salingar, *Shakespeare and the Traditions of Comedy* (Cambridge 1974) 94. Two new studies suggest that Dionysus himself in the *Bacchae* stages and directs the proceedings of the play from within, functioning both as a character within the drama and as the god of the theater. See Helene Foley, "The Masque of Dionysus", *Transactions of the American Philological Association* 110 (1980) 107–33, and Charles Segal, "Metatragedy: Art, Illusion, Imitation", forthcoming in *Dionysiac Poetics and the Bacchae* (Princeton 1982). The *Thesmophoriazousae* precedes the *Bacchae* by about seven years, a fact which provokes speculations as to the relationship of the tragedy to the comedy.

30.   This opposition between Dionysiac and Demetrian modes is not as stable as I suggest for the purposes of this analysis, since any situation which places women "on top", even for legitimate cultic purposes, invokes the anxiety that women will do violence to men in the Bacchant or the Amazonian way. Two historical anecdotes, in fact, tell such a tale of men who infiltrated the mysteries of the Thesmophoria, one in Cyrene and the other in Laconia. See further, M. Detienne, "Violentes 'eugénies', en pleines Thesmophories: des femmes couvertes de sang", in M. Detienne and J.-P. Vernant, eds., *La cuisine du sacrifice en pays grec* (Paris 1979) 183–214.

31.   Salingar, 104.

32.   For Helen as the Korē, see J.-P. Guépin, *The Ritual Paradox* (Amsterdam 1968) 120–22, 128–33, 137–42. The motif is also treated by Wolff and Segal.

33.   Strictly speaking, Pallas Athena has no place in the rites of the Thesmophoria, but it is entirely in keeping with the political orientation of Old Comedy that she have the pride of place as the virgin figure, par excellence, in the city. Similarly, the myth of the Thesmophoria involves a relationship between a mother and daughter (Demeter-Korē), but the women, in the parabasis, when they boast of their maternal function, refer to the hoplite sons they have borne for the city. I am indebted to Nicole Loraux for raising this issue.

34.   On the nature and types of *aischrologia*, see Hanns Fluck, *Skurrile Riten in griechischen Kulten* (Endingen 1931). For further discussion of the issue within the social and cultural parameters of women's lives, see my piece, "Cultic

Models of the Female: Rites of Dionysus and Demeter", forthcoming in *Arethusa*, Spring 1981.

35. On Stesichorus (and especially in relation to Euripides' *Helen*), see the discussion with bibliography in Kannicht, 26–41. Some recently discovered papyri suggest the possibility of a second palinode, but Kannicht persuasively argues for one.

36. We learn from ancient testimony that in Stesichorus' version, Tyndareus, the father of Helen and Clytemnestra, had forgotten to sacrifice to Aphrodite while giving worship to other gods. The goddess, angered by his neglect, predicted that his daughters would be twice-wedded (*digamoi*) and thrice-wedded (*trigamoi*), i.e. that they would experience an excess of Aphrodite to compensate for their father's underestimation of the goddess and her power. The slander of Helen, then, perhaps lay in the lubricious sexuality attributed to her, a trait which now belonged to her by "nature", as it were, rather than to the circumstantial facts of the myth itself. See further, Kannicht, 39–41.

Euripides himself may be said to have composed a "palinode" when he offered a second version of the *Hippolytus* in circumstances which resembled those of Stesichorus. The first *Hippolytus* (known to us from fragments and other evidence) caused a scandal in Athens because of its shameless Phaedra, to whom Aristophanes, in fact, refers in the *Thesmophoriazousae* and in the *Frogs* (see note 8). In response, Euripides revised his representation of Phaedra to that of a noble woman who struggles heroically to suppress the fatal passion with which Aphrodite has afflicted her.

Stesichorus' blindness may be a "sacralized" version of Euripides' violation of literary decorum. Blindness is a punishment for mortal men who mingle with goddesses or who view them naked at their bath, but blindness is also an attribute of poets and prophets.

37. L.L. Clader, *Helen: The Evolution from Divine to Heroic in Greek Epic Tradition* (Leiden 1976) 8.

38. Helen's skill may be compared with that of the Delian maidens whose extraordinary talents are related to us by the Homeric Hymn to Apollo: "And there is this great wonder besides — and its renown shall never perish — the girls of Delos, hand-maidens of the Farshooter (Apollo); for when they have praised Apollo first, and also Leto and Artemis . . . (i.e., sacred hymns), they sing a song calling to mind men and women who lived long ago (i.e., epic) and thus they charm the tribes of men. Also they can imitate the tongues of all humankind (*anthropoi*) and their chattering speech. Each one would say that he himself were uttering the sound, so well is the beautiful song fitted to them." (*HH Ap.* 156–64). The mythic Echo is relevant here, especially the version of her relationship to Pan (Longus 3. 23). See the interesting feminist discussion of Echo by Caren Greenberg, "Reading Reading: Echo's Abduction of Language", in S. McConnell-Ginet *et al.*, eds. *Women and Language in Culture and Society* (New York 1980) 300–09.

39. For two excellent but different treatments of these stories, see Roselyne Dupont-Roc and Alain Le Boulluec, "Le charme du récit", in *Ecriture et théorie poétiques* (Paris 1976) 30–39, and Ann L.T. Bergren, "Helen's 'Good Drug', *Odyssey* iv 1–305", *Contemporary Literary Hermeneutics and the Interpretation of*

Classical Texts, ed. Stephen Kresic (University of Ottawa Press 1981) 201–14.

40.   Space does not allow a more detailed discussion of the ambiguities of persuasion and the *logos* in connection with the feminine and with *eros*. See further, P.L. Entralgo, *The Therapy of the Word in Classical Antiquiry*, ed. and tr. L.J. Rather and J.M. Sharp (New Haven and London 1970) 51–69, M. Detienne, *Les maîtres de vérité dans la Grèce archaïque* (Paris 1973) 51–80, and L. Kahn, *Hermès ou les ambiguités de la communication* (Paris 1978) 119–64. For art and literature, see also J. Svenbro, *La parole et le marbre: aux origines de la poétique grecque* (Lund 1976), and Zoe Petre, "Une âge de la représentation — artifice et image dans la pensée grecque du VIe Av. N.E.", *Revue Roumaine d'Histoire* 2 (1979) 245–57.

4ì.   The more perjorative notion of art as a counterfeit imitation of the real owes more, of course, to Platonic aesthetic theories. Craft includes and even gives first priority to artisanal skill. But this is a category which is not without its ambiguities for Greek thought in which the artistic product is far more admired than the artist who produces it. Poetry claimed a higher status than representational art, but greater consciousness of the poet as *poiētēs* (maker) introduces comparisons with artisanal activity. The *Thesmophoriazousae* itself reproduces, in fact, the two opposing notions of poetic composition in its comic presentation of Agathon, where the sacred, as discussed above, is juxtaposed with technical terms drawn from the more homely métiers (52–57).

42.   P. Pucci, *Hesiod and the Language of Poetry* (Baltimore and London 1977) 100–01.

43.   Citations from Gorgias, *Encomium of Helen*, fr. 11 in Diels-Kranz, *Die Fragmente der Vorsokratiker*, vol. 2 (Dublin and Zurich 1966) 288–94. Relevant work on Gorgias includes M. Untersteiner, *The Sophists*, tr. K. Freeman (Oxford 1954) 101–201, T. Rosenmeyer, "Gorgias, Aeschylus, and *Apate* (Deceit)", *American Journal of Philology* 76 (1955) 225–60, Charles Segal, "Gorgias and the Psychology of the Logos", *Harvard Studies in Classical Philology* 66 (1962) 99–155, J. de Romilly, "Gorgias et le pouvoir de la poésie", *Journal of Hellenic Studies* 93 (1973) 155–62, and relevant sections in Entralgo and Detienne.

Could Greek women read and write?

SUSAN GUETTEL COLE

University of Illinois, Chicago Circle

THE GENERAL TOPIC of Greek literacy has often been considered during the last fifteen years, but little attention has been paid to a more specific topic, the literacy of Greek women.[1] Granted, there is not a great deal of evidence for female literacy in antiquity, but women appear among the earliest examples of readers of books on Athenian vases, fourth-century writers often discuss the topic of the education of women, and references to women who read and write often appear in later literature. The evidence for female literacy comes from a variety of sources. Because the evidence is random and haphazard, no single method of analysis could yield reliable statistical results and any conclusions must be offered with care. Generally speaking, however, it is clear that literacy is not universal in antiquity, that the level of literacy varies from place to place and from time to time, but that in all places women are less likely to be literate than men. For the purposes of this paper, I will be concerned with women who spoke Greek, and the nature of the evidence is such that the chronological and geographical limits will be broad: from the seventh century B.C. to the fourth century A.D. and from mainland Greece to the Black Sea, Asia Minor, and Egypt.

Literacy is understood as knowledge of the alphabet and the ability to write one's own name and to read simple formulaic expressions. The Greek word *grammatikos* ("literate") originally meant "knowing the alphabet," and it is significant that the word appears for the first time in Xenophon (*Mem.* 4.2.20), a writer

219

of the fourth century B.C. *Agrammatos* ("not knowing the alphabet," therefore "illiterate") also appears for the first time in the same passage. Distinctions between the literate and the illiterate, therefore, are not socially important before the late fifth or early fourth century B.C.[2]

There are problems with discussing literacy in antiquity. First, the sources for reading are not the same as the sources for writing. Reading and writing are separate skills, and ability in one does not automatically imply ability in the other. Second, the nature of ancient books and ancient writing materials was such that reading a long text was awkward, and writing a laborious and inconvenient task. Ancient books consisted of long rolled strips of papyrus. The roll was unrolled from the right and rolled up with the left hand as the reader progressed through the text. Papyrus was expensive. People inscribed casual messages on scraps of pottery. For temporary writing needs, waxed tablets served. Two pieces of wood, covered with wax on one side and attached together with a piece of leather, formed a double table or diptych. Writing was done with a stylus, a sharpened piece of wood, and could easily be erased. The act of writing itself, whether on pottery, a wax tablet, or with a brush on papyrus, was sufficiently awkward, difficult, and slow that messages were of necessity short. Third, as literature developed, the variety and volume of reading material changed and increased. In the fifth century B.C. the only extensive texts available were texts of poets and state inscriptions carved in stone. The limited amount of reading material at the time suggests that people would have had no need to develop methods of fast reading, and in fact, most reading was probably done aloud.[3] Fourth, it is rare to find references to illiterate people in literature. Harvey finds this fact significant and argues that illiteracy was therefore rare, at least at Athens.[4] The reverse is just as likely to be true. Illiteracy may have been so common as to go almost unmentioned. Literature is generally the product of the upper classes, and therefore the literate people about whom we hear in literature may be the exception and not the rule.

The earliest Athenian inscriptions, inscribed on pottery, date from the last quarter of the eighth century B.C. During the seventh and sixth centuries, writing was used for religious dedications,[5] personal messages (e.g., "Thamneus, put the saw under the threshold of the garden gate."[6]), to mark ownership, and to give compliments or to make insults. Women's names occur often among these early examples. Women are designated as making dedications,[7] as owners of vases,[8] as objects of affection,[9] and as objects of sexual insult.[10] It is important for our knowledge of Athenian social life that women's names appear among these early examples of Athenian writing, but it is impossible to determine, even in the case of owner's marks, whether the women themselves could actually write. Three other examples are suggestive, but inconclusive. One is a sherd from the Athenian agora, dating from the late eighth or early seventh century B.C.[11] The sherd is inscribed with a woman's name in the dative case. Lang has suggested that the sherd was a label for a package addressed to Menesthō, but it would have been the person who delivered the package, not Menesthō herself, who would have had to read the label. The other two examples, from the fifth century B.C., are compliments: "Ianthis (female) thinks that Lykomachos (male) is handsome." and "Alkaios (male) appears handsome, therefore, to Melis (female)."[12] These examples are variations of a typical formula. It was customary for people to write the name of a beloved on a vase with the phrase "So and so is beautiful,"[13] but customarily it is a male who writes the name of his beloved (either male or female). It is unusual to find women's affections expressed in this manner. While there is always the possibility that these pots were inscribed by third parties, it is not impossible that Ianthis and Melis themselves wrote the inscriptions. Whatever the case, both women are almost certainly prostitutes or *hetairai* because it was almost impossible for Athenian women of citizen class to become acquainted with men outside their immediate families.

Harvey assumes that because Athenian women did not participate in the political life of the city, they would have had little need for reading and writing,[14] but even at Athens, it is clear from the graffiti that the earliest uses of writing were not political. One should not assume that because women were excluded from politics, they had no need for writing. Conversely, one should not assume that men were literate simply because they were involved in politics. The institution of ostracism is a case in point.

Ostracism was introduced at Athens early in the fifth century B.C. for the purpose of annually expelling the most unpopular citizen from the city. In order to select a person for expulsion, each citizen voted by inscribing a name on a potsherd (*ostrakon*). Vanderpool, who has studied *ostraka* from the Athenian agora, assumes that the very existence of such a custom means that Athenian men of the fifth century were "largely literate."[15] His own evidence contradicts this hypothesis. Many of the early fifth century examples show that even those who could write did not write easily and that writing itself had not yet become standardized. The published *ostraka* show uncertainties about the direction of the lettering and awkward and uneven letters.[16] In addition, one hundred and ninety *ostraka*, inscribed with the name of Themistokles by only fourteen different hands were found in a well on the Akropolis.[17] It seems fair to assume that these were either prepared honestly for people who did not know how to write and wanted to vote for Themistokles, or that they were prepared dishonestly by Themistokles' enemies for men who not only did not know how to write, but also did not know how to read. Whichever is true, Themistokles' enemies, fourteen of whom could write very well indeed, had a cynical estimate of the reading and writing ability of at least some of the Athenian electorate.[18] Themistokles was often a candidate for ostracism (over one third of all known *ostraka* are inscribed with his name), and he was finally ostracized in 471 B.C. The *ostraka* from the well could have been inscribed any time during the previous twenty years. Clearly then, even in the early fifth century many Athenian men were illiterate.

Plutarch tells an anecdote about one such person, an Athenian peasant who wanted to vote against Aristides (ostracized in 482 B.C.), but who could not write Aristides' name (*Arist.* 7.5-6). Harvey thinks that the story indicates that only one Athenian was illiterate,[19] but the anecdote seems more likely to show that in the early Classical period, rural residents (Plutarch calls the man *agroikos*) were less likely to know how to write than those in the city.[20] By the end of the century, however, literary evidence indicates that literacy among Athenian men was becoming more common. Even Aristophanes' Sausage-seller knows his letters (*Eq.* 188-89), his Strepsiades can read his accounts (*Nub.* 18-20), and his Demosthenes can read an oracle (*Eq.* 118, 128-43).

The earliest evidence for the reading ability of Athenian women is from vase painting. Vases showing women holding or reading book rolls are among the earliest evidence for the reading of literary texts. All of the examples showing women, except for one white ground lekythos, are red-figured vases.[21] Of the thirty-two examples which definitely show women with book rolls, nineteen (dating from 450 to 360 B.C.) show women who can be identified as Muses,[22] and thirteen (dating from 460 to 390 B.C.) show women in domestic scenes.[23] Even if the scenes showing Muses are excluded, scenes showing ordinary women with book rolls are almost as common as scenes showing men and boys with book rolls. If the scenes showing Muses are included, then the total number of vases showing women with book rolls far exceeds the number of vases showing men with book rolls.

Some of the book rolls on the vases are inscribed with lines of poetry, and Immerwahr argues that the vase paintings not only constitute evidence for the literacy of contemporary Athenian women, but also show that these women may have had an interest in literature.[24] Although the vases may indicate that some women had an interest in poetry, it is well to exercise some caution when interpreting these scenes. The prevalence of a specific motif in art may be the result of a tendency towards idealization rather than a reflection of contemporary practice.[25] Also, the Muses are associated with oral poetry long before poetry appeared in written form. This practice may have set a precedent for the association of poetry in written form with the Muses, and the association of written poetry with women in general may have been a natural consequence. The book rolls on the vases are used not for solitary reading, but as aids to recitation. The typical scene shows one woman reading from a book roll either to a maid or to a group of women; sometimes one of the listeners holds a lyre. One of the

readers is actually identified as Sappho.[26] The vase on which
Sappho appears is certainly meant to commemorate a famous
poet and cannot be considered as representing a familiar or typical
domestic scene.

Many of the vases may represent idealized situations, but there
are seven vases which include household furniture, two of which
show children as well as women. Pomeroy has suggested that these
two details indicate domestic scenes depicting Athenian women
of citizen class.[27] These vases do seem to show the women's
quarters (gynaikōnitis) where women and young children spent
most of their time. One of the vases, where on one side a little
boy is being spanked with a sandal while on the other a group of
women listen to a recitation, seems to be intended to show a scene
from daily life rather than an idealized situation.[28] These domestic
scenes are of interest because they show that reading was a normal
activity for at least a limited number of Athenian women. It may
be of significance, however, that although writing materials are
often depicted hanging on the wall in scenes of the gynaikōnitis,[29]
the vases never show women in the actual act of writing.[30]

The evidence of Greek tragedy is inconclusive. Only one woman
in Greek tragedy knows how to write. Euripides' Phaidra can
write; her note is absolutely essential to the plot (Hipp. 856-81),
but his Iphigeneia must ask someone to write a letter for her (IT
582-87). Because Agamemnon writes two letters to Clytemnestra
in another play, it has been suggested that she can read.[31] However, she does not read on stage, and as a matter of fact the
messenger memorizes the second letter so that he can deliver it
orally (IA 115-23). Harvey argues that Sophocles' Deianeira cannot read,[32] but the tablet whose text confuses her records not
simple Greek prose, but an oracle (Trach. 155-63). Herakles left
with her a tablet on which he had noted down a prophecy given to
him at Dodona. Deianeira describes the tablet as παλαιὰν δέλτον
ἐγγεγραμμένην ξυνθήμαϑ᾽ ("an ancient tablet inscribed with signs")
and says that Herakles had to explain it to her. Herakles' tablet is
not the same sort of tablet as those actually found at Dodona.
These record inquiries, written in ordinary Greek prose, of people
who came to consult the oracle. Herakles' tablet records not his

request, but the oracle's response. The word ξύνθημα, which in later Greek means "code" or "cipher," refers to the enigmatic expressions of the oracle which Deianeira cannot understand, not to the words of a text which she cannot read.

It is perhaps ironic that there is no firm contemporary evidence that Aspasia, the most famous woman of fifth century Athens, knew how to read and write. She was the mistress of Perikles and was reputed to have been of great intellectual influence. Not an Athenian by birth, but from Miletos in Asia Minor, Aspasia had a reputation for being able to compose successful orations, and Plato, the earliest writer to mention her, makes her the author of a funeral oration in one of his dialogues (*Menex.* 235e-236c). As Socrates reports her technique, although the actual delivery of the speech was intended to be oral,[33] the method of composition implies the use of writing materials. He says that she composed the speech by making up some new material and incorporating with it some material from an earlier speech. Plato uses the word συγκολλᾶν ("to glue together") to describe Aspasia's weaving together of the separate passages. Κολλᾶν is the word commonly used to describe the gluing together of papyrus sheets to form or mend a book roll.[34] Plato's use of the term in this context may be metaphorical, but there is a possibility that he is referring to the process of gluing together separate pages of papyrus to make a continuous text. Unfortunately, he was writing at least two generations after Aspasia's death, and there is no way of knowing whether the technique refers to fifth- or fourth-century practice. The distinction between the two periods is important because there is no evidence for written speeches before the fourth century.[35] Unfortunately, Plato's description is not a reliable indication of Aspasia's own literacy.

Although in the fifth century a literate women must have been the exception and not the rule, it is fair to ask how any woman could have learned to read and write at this time. There is no evidence for regular instruction in reading and writing for girls in the Classical period. On the basis of the availability of written texts, both epigraphical and literary,[36] it seems likely that reading and writing must have been regularly taught, at least to boys, by the end of the fifth century, but apart from a vase showing boys being instructed in writing,[37] the only reference to schools where reading and writing were part of the curriculum refers to a place outside of Athens.[38] The earliest contemporary reference to the teaching of letters outside the home at Athens is found in Plato (*Prt.* 325e-326d)[39] and Demosthenes (18.258). Schools were not public; according to Xenophon (*Mem.* 2.2.6), parents sent their children to private tutors. The single piece of evidence for a girl going outside the home for instruction in writing during the Classical period is a vase which shows a girl carrying a writing tablet.[40] She is accompanied by another girl, probably a slave. The scene has been interpreted as showing a young girl on her way to school,[41] but the girl, who is as tall as her maid, is not young. The vase shows that a girl might be able to write, but it says nothing about schools for girls. Only families of exceptional means would have found it worthwhile to educate a daughter. From a remark in a speech by Lysias, it is clear that families spent money to provide maids as companions for their daughters, but the speaker makes a distinction between the *paidagōgos* who accompanies two boys to school and a maid (*therapaina*), who is strictly only a companion for their sister (32.28).[42]

If girls were not sent to school during the Classical period, any girl of citizen class who learned to read and write must have done so at home. There is no fifth-century evidence for the actual instruction of girls by their mothers. The only such evidence is much later: a Hellenistic terracotta statuette of a woman and little girl reading together from a book roll.[43]

Although there is no Classical evidence for girls learning reading and writing from their mothers, there are two pieces of information which indicate that some mothers are capable of such instruction. As chance would have it, the student in both examples is a boy. The first item is a vase which shows a woman looking at a book roll with a young boy facing her. Immerwahr has suggested that the boy is reciting and practicing before his mother or some other woman in the household.[44] The second item is an account by Herodotus. He relates that Skyles, a Skythian king, was enamored of Greek customs and Greek religion because he had learned the Greek language and letters (*grammata*) from his mother (4.78). Skyles was not Greek, but his mother was. She came from Istria, a Greek city on the western coast of the Black Sea. Istria had been settled in the seventh century by Greek colonists from Miletos and remain throughout antiquity an outpost of Greek culture in the north. Skyles' mother, only one of several wives of Skyles' father, may have been a Greek captive. Skyles' date is not known, but he must antedate Darius' expedition to Skythia, a fact which would place him in the sixth century B.C. This is earlier than the period under discussion, but the story does give a piece of cultural information not available elsewhere: the fact that Skyles learned the Greek language and alphabet from his mother. Whether the literacy of Skyles' mother is an invention of Herodotus himself is not necessarily an issue. An anecdote of this sort is more likely to reflect the culture of the author than the society of the subject. At least Herodotus, writing in the fifth century, does not find it unusual for a Greek woman to know the alphabet.

The education of women is a topic which is discussed several times during the fourth century, and opinion on the subject is divided. Plato advocates equal education for women in the *Republic*, and even after retracting some of his more radical ideas on other subjects, still speaks in the *Laws* of "educated women" (658d). Theophrastos, two generations later, says that instruction in letters is necessary for women, but he qualifies his statement by saying that instruction should be limited to those items which are necessary for running a household. He says that intensive study makes women "lazy, babbling, and meddlesome" (Stobaeus IV, 193, no. 31 Meineke). An unknown writer of New Comedy is far more spiteful. He says that teaching a woman letters does no good: "It's just like giving venom to a viper!"[45]

If more women were learning to read and write in the fourth century, their number was probably still small. The actual evidence is quite limited. Demosthenes says that the wife of Polyeuctes left written records when she died, but it is not clear whether she wrote them herself (41.9, 21). Pomeroy claims that Diodotos' wife, daughter of Diogeiton, is literate because when she argues for her children's inheritance before a group of male relatives, she seems to be acquainted with written documents (Lysias, 32.14-15).[46] Diodotos' wife mentions that she had in her possession a notebook (*biblion*) which her children had found, and she does seem to be well acquainted with the accounts and figures recorded there. Xenophon's Ischomachos prides himself on the fact that when he married his bride (when she was fourteen years old), she came to him in a state of almost total ignorance, but he does insist that she be able to catalogue the furniture and utensils in his house by writing down each item when distributing it to the servants (*Oec.* 7.5 and 9.10). One wonders about Aeschines' mother. Demosthenes accuses Aeschines of helping his mother conduct initiation ceremonies by reading the text to the initiates while she presided (18.259; 19.199). The accusation may not mean that Aeschines' mother cannot read, however, because she would be otherwise occupied with cult activities during the ceremony.

There is little evidence for the literacy of women outside of Athens during the Classical period. Although the reputation of the Spartans for literacy is not very high, Plato says that both Spartan men and Spartan women took pride in their education (*Prt.* 342d). Women's names appear on Spartan pottery before 500 B.C., and there are many dedications by Spartan women in the Hellenistic period,[47] but there is nothing to indicate that the letters which Plutarch says Spartan mothers wrote to their sons are anything but fictitious.[48] Herodotus does say that Gorgo, the wife of Leonidas, figured out how to read a secret message written under the wax layer on a waxed tablet (she suggested scraping off the wax), but he does not say that Gorgo could read the message herself (7.239).

There are several late traditions about women who become students of philosophers. For the fourth century there is Lastheneia of Mantinea and Axiothea of Phlius,[49] both of whom are said to have gone to Athens to attend lectures of Plato. Axiothea seems relevant because a late anecdote describes her as having become attracted to the philosophy of Plato when she read one of his works on politics. She is said to have left home and travelled to Athens, where, disguised as a man, she became a student of Plato. Pomeroy assumes that the story of Axiothea is true,[50] but although it is of interest to notice the report of a fourth-century woman who reads Plato in her spare time, there are several problems with this item. First, it is unlikely that texts of Plato's works actually circulated widely during his lifetime.[51] Second, the story is preserved only by Themistios, a very late author whose reliability for the fourth century B.C. is questionable; Riginos has shown that the anecdote was probably a late invention.[52]

There is also a tradition that women associated with the Pythagorean circle were literate. An anecdote about Pythagoras himself (who may have left no writings) describes how he tricked his followers into believing that he had not only gone to the underworld and returned safely, but knew what had happened at home in his absence. He is said to have gone down into an underground chamber in his home after requesting that his mother stay behind and take notes on all that transpired while he was gone.[53] The story is obviously an invention meant to discredit Pythagoras himself, and the detail which requires the literacy of his mother is therefore likely to be a reflection of the habits of a later period.[54] Several essays purportedly written by female followers of Pythagoras are included in the Hellenistic corpus of Pythagorean writings, but even though one of the writers is said to have been Pythagoras' own wife Theano, none of these essays is likely to antedate the third century B.C.[55] The topics of these essays are directed at a female audience,[56] a fact which in itself seems to indicate that women in the Pythagorean associations of the Hellenistic period could read. Nevertheless, the women's names used to identify the writers of the essays are almost certainly fictitious.

There is some limited archaeological evidence for the fourth and third centuries B.C. which indicates that some women had a use for reading and writing. In Hipponion, a Greek colony in southern Italy, an inscribed gold tablet was found in the grave of a woman.[57] The tablet, dated reliably to about 400 B.C., is addressed to the dead person, giving specific directions for reaching a privileged place in the underworld. The appearance of such tablets attaches a definite importance to the use of written texts in a religious context, but there is no way of knowing whether the woman herself would actually have been able to read such a text while alive.[58] A lead tablet from Dodona, dated to the fourth or third century B.C., seems a stronger piece of evidence. Nikokrateia asks the oracle to which of the gods she should sacrifice in order to be rid of her disease. Nikokrateia's tablet is a rare example of a question put to an oracle by a woman. Because the confidentiality of the oracle would require that the inquirers write their own requests, the tablet from Dodona is almost surely in Nikokrateia's own hand.[59] Another lead tablet, found in a grave near Athens and dated to the fourth century, carries a curse and includes the name of the woman who wrote the curse, Onesine. She is called *molybdokopos*, inscriber of lead tablets.[60]

The earliest clear evidence for the schooling of girls comes from the Hellenistic period, but even before that time certain exceptional women seem to have been literate. For instance, Alexander the Great wrote letters to his mother Olympias while on his eastern expedition.[61] It is difficult to imagine that Olympias, so famous for her intrigue in the Macedonian court, would not have been able to read them. Olympias was one of the wives of Philip II. Philip's mother Eurydikē is said to have made a dedication to the Muses with an epigram where she describes how she learned to read and write only after her children were born (Plut. *De lib. ed.* 14b-c). Plutarch thought that she did this to set a good example for her children.

The mother who takes an interest in her child's education at school makes her first appearance in Greek literature some time during the Hellenistic period. Herondas presents a sketch of a mother who is frustrated by her son's laziness when she tries to help him with his homework.[62] She marches him to school and demands that the teacher punish him. It is clear from her tirade to the teacher that the father of the child had the responsibility of helping the boy with his letters, but that the mother herself was knowledgeable enough to listen to his recitations. His grandmother, however, is held up as an example of a complete illiterate who knows no more than a slave. The mother obviously considers herself to be somewhere between the father and the grandmother as far as education is concerned, but from the discussion available, it seems that the father is the educational authority in the family. The mime of Herondas illustrates two things: the importance of education in a period of relative social mobility and the fact that women are not necessarily totally excluded from participation in the educational process. The mother in the story may never have been to school herself, but she knows enough to be able to judge her son's performance.

Subsidized education is introduced in many cities during the Hellenistic period, and it is clear from the epigraphical evidence that young girls as well as boys benefitted from these local schools. The evidence comes from Greek cities in the east where there were classes for girls. At Teos in the second century B.C. free boys and girls were taught together for the first three grades by *grammatodidaskaloi*.[63] At Teos girls apparently received instruction only at the elementary level and only in reading and writing, while boys went on to study music and to receive training as *ephēboi*.[64] At Pergamon girls received instruction and were awarded prizes in epic, elegiac, and lyric poetry, and in reading and penmanship (*kalligraphia*).[65] At Dorylaion in the Imperial period a woman is honored together with her husband for serving as *gymnasiarchos*; her husband filled the office of *gymnasiarchos* of the boys, both slave and free, while Antiochis herself served as *gymnasiarchos* of the women.[66] Female *gymnasiarchoi* are not unusual,[67] but literacy was not a requirement for serving in that office. The requirement was financial.[68] The important thing about Antiochis is not her title, but the women which she served; they must have been young women who attended classes at the' *gymnasion*.

Although girls appear as students in this period, it should be pointed out that the curriculum for girls, as far as can be ascertained from the available evidence, seems confined to reading, writing, and the study of poetry. Girls apparently did not commonly study rhetoric or mathematics. That young girls were taught to read and write is indicated by the many terracotta statues of girls who carry writing tablets or sit with diptychs or book rolls on their knees. Such statuettes are found in Greece, Asia Minor, and Egypt.[69] The gravestone of a young girl named Abeita shows her sitting on a chair and reading from a book roll. Her pet dog sits at her feet. Abeita was only nine years old when she died, but apparently she already knew how to read.[70] How unusual the schooling of young girls was in this period is not certain. Pomeroy argues that it was more general than the limited epigraphical evidence indicates,[71] but Plutarch, writing in the late first century A.D. about the education of children, definitely thinks only of the education of boys.[72] Another essay, attributed to Plutarch by Stobaeus, argues for the education of women.[73] Plutarch would hardly believe such an argument necessary if education for girls and women were common, but he may be arguing not for education in reading and writing at the elementary level, but for education in mathematics and philosophy on the higher level. Like Musonius Rufus, his Roman counterpart, Plutarch assumes that women are capable of studying philosophy. In a long essay of advice about marriage, he urges that husbands become tutors to their wives. Husbands must select texts on philosophy, geometry and astronomy so that their wives will avoid the ignorance and superstition commonly associated with women.[74] Plutarch specifically advises wives to read the writings of Timoxena to Aristylla, an essay discouraging vanity. He therefore believes that a literate and educated wife contributes to the happiness of marriage.

Phaidra may be the only woman who can write in Greek tragedy, but the literature of later periods is full of examples of women who read and write. Literary anecdotes must be used with caution, but the occasional representation of literate women in Greek literature of the Hellenistic and Roman periods seems to be a sign that reading and writing were becoming more common and that some women were assumed to have these skills. For instance, the inscribed apple used as a love gift appears first in Kallimachos. One of his poems tells the story of a young man who embarrassed a girl by sending her an apple inscribed with an offering of marriage. Kydippe, the girl, read the inscription and threw the apple away.[75] Writing is a necessary skill for two of Plutarch's heroines.

When the women of Elis are brutally imprisoned, the tyrant Aristotimos tries to force them to write letters to their husbands to trick them into withdrawing from battle (*De mul. virt.* 15). In another episode Polykrite of Miletos, captured by the Erythraians, saves her friends by sending to her brothers a note inscribed on a piece of lead and hidden in a cake (17). Both of these stories, although associated with historical events, are in themselves only legends meant to illustrate extraordinary heroism, but the fact that these women are assumed to be able to write indicates that literacy is not beyond the reach of Plutarch's female contemporaries. In the epistolographical exercises so popular in the second century A.D., letters supposedly written by women appear several times. Most of these fictitious letters, actually by Lucian, Philostratos, and Alciphron, are imagined to have been written by disgruntled wives, prostitutes, courtesans, or women in the throes of love affairs.[76] The letters themselves are not evidence for the literacy of women, but certain incidental details in the letters imply that writing and reading are not unusual skills for women at this time. One woman mentions that she read a letter,[77] another receives an inscribed apple,[78] and prostitutes in Athens are represented as reading and writing messages scribbled on a cemetery wall.[79] Lucian, however, describes a conversation which provides a rare glimpse of the tacit acceptance of illiteracy. A woman who receives a note from her lover must ask a girl friend to read it to her. She says, "Take it and read it, for you, at least, know your letters."[80]

The general increase in educational opportunity for both men and women in the Hellenistic and Roman periods should not cloud the fact that a good part of the population still remains illiterate. The only place where there is enough evidence to form judgments about the illiteracy of the general population is Egypt. Among the papyri preserved in Egypt are thousands of documents and personal letters written by and for the people who lived there. Legal documents are usually written out by professional scribes, but the partners to a legal transaction must sign the document themselves, or, if illiterate, have someone else sign for them. If illiterate, they are called in the papyri "unlettered" (ἀγράμματα).[81] Those who are able to do little more than sign their names are described as "writing slowly" (βραδέως γράφοντες).[82] Because women in Graeco-Roman Egypt could and did own property, women's names appear often in contracts and legal documents. A high percentage of the women who appear in the documents fall into the first category, and very few in the second.[83] If a woman is *agrammatos*, her *kyrios*, guardian, usually her husband, father, or son, writes for her.[84] If her *kyrios* is also illiterate, someone else writes for both.[85] A man can act as *kyrios* without knowing how to write himself.[86] In fact, it was even possible for a literate woman to have as *kyrios* an illiterate husband.[87] More common is a literate man with an illiterate wife, but the husband may be only a slow writer. The case of Stotoetis and his wife Thases is an example. Thases is selling a camel and a contract of sale is drawn up by a professional. Stotoetis signs it by saying, "Stotoetis, her *kyrios*, has written here." He cannot spell either *kyrios* or the verb "written" and his lettering is childish and uneven.[88]

Women appear in legal documents pertaining to property, marriage, divorce, and professional duties. In none of these categories must a woman sign for herself. An early Hellenistic marriage contract even stipulates that both husband and wife keep a copy to produce if either should default, but the wife would not have had to be able to read her copy.[89] The fact that she receives a copy indicates only the importance of the written document itself. The contract twice mentions "those acting with Demetria," implying that she is incapable of initiating legal action herself and suggesting that she would not have had the responsibility of reading her own contract. Women often enter contracts about professional duties, but rarely sign the contract themselves. A common job for a woman is that of wet-nurse; two examples will show that the woman in whose name the contract was written, did not have to write herself. In 13 B.C. a brother signed for his sister a document written by a scribe, and in the second century A.D. the receipt for wages received for wet-nursing was signed by the woman's husband.[90]

In addition to the many legal documents signed by both men and women there are scores of private letters from Egypt. One of the difficulties in arguing for literacy on the basis of the wide use of personal letters is that letters written by professional scribes, unlike legal documents, are not likely to have this fact mentioned. For instance, one letter from a woman to her brother has a post-script from their father, but the entire letter, described by the editor as "very ungrammatical" is written in a single hand.[91] Did the woman write the whole letter simply adding her father's message? Did her father write the entire letter? Or did they employ a poorly qualified scribe? Illiterate people often relied on others, barely literate themselves, to write letters. In 209 B.C. an illiterate Macedonian woman, resident in Egypt, sent a letter to another woman, but the letter, described by the editor as written in "a heavy ill-formed hand" is written by a man.[92] The woman to whom the letter was addressed probably had to ask someone else to read it for her. Even people who themselves knew how to write perfectly well might employ a professional to write a more elegant script.[93]

Although it is impossible to determine just how many of the personal letters to and from women were read and written by the women themselves, the proliferation of such letters shows that women have a need for written communication. There are letters from husbands to wives,[94] a wife to her husband,[95] sons to mothers,[96] mothers to sons,[97] women to their sisters and brothers,[98] from women to their mothers,[99] and even a letter from a slave to her mistress.[100] Women seem on the whole more likely to receive letters than to send them, a fact which in itself is a sign of limited literacy. The topics of the letters are often con-fined to the sending and receiving of parcels of foods or clothing, but some women have an interest in financial matters, others have professional interests,[101] and one mother, who is concerned about her son's education, asks what book he is reading at school.[102] In general, however, the subject matter of letters to and from women tends to relate to family affairs, and even a letter where a woman offers to go and collect the rents from her sister's tenant farmer includes a note about a jar of pickles sent as a gift and advice on how to eat them.[103] The topics of women's letters are of interest because they raise the issue of the social uses to which writing is put. The women of Graeco-Roman Egypt have a use for written communication even though they have no political power and even though they do not participate in the administration of government. Nevertheless, the use of written communication must be distinguished from literacy. Women in the papyri have a need for written communication, but because they do not always write their own letters or sign their own documents, it is clear that widespread literacy is not always the consequence of a general and widespread use of written documents.[104]

There are many examples of literate women in Egypt during the Roman period. A letter from a man to his brother mentions books belonging to their sister.[105] In another text a military officer is instructed to provide a reading book for his daughter.[106] A woman named Hermione, known from her mummy portrait, has her occupation recorded on her portrait: γραμματική ("secretary").[107] Hermione died about A.D. 200. In 245 Aurelia Thaïsous writes to her prefect petitioning to be released from the requirement of having to have a *kyrios* to represent her in legal affairs. This is a perfectly valid request. Egypt was part of the Roman Empire, and according to a Roman law, the *ius trium liberorum*, a woman who had three children could act without a *kyrios* in legal matters. Aurelia Thaïsous says:

(Laws have been made), most eminent prefect, which enable women who are honored with the right of three children to be independent and act without a guardian in all business which they transact, especially those women who know how to write. Accordingly, I too, fortunately possessing the honor of being blessed with children, and a writer who is able to write with the greatest of ease . . .[108]

We know from a document dated four years later that her request was granted,[109] but her writing ability, although it is certainly an asset, has nothing to do with her eligibility for legal independence. Sijpesteijn has collected eighty-three examples from the papyri of women who act without a *kyrios* by virtue of the *ius trium liberorum*. Of the eighty-three he finds only five who are described as knowing how to write, and all of these are from one place.[110] Of the remainder, twenty are called *agrammatos*.[111] Aurelia Thaïsous' writing skill is interesting not because she thinks it strengthens her case, but because she takes such pride in it. What we can conclude is that in third-century Egypt, writing easily (this means only the ability to form neat and even letters) was a skill possessed by few women.

It is difficult to estimate just what proportion of the female population of Graeco-Roman Egypt could actually read and write. Pomeroy argues that the literate women of the papyri represent a far smaller proportion of the total female population than do the literate men with respect to the total male population.[112] This is certainly true, but women simply appear in the documents far less often than do men. Fewer women than men know how to write, but as Calderini's statistics show, fewer women than men are described as *agrammatos*.[113] The same is true of the numbers described as "writing slowly." In the first and second centuries A.D of twenty-six people whom Calderini finds described as βραδέως γράφων, only five are women.[114] That fewer women than men are described as *agrammatos* is not an indication that women are more apt to be literate, but simply a reflection of their less frequent appearance in the documents.

It is difficult to compare the total number of illiterate women with the total number of illiterate men in the population as a whole. Where evidence is available, it is clear that in the later period, most people did not know how to write. For instance, in the third century A.D. in Oxyrhynchus, an area where there was a great respect for written records, two-thirds of the men who applied for the grain dole could not write their own names, and these applicants were not from the poor, but from the middle class.[115] There is not enough evidence to estimate what proportion of the corresponding female population at Oxyrhynchus was illiterate, but conclusions reached by Duncan-Jones concerning the extent of illiteracy in the western Roman Empire indicate that the proportion of illiterate women would be much higher than the proportion of illiterate men.[116] The actual numbers, as counted in the available papyri, are not always reliable indicators; the random nature of the evidence distorts even available figures.[117] For instance, Calderini finds that in the second and third centuries A.D., the percentage of women mentioned in the papyri who know how to write increases slightly although the total number of men who know how to write actually decreases in the same period.[118] It would be unwise to assume, on the basis of the limited evidence available, that there was actually a sudden surge in interest in the education of women in this period. As far as popular attitudes go, a literate woman is still an object of amusement. A schoolchild's copybook of the third or fourth century A.D. preserves a maxim expressing the same sentiment which appeared earlier in Athens of the fourth century B.C.: "Seeing a woman being taught her letters, he said, 'What a sword she's sharpening!' "[119]

ACKNOWLEDGEMENTS

The author wishes to thank Bernard Knox, Mae Smethurst, and Jon Billigmeieer for their helpful comments in the preparation of this article which was written with the assistance of a fellowship from the National Endowment of Humanities.

Notes

1. F. D. Harvey, "Literacy in the Athenian Democracy," *REG* 79 (1966) 585-635; E. A. Havelock, "Prologue to Greek Literacy," *Cincinnati Classical Studies* 2 (1966-70) 331-91, *Origins of Western Literacy* (Toronto 1976), "The Preliteracy of the Greeks," *New Literary History* 8 (1977) 369-91; P. A. Cartledge, "Literacy in the Spartan Oligarchy," *JHS* 98 (1978) 25-37; T. E. Boring, *Literacy in Ancient Sparta* (*Mnemosyne* Supplement 54, 1979).
2. Euripides' description of an illiterate man who cannot read Theseus' name (Fr. 382 Nauck) would not have made sense to a completely illiterate audience, but it would hardly have had any point if people who could not read were unusual. Because Euripides can show such a person on stage it is clear that the audience is conscious of distinctions between literate and illiterate people. Harvey (*op. cit.*), 603-604 comments on this passage.
3. For the evidence on silent reading, see B. M. W. Knox, "Silent Reading in Antiquity," *GRBS* 9 (1968) 421-35.
4. (*op. cit.*, note 1), 592-93.
5. M. L. Langdon, *A Sanctuary of Zeus on Mount Hymettos* (*Hesperia* Supplement 16, 1976) 13-41.

6. M. Lang, *The Athenian Agora* XXI (Princeton 1976) 8, no. B1.
7. Langdon (*op. cit.*, note 5) 15, no. 9.
8. Lang (*op. cit.*, note 6) 30; of one hundred forty six owners whose sex can be determined, one hundred twenty seven are male and nineteen female. Lang leaves open the possibility that the women wrote their own names. For a vase from Cumae perhaps inscribed by a woman (sixth century B.C.), see C. D. Buck, *The Greek Dialects* (Chicago 1928) 192, no. 10.
9. *ibid.*, 12, no. C3; 13, no. C11.
10. *ibid.*, 14, no. C27; 15, no. C33.
11. *ibid.*, 17, no. D2.
12. *ibid.*, 13, nos. C10 and C19.
13. Love names are usually printed on the vase before firing, for which see D. M. Robinson and E. J. Fluck, *A Study of the Greek Love-Names* (Baltimore 1937) and K. J. Dover, *Greek Homosexuality* (London 1978) 114-22. The examples published by Lang are scratched on the vase after firing, presumably by the owner, not the person who made the vase.
14. (*op. cit.*, note 1) 621.
15. E. Vanderpool, "Ostracism at Athens. I. The Ostraca," *Cincinnati Classical Studies* 2 (1966-70) 229.
16. *ibid.*, 229 and 243.
17. O. Broneer, "Excavations on the North Slope of the Akropolis," *Hesperia* 7 (1938) 228-43.
18. Vanderpool, (*op. cit.*, note 15) 225, thinks that the *ostraka* were inscribed in advance for people too busy to make their own. Harvey, (*op cit.*, note 1) 591-92, has a different view.
19. *ibid.*, 592-93.
20. The illiterate man in Euripides' *Theseus* (*op cit.*, note 2) is called βοτήρ ("herdsman"); Harvey discusses the rural origin of these characters (*op. cit.*, note 1) 620.
21. H. R. Immerwahr, "Book Rolls on Athenian Vases," *Classical, Mediaeval and Renaissance Studies in Honor of Berthold Louis Ullman* (Rome 1964) 17-48 and "More Book Rolls on Attic Vases," *AK* 16 (1973) 143-47; A. G. Beck, *Album of Greek Education* (Sydney 1975) 56-58, adds two more examples.
22. Immerwahr, nos. 20-28, 28a, 28b, 29-32, 32*bis*, 33-35.
23. Immerwahr, nos. 9, 12, 12*bis*, 12*ter*, 12*quater*, 13-16, 16*bis*, 17, *AK* 146 and pl. 33.3-4; Beck, no. X.33. Two other vases may belong to this group. *ARV*^{2} 852.5 (Beck, no. X.2) is "very much restored" and therefore ambiguous. *ARV*^{2} 1076.14 (Immerwahr, no. 24*bis*) depicts three women, one with a book roll, but there is no information about the context.
24. "Book Rolls," (*op. cit.*, note 21) 27.
25. As a point of comparison, H.-I. Marrou, *Mousikos Anēr* (Grenoble 1938), for scenes of intellectual activity as represented on funeral monuments of the late Roman Empire. While not concerned with literacy itself, this study does offer many examples of people engaged in reading or writing and occasional examples of young girls learning to write and of women holding or reading *volumena* (e.g., nos. 1, 8,

10, 13, 20, 52, 71, 88). In any given case it is impossible to tell whether the specific individual was as interested in literature as the tomb monument implies. Although Marrou's collection shows that many people aspired to the intellectual life, other evidence indicates that there may have been a shortage of good texts for serious scholars. See A. F. Norman, "The Book Trade in Fourth-Century Antioch," *JHS* 80 (1960) 122-26.

26. *ARV²* 1060.145 (Immerwahr, no. 18; Beck, no. X.27).
27. S. B. Pomeroy, "Technikai kai Mousikai," *AJAH* 2 (1977) 51.
28. Leningrad 317; Beck, 58, no. 33 (+ 46, no. 8), Figures 268 and 372.
29. Immerwahr, "Book Rolls," (*op. cit.*, note 21) 27-28, note 4.
30. Immerwahr (*ibid.*) note 4, (Furtwängler, *Antike Gemmen*, pl. 31.12) has been shown by Pomeroy (*op. cit.*, note 27) 63-64, to be a Muse.
31. Harvey (*op. cit.*, note 1) 622, where he also discusses the other passages from Greek tragedy.
32. *ibid.*, 622.
33. After practicing the speech by reciting it from beginning to end, she made Socrates learn it by memorizing it on the spot (236b-c).
34. N. Lewis, *Papyrus in Classical Antiquity* (Oxford 1974) 13, note 14.
35. The remark in Suidas, s.v. "Perikles," where Perikles is said to have been the first person to use a written speech in court is not considered reliable. See E. G. Turner, *Athenian Books in the Fifth and Fourth Centuries B.C.* (London 1952) 18. The earliest reference to a manuscript of a written speech is found in Plato (*Phdr.* 228d-e).
36. Official decrees carved in stone are especially numerous by the middle of the fifth century; see B. D. Meritt, *Epigraphica Attica* (Cambridge 1940) 90-92. Literary texts must have been in circulation much earlier, as the evidence of the vases indicates, but the earliest reference to the buying and selling of such texts is found in Plato, *Apol.* 26d.
37. The earliest Athenian evidence for schools is the vase by Douris (490-80 B.C.), *ARV²* 431.48, discussed often, and in particular, by F. A. G. Beck, *Greek Education* (London 1964) 82 and 89; see also Immerwahr, "Book Rolls," (see note 21) 18-19, no. 1 and K. J. Freeman, *Schools of Hellas* (London1922) 52 and pl. I.A-B. Havelock, "The Preliteracy of the Greeks," (see note 1) 385-387, argues that the Douris cup does not represent a school and specifically, that the scene where a man is writing on a diptych while a boy looks on is not a writing lesson. His argument is forced and not convincing. The reason for his argument is his belief that writing was not formally taught at Athens until much later, but he does not hesitate to distort evidence which does not support his thesis. For instance, he thinks that the earliest representation of a solitary reader in Greek art is the grave stele in the Abbey of Grottaferrata, discussed by G. M. A. Richter, "A Stemmed Plate and a Stele," *MDAI* 71 (1956) 141-44 and pls. I-III, dated 430-420 B.C. However, there are two representations of solitary female readers which are slightly earlier: *ARV²* 1199.25 (Immerwahr, no. 15) and *ARV²* 923.28 (Immerwahr, no. 9). Immerwahr calls the second reader a boy, but Beck, *Album of Greek Education*, 56, no. 6 (Figure 353) recognizes a girl. For the earliest

literary references to schools, see Beck, *Greek Education*, 77-79 and
K. J. Dover's introduction to Aristophanes' *Clouds* (Oxford 1968) lviii-lx.

38. Of the references to schools in the fifth century (Paus. 6.9.6, Asty-
palaia, 496 B.C.; Hdt. 6.27, Chios, 494 B.C.; Plut., *Them.* 10, Athenians
at Troizen, 480 B.C.; Thuc. 7.29, Mykalessos, 413 B.C.) only Herodotus mentions reading and writing. Aeschines (1.9) does attribute to
Solon laws about the management of schools in Athens, but does not
mention the curriculum.

39. Discussed by E. G. Turner, "Athenians Learn to Write: Plato, *Prota-
goras* 326d," *BICS* 12 (1965) 65-67 and F. D. Harvey, "Greeks and
Romans Learn to Write," *Communication Arts in the Ancient World*,
E. A. Havelock and J. P. Hershbell, eds., (New York 1978) 63-78.

40. *ARV²* 908.13.

41. Beck, (*op. cit.*, note 21) 56, no. 3 and Figure 350; Pomeroy (*op. cit.*,
note 27) 64, note 8, where it is suggested that the girls may be *hetairai*.

42. S. F. Bonner, *Education in Ancient Rome* (London 1977) 38 suggests
that the passage from Lysias implies that the *paidagōgos* was in charge
of the girl as well as her brothers, but the text does not support this
interpretation.

43. Daremberg-Saglio, s. v. "Educatio," 477, Figure 2605.

44. "More Book Rolls" (see note 21) 144.

45. [Menander] 702 (Kock); the fragment is not included by A. Koerte,
Menander. Reliquiae (Leipzig 1953). For comments on the relevance
of this fragment to the literacy of women, see Harvey (*op cit.*, note 1)
621 and Pomeroy (*op. cit.*, note 27) 61.

46. *op. cit.*, note 27, 51.

47. Boring (*op. cit.*, note 1) 15.

48. Cartledge (*op. cit.*, note 1) 31.

49. Lastheneia: Diog. Laert., 3.46; Axiothea: Diog, Laert., 3.46 and Themistios, *Or.* 23, 295c = Aristotle, *Nerinthos* fr. 1 (Ross, 23).

50. *op. cit.*, note 27, 58.

51. G. C. Field, *Plato and his Contemporaries* (London 1930) 47-48, argues
for a library of Plato's works in the Academy and even thinks there
may have been a lending library of some sort, but he has no firm
evidence. He cites the story of the Corinthian farmer who was converted to philosophy when he read the *Gorgias*, but the story is preserved only in the passage of Themistios (*op cit.*, note 49); although
Themistios mentions Aristotle by name, the anecdote is so close to the
one about Axiothea that it seems likely that they are both folktales.
Zenobius says that Hermodoros, a pupil of Plato, took to Sicily arguments put together by Plato (no. 6, Leutsch-Schneidewin, *Corp.
Paroem. Gr.* I, 116). Cicero, *ad Atticum* 31.21a, quotes part of a
proverb about Hermodoros and says that Hermodoros did not publish
without Plato's permission. From these two bits of information it seems
likely that Hermodoros distributed works of Plato, but clearly nowhere
else than Sicily.

52. A. S. Riginos, *Platonica* (Leiden 1976) 183-84.

53. Diog. Laert. 8. 41.

54. Some think that this story is earlier than its source, Hermippos (third century B.C.), but the detail which requires the literacy of Pythagoras' mother is a sign that it must be late. See W. Burkert, *Lore and Science in Ancient Pythagoreanism* (Cambridge 1972) 156 and 200.

55. H. Thesleff, *An Introduction to the Pythagorean Writings of the Hellenistic Period* (Abo 1961) 106, 113; Pomeroy (*op cit.*, note 27) 57-58. The Pythagorean bluestocking may have been a figure of fun as early as the fourth century B.C. According to Diogenes Laertios (8.37), Kratinos wrote a comedy entitled Πυθαγορίζουσῃ.

56. Pomeroy (*op. cit.*, note 27) 57.

57. G. Foti and G. Pugliese-Carratelli, "Un sepolcro di Hipponion e un nuovo testo orfico," *PP* 29 (1974) 91-126.

58. E. G. Turner, *Greek Papyri* (Princeton 1968) 76-77, for salutary comments on the relation of texts found in graves to literacy.

59. *SIG*³ 1161 = H. W. Parke, *The Oracles of Zeus* (Oxford 1967) 268, no. 15. On page 101 Parke notes the dialectical variation on the tablets from Dodona and suggests that individuals inscribed their own tablets.

60. *IG* III, part III, Appendix, no. 100.

61. Plut., *Alex.* 39.4-5; J. R. Hamilton, *Plutarch. Alexander* (Oxford 1969) 103. Hamilton's scepticism about the genuineness of the specific letter quoted does nothing to invalidate the tradition that Olympias wrote letters. The sources for the letters to Alexander and Olympias have been collected by A. Zumetikos, *De Alexandri Olympiadisque epistularum fontibus et reliquiis* (Diss. Berlin 1894).

62. Herondas 3.

63. *SIG*³ 578. The subject of schooling for girls in the Hellenistic period is discussed by M. P. Nilsson, *Die Hellenistische Schule* (Munich 1955) 47; H.-I. Marrou, *A History of Education in Antiquity* (London 1956) 111; Pomeroy (*op. cit.*, note 27) 52.

64. The inscription from Teos says that there will be three *grammatodidaskaloi* to teach both *paides* and *parthenoi*. Later, when the pay for the music teacher is discussed, only *paides* are mentioned. Pomeroy, (above) 52, argues that in the second case *paides* refers to both boys and girls and that girls therefore received instruction in subjects other than reading and writing. This is unlikely. If the sexes are distinguished in the first place, there is no reason to assume that the distinction is not maintained throughout the inscription.

65. *MDAI* 35 (1910) 436, no. 20; 37 (1912) 277-78, no. 1; L. Robert, *Études anatoliennes* (Paris 1937) 58-59, shows that these two texts are parts of the same inscription. An inscription from Pergamon (*IPerg* 463) includes among a list of students of the *gymnasion* the person who is in charge of the *eukosmia* of the young girls and the young girls themselves. A similar official also appears on the inscription found in Smyrna, *CIG* 3185, but Robert argues, p. 59, that the Smyrna inscription came originally from Pergamon.

66. *MDAI* 22 (1897) 480-81; E. Ziebarth, *Aus dem griechischen Schulwesen* (Leipzig 1909) 32.

67. Marrou (*op. cit.*, note 63) 388, note 29; H. W. Pleket, *Epigraphica* II (Leiden 1969) 28, no. 13.
68. Pleket, 29-30, no. 16.
69. Beck (*op. cit.*, note 21) 57, nos. 15-17, Figures 357-58; For more references, see Pomeroy (*op. cit.*, note 27) 64, note 9 and Marrou (note 63) 396, note 7.
70. *BMI* 1127; Beck (*op. cit.*, note 21) 57, no. 19, Figure 359.
71. *op. cit.*, note 27, 52.
72. *De lib. educand.* 4a and 9f. The essay may not be by Plutarch; see Marrou (*op. cit.*, note 63) 397, note 14.
73. Frgs. 128-33 (Sandbach); cf. Musonius Rufus, "Should Daughters Receive the Same Education as Sons?" Cora Lutz, ed. (New Haven 1947) 42-48. For a summary of references to literate and literary women in Rome, see S. B. Pomeroy, *Goddesses, Whores, Women, and Slaves* (New York 1975) 170-76. For slave women as professional secretaries and readers in Rome, see Susan Treggiari, "Jobs for Women," *AJAH* 1 (1976) 78, 90.
74. *Conj. praec.* 145a-d.
75. Frgs. 67-75 (Pfeiffer); Harvey (*op. cit.*, note 1) 622. The literary sources for inscribed apples are collected by A. E. Littlewood, "The Symbolism of the Apple," *HSCP* 72 (1967) 167-68. Except for a story dubiously attributed to Hesiod in a scholion to Homer, Kallimachos is the earliest.
76. e.g., Alciphron, *Epist. piscat.* 6, 11, 12; *Epist. rust.* 6-7, 18, 31, *Epist. amat., passim.*
77. Lucian, *Dial. meret.* 10.3.
78. Philostr., *Epist.* 62.
79. Lucian, *Dial. meret.* 4.2-3.
80. *ibid.*, 10.2.
81. H. C. Youtie, "ἀγράμματος: An Aspect of Greek Society in Egypt," *HSCP* 75 (1971) 161-76, republished in *Scriptiunculae* (Amsterdam 1973) II, 611-27.
82. H. C. Youtie, "βραδέως γράφων; Between Literacy and Illiteracy," *GRBS* 12 (1971) 239-61, republished in *Scriptiunculae* II, 629-51.
83. Rita Calderini, "Gli ἀγράμματοι nell'Egitto greco-romano," *Aegyptus* 30 (1950) 23 and 34.
84. *ibid.*, 31.
85. *ibid.*, 32.
86. Youtie (*op. cit.*, note 81) 166; in another article, "ὑπογραφεύς: The Social Impact of Illiteracy in Graeco-Roman Egypt," *ZPE* 17 (1975) 213, Youtie demonstrates that a *kyrios* was chosen on the basis of family relationship. Literacy was not a necessary qualification.
87. *POxy* 1463; Youtie, "ὑπογραφεύς," (above) 216, note 42; cf. *PTebt* 397.
88. *PAmh* 102; Youtie, "βραδέως γράφων," (*op. cit.*, note 82) 249.
89. *PEleph* 1 = A. S. Hunt and C. C. Edgar, *Select Papyri* (hereafter *SP*) I. 1; 311 B.C.
90. *BGU* 1107 (*SP* I. 16) and *PTebt* 399.

91. *POxy* 1067. The editor suggests that the woman and her father used a scribe.
92. *PTebt* 821.
93. *POxy* 3313.
94. *POxy* 528 (*SP* I. 125), 744 (*SP* 105), 1070, 1159; *JEA* 12, p. 61 (*SP* I. 155).
95. *PLond* 42 (*SP* I. 97).
96. *POxy* 1293, 1481, 1678; *CP* 22, p. 243 (*SP* I. 111); *BGU* 846 (*SP* I. 120); *Rev. Eg.* 919, p. 204 (*SP* I. 121). Hunt and Edgar remark, with respect to the last example, that the letter was included on the same sheet as a letter to a brother, but that the sheet was addressed only to the brother; the mother probably did not read.
97. *PFlor* 332 (*SP* I. 114); *POxy* 930 (*SP* I. 130).
98. *POxy* 1215, 1291, 2680; *PTebt* 414.
99. *BGU* 1680 (*SP* I. 134); *PFay* 127; *POxy* 295.
100. *PTebt* 413.
101. *POxy* 2593, a business letter from a woman who is a professional spinner.
102. *POxy* 930 (*SP* I. 130).
103. *POxy* 2680.
104. The same point is made by Cartledge with respect to the Spartans (*op. cit.*, note 1) 37.
105. *PTebt* 422.
106. Marrou (*op. cit.*, note 63) 144.
107. M. H. Swindler, *Ancient Painting* (New Haven 1929) 323 and pl. xv; K. Parlasca, *Mumienporträts und verwandte Denkmäler* (Wiesbaden 1966) pl. 15, no. 1. Cf. Eusebius, *Hist. Eccl.* 6.23, for girls trained in penmanship who helped record Origen's commentaries.
108. *POxy* 1467, translated by Grenfell and Hunt; discussed by Youtie (*op. cit.*, note 81) 166-67 and (*op. cit.*, note 86) 221, note 62.
109. *POxy* 1475.
110. P. J. Sijpesteijn, "Die χωρὶς κουρίου χρηματίζουσαι δικαίῳ τέκνων," *Aegyptus* 45 (1965) 176.
111. *ibid.*, 180-87.
112. *op. cit.*, note 27, 64, note 16.
113. *op. cit.*, note 83, 23: 1365 men, 373 women.
114. *ibid.*, 34-35; four have Greek names and the other a Roman name.
115. Grain was not distributed on the basis of need. Eligibility was a privilege reserved for ἐπικριθέντες and those who had performed liturgies. For a discussion of the requirements, see J. R. Rea, *The Oxyrhynchus Papyri* XL (London 1972) 2-5. The observation on the illiteracy of the applicants was made by J. D. Thomas, *CR* n.s. 26 (1976) 111.
116. "Age-Rounding, Illiteracy and Social Differentiation in the Roman Empire," *Chiron* 7 (1977) 333-53; Duncan-Jones attempts to establish a statistical method for determining the rate of illiteracy in the western Roman Empire. He analyzes the age at death as given on tomb inscriptions and determines that ages divisible by five occur with greater

frequency than should be expected. He argues that many people do not actually know their ages and that there is a relation between age-rounding and illiteracy. He finds that slaves round their ages more often than citizens, that women tend to round their ages more than do men, and that among rural populations in the provinces, age-rounding increases with distance from the capital city.

117. Another problem is the fact that Egyptian culture of the Hellenistic and Roman periods is bilingual, and although Greek is the official language, Demotic (Egyptian) continues to be written by the native Egyptian population. Youtie, "Because They Do Not Know Their Letters," ZPE 19 (1975) 101-110, has demonstrated that the term *agrammatos* as used on Greek documents refers only to illiteracy in Greek. There is no way to determine just how many of those who are illiterate in Greek can actually write the Demotic. It is of interest to notice that one of Youtie's examples, *PTebt* 383, records a husband who can sign in Demotic and his wife who cannot write in either Demotic or Greek. Finally, almost all known papyri originate in rural districts; very few come from the urban centers. If the Greek city of Alexandria were better represented, the picture would certainly be different.

118. *op. cit.*, note 83, 37.

119. *PBouriant* 1, printed also by E. Ziebarth, *Aus der antiken Schule* (Bonn 1913) 21-24, no. 46, f. VI-VIIIʳ, no. 2: Ἰδὼν γ[υν]αῖκα διδα[σκ]ομένην γράμματα εἶπεν· οἷον ξίφος ἀκονᾶται. Cf. no. 3: Ἰδὼν γυν[α]ῖκα γυ[ν]αικι συμβουλεύουσαν εἶπεν· ἀσπὶς παρ' ἐχίδνης φάρμακον πορίζεται. The latter is actually attributed to Diogenes of Sinope (ca. 400-325 B.C.) and no. 2 is in Diogenes' style. See *FPG* II, 304, no. 56 (Mullach). P. Jouguet and P. Perdrizet, "Le papyrus Bouriant, no. 1," *Studien zur Palaeographie und Papyruskunde* 6 (1906) 148-61, suggest that the comic fragment discussed above (see note 45) is a conflation of the two: γυναῖχ' ὁ διδάσκων γράμματ' ⟨οὐ⟩ καλῶς ⟨ποιεῖ⟩ / ἀσπίδι δὲ φοβερᾷ προσπορίζει φάρμακον.

Home before lunch: The emancipated woman in Theocritus

FREDERICK T. GRIFFITHS
Amherst College

THE WOMEN of Ptolemaic Alexandria enjoyed an advance in their condition sufficient to inspire modern talk of emancipation and a new spiritual freedom. After the low point reached in the age of Pericles, the flowering of vast new metropolises a century later diminished the male monopoly on the marketplace, the law court, the palaestra, the stoa, and the throneroom, as papyrus fragments (deeds, marriage contracts, even some letters) reveal in unprecedented detail.[1] We remain curiously uninformed, however, about the feelings, aspirations, and values of the "New Woman"[2] because usable literary evidence now becomes scarce. As respectable women ventured into the streets, poets were disappearing into libraries to cultivate a style that says everything about art and remarkably little about character. The intellectual toys of a learned age — geographical arcana, quaint outcroppings of saga, recherché vocabulary, literary criticism — all find their way into refined and allusive verse. Only a small handful of poems give voice to the women of the age in any direct and extensive fashion.

Chief among the sources concerning Hellenistic women is the Syracusan Theocritus, who was writing in Ptolemaic literary circles in the 270's B.C. From him we have versified vignettes of daily life (mimes) which combine psychological depth with credible realism about life in Hellenistic cities. Two such poems are acknowledged masterpieces: Critics since Racine[3] have attested to the emotional impact of the *Sorceress* (*Idyll* 2), in which a most ordinary young woman attempts by black magic, imprecation, and finally self-reflection to deal with her feelings toward an elegant youth who has loved (at her invitation) and abandoned her. What the *Sorceress* reveals about the inner life of women is complemented by the social observation of *Idyll* 15, *The Syracusan Women* or *Women at the Adonis Festival*, which depicts two Syracusan immigrants to Alexandria as they pry themselves loose from demanding households to spend a morning at Queen Arsinoe's Adonis festival. As the two housewives trek from dusty suburban lanes to the palace and encounter women from nursemaids to queens, they provide our fullest profile of ancient Alexandria. The two poems have earned Theocritus a central place in virtually all surveys of the life of Hellenistic women, along with commendation as "an intelligent and sensitive feminist"[4] and "one of the great discoverers of woman's soul."[5]

As social documentation, however, the two pieces contradict each other beyond any resolution. Simaetha, the fledgling sorceress of *Idyll* 2, does indeed enjoy unprecedented opportunities to venture out into the city unchaperoned, to reflect at leisure on the problems that she has caused herself, and to guide her life, dispiriting as it may be without the interference of men. Yet in *Idyll* 15 Gorgo and Praxinoa, the housewives, must devote a rare day of festal freedom to threading an obstacle course around demanding infant sons, charging cavalry in the streets, censorious men in the crowd (along with some who flirt), and husbands who, festival or no festival, will be wanting their lunch. Where Simaetha has free access to sexual partners, Gorgo and Praxinoa cannot even do their own shopping. *The Syracusan Women* excludes those possibilities for female autonomy which the *Sorceress* casually assumes.

As to woman's "soul," Theocritus seems as capable of discounting as of discovering it. The *Sorceress* does present the desired case of a Hellenistic poet taking a female subject seriously in a way that his classical predecessors would not have. Theocritus has found almost tragic stature in a woman of his own day and, indeed, one from a social milieu so lowly that the boundaries of slave and free are blurred.[6] A woman no longer need be monumental like Antigone, Clytemnestra, or even Lysistrata to compel a poet's attention; nor is her life of interest only as she is impinging on men's affairs by seduction, treachery, or defiance. Theocritus explores Simaetha's commonplace experiences entirely for their own sake and without involving any male characters beyond her memory of the faithless

Delphis. In *The Syracusan Women*, on the other hand, Gorgo and Praxinoa take themselves far more seriously than does the poet. After Simaetha's moving aria, what are they but chattering viragoes whose major contribution to human happiness can never go much beyond fixing their husbands' lunch? And Praxinoa should stop snapping at her baby and maid. Where Simaetha demonstrates the extraordinary inner life of an ordinary person, Gorgo and Praxinoa leave us with the distinct impression that there is less here than meets the eye. For example, in remembering her deflowering Simaetha visualizes herself as a sleeping baby whimpering for its mother and as the stiff, lifeless figure of a doll (*Idyll* 2. 108–110). These fresh, highly individual images are worlds away from the clichés of the sexually hungry female that earlier Greek poets would have applied to a woman who, like Simaetha, had pursued the man. Without pretending to innocence, she shows herself as childlike and not voracious; more vulnerable than monstrous; less thrilled (as the man might fancy) by the display of male potency than preoccupied with her own ambivalence. Indeed, the closest thing we find to phallic symbolism is the image of the stiff doll, which she applies to herself. By contrast, poor old Praxinoa, obviously frustrated and obviously obsessed with male power and size, confesses her fear since childhood of horses and snakes (*Idyll* 15. 57–59) — a familiar kind of swipe at female phallicism. She is a comic stereotype in a way that Simaetha conspicuously is not.

Where Simaetha relies finally on her own emotional resources, Gorgo and Praxinoa find spiritual solace in the festival's tableau of lovely young Adonis dead in the arms of Aphrodite. Yet this mawkish spectacle, gotten up for the consumption of the masses, parallels the Gothic novels and soap operas of our own day in symbolizing the housewife's failure of imagination. The two women's fleeting experience of freedom demonstrates how little capable they are of using more. Where Simaetha rises above her condition, Gorgo and Praxinoa show themselves completely the creatures of their bourgeois surroundings. Yet the details of daily life seem as credible in one poem as the other.

The rest of the *Idylls* confirm the impression of a poet as unpredictable as he is adroit in the delineation of sexual roles. Theocritus wrote some ambitious adaptations of Sappho (*Idylls* 29 and 30) —

as pederastic poems. He may have used Erinna's *Distaff* in a poem to the wife of his friend Nicias (*Idyll* 28) — but no poet she, and woman's place is in the home. Yet in celebrating Helen's marriage in *Idyll* 18 an imposing and athletic chorus of Spartan maidens grants the bridegroom Menelaus no more than drone status. The famous pastorals, on the other hand, depict an entirely male world in which the sense of freedom often derives from nothing so much as freedom from women, and in which sexual energy erupts freely and without particular need of female or even human objects. In all, we can be sure that Theocritus, well as he understands the stereotypes of the battle of the sexes, is as capable of exploiting them for laughs in *The Syracusan Women* as of transcending them in the *Sorceress* or of translating them in the pederastic and pastoral idylls to a milieu where sexual roles do not derive from gender. Perhaps we should not be surprised. After all, Alexandria was Alexandria for over two thousand years before Cavafy and Durrell gave us the details.

Must we abandon the *Idylls* as evidence for the life of Hellenistic women? No. Indeed, they doubtless have been used far less than prudently can be done. We must, however, recognize one pitfall in working with Theocritus: Unlike most Hellenistic poets, he is excerptible. To all appearances commonplace people say simple things in realistic settings. The anthologist may proceed without footnotes. Especially when Theocritus' utterly artificial Greek is translated into simple English, the casual reader may well not suspect that the picture of simple folk like Praxinoa or Simaetha may be literarily no simpler than Joyce's portrait of the unremarkable Leopold Bloom. Theocritus anticipates Joyce and other moderns in using the accumulated resources of a rich literary tradition to make ordinary life as interesting as it is insignificant.

It is with the Hellenistic poets, the writers of mime particularly, that the social historian first encounters a kind of literary realism which should simplify the relationship of poetry to life and in fact does quite the opposite. For Theocritus and his generation applied their new veristic techniques first to the subjects furthest away from what we know to have been their experience and can expect to have been their sympathies. Virtuosity lay in the elegant execution of once subliterary topics. For orientation the reader may ponder the scene of the Ptolemies throned in pharaonic splendor as they amuse themselves with poets' impressions of street life and barnyard such as royal eyes never see: herdsmen squabbling over a goatskin (*Idyll* 5), matrons visiting the cobbler to select sexual devices (Herodas, *Mime* 7), love on a budget (*Idyll* 14), a schoolboy getting thrashed (*Mime* 3), a pimp in court (*Mime* 2), the woes of a suburban Medea (Simaetha in *Idyll* 2), and even the sublime bad taste — at once ignorant and pretentious — of the tourists that one sees filing through the palace (Gorgo and Praxinoa in *Idyll* 15). Sophisticated Alexandrian audiences, who obviously took pleasure in the nitty-gritty of the grinding lives they were spared, wanted authenticity along with amusement. We can probably trust Theocritus, therefore, about the details of domestic life: households kept weasels to control pests; the servant problem continued; textiles were available, but not cheap, and women did their own tailoring; festivals still offered them their major chance for freedom. The larger literary point, however, was for declassé subjects to show themselves funny, titillating, or perhaps a bit poignant. The emotional realities of living in the poorer or female part of society, if known, may get lost in the telling. In sum, street life is, yes, observed closely as never before, but from above and for reasons that have nothing much to do with the values of the people being watched.

Still, the more we temper our hopes for documentary accuracy from these evasive poets, the more we confront the equally important matter of explaining what in the new society of Alexandria caused writers to perceive women in new ways. In accounting for Theocritus' attitudes we may begin with two clear facts of an otherwise sketchy biography: He invented the pastoral and he wrote for the Ptolemies. These are, I submit, related phenomena and both of material interest to the feminist critic. Let us begin with the latter, for the Ptolemaic influence on Theocritus' verse seems to derive largely from the remarkable Arsinoe II.[7] We can, after all, reasonably expect a poet writing for a female patron to start seeing his women characters in a new light.

Arsinoe was born to the founder of the dynasty, Ptolemy I, in 315 B.C. At fifteen or sixteen years of age she was married off to the much older Lysimachus, king of Thrace, to whom she dutifully set about bearing heirs. He had a son slightly older than Arsinoe, whom she may have loved and probably poisoned. Some years later, Lysimachus was overthrown, and she escaped only by dressing as a beggar and leaving a maid to be slain in her own royal robes. Finding herself a young widow with three children to support and no throne, she exercised her best option and married her half-brother, Ptolemy Ceraunus, now king of Macedonia and Thrace. It was not a happy match, for Ceraunus, who had his own dynastic motives, killed her two younger sons on their wedding day. In the wake of this second marital disappointment, Arsinoe found herself again a refugee — pushing forty, twice a queen, and with nothing to show for it. Returning home to Alexandria, she took shelter in the household of her brother Ptolemy II, where she made herself useful in her later years by ruling Egypt. She pruned the dynasty of Ptolemy's first wife (her former step-daughter, as it happened) and two of their brothers, but did allow her bumbling younger brother to stay on the throne as her husband, Ptolemy Philadelphus, "Ptolemy Who Loves his Sister". Since the pharaohs had always married their sisters, the indigenous Egyptians were touched that the Greek overlords were finally going native. The Greeks apparently felt otherwise, and the wag Sotades is reported to have quipped that "Ptolemy has dipped his *kentron* (prod) in an unholy hole".[8] Ptolemy and Arsinoe were not amused. Sotades visited the harbor bottom in a leaden coffin. And all over Egypt poets suddenly discovered the brighter side of incest. The best sort of Greeks had not, to be sure, ever done this sort of thing, but their gods certainly did: Zeus and Hera, for instance. Moreover, the Ptolemies eased the comparison by deifying themselves as the Theoi Adelphoi, "the Brother and Sister Gods". In the best Greek families godhead was, in fact, traditionally no more commonplace than incest. Then again, cagey arrivistes proceeding with the right combination of style and omnipotence might just get two wrongs to add up to one right. In any case, the Ptolemies did not rule Egypt so much as own it, and set about building its new cities as their shrine, even as they caused classical Greek poetry to flower a final time on their payroll.[9] Their traces were to be found in every temple and every street corner, for they initiated the naming of streets for political purposes. When Theocritus' Gorgo and Praxinoa walk to the palace they may have gone through Arsinoe the Queen Street to Arsinoe Goddess of Pity Street to Arsinoe Consummator, Arsinoe of the Brazen House, Arsinoe the Bearer of Bounty, and even Arsinoe Victor — a title earned in her skillful management of Egypt's wars. The queen, apparently, was by this point not much worried about being overlooked, and hence to compliment her Theocritus in *The Syracusan Women* need only note the long shadow that she casts over Alexandrian society. One suspects that the very busy Arsinoe was not exactly waiting for a mere poet to reassure her that she was doing a good job as regent, field marshal, city planner, owner of Egypt, wife, sister, stepmother, and several goddesses.

Theocritus' courtly intentions emerge only in the second half of the poem, which anthologists and social historians routinely omit and ignore. Yet to present an Alexandria without Arsinoe amounts to an odd distortion of women's impact in these years and obscures the possibility that *Idyll* 15's female characters may demonstrate far less about the age than does its female audience. For how women are handled in this poem may have quite a bit to do with what Arsinoe was ready to hear.[10]

THE SYRACUSAN WOMEN

The action of the piece unfolds in a simple plan: Gorgo arrives to pick Praxinoa up at home; they walk to the palace and enter; there they admire the tapestries and tableaux; finally a singer laments Adonis and in the process praises the Ptolemies; Gorgo has the last word as she salutes Adonis and remembers her husband's lunch. As the women move from household to street to palace, the poem widens its perspective from private to public concerns and thereby outlines the relationship of the Ptolemies, at the top of society, to everything beneath. What begins as a comic episode in the battle of men and women modulates into a portrait of the harmonious relationship of the rulers and the ruled, in this case with a female ruler.[11] By the end we are alerted to the extent that household and palace are opposite, complementary, and equally feminine realms.

What is distinctive in the opening domestic scenes is the extent to which the perspective is already political or, more precisely, the extent to which social relations reduce themselves to struggles for power. Family life, it seems, is warfare conducted by other means. It is not mother love nor marital harmony that binds the household together, but reciprocal quests for dominance. Praxinoa retaliates against her husband with verbal abuse ("that lunatic of mine" v. 8)[12] so violent that it frightens her infant son. He, in turn, seems a tiny tyrant whose tears at her departure would deprive her of one of her few chances for freedom. She also tries to bolster her uncertain control over her maid by more strong words (vv. 27–31): "I'll teach you! . . . you thief . . . Idiot!". Both she and Gorgo see their husbands' purchases, of houses and dry goods, as directly calculated to reinforce their domestic servitude.

The women's progress out into the street simply allows the sexual warfare to take on larger social dimensions. Here the ranks of oppressive males are joined by Egyptian pickpockets, cavalrymen, and a bystander in the palace who chides the women for chattering away in their rustic Sicilian dialect, thereby allowing Praxinoa a much treasured opportunity to talk back to a man, as she does at length. We also encounter our first positive image of a male in the poem: good king Ptolemy, who has made the streets somewhat safer.

Finally, Gorgo and Praxinoa enter Arsinoe's grotto, where the various lines of social tension converge and are transcended. The mob, seen as ants (v. 45) and pigs (v. 73) outside, can here join in communal activity as they celebrate the linked myths of personal immortality and redemptive kingship. If Gorgo and Praxinoa usually feel a deep sense of powerlessness as women, here they see in the Adonis festival an affirmation of female power and self-sufficiency. For the immensely powerful Queen Arsinoe is celebrating this festival of Aphrodite on behalf of her now deified mother Berenice. It was women who made the tapestries; it is a woman who sings the hymn. Like Arsinoe, she is identified in terms of her mother, not her father (v. 97), and she got her starring role not by being someone's favorite, but by proving her ability in a singing competition. Arsinoe's household offers all the autonomy that women lack in their private lives.

The fantasies here depicted create a similar escape from the man's world outside. Instead of the pickpockets and soldiers of the streets, in this grotto one finds only flights of cupids. There are no more cranky children here, only the obliging boy Ganymede being borne by eagles of white ivory to Zeus, whose heart he has stolen. Domineering husbands are replaced by the lovely, passive Adonis, a symbol of the male principle submissive to a powerful goddess of generativity. The union of Aphrodite and Adonis, whom she yearly causes to die and be reborn, symbolizes not marriage, but anti-marriage, as Detienne[13] suggests in his analysis of the festival. If the Thesmophoria celebrates the strength of the marital bond, the Adonis festival explores the fantasy of liberation from that institution. Here woman's self-sufficient power to give life can even reverse death: it was Aphrodite, not Zeus, who deified Berenice and who shows particular care for Arsinoe. It is implied that Arsinoe, like Helen, to whom she is compared (v. 110), can also look forward to immortality. Meanwhile Zeus has been overwhelmed by the love of the mere child Ganymede, and Adonis, though only the consort of a powerful goddess, surpasses paragons of assertive masculinity like Ajax and Agamemnon (vv. 137–142), for he alone participates in the triumph of the cyclic female principle over death. Earlier we were reminded of the parallel conquest of death by Demeter in rescuing her daughter Persephone from Hades (v. 94).

Household and palace are linked, then, by a whole network of inversions. The women must pinch pennies at home, but in the palace they witness how hard and fast systems of exchange break down at the central point in the society. Praxinoa, for one, is perfectly aware of the social stratification involved when she petulantly remarks (*Idyll* 15.24), "Everything's grand in grand houses". But in this royal and divine realm, it is generosity that yields a profit. The people of Alexandria and indeed of the whole empire bring their tributes to Adonis, hence indirectly to the monarchs, who somehow mysteriously generate prosperity for the whole society as good kings have always done.[14] Similarly, Gorgo's and Praxinoa's practical interest in sewing focuses itself now on the tapestries, which force them to think in aesthetic as well as technical terms. Things experienced mundanely in the household find their sublime idealization here in Arsinoe's palace. And what the women see here is a festival where women are so fully in charge that they need not exclude men.

Given the sensitive project of describing Arsinoe's cultural and religious program, why has Theocritus picked observers as limited as Gorgo and Praxinoa obviously are? For one thing, they allow him to imply a healthy and just relationship between the rulers and the ruled, for the women show real affection for the royal house and think it natural that it should be central to the society in the way that it is — by no means an inevitable attitude in Greek poetry, given the democratic outlook of most fifth century poets. Gorgo's and Praxinoa's bland acceptance of the Ptolemies' incest, self-deification, and autocracy suggests that these are not inflammatory issues even for the most limited bourgeois sensibility. The women are better able to bear their oppressive homelives because of periodic enjoyment of such escapist fantasies, while their pronounced limitations as people confirm the essential justice of the social stratification. Arsinoe is a good deal better to her subjects than Praxinoa is to her maidservant. The dreariness of their lives in itself heightens the glamor of the palace.

Gorgo and Praxinoa do not see beyond the façade that Arsinoe erects to capture the imagination of the masses and sustain their loyalty. The rococo flamboyance of the festival epitomizes bad taste, and therefore Theocritus can share a laugh with his patron by memorializing the masses' susceptibility to such vulgarity in his own impeccably refined verse. Yet he also implies some very gratifying things about what lies behind the façade, about realities obvious to the court, if lost on such as Gorgo and Praxinoa. The final surprise in this study of the political uses of illusion is that Arsinoe surpasses in actuality the contrived image that she purveys to the masses. For beyond the fantasy of female supremacy in Aphrodite lies the historical reality of Arsinoe, who so overshadows her husband, brother, co-regent, and fellow god, Ptolemy II. The fact that Gorgo and Praxinoa behave as women always have in the festivals of Old Comedy and Mime belies how utterly new are the political circumstances of this festival in ways to which they are oblivious. Hitherto women's festivals in Greek literature have tended to be at the margins of society; this Adonis festival is in the palace itself. The kind of female conspiracies (e.g., Aristophanes' *Lysistrata*) to which Gorgo and Praxinoa show a mild inclination have always found a check in the final and welcome assertion of male authority. *Idyll* 15, however, suggests no larger male context for the women's activities and presents in the political sphere no oppressive males against whom to conspire. That Gorgo and Praxinoa have to hurry home to their husbands makes all the stronger reminder that Berenice, Arsinoe, and Aphrodite are not shown as answering to any male. What delights the masses is a fantasy of female self-sufficiency; what stages the fantasy is the reality of the same. Though the world of festival customarily inverts daily realities (e.g., in the Saturnalia or Sadie Hawkins Day), Arsinoe's Adonis festival instead mythologizes the real, if perhaps unadmitted working principles of the permanent government. For it is not just one day a year that the Ptolemies become like gods or that Arsinoe overshadows Ptolemy. Arsinoe as Helen is not just the face which launched a thousand ships; she is also the admiral who commands them.

The presence of Arsinoe at one end of the poem does much to explain the treatment of Gorgo and Praxinoa at the other. Their oppressed femininity serves as a foil for her unusual attainment. Similarly, the battle of the sexes which dominates the first part of the poem is not a self-contained theme and surely not the final concern of the poem, but rather presents conflicts susceptible of resolution in the larger social relationship of the rulers and their subjects, here seen as harmoniously interdependent. Though it is keen observation on Theocritus' part to see the household more as battlefield than as protective nest, he does so primarily to prepare a link to the world of the palace where absolute power can be seen as benign and constructive. When struggles for domination prove so pernicious between man and wife, master and slave, how fortunate that the Ptolemies' absorption of all political power protects society at large from comparable disturbance! The streets of Alexandria clearly cry out for law and order. Male dominance in the exogamous marriages of the masses is balanced by female supremacy in the incestuous royal sphere with its numerous similarities to the Olympians. Similarly, the self-encumbering fecundity of housewives is complemented by Ptolemy's and Arsinoe's childless sibling union, whose generativity sustains and enriches the whole society. Though these relationships are only sketched in here, other courtly poems fill out the picture, and, in any case, Theocritus need not belabor the matter for an audience itself in the process of inventing this mythology.

Does *Idyll* 15, then, give us the Alexandrian "woman in the street"? Theocritus would not give a contemporary audience any but credible details, so these must stand, and they present a picture of domestic life very like that of fifth century Athens. Men and women may mingle a bit more freely in public than previously, and we may deduce a degree of emancipation thereby.[15] Festivals, however, are notoriously unreliable indices of daily life. It should be noted that Praxinoa summons the courage to talk to a strange man only on the threshold of Arsinoe's palace, and the exchange may derive more from the symbolism of that space than from actual Alexandrian manners. As examples of female talent and efficaciousness, Gorgo and Praxinoa offer no competition to Arsinoe. The larger myths of kingship, which the poem is ultimately designed to sustain, naturally do not highlight the untapped talents of the subjects or their capacity for progressive social change. If a new egalitarianism was transforming the Hellenistic world, courtly poetry would be the last form to reflect it. What *The Syracusan Women* establishes above all is that nature has picked its housewives well, even as it has picked its queens.

Just as the view of housewives here is essentially traditional, so to a surprising extent is that of queens. Even in delineating Arsinoe's unprecedented power, Theocritus avoids any but the most conventional and genteel view of her own nature. The poem manages to locate Arsinoe at the very center of political and religious power in the society without making her seem in the slightest *unladylike*. One thinks of the parallel of the *Odyssey*'s Penelope, who can control Ithacan society with unimpeachable femininity and no compromise of honor because the volatile elements of that society, the suitors, have gathered in her hall and in courting her voluntarily submit to her influence.[16] She has not sought power. Operating at home, she can make control of these dangerous young men simply an extension of household management. What power we see Arsinoe exercising is similarly in her own household. Like Penelope, she stays offstage and largely leaves things to the crowd's imagination. Though the festival amounts to a form of political control, its use of beauty and illusion is acceptably feminine. Likewise, Arsinoe's chief medium of influence here is religion, traditionally the form of social power open to women.

Indeed, it is Arsinoe's very divinity, here broadly anticipated and a central assumption of other courtly verse, that spares her the appearance of infringing on male prerogative. Oddly enough, it is only her brother who receives commendation from poets for the political and military acumen that he may have had in smaller measure than his wife (e.g., *Idylls* 14 and 17),[17] while Arsinoe, like the queens after her, almost always appears in verse as a goddess.[18] But, then, it is doubtless less unsettling to worship Arsinoe as a great deity than to acknowledge her as even a good general. As goddess, Arsinoe naturally poses no threat to the men of the society and offers no imitable model to the women. Divinity, we recall, was to enjoy a long literary career as one of the pedestals on which ladies could be put to keep them out of trouble. Though the Ptolemies were gods at their own insistence and Arsinoe far the most popular of the new Olympians, their poets' skittishness about the queens' (but not the kings') human and political aspect may reflect an inability to escape the old Greek penchant for portraying powerful women as somehow masculinized and monstrous (e.g., most memorably Clytemnestra).[19]

In all, then, the only "New Woman" that *Idyll* 15 illustrates for us is Arsinoe, and even she is portrayed so conservatively that one might easily overlook the unprecedented scale of her power. Gorgo and Praxinoa do not mark a radical new departure nor, however, do they in the slightest disprove the notion of increasing emancipation. The women of Alexandria could be making great strides without Theocritus' having any reason to note the fact, given his courtly intentions, or even particularly knowing about it. As ever we must reckon with the possibility that Greek men kept through life childhood impresssions of the domestic life of which they saw so little as adults. For Theocritus, that means Syracuse not Alexandria, where in any case he would know the Simaethas far better than the Praxinoas. While the particular details of *The Syracusan Women* are surely credible, the larger outlook is informative only about Arsinoe — as if she were not quite enough.

THE SORCERESS

Idyll 2 presents the tawdrier aspects of the same urban setting seen, ironically, from a much more innocent perspective. For all the violence of her feelings toward the faithless Delphis, Simaetha shows no interest in the pernicious inequalities between men and women or rich and poor. Delphis, in fact, comes from the cream of society as she from its margins, and as she quotes him, the audience realizes that he congenitally commands the sophisticated style and diction which Simaetha still clumsily affects.[20] There are lessons to be drawn here about the exploitation of women and the poor, such as Gorgo and Praxinoa would not fail to note. Yet when Simaetha finds spiritual solace in ignoring such issues, the audience may likewise feel absolved of the need to consider the inequities of class and sex. Whatever social ills may in fact have cheated her of happiness, Simaetha seems to find a profounder peace in contemplating the serene face of the moon. In radical contrast to *The Syracusan Women,* the technique of the poem is studiously apolitical in much the same way that Theocritus' pastorals are apolitical. Let us turn, therefore, from Theocritus the court poet to Theocritus the pastoralist.

Like Simaetha, Theocritus' herdsmen are obsessed with momentary problems. They resemble other mortals in getting enslaved, enraged, enamoured, wounded, cheated, raped, and spurned. Yet none of these woes preoccupies their labile minds for more than a few minutes at a time. There emerges a vision of life made not euphoric, but simple, and of human ills not denied, but shrunk into innocuousness. Theocritus' countryside is not an Eden walled off from death; it merely accommodates moments in human life when people are devoting earnest attention to reassuringly trivial problems. It is by having these simple folk take life so very seriously that the poet can establish with his refined audience a tone of mock-seriousness. The bucolic myths of freedom and pleasure operate by omission, by the larger anxieties which cast the merest shadows on the pleasance.

Simaetha has a good deal more to complain about than do most herdsmen and no trouble in attaining the requisite volume. Yet critics, variously heartened or disappointed, uniformly wonder why this fine young woman is not committing ot at least threatening suicide *comme il faut* after seduction and abandonment. Well, on closer examination we find that she leads what is, apart from utter wretchedness, quite a charmed life. In Greek literature the fallen woman must at the very least expect loss of honor and of family, and often enough pregnancy, madness, and murder (committed or suffered), as well as suicide. When in fact Simaetha walks away from the situation sadder, but wiser and otherwise intact, we may well have the sense conveyed by the pastorals of the essential harmlessness of life's injustices, of their tendency to issue in moments of fervent song without leaving permanent scars. It is all very well for Simaetha to fancy herself in the company of Circe and Medea (vv. 15–16), but if she's to be a proper heroine she must not end up crooning to the night sky at a moment when she should be tying a noose. The final tone seems somehow mock-tragic without being dismissive. As in the pastorals, Theocritus is not undercutting the character, but rather the character's obessions. To be sure, Simaetha's urban surroundings are not delightful in the way that the countryside is. But for Theocritus' elite audience they may be equally distant and exotic in their simplicity. And in both cases the suggestion of spiritual freedom in humble circumstances may derive more from the fancies of the educated than from the actual lives of the poor. The benign confidence that people can live in poverty without being degraded thereby may indicate an expansion of poetic sympathies — and Theocritus does handle such characters with obvious affection — or it may indicate that increasing social stratification had simply removed the unwashed masses to a distance where they could be quaint without being troubling.

Simaetha's durable innocence is even more remarkable than that of the herdsmen, since she maintains it in the midst of the demimonde. She rehearses for us a scene of seduction where one partner knows the rules and the other does not. She went to the Artemis festival where nothing, not even the lionesses, caught her eye so much as Delphis' glistening muscles (82): "I saw, and madness seized me, and my hapless heart was aflame". These are *almost* the correct symptoms, for love at first sight belongs more properly to the man. Delphis when summoned makes a point of pretending that it had already struck him. While she had a woman's proper physical reaction to an illicit love — wasting paralysis and hair-loss — she flouts even courtesan etiquette in simply sending for the young man. In accepting her flat invitation, Delphis tries to normalize the situation by claiming that he was already in the process of taking the initiative (has he even noticed her before?) and by pretending that she remains to be seduced. He treats her to a full-scale version of his polished "line", which shows a real mastery of the erotic clichés which Simaetha even now imitates with mixed success. He mentions the feminine resistance that adds savor to this sport; she offers none then nor three and four times a day thereafter. She has simply not figured out the rules nor even, in her naiveté, that there are rules. Delphis announced himself a competitor from his first words (vv. 114–116): "With thy summons to this house thou didst outrun my coming by no more than I of late outran the charming Philinus". Yet Simaetha has not perceived that this kind of liaison is a game with winners and losers, and that her lack of subtlety and device (not to mention wealth, social position, or even perhaps beauty)[21] destined her to disappointment from the first. A scene that should show her being corrupted in fact serves above all to establish her unassailable purity of heart. Whatever social codes she is violating, she is so little aware of them and such a stranger to guilt that one scarcely feels tempted to judge her. Indeed, nothing underscores the depth of her innocence so much as the forthrightness of her sexuality. She does not pursue Delphis for the sake of security, prestige, or money; nor does she use him in the total absence of other men in her life to define her values or goals. On the contrary, it is Delphis who fulfills the stereotypically feminine role of being devious, manipulative, and duplicitous.

By the end Simaetha has attained a kind of spiritual freedom. She has dispelled her delusions about Delphis and stops using language like his; all that can be done about longing, she now realizes, is to bear it. She ends with a delicate image of the beautifully throned Moon and the stars which surround the chariot of Night. The wild passions of the poem seem finally to have distilled themselves into aesthetic sublimation. Having lost in love, she would show herself fully victimized if she elected to continue playing the game in the same way. Instead she chooses to be honest with herself and to reject the vicious values and seductive delusions of the corrupt milieu into which she has fallen. Theocritus' other city dwellers, oblivious to the world beyond the city gates, trap themselves entirely in society and its vanities. Simaetha alone joins the herdsmen in letting nature clarify and deflate her current obsessions.

Simaetha's naiveté leaves her in a world which, for all its surface verism, is as simplified as that of the pastorals. We see it only through her eyes, and she shows no interest in money, social status, or any aspect of power. She cannot finally accept love relationships as essentially a matter of dominance and submission and accordingly abandons her sorcery halfway through the poem. As noted above, she could easily amplify her charges against Delphis as male exploitation of woman or upperclass exploitation of the disadvantaged. Her clear focus on her own emotions instead precludes a more complex view of society.

Such people have actually walked the face of the earth, so we are not yet beyond the realm of possibility. It is not, however, only Simaetha's heart that has remarkable simplicity in this poem, but also her circumstances — and here we run into grave problems if we ever mean to use the poem for social documentation. Not only is Simaetha refreshingly oblivious to money, but she also lives with no visible means of support and no apparent fears of being trapped in the demimonde or being sold into slavery. She has paid a large emotional price for her sexual indulgence, but has also somehow escaped the fact or fear of pregnancy.[22] She feels embarrassed before her friends, but does not fear ostracism or any substantial compromise of status. Most remarkably, she lives in a totally female milieu with no men in sight apart from the shadowy Delphis. Her single-sex world resembles the bucolic poems' all-male society which women enter only as a subject for song, and may be about as improbable.

Simaetha's freedom from supervision by father, brother, husband, or son has served as the chief literary evidence for a class of "liberated women" in these years.[23] But what precisely is she? Her but recently lost virginity compromises her credentials as a *hetaera*, as does her lack of commercial interest or *savoir faire* in dealing with Delphis. The diagnosis of "would-be courtesan" does not fit the end of the poem very well, as we have seen. Her wide-eyed reaction to the Artemis festival and need to borrow a cloak to attend it do not suggest someone (e.g., a flute girl) familiar with public life. Most often Simaetha is taken to be something like an orphan without male relatives, as could happen in the first generation of immigrants to the Ptolemaic cities. Yet such cases cannot have existed in sufficient numbers to make Simaetha broadly representative of the women of her age.

Gow[24] cites similarly free but impoverished women in the Athenian New Comedy of the preceding century. But the comedians, I submit, demonstrate the very thing we might suspect in *Idyll* 2: the juggling of facts to get plots to run. For Greek women, respectability directly excluded the latitude for action needed in a dramatic character. Yet the free and resourceful women in society, basically the *hetaera* class, had smaller claims on the audience's sympathies and were entitled to less happiness in the happy endings. In comedy, then, every use is made of those odd mischances (mistaken identities, temporary absences) which might give an honorable woman scope for independent action. Likewise Theocritus may be using a possible, but exceptional living arrangement to create an observer of the demimonde who does not alienate the audience by being fully part of it. Like the respectable women of New Comedy, Simaetha shows a miraculous ability to experience the larger world without finally being tainted by it. Herodas' *Mimes*, more or less contemporary with Theocritus, depict characters in this same urban milieu who lack Simaetha's spiritual distance from her corrupt surroundings, and to them we can react only with condescension and prurient amusement. Simaetha has far greater profundity as a portrait of the human soul, but as such may say little about the daily indignities of being poor, female, and alone.

Hard as it is to parallel Simaetha in historical terms, she may prove even more anomalous literarily. In Greek poetry other than Sappho, women invariably pursue love through a network of conflicting male claims. What choice the woman has is a choice of masters. She enters an illicit relationship with one male only by betraying another (usually father or husband); the end of the affair exposes her to the consequences of this betrayal (e.g., exile or the retribution of the wronged male). Even a symbol of female self-determination like Medea confronts no choices but those about men. To follow Jason, she betrayed her father and killed her brother. To repay Jason's perfidy, she killed her sons. To achieve a triumphant and safe departure, she relied on her grandfather's (Helius') chariot and the hospitality of Aegeus (with his need for male heirs). Though a figure of pure suffering, Simaetha has the immense advantage of having betrayed no one but herself; no men will now intercede to resolve her plight, for better or worse. She now has a luxury shared only by Sappho among Greek literature's amorous women: the chance to reflect on the matter at leisure afterwards. We know of no precedents for Simaetha's immunity to male influence, and even later poets who depict the lament of the abandoned woman cannot resist painting a man into the canvas somewhere. In adapting *Idyll* 2 in *Eclogue* 8, Virgil added the possibility of the returning lover's footstep heard on the threshold, and in any case it is a man who sings the woman's part here in the bucolic singing match. Catullus' Ariadne in *Peleus and Thetis* (64) has some moments of solitude on the shore, but Dionysus impends. Even in Hades Virgil's Dido, who in committing suicide has certainly earned her privacy, in fact goes off to the protection of the shade of her husband Sychaeus. The common experience of these women is that it is easy enough to get abandoned by a lover, but nearly impossible to shake loose of men altogether.

Simaetha alone presents a totally self-defining female consciousness. She acts for herself and thinks for herself. Her sensibilities are not lost in a network of overlapping and conflicting male relationships, as is the case for all the great heroines. She alone can peer into her own soul without finding the internalized images of father, brother, husband, or son to impose standards on her. Her social values derive entirely from her women friends; her religious thinking entails an exclusively female pantheon (Hecate, Artemis, the Moon). Even Sappho in eliminating men as objects for love defines herself against them as erotic competition. The *Sorceress* almost seems to raise the speculation: What would be left in a female character if one stripped away the roles of daughter, sister, wife, and mother?

From a male poet the probable answer is "a man", and we must admit that Simaetha does reflect some suspiciously masculine attitudes. She did the pursuing; Delphis' role was to be beautiful and fickle. What caught Simaetha's fancy was his well-oiled muscles, a susceptibility familiar in ancient men (e.g., in the sharp eyes of the Socratic circle), but not in women so far as we hear. Delphis' language about himself is sexually ambiguous;[25] in proper Sapphic fashion Simaetha compares his splendor to the Moon (v. 79).[26] She does not know whether she has been replaced by a man or a woman, that is, whether Delphis is playing the active role with a woman or the passive *eromenos* role with an older man.[27] Indeed, Simaetha's disillusionment and resignation echo nothing in the *Idylls* so closely as the laments about the inconstancy of boys that we hear from the aging pederasts of *Idylls* 29 and 30. Her passionate self-reflections and allusions to Sappho draw the poem close even in form to these Aeolic idylls, and *Idyll* 30, in particular, offers far the closest parallel in Theocritus, indeed in all of Greek literature, for Simaetha's dawning awareness that love is a disease caused by illusions whose virulence may have little to do finally with the particular beloved.

Simaetha's distress does not result, as noted above, from feminine vulnerabilities like pregnancy, loss of honor, or financial dependency, but seems the inevitable experience of any romantic soul in the process of being disillusioned. Theocritus likes this theme and dramatizes it in at least another half dozen sentimental lovers, all male, who are being evaded by love objects with more wit and less feeling than themselves. Some versions of this romantic impasse (e.g., *Idylls* 3, 6 and 14; cf. 13) draw on a polarity between male straightforwardness and female guile which, if applied to *Idyll* 2, puts Simaetha in the role of the feckless suitor. If woman's lot is to be "used" and abandoned, the willing Simaetha was not "used" and all of Theocritus' male lovers get abandoned too. She joins the men of Greek literature and fewer of the women in yielding to the simplest sort of bait: a pretty face and fetching manner. Other things that Greek women customarily seek from a man — protection, position, approval — do not for the moment preoccupy her, though she does mention marriage in passing. None of the women but Simaetha seeks or can offer the one thing eternally hoped for by the men: a free and unencumbering exchange of sexual gratification.

At this point, lest Theocritus' preeminently ordinary Simaetha start seeming rather bizarrely transsexual, let us recall that in Greek literature characters may routinely be female without being entirely so. Audiences experienced the great women of the *Iliad* and the *Odyssey* as impersonated by bard or rhapsode; Clytemnestra, Antigone, and Lysistrata were, of course, played by men. Indeed, in symposia and elsewhere quite a lot of singing was done by transvestite singers,[28] and *Idyll* 2 would doubtless be performed, if at all, by a man.[29] A male character sings Virgil's imitation of it in *Eclogue* 8. In all, the Greek audience would not construe the femaleness of characters literally in the way that we do. Having elsewhere presented only male lovers, Theocritus will naturally cut Simaetha from the same cloth. Hellenistic love poetry in general celebrates little but *hetaerae* and beautiful youths, and both of these groups in themselves encouraged the dismantling of sexual stereotypes, for the *hetaerae* discredited the entrepreneurial spirit as an exclusively male trait, and in tormenting their suitors lovely youths provoked the paranoia that men of other cultures have reserved for women.

Once again Theocritus' herdsmen may provide a helpful analogy. They come from the lowest stratum of society, but regularly "live above their intellectual means"[30] in singing like the most cultivated of *litterateurs*. They embody the charming paradox of spiritual richness in the midst of poverty, of great freedom in lives which present no real choices. In their elemental solitude they can still sometimes experience the world as it was before the advent of women, untroubled by the opposition of male and female and careless of the boundary between animal and human. Like them, Simaetha exemplifies human universality in a humble particularity. She is poor, but we forget that. She uses the language of the streets, but also of Homer and Sappho. And though she starts out with the witchcraft that only women use, she finally demonstrates something far more universal about the capacity of the human soul to understand and heal itself. The absence of men from her life as anything but an emotional indulgence neutralizes gender distinctions as an active issue in the poem and thereby makes Simaetha, like the herdsman, capable of speaking for all people. If the rustic is moment by moment variously philosopher, fool, king, criminal, artist, or savior, Simaetha, for all the improbable simplicity of her circumstances, merges traces of the erotic experience of *hetaera*, mythic heroine, pederast, and maiden. Poetically she is a triumph. But for documentary purposes, in escaping conventional femininity Simaetha also escapes usefulness. Her financial and spiritual autonomy may be no more than a happy fantasy clothed in credibly dreary details.

Finally, in comparing the two idylls we should note that they share the distinction of being the two poems from antiquity which most fully delineate the possibilities of a female world that runs itself. Both move their women characters from situations where they are at a disadvantage to men into a realm of unchallenged female predominance. So much is evident in Arsinoe's palace. Simaetha's attention similarly shifts from the world of society where one encounters such as Delphis (along with his gods and heroes: Dionysus, Heracles, Hephaestus) to the consoling world of nature, which is female in all of its aspects: Aphrodite, Artemis, Hecate, Dawn, Moon. Simaetha had initially felt herself alienated from this realm (vv. 38–39): "Lo, still is the sea, the breezes still; yet not still the torment in my breast". By the end, of course, she is in harmony with the moon and peaceful sky and thereby immersed in a triumph of the female principle as solacing to her as Arsinoe's festival is pleasantly distracting for the housewives.

It is, therefore, perfectly understandable that these two poems should routinely be taken *faute de mieux* as an ancient anticipation of feminism, when, in fact, they are if anything a call to complacency about the status of real women. *Idyll* 15's reassurance that nature has picked its queens well implies that the election and exploitation of housewives is comparably just and inevitable. There are no Arsinoes at one end of society without Praxinoas at the other. Likewise, Simaetha's gradual and surprising growth from a social "type" into a sensibility of universal appeal, and with it the reperception of her surroundings from low-rent district to lovely starry night, leaves questions posed initially about manners and class to be answered at last in spiritual and aesthetic terms or, if you will, not answered at all. Overshadowed as she is by the moon, the heavens, and Mother Nature, even Simaetha senses the negligibility of her afflictions. That she does not put anything like a feminist reading on her own experiences largely prevents the audience from doing so. God's in Her heaven; all's right with the world.

What I think we are seeing at work here in relation to sex are functions of pastoral and courtly myths already well understood in relation to social class. As critics started noting with Puttenham's *Arte of English Poesie* (1589) and stopped denying after the work of Poggioli and especially Empson,[30] the pastoral refuge to the apolitical realm of nature is itself susceptible of a political reading in that the form implies "a proper or beautiful relationship between rich and poor",[31] as between ruler and ruled. Amidst the riches of nature, herdsmen rule their sheep; Marie Antoinette roamed Versailles dressed as a shepherdess. The harmony between these social polarities, king and shepherd, suggests the compatibility of the orders in between, as well as the naturalness and inevitability of the ranking. Thieves can serve in place of shepherds (Empson adduces Gay's *Beggar's Opera*) as can children (*Alice in Wonderland*), since both the underworld and the nursery appear to outsiders as topsy-turvy inversions of usual and anxious experience, refuges for wise fools. Indeed almost any sort of humble circumstances can spawn myths of liberating simplicity as long as they are sufficiently unknown to the audience. Already Theocritus finds such lives as easily in the city as in the country (in *Idyll* 14, as well as 2 and 15).

The fantasies that the privileged harbor about everyone else of course tell us quite a bit about what men suspect of women. Theocritus is only the first to attribute equally to women and herdsmen qualities of carefree powerlessness (charmingly shielded by constant distraction), childlike resilience, and proximity to nature. Like Simaetha, his rustics do fall perishingly in love (*Idylls* 3, 6, 10, 11) — but without any possible threat of success. Simaetha and the rest may all wake up on the morrow still tragically in love, but not necessarily with the same person. Some of his herdsmen, like Gorgo and Praxinoa, are more capable of staying constantly upset than of remembering exactly why. Gorgo, Praxinoa, and Simaetha are all ter-

ribly stirred up by women's usual experience, and the poet notes
their troubles carefully and with sympathy. Neither poem suggests
by its end, however, that we are dealing with more than a tempest
in a teapot. Tomorrow will be another day. And are we surprised
if a poet who can envy shepherds their poverty can also unsee the
inequities of sex?

   Still and all, we remember Simaetha as a female character and
one who compels respect. Gorgo and Praxinoa may be a poetic trifle,
but they are human and memorable in a way that the baroque masterpieces of the Alexandrians are not. The formidable Arsinoe we ignore at our own peril. Whatever their motives, Theocritus and his
contemporaries are at least paying women the compliment of new
sorts of attention, even if that attention yields little of direct
documentary value. We must only keep in mind that from poets as
ironic and as snobbish as they attention may be a left-handed compliment, as we often see with the other new subject matters of
Alexandrian high literature: the very old and the infantile;
herdsmen, of course; enchanted beauties and the monstrously ugly;
slaves; oracular foetuses; talking crows; the urban poor. The imposing heroes and their ladies who had monopolized Greek literature
were now boring and inimitable. But the colonization of new poetic
areas entailed both curiosity and condescension, sympathy and dismissive irony. An educated female audience influenced literature as
never before, sometimes by patronage, but the innocuous and divine
image of the great queens suggests their hope that men not resent
nor women presume to their new-found powers. The single and famous example of pastoral poetry should sound a sufficient warning
about the other new subjects, for here modern critics have found the
model case of surface simplicity harboring a bewildering mix of poetic attitudes. Line by line a herdsman can change from the poet's
ideal to his fool; irony made flesh, then noble savage; royal, rude,
wry, then dense. Properly underestimated, women subjects, as we
have seen, fall prey just as easily to "the pastoral process of putting
the complex into the simple",[32] and that is one of literature's most
complicated operations. When in Alexandria the New Women enter
literature in the same mysteriously mixed ranks of queens and
shepherdesses (or their urban sisters), scenes apparently drawn

from life reveal, on closer examination, immensely complex sub-
texts. The static and credible cultural datum that Praxinoa's husband is a tyrant ultimately serves the demonstration that Arsinoe
is not. Though the fully autonomous Simaetha might exemplify a
real (though necessarily rare and otherwise unattested) possibility
for Hellenistic women, as a poetic voice she speaks with Teiresian
range for the erotic experience of both sexes, and the social historian
cannot circumvent the lingering suspicion that the man in
Simaetha's life is herself. Those who have sensed emancipation in
this verse — despite all of its crabbed and erudite deviousness —
were surely right to do so. But we sense that freedom also in
herdsmen, in mythic heroes and monsters (the Cyclops becomes a
lover as well as a cannibal), in infants and Olympians. That sense
of emancipation may derive less from new social realities than from
the poetic project of liberating literature, now turned playful, from
its direct relationship to life. Women's problems inevitably look less
grave in a poetry that takes few problems seriously but those of style
and patronage.

Notes

1. See Claire Préaux, "Le Statut de la femme à l'époque hellénistique, principalement en Egypt", *Recueils de la Société Jean Bodin* 11: *La femme* (1959) I.
   127–175, and Claude Vatin, *Recherches sur le mariage et la condition de la femme
   mariée à l'époque hellénistique* (Paris 1970) 241–254.
2. The term used by Charles Seltman, *Women in Antiquity* (London and New
   York 1956) 138–158.
3. Earlier work on *Idyll* 2 is surveyed by Peter Henkel, "Zu Theokrit, Id. II. VV.
   38–42 (28–32)", *Serta Philologica Aenipontana*, ed. Robert Muth (*Inns-
   brucker Beiträge zur Kulturwissenschaft* 7–8 [1962]) 191–214. See most recently
   Charles Segal, "Simaetha and the Iynx (Theocritus, Idyll II)", *Quaderni Urbinati di Cultura Classica* 15 (1973) 32–43.
4. So Seltman, *op. cit.*, p. 155.
5. "Einer der grossen Entdecker der Frauenseele" — Carl Schneider, *Kulturge-
   schichte des Hellenismus* (Munich 1969) I. 107. Among recent publications,
   Schneider's chapter "Die Frau und das Frauenbild des Hellenismus" (pp.
   78–117) puts the literary evidence, especially Theocritus, to fullest and best
   use. Other recent works which make use of him are Verena Zinserling, *Women
   in Greece and Rome*, trans. L.A. Jones (New York 1972) 36–37; Sarah B.
   Pomeroy, *Goddesses, Whores, Wives, and Slaves* (New York 1975) 147–148; and
   Mary R. Lefkowitz and Maureen B. Fant, *Women in Greece and Rome* (Toronto

and Sarasota 1977) 88–90 and 100–101. On Theocritus' view of women, cf. also Anna Rist, *The Poems of Theocritus*(Chapel Hill 1978) 38.

6. I have dicussed Theocritus' relations with the Ptolemies at length in *Theocritus at Court* (Leiden 1979), to which I refer the reader for documentation of positions presented here in summary fashion.

7. Arsinoe II's life is well recounted by Grace Macurdy, *Hellenistic Queens* (Baltimore 1932), and most recently by Gabriella Longega, *Arsinoe II* (Rome 1968).

8. Athenaeus xiv. 621 B = Powell, *Coll. Alex.* 238.

9. See in general P.M. Fraser, *Ptolemaic Alexandria* (3 vols., Oxford 1972).

10. See Sarah B. Pomeroy, "Technikai kai Mousikai: The Education of Women in the Fourth Century and in the Hellenistic Period", *American Journal of Ancient History* 2 (1977) 60–61.

11. Exactly the same pattern is to be found in Theocritus' tribute to Ptolemy II in *Idyll* 14; see Griffiths, *op. cit.*, pp. 109–116.

12. This and following translations are by A.S.F. Gow, *Theocritus*[2] (2 vols., Cambridge 1952; reprinted 1965).

13. *The Gardens of Adonis: Spices in Greek Mythology*, trans. Janet Lloyd (Atlantic Highlands, N.J. 1977).

14. This theme is developed very much more explicitly in the *Encomium of Ptolemy*, *Idyll* 17. 77–85, again in the mode of paradox, for rainless Egypt is the most abundant of lands.

15. So Pomeroy, *Goddesses*, p. 148.

16. On the political situation in Ithaca, see Helene P. Foley, "'Reverse Similes' and Sex Roles in the *Odyssey*", *Arethusa* 11 (1978), 7–26.

17. For example, in *Idyll* 14. 60–64 he is described in conversation: "The very best — kindly, cultured, gallant, as pleasant as may be; knows his friend, and knows his enemy even better. As a king should be, he's generous to many, and doesn't refuse when asked . . ."

18. See Rudolph Pfeiffer, "Arsinoe Philadelphos in der Dichtung", *Die Antike* 2 (1926) 161–174. I would add *Idyll* 18, *The Epithalamium for Helen*, to the list of poems celebrating Arsinoe in her divine aspect; see Griffiths, *op. cit.*, pp. 52–57 and 86–91.

19. This phenomenon is very evident in Callimachus. See Konrad Ziegler, "Kallimachos und die Frauen", *Die Antike* 12 (1937) 20–42.

20. I have elsewhere discussed the relationship of style and characterization: "Poetry as Pharmakon in Theocritus' *Idyll* 2", in *Arktouros: Hellenic Studies Presented to Bernard M.W. Knox on the Occasion of his 65th Birthday*, edd. G.W. Bowerstock, W. Burkert, and M.C.J. Putnam (Berlin and New York 1979) 81–88.

21. So suggests her name: *simos* means "snub-nosed"; -*aetha* shows up in Theocritean animal names (*Idylls* 1. 151, 4. 46, and 5. 102).

22. Kenneth J. Dover, *Theocritus* (Basingstoke and London 1971) 96, speculates about Greek advances in contraceptive and abortifacient techniques, but Simaetha's naiveté and recklessness in sexual matters diminish the likelihood of her technical mastery here. Infanticide remained an option, but would we expect casualness about the prospect to the point of omission from a young woman so sentimental about babies and dolls and so unsparing in her bill of particulars against Delphis?

23. See Ulrich von Wilamowitz-Moellendorff, "Des Mädchens Klage", in *Kleine Schriften* (Berlin and Amsterdam 1971) II. 114. Dover, *op. cit.*, pp. 95–96, provides a helpful summary of the arguments adduced by other commentators (Legrand, Cholmeley, Gow, and Monteil).

24. *Op. cit.*, II. 33. See also the excellent collection of evidence of Elaine Fantham, "Sex, Status, and Survival in Hellenistic Athens: A Study of Women in New Comedy", *The Phoenix* 29 (1975) 44–74; esp. 61–62.

25. He compares his passion to that which "scares a maiden from her bower, and a bride to quit her husband's bed ere it be cold" (vv. 136–137).

26. *Idyll* 2's extensive allusions to Sappho have inspired speculations about her possible Lesbianism from George Devereux, "The Nature of Sappho's Seizure in Fr. 31 LP as Evidence of her Inversion", *Classical Quarterly* N.S. 20 (1970) 17–31. He diagnoses "manifest homosexual overtones" in her reference to Delphis' own sexual ambivalence, her manifest anxiety (taken to by symptomatic of crises of pederastic, but not heterosexual love), and her use of black magic (a symptom of anxiety among primitives). His contention that "what really matters is not Simaetha's love-sorrows and jealousy, but her anxiety" (p. 25) may not persuade many readers of the poem, who are therefore directed to the counterarguments of F. Manieri, "Saffo: appunti di metodologia generale per un approccio psichiatrico", *Quaderni Urbinati de Cultura Classica* 14 (1972) 46–64.

27. See Kenneth J. Dover, *Greek Homosexuality* (Cambridge, Massachusetts 1978) 67.

28. See Andreas Rumpf, "Zu einer Vase der Sammlung Robinson", in *Studies Presented to David Moore Robinson*, edd. G.E. Mylonas and D. Raymond (Saint Louis 1953) II. 84–89.

29. Presumably by Theocritus, who in *Idyll* 7 apparently uses a pseudonym, "Simichidas", strangely reminiscent of "Simaetha".

30. Bruno Snell, *The Discovery of the Mind*, trans. Thomas Rosenmeyer (Oxford 1953) 286.

31. William Empson, *Some Versions of Pastoral* (Norfolk, Connecticut 1960) 11.

32. *Ibid.*, p. 23.

Asclepiades' girl friends

ALAN CAMERON

Columbia University

I

THE SOCIAL, moral and marital status of the ladies of the Roman love elegists has been long and solemnly debated — if to little avail.[1] By contrast, no attention at all has been paid to the women of a genre that is known to have exerted considerable influence on the elegists, hellenistic love epigram.[2]

It is easy to see why. Of its three most distinguished and prolific exponents, Meleager's fantastic arsenal of Cupids, arrows and torches is directed with no discernible difference of tone or circumstance against boys and girls. Callimachus writes only of boys. And as for Asclepiades of Samos, though he writes only of women,[3] in many different moods, it has always been taken for granted that they are 'hetairas'.

Critics prefer the word 'hetaira' because it suggests something more glamorous and less sordid than 'prostitute'. Now some of the hetairas of fifth and fourth century Athens do seem to have been women of education and culture who could supply Athenian males with the sort of intellectual as well as sexual companionship that they did not usually get from their wives.[4] However, we must beware of swallowing uncritically the romanticised (and still current) picture of the Intellectual Whore, more poet and philosopher than sexual gymnast. There can be little doubt that many hetairas acquired and used their culture in order to ensnare and fleece more cultivated and therefore wealthier clients, like the courtesans of Renaissance Rome and Venice[5] and the 'pretty Horsebreakers' of nineteenth century London and Paris,[6] to name two other brief moments in history when a small number of high class prostitutes acquired not only great wealth but also a surprising degree of social acceptance. But at all times and places, and certainly in their golden age at Athens, even the most accomplished courtesans were best known for their rapacity.

Did this Athenian 'Hetärenwesen' (as the Germans nicely call it) survive in all its glory into the hellenistic age? So most scholars have presumed. Yet the abundant (if suspect) information on hetairas in Book XIII of Athenaeus' *Deipnosophists* was collected almost entirely from Attic comedy and the Attic orators. It was originally put together by hellenistic scholars evidently fascinated by the flamboyant *femmes fatales* they had read about in their classics. Athenaeus supplies an illuminating bibliography: 'Aristophanes, Apollodorus, Ammonius, Antiphanes and Gorgias of Athens, all of whom have written on the hetairas of Athens' (567A). Aristophanes was apparently first in the field, but the later writers were able to add substantially to his total of 135 hetairas (583E). Another earlier writer laid under heavy contribution by Athenaeus is Machon.[7] The obvious implication is that the radiant charmers of Athenian society were *not* still to be found at every hellenistic symposium. Prostitution itself will naturally have continued to flourish, especially in a great seaport such as Alexandria.[8] But what was the social standing of even the most expensive? Did the jeunesse dorée still fight over the honour of squandering fortunes on them, as they did in fourth century Athens and were to again in nineteenth century London?[9] In most ages not even poets (who seldom have the money anyway) are prepared to admit that they patronize prostitutes and even to boast of being their slaves. It may be significant that almost all the hetairas known by name after the fourth century were mistresses[10] of hellenistic kings, whom we should not lightly presume to have kept open salon.

Nonetheless his commentators have taken it for granted that Asclepiades (who wrote mostly in early third century B.C. Alexandria)[11] moved in the same erotic world as the feckless young heroes of New Comedy. Conspicuously so the authoritative edition of Gow and Page,[12] though no one perhaps has put it quite so bluntly as P.M. Fraser:[13]

this world of venal love, in which the young of both sexes refuse and grant their
favours with equanimity and impartiality, on a cash basis.

Is this really the world Asclepiades wrote of? Even as a fictive world,
is it credible in any age?

The underlying assumption is presumably that no woman mentioned in an erotic poem can be respectable;[14] that even without
specific pointers contemporary readers would automatically and in-
stinctively have identified Asclepiades' girlfriends as prostitutes.
Now in fifth and fourth century Athens this presumption may not
have been far off the mark. There it may well have been true that
"unmarried men had no opportunities for heterosexual activity except with prostitutes and slaves".[15] This is why it was only at religious festivals that the respectable girls of New Comedy got pregnant.[16]

But Athens was unusually repressive in this respect. By the third
century elsewhere in the Greek world the status of women was im-
proving.[17] More specifically, there is evidence for a growth in education of women outside the home,[18] giving respectable women one of
the advantages till then enjoyed by hetairas alone. Thus we need
not automatically assume that any woman present at a symposium
was a hetaira. For example, there is nothing in the poem itself to
suggest that the girl Cynisca who participates in the rustic symposium of Theocritus XIV is a hetaira.[19] Æschinas is distressed to
have lost her, but there is no question of the depth and sincerity of
her passion for Lykos. Gorgo and Praxinoa in Theocritus XV are
bourgeois housewives who move freely about Alexandria on foot,
bumping into and talking with strange men whom they meet on the
way.[20] Simaetha in Theocritus II is a poor but respectable girl who
lives alone with a maid, a virgin until she gave herself to the faithless
Delphis.[21] The so called *Fragmentum Grenfellianum* is a lament sung
by a girl who has walked through the streets at night (naturally with
an attendant, 1.25) to the house of the beloved who has left her to
sleep alone.[22]

The pages that follow have the limited aim of suggesting (1) that
there is seldom the slightest indication in the poems that
Asclepiades' girlfriends expect money in return for their favours;

and (2) that on the contrary, many of his poems make much better sense if we assume that they do not. The girls may not all be chaste, but with one or two exceptions that prove the rule, they are certainly not prostitutes.

II

We may begin with a simple case, Asclepiades III (*AP* v. 153):

> Νικαρέτης τὸ πόθοις βεβλημένον ἡδὺ πρόσωπον
> πυκνὰ δι' ὑψηλῶν φαινόμενον θυρίδων
> αἱ χαροπαὶ Κλεοφῶντος ἐπὶ προθύροισι μάραναν,
> Κύπρι φίλη, γλυκεροῦ βλέμματος ἀστεροπαί.

The bright lightning of the sweet eye of Cleophon blasted
Nicarete's sweet face, smitten by the Desires,
appearing often through the high windows,
as he stood at the threshold, dear Cypris.

'The fact that Nicarete is often to be seen at her window probably indicates that she is a hetaira, or at least not unduly modest', remarks Gow primly. It is true that a prostitute might be pictured beckoning to potential customers through an open window, but that can hardly be the case here. In line 1, P (the only manuscript) offers πόθοισι. All editors since Wilamowitz have objected both to the prosody βεβλημένον and to the description of Nicarete as 'smitten with desire'. Hence Wilamowitz' generally accepted conjecture βεβαμμένον, 'bathed *in* desire' — more appropriate to the presumed beckonings of the whore. Yet a simpler and more satisfactory way to correct the prosody (if correction is needed) is Pfeiffer's πόθοις.[23] And far from the announcement that Nicarete is 'smitten with desire' anticipating 1.3 'unsuitably' (Gow), on the contrary it alerts us for the eventual revelation of the source of her passion. For the point of the poem is surely that it is a one-way passion. It is Cleophon's flashing eyes that 'wither' her from the porch. No doubt he is staring up at her flirtatiously, but there is no hint in the poem that he reciprocates her passion — or indeed that he has ever actually spoken to her. The fact that her face is *often* at an upstairs (ὑψηλῶν) window suggests that this is the only way she can get to see him. In fact, it is clearly a story of (? first) love at a distance. Far from being a hetaira luring clients in off the streets, Nicarete is an innocent young girl kept in seclusion by her parents who is devastated by the sight of a handsome youth on the doorstep (perhaps a delivery boy), and forced to spend her days looking out of her bedroom window for his visits.

Before passing on we ought perhaps to consider frag. 8 of Praxilla,[24] which is often held to have been Asclepiades' source:

> ὦ διὰ τῶν θυρίδων καλὸν ἐμβλέποισα
> παρθένε τὰν κεφαλὰν τὰ δ' ἔνερθε νύμφα.

You who look prettily in through windows,
maiden in your head, bride below.

Most commentators have inferred from 1.2 that the girl is a whore with the face of a virgin. Obviously, if Praxilla's poem is about a whore, this will have a bearing on the interpretation of Asclepiades' poem. But why is the girl looking *in* rather than out of the windows? Perhaps ἐκβλέποισα, 'looking out,' remarks Page in his note, unless (he adds) the girl is so shameless that she is wandering down the street looking in windows to lure prospective clients out of their very front doors. Such aggressive salesmanship might astonish even in Times Square. W. Aly came up with an ingenious and attractive alternative:[25] no mortal girl at all, but Selene, the Moon, who gazes in through peoples' windows (explaining the plural) as she sweeps across the night sky 'in maidenly inaccessibility'; and when she is below the horizon during the day — τὰ δ' ἔνερθε — is Endymion's wife. This may be thought a shade too fanciful; it explains the 'below' to perfection, but 'maiden as to your head' rather less well. Yet the traditional explanation is no more satisfactory. While one can say in most languages that a girl has the face of a virgin but the heart or body of a whore, it is surely very odd to say that she has the head of a virgin but is a *bride* (or married woman) *beneath*. Marriage marks the end of virginity, to be sure, but most people consider it respectable enough. If we had the rest of Praxilla's poem these two lines might take on a meaning we could never have guessed: perhaps, for example, a creature with the head of a mortal maid but quite literally a nymph (an immortal) lower down. At all events, whether or not Asclepiades knew the poem, the interpretation of these two lines is far too uncertain to warrant importing the notion of an unchaste woman into Asclepiades. Depending on the interpretation, Asclepiades may have nothing in common with Praxilla beyond a reference to windows. More relevant, in fact, is the scene in Aristophanes' *Ecclesiazusae* (884 f.) in which a young girl peeps out of an upper storey window. To be sure this girl is behaving more provocatively than Nicarete; she is hoping — unsuccessfully in the event — that her boyfriend will pop up while mother is out. Yet it would be ruinous to the plot of the play if she were a prostitute.[26]

That some at least of the girls Asclepiades wrote of were not merely respectable but actually virgins is proved by II (v. 85), open-φείδῃ παρθενίης;

> Pretty maiden, what's the good
> of hoarding up your maidenhood?

in Phillimore's translation,[27] concluding with the reflection that was to be urged so often in future centuries on reluctant virgins,

> Once in Acheron we must,
> maiden, come to bones and dust.

Compare too the charming description of a young girl called Eirenion in XXXIV (v. 194, ascribed to 'Asclepiades or Posidippus'), with whom all the boys are in love.[28] The attentions of the young men are inspired by the arrows of the Erotes, not her own coquettishness, and especially in view of the reference at 1.4 to her 'maidenly charms' there seems no reason to see her as a hetaira. Compare too *AP* v. 199 by Asclepiades' disciple Hedylus, about a girl (ironically called Aglaonice, 'Spendid Victory') who has lost her virginity after a party, undone by wine and the love of Nicagoras.[29] 'On the hetaira Aglaonice', sternly remarked the corrector of the Palatine manuscript; for once even Gow was moved to concede that this was 'not necessarily' so. Young girls who go to riotous parties may not be as modest as their parents might wish, but they do not have to be prostitutes.

III

Next IV (v. 158):

> Ἑρμιόνη πιθανῇ ποτ' ἐγὼ συνέπαιзον ἐχούσῃ
> зώνιον ἐξ ἀνθέων ποικίλον, ὦ Παφίη,
> χρύσεα γράμματ' ἔχον· 'διόλου' δ' ἐγέγραπτο 'φίλει με,
> καὶ μὴ λυπηθῇς ἤν τις ἔχῃ μ' ἕτερος'.

> I played once with obliging Hermione, and she wore
> a girdle of variegated flowers, Paphian queen, with
> golden letters. All around it was written: "love me—
> and don't be upset if another has me".

'On a hetaira whose inscribed girdle warns the lover against jealousy' (Gow). 'The adjective is somewhat surprising', he remarks on πιθανῆ. It is in fact a good example of a characteristic device of Asclepiades, a word or phrase in the first line that (for the alert reader) anticipates or foreshadows the conclusion of the poem.[30] Hermione is obliging, pliant, suggestible, accommodating. That is to say she gives in too easily. The point is caught nicely in Phillimore's version,

> Once as I toyed with that Hermione
> whose tender heart no suitor could not melt,

but his explicitness destroys Asclepiades' subtlety. The reader cannot be sure which of the possible meanings of πιθανῆ to choose until he has got to the end of the poem. In the same way, it is not till he has got to the end of the Nicarete poem that the reader appreciates why she is smitten with desire. Compare too VII where the apparently casual information that the women named are from Samos (an island proverbial for female licentiousness) prepares us for what is to come. One or two further examples will be quoted below.

The point of the poem is that Hermione is *not* a whore. Indeed the poet takes her for a respectable woman. Although he has already noted her complaisance while they 'play together', he is apparently surprised by the announcement of her promiscuity. If she had been a whore, obviously he would have expected both as a matter of course. συνέπαιζον certainly implies 'amorous dalliance' (as Gow archly puts it), but clearly not (in the context) actual sexual intercourse.[31] The girdle is of course an undergarment; it is not till he has partially undressed the girl that he comes across the gold letters.[32] We are hardly intended to think him too naive till then to see her true nature (that is the theme of poem VIII). It is by her promiscuity and avarice that a hetaira reveals her nature, not by discreet advance warnings.

Like several others of Asclepiades' poems, this one is about a specific type of girl. Nothing so general as a hetaira, who is mercenary as well as promiscuous. She is simply a flirt, the girl who 'can't say no'. The poet should have guessed that a girl who gave way so easily to him would give way as easily to another. Provided he can accept this, he is free to love her with all his heart — scarcely the advice of a hetaira.

IV

Perhaps the most puzzling of Asclepiades' poems is IX (v. 7):

> Λύχνε, σὲ γὰρ παρεοῦσα τρὶς ὤμοσεν 'Ηράκλεια
> ἥξειν κοὔχ ἥκει· λύχνε, σὺ δ᾽ εἰ θεὸς εἶ
> τὴν δολίην ἔ πάμυνον· ὅταν φίλον ἔνδον ἔχουσα
> παίзῃ ἀποσβεσθεὶς μηκέτι φῶς πάρεχε.

> Lamp, three times Heracleia swore in your presence
> to come, and comes not. Lamp, if you are a god,
> assist her trickery. When she has a friend at home
> and is sporting with him, go out and provide no more light.

Commentators have made extraordinarily heavy weather of this poem, 'une des épigrammes les plus controversées de l'Anthologie' according to Giangrande.[33] Is the lamp by which Heracleia perjures herself in her room or the poet's? Or are there two different lamps;

do lamps 'make common cause, [so] that the poet's lamp can control
the behaviour of Heracleia's' (Gow, with a variation, capitalizing
Λύχνος, by M. Marcovich)?[34] Or is the poet 'waiting neither in his
house nor in hers but in a room which she uses for assignations'
(Gow, developed by Giangrande)?

These explanations all share one fatal flaw. The one thing they
do not explain is the climax of the poem: in what way does the extinction of the lamp pay Heracleia back for her trickery?

'Lovers keep the lamp alight', comments Page, on a rather different poem by Meleager.[35] It is true that Greek and Roman poets frequently refer to lamps as witnesses of lovemaking,[36] but that is because people normally make love in private at night. So the bedroom
lamp witnesses what others do not. The lamp may be called the
'guardian' of the poet's beloved; sometimes the poet will guess from
the light in her window that his girl is with another man; and, like
everybody else, lovers extinguish the lamp when they are ready for
sleep. But none of these variations on the motif is quite the same as
saying that lovers prefer actually to make love with the light on. This
was surely a matter of taste. As one poet admitted, while he liked
'ludere teste lucerna', his modest wife preferred the light off (Martial, xi.104.5–6). After all, the lamp will usually have 'witnessed'
quite enough to compromise the lovers even if they extinguish it before actually getting into bed.

To return to Asclepiades IX, whether Heracleia and the poet's
rival are already making love or only about to, they are not going
to stop or abandon the idea just because the lamp goes out. The
climax of the poem cannot rest on such an improbable assumption.[37]
Most relevantly, on the universal assumption that Heracleia is a
prostitute, are we to believe that the client will ask for his money
back if the light goes out? For that is the only way a prostitute could
be punished effectively.

I suggest that Heracleia is not a prostitute, but another female
type: this time the tease. Neither the poet nor the rival are 'clients'
(note that the latter is described merely as a 'friend'), but admirers
whom she has so far kept at arm's length. It was during a visit by
the poet to her apartment to pay court to her that Heracleia (falsely)
swore by the lamp to spend a night with him. To get his own back

he envisages an occasion when she is 'playing her game' with a rival: that is to say making him too promises she has no intention of keeping. παίζῃ again of flirting or petting rather than intercourse itself. It is at this moment that the poet wants the lamp to extinguish itself. How will the rival take it?

Naturally he will assume that Heracleia has turned it out. Now people do not normally turn their lamp out until they are ready for bed. The rival will hardly take it as a hint to leave or sleep in the spare room. He will assume that the 'play' of 1.3 was meant in earnest — and pounce.

On this interpretation it is a far more subtle poem: Heracleia's teasing really will be her undoing. And in support consider more closely the first verb in 1.3. P offers ἀπάμυνον, which editors all interpret in the otherwise unparalleled sense 'punish'; elsewhere it always means 'keep off', 'ward off', 'repel', meanings wholly unsuitable here. But Planudes has ἐπάμυνον which 'should mean *assist* and is therefore improbable' (Gow). Not on my interpretation.[38] The lamp does in fact 'assist' Heracleia's 'trickery', in the sense that it furthers the course of action Heracleia had been *pretending* to follow. She is giving the rival her usual deceitful encouragement; the lamp makes him think it is genuine.

Poem X (v. 150) ought perhaps to be considered together with this poem:

'Ωμολόγησ' ἥξειν εἰς νύκτα μοι ἡ 'πιβόητος
Νικὼ καὶ σεμνὴν ὤμοσε Θεσμοφόρον,
κοὐχ ἥκει, φυλακὴ δὲ παροίχεται. ἆρ' ἐπιορκεῖν
ἤθελε; τὸν λύχνον, παῖδες, ἀποσβέσατε.

That Niko that people talk about[39] agreed to call on
me at night, and swore by holy Demeter the lawgiver.
She comes not and the watch is passing. Did she
deliberately perjure herself? Boys, put out the lamp.

This lady looks somewhat shadier, but Gow was wrong to proclaim her a hetaira on the strength of the name, which was common among respectable women, most relevantly in his own Boy Meets Girl idyll XXXVI (v. 209). There are two details in the poem that need clarification. First, we are meant to appreciate how differently the lover reacts to his disappointment this time. Instead of getting angry or giving way to despair or plotting revenge, he coolly gets ready for bed. If Niko was playing hard to get, it was a play that failed. Secondly, the oath. As Gow remarked, Aphrodite, who notoriously laughed at lovers' perjuries, might have been expected rather than the more respectable Demeter Thesmophoros (note especially the epithet σεμνήν, the vox propia for Demeter).[40] The Thesmophoria (which we know to have been celebrated with great pomp in Ptolemaic Alexandria)[41] was restricted to respectable married women (as explained in Callimachus, fr.63. Pf.) and required, moreover, sexual abstinence before and during the festival. So which was the more sacrilegous, the making or the breaking of Niko's oath? The lover takes his deception so philosophically because he realizes that he should have guessed from so perverse an oath.

Connected with this poem is XIII (v. 164):[42]

Νύξ, σὲ γάρ, οὐκ ἄλλην, μαρτύρομαι, οἷά μ' ὑβρίζει
Πυθιὰς ἡ Νικοῦς οὖσα φιλεξαπάτις.
κληθείς, οὐκ ἄκλητος, ἐλήλυθα· ταὐτὰ παθοῦσα
σοὶ μέμψαιτ' ἐπ' ἐμοὶ στᾶσα παρὰ προθύροις.

Night, it is you I call upon, no other, to witness
what wrongs Pythias, Niko's girl, has done me, lover
of deceit that she is. I came not uninvited, but at
her invitation. May she suffer the same as she stands
outside my door and complains to you about me.

'Niko's girl' is surely not meant to name the bawd whose house Pythias works from (so Gow, literal-minded as ever). It is an allusion to the preceding poem; the reader is meant to recall the faithless Niko and reflect 'like mother like daughter'. The poem closes with a restrained treatment of that motif so mercilessly worked to death by later erotic poets, Greek and Latin, the rejected lover telling his girl that in time she too will love and be rejected (see Nisbet and Hubbard's ample commentary on Horace, Odes i.25, oddly not quoting this the earliest example). It was one thing if a girl did not invite in a lover who called unexpectedly; but to invite him and then bar the door, that was a calculated slight, incredible (or at any rate imprudent) for one who earned her living that way. There is nothing in the poem to suggest either that the poet cannot pay her price or that she was already entertaining a richer lover who had arrived first. Either Pythias does not reciprocate his passion; or she is playing hard to get; or she has chosen the most public and hurtful way of letting him know that the affair is over.

V

XXV and XXVI (v. 181 and 185) both present us with hosts going over their shopping lists for a party. The text of 181 is often uncertain, but the general sense of the first eight lines are clear and it will suffice for our purpose to give the Wallaces' translation, which conveys something of the detail and vividness of the original. The host, Bacchon, is discussing the prices with his slave:

> Three quarts of nuts — when will he come? —
> and five rose wreaths — what now? Be dumb!
> You've got no money, I suppose.
> O God! I'm ruined! Will none dispose
> of this great brute? A thief, it's plain
> I have, no servant. You complain
> you haven't robbed me? No, not you!
> Bring me your cash-book to go through.
> Phryne, go get it . . . Oh, the cheat!
> For wine, five drachmas . . . two for meat;
> oysters and honey, cakes and trout . . .
> tomorrow we'll get it straightened out.

It is the last four lines that cause problems:

> αὔριον αὐτὰ καλῶς λογιούμεθα, νῦν δὲ πρὸς Αἴσχραν
> τὴν μυρόπωλιν ἰὼν πέντε λάβ' ἀργυρέας·
> εἰπὲ δὲ σημεῖον Βάκχων ὅτι πέντ' ἐφίλησεν
> ἑξῆς, ὧν κλίνη μάρτυς ἐπεγράφετο.

> Now go to the perfume-seller Aeschra and get five
> silver flasks. And for identification tell her
> that I am the Bacchon who made love to her five times
> in a row: the bed is a certified witness.

First the motif of the σημεῖον. In a number of private letters preserved on papyrus the writer introduces with the formula σημεῖον
a proof of his identity that could only be known to his correspondent
and himself.[43] R. Merkelbach[44] at once appreciated the relevance of
this usage both to this poem and to *AP* v. 213 (discussed below). Unfortunately Merkelbach's own discussion of both poems seems to me
not quite to hit the nail on the head.

The σημεῖον is clearly the number of times Bacchon and Aeschra
had made love, a figure known only to them — and the bed. But
what of the ἀργυρέας which has so exercised commentators? The
Wallaces saw a reference to 'five pieces of silver which are either to
be paid to or borrowed from Aeschra', translating 'Bacchon will pay
for his kisses yet'. It will be noticed that behind any such interpretation there lurks the assumption that Aeschra trades her favours
for cash. As Meineke saw, the obvious solution is to understand
ληκύθους, 'silver phials'. Gow thought it 'most unlikely that perfume would be brought in silver λήκυθοι and that a host purchasing
perfume for his guests would buy it in separate receptacles'. But
surely the point and climax of the poem is precisely that, after all
the itemizing and penny-pinching of the first 8 lines, the poet sends
out a slave, who has already stated that he has no money left, for
a ridiculous extravagance, an individual silver perfume pot for each
guest. And the reason, of course, is that this is the only shop where
he can get *credit* — because of the hold he has over the girl who works
there. This is why he humorously adds, as though she might try to
deny it, that there was a witness of their love-making — the bed
(ἐπιγράφεσθαι 'is technical of the endorsement of witnesses on a de-
position', Gow).

Aeschra is not chaste — but not a prostitute either. She is a working woman, and in a luxury trade too.[45] It is the poet who is the
sponger, trying to exploit *his* favours for gain.

Before considering Aesclepiades' other shopping list poem, a
word on the evidently related poem *AP* v. 213 by Posidippus. The
poet is apparently addressing that indispensable figure in later erotic
elegy, the maid:

Πυθιὰς εἰ μὲν ἔχει τιν' ἀπέρχομαι· εἰ δὲ καθεύδει
ὧδε μόνη μικρὸν πρὸς Διὸς εἰσκαλέσαι.

εἰπὲ δὲ σημεῖον, μεθύων ὅτι καὶ διὰ κλωπῶν
ἦλθον Ἔρωτι θρασεῖ χρώμενος ἡγεμόνι.

If Pythias is with someone, I'm off. If she's
sleeping alone, let me in for a moment, for God's
sake. Tell her in identification that I'm the one
who came drunk, through footpads, with the boldness
of Love as my guide.

In the light of the σημεῖον motif, it should be clear that we must restore P's ἦλθεν (universally rejected by editors) to the text in 1.4,
in place of the early modern conjecture ἦλθον.[46] The poet is not
speaking of his present visit, but of the earlier occasion from which
he hopes that Pythias will remember him.

Gow remarks that μεθύων, drunk, is 'unexpected, since that is
the usual condition of comasts'. That (of course) is precisely the
point. The poem fits into that well known category, the
paraclausithuron. To judge from the dozens of examples studied by
F.A. Copley in his useful monograph,[47] the streets of hellenistic cities
were packed with young men driven by liquor and lecherousness to
brave footpads in laying siege to the doors of any presentable female,
respectable or not (Pythias clearly not). Posidippus' description
would have fitted 75% of Pythias' clients. It is as though a young
man today, in a similar situation, had told the maid: she'll remember
me, the football fan who called once a bit drunk on a Saturday night.

Posidippus was much influenced by the work of Asclepiades,[48]
and there can be no doubt that it was from this very poem of
Asclepiades that he took the σημεῖον motif. But he has adapted it
more cleverly than has been appreciated. Whereas the reader of
Asclepiades' poem feels that Bacchon may well get his silver perfume pots, Posiduppus' young man is surely going to have Pythias'
door slammed in his face.

Now to the second of Asclepiades' shopping lists, XXVI (v. 185):

Εἰς ἀγορὰν βαδίσας, Δημήτριε, τρεῖς παρ' Ἀμύντου
γλαυκίσκους αἴτει καὶ δέκα φυκίδια
καὶ κυφὰς καρῖδας—ἀριθμῆσαί σε δεῖ αὐτόν —
εἴκοσι καὶ τέτορας. δεῦρο λαβὼν ἄπιθι,
καὶ παρὰ Θαυβαρίου ῥοδίνους ἓξ πρόσλαβε...
καὶ Τρυφέραν ταχέως ἐν παρόδῳ κάλεσον.

> Go to the market, Demetrius, and get from Amyntas
> three small herrings, ten wrasses and two dozen prawns
> (be sure to count them yourself). Then come straight
> back. Pick up six rose garlands at Thaubarius' stall
> and, since it's on your way, invite Tryphera.

This time the slave is given very precise instructions about which shops to go to as well as how many of each item to get. But what of the last item on the list? 'A hetaira to entertain the party' runs the predictable note of Gow, again reflecting the general opinion of commentators and translators.

But is Tryphera really just a cynical afterthought on a level with the garlands? Surely the point of the poem is precisely that, in Giangrande's words, 'the most important ingredient, as it were, is left with apparent nonchalance to the very end'.[49] But not just because no good party was complete without a hetaira. Another dimension is added to the poem if we suppose that Tryphera is not a hetaira but the poet's latest flame; that he is only throwing the party so that he can invite her. But the bashful youth does not wish to seem to be attaching too much importance to the occasion, even in the eyes of his own slave. Hence the affectation of casualness. But we should not be misled. By telling the slave exactly which shops he should go to he has made sure that Tryphera's house will in fact be 'on the way'.

VI

XX (xii. 161):

> Δόρκιον ἡ φιλέφηβος ἐπίσταται ὡς ἁπαλὸς παῖς
> ἔσθαι πανδήμου Κύπριδος ὠκὺ βέλος
> ἵμερον ἀστράπτουσα κατ' ὄμματος,   ἡδ' ὑπὲρ ὤμων
> σὺν πετάσῳ γυμνὸν μηρὸν ἔφαινε χλαμύς .

> Dorkion, who loves ephebes, knows, like a young
> boy, how to launch the swift dart of Aphrodite who
> welcomes all, flashing desire down from her eye;
> with her (ephebe's) hat over her shoulder her
> cloak revealed a bare thigh.

This poem too has caused many problems. First, it should be noticed that we have yet another ambiguous anticipatory phrase in line 1: 'like a young boy'. For it is not till the last line that the poet discloses that Dorkion not only behaves like a boy (nothing so outrageous or even perhaps unusual) but actually *dresses* like one. Anyone familiar with the hundreds of representations of chlamys-draped youths (less often wearing or carrying round their necks the petasos, the characteristic hat of the ephebe) on Attic vases[50] will appreciate the revelation contained in the final word of the poem. The last line and a third have been much vexed and misunderstood. The expression is abrupt, but with ἡ for P's ἥ yields perfectly acceptable sense. Gow supposed that Dorkion 'wore this provocative costume in such a manner that it did not conceal her charms'. Giangrande was more explicit, arguing that her chlamys was worn so high that it betrayed her sex (adding the grotesque extra suggestion that πέτασος was an obscene double entendre for the vagina).[51] Yet it is clear from the vases that the chlamys was a short cloak worn across the back; the petasos too was worn across the back if not on the head. There is no conceivable way that this costume, not at all 'provocative' in itself, could have concealed either the breasts or the genital area of a girl. It goes without saying that, unlike the idealized youths on the vases, Dorkion will have been wearing the customary short chiton underneath, naturally (given her imposture) the short boy's chiton. The combined reference of hat, cloak and shoulders makes it clear that it is the back rather than the front of Dorkion that the poet has in mind. Now even if she had hoisted chiron as well as chlamys, this is the last viewpoint from which a slim girl was likely to betray her sex. Especially since her object was to conceal her sex and attract lovers who would take her for a boy. This, surely, is why the poet focuses on the view from the rear: the best way she can achieve her object is by deflecting the eyes of potential admirers *away* from her front. By wearing the chlamys and the short boy's chiton with its split sides she will display an attractive amount of thigh as she walks, and Greek pederastic writings wax warm on the attractions of the thigh.[52] The scene is caught to perfection in the following lines (surely known to Asclepiades) of the tragic poet Chaeremon (incidentally perhaps explaining the imperfect ἔφαινε which has puzzled commentators in Asclepiades):[53]

ἡ δὲ ῥαγέντων χλανιδ ίων ὑπὸ πτύχας
ἔφαινε μηρόν.

she, meanwhile, her robes all torn, *showed her thigh* from beneath its folds.

In both cases all that is meant is a tantalizing glimpse of more thigh than would ordinarily be proper or expected.

So the poem describes the success, not the failure[54] of Dorkion's ruse. According to W. Ludwig, the name Dorkion "war bei Hetären verbreitet".[55] Connoisseurs of Greek names such as A. Wilheim[56] and L. Robert[57] have insisted time and again that there are no names 'common to' or (if unattested) 'suitable for' hetairas, and the truth in this case is that the name Dorkion (diminutive of Dorkas, 'little gazelle') is found once elsewhere, in a fragment of Roman comedy, not obviously of a hetaira. Dorkas is common, always (it seems) of respectable women.[58] Since the gazelle won his name because of his large, bright eyes and is proverbially one of the slenderest of creatures, the diminutive Dorkion is doubly appropriate for the boyish girl with fetching eyes of our poem. Neither her name nor her come hither looks prove Dorkion a hetaira. After all, a hetaira depended for her livelihood on fees or presents from clients. Dorkion could hardly have counted on gifts from her indignant ephebes when they discovered (as sooner or later they were bound to) that she was not what she seemed.

VII

Next some poems where Asclepiades does not even claim to be describing his own experiences. In XIX (xii.153) a girl laments that Archeades, whom she used to tease, now does not look at her even in play; the course of honeyed Love does not run always sweet; the god often seems sweeter to those he has hurt. Clearly a respectable girl. The statement that Archeades is not interested in her οὐδ᾽ ὅσσον παίζων suggests that, while no longer sweethearts, the couple still meet socially.

Next I (v. 169):

'Ηδὺ θέρους διψῶντι χιὼν ποτόν, ἡδὺ δὲ ναύταις
ἐκ χειμῶνος ἰδεῖν εἰαρινὸν Στέφανον·
ἥδιον δ' ὁπόταν κρύψῃ μία τοὺς φιλέοντας
χλαῖνα, καὶ αἰνῆται Κύπρις ὑπ' ἀμφοτέρων.

Sweet is a cool drink in summer for the thirsty;
sweet for sailors the (rising of the Northern) Crown
after winter; but sweeter still when one blanket
covers two lovers and the Cyprian is honoured by both.

This fine priamel (which inspired a famous passage in Catullus) stands in no need of comment. Its conclusion is echoed in the conclusion to **XXVI** (v. 209), the story of how Cleander caught sight of Niko swimming off the 'Paphian shore' and was consumed by passion for her. The goddess heard his prayer and 'now their love for each other is equal' (line 7, νῦν δ' ἴσος ἀμφοτέροις φιλίης πόθος). Compare too the opening of the girl's lament in the *Frag. Grenfellianum*: ἐξ ἀμφοτέρων γέγονεν αἵρεσις . ἐζευγίσμεθα ('from both of us came the choice; we are yoked together'). This is a far cry from the cynical commercialism perceived by Fraser.

VIII

Now for the exceptions that prove the rule. First VIII (v. 162):

'Η λαμυρή μ' ἔτρωσε Φιλαίνιον, εἰ δὲ τὸ τραῦμα
μὴ σαφές, ἀλλ' ὁ πόνος δύεται εἰς ὄνυχα.
οἴχομ', "Ερωτες, ὄλωλα, διοίχομαι, εἰς γὰρ ἑταίραν
νυστάζων ἐπέβην, οἶδ', ἐθίγον τ' ἀίδαι.

Cruel Philaenion has bitten me. Though the bite does
not show, the pain reaches to my finger-tips. I am
gone, Loves, finished, past hope. For half-asleep I
trod on a whore, I know it, and her touch was death.

Here the girl bears a name formed from that of a particularly notorious hetaira, Philaenis, author of the first extant sex manual.[59] She is described as λαμυρή, which has been defined as 'wantonly and

insatiably gluttonous', whether for food or sex.[60] In this case the first
line epithet prepares us for the worst. A recent paper by E.K. Borthwick has fascinatingly illustrated the comparison between the harlot
and the viper that runs right through the poem:[61] the invisible but
poisonous bite (1-2) got by treading inadvertently (4). P. Waltz,
however, thought that still greater explicitness was desirable and
conjectured ἔχιδναν, 'viper', for ἑταιραν at the end of 1.3, and he
has been generally followed, notably by Gow and Page. Their argument is revealing: 'a stylist does not say "I have inadvertently en-
countered a harlot" when the harlot in question is the subject of his
epigram'. That is to say, taking it for granted that all Asclepiades'
girlfriends were hetairas, they found 'hetaira' a very lame climax
after three lines of preparation. Yet this is to pay too little attention
to the metaphor in νυστάζων, literally 'dozing'. Just as someone
walking in a field without due caution might tread on a snake, so
the poet blundered into this unfortunate relationship unawares.
Philaenion did not just turn out to be more mercenary or promiscuous than he had counted on; he was naive enough not to have
realized that she was a hetaira at all. The recognition that he was
involved with a hetaira was indeed a climax. How flat, by comparison, to spell out with ἔχιδαν the metaphor so unmistakably
suggested already by more subtle means.

Ovid *Amores* i.10 makes a suggestive comparison. The poet describes how all his romantic ideals (skilfully built up by a series of
mythical exempla) collapsed the moment his girl started asking for
presents. Here the interesting point is his complaint that, unlike the
common prostitute, she does not *need* the money in order to live. By
analogy we might guess that Philaenion was not a regular professional (who would probably have asked for her money in advance)
but a schemer who similarly won the poet's love before asking for
presents. Hence his bitterness when he realizes the truth. Compare
too the long fragment from Anaxilas' comedy *Neottis*, 'The Chick'
(*Com. Att. Frag.* ii.270 Koch = Athenaeus xiii, 558A):

ὅστις ἀνθρώπων ἑταίραν ἠγάπησε πώποτε ,
οὗτος οὐ γένος δύναιτ' ἂν παρανομώτερον φράσαι .
τίς γὰρ ἢ δράκων ' ἄμικτος ἢ χίμαιρα πυρπνόος
ἢ χάρυβδις ἢ ... λέαιν ', ἔχιδνα ...

Anyone who has ever been in love with a hetaira would be
unable to name a more lawless creature. For what savage
dragon, what fire-breathing Chimaira, or Charybdis . . .
lioness, viper . . .

Here as well (cf. too line 29 of the fragment) the emphasis falls on
the folly of falling in love with one who only pretends to love for gain.
Then there is XLI (vii.217):

'Αρχεάνασσαν ἔχω τὰν ἐκ Κολοφῶνος ἑταίραν,
ἇς καὶ ἐπὶ ῥυτίδων ὁ γλυκὺς ἔζετ' Ἔρως.
ἇς νέον ἥβης ἄνθος ἀποδρέψαντες ἐρασταί
πρωτόβολοι, δι' ὅσης ἤλθετε πυρκαϊῆς.

Archeanassa have I, the hetaira of Colophon on whose
very wrinkles sweet Love still sits. You lovers
who plucked the fresh flower of her youth, you who were
first struck, through what a furnace you passed!

It is strange that Fraser should have revived[62] (after the refutations
of Ludwig and Gow) the old view that this is an erotic poem commemorating a night Asclepiades spent with the elderly Archeanassa.
There can be no doubt (as all the ancient anthologists thought) that
it is an *epitaph*, and that the speaker (as so often) is the tomb. All
that concerns us here is the way Asclepiades describes her bluntly
as a hetaira and emphasizes the large number of lovers she had
had.[63]

By Asclepiades' day there was beginning to develop the literature
on hetairas to which reference has already been made. As may easily
be seen from the liberal' excerpts from it preserved in Athenaeus
XIII, it focussed not on their intellectual accomplishments but on
the number and variety of their lovers, their prices (a subject on
which we are singularly well informed),[64] their witticisms (invariably obscene double entendres) and the sexual positions in which
they specialized. Asclepiades VI (v. 203) is an early example of this
genre:

Λυσιδίκη σοί, Κύπρι, τὸν ἱππαστῆρα μύωπα
χρύσεον εὐκνήμου κέντρον ἔθηκε ποδός,
ᾧ πολὺν ὕπτιον ἵππον ἐγύμνασεν, οὐδέ ποτ' αὐτῆς
μηρὸς ἐφοινίχθη κοῦφα τινασσομένης.

ἦν γὰρ ἀκέντητος τελεοδρόμος, οὕνεκεν ὅπλον
σοὶ κατὰ μεσσοπύλης χρύσεον ἐκρέμασεν.

Lysidice dedicated to you, Cyprian, the golden
goad of her shapely foot, with which she has exercised
many a stallion on his back while her own thigh was
never reddened, so lightly did she bounce. For she
would finish the course without applying the spur.
So she hung this her weapon of gold on the gate (of
your temple).

Evidently Lysidice is a κελητίζουσα, an 'equestrienne';[65] that is to
say she specializes in the superior position.[66] According to Gow she
dedicates the spur to Aphrodite 'in gratitude for the proficiency she
has been enabled to display in her profession'. But (followed by
Fraser)[67] he found the poem 'puzzling in detail', thought that in the
last couplet 'the rider is the man and the spur seems to have been
transferred to him', and even toyed with the idea that the last couplet
is spurious. All this is quite wrong.

In a normal dedication (as can be seen from the hundreds of examples in *AP* vi) the dedicatee presents to the deity some object for
which (s)he has no further use, usually on retirement. So here,
though the twist is that Lysidice is so skilful at bringing her men off
that she does not *need* a spur. All that is wanted to keep Lysidice on
top[68] (as we must) is to interpret ἀκέντητος not 'ungoaded' but 'not
goading'. Many examples of similar variation between active and
passive in adjectives of precisely this form could be cited:[69] e.g. ἀβοή-
θητος, which can mean both 'helpless' and 'unhelpful'; ἀνόνητος,
both 'unprofitable' and 'taking no profit from'; ἀδέητος, 'not wanting' and 'inexorable'. It is precisely the fact that the poem is a perversion of the usual dedication that eliminates the possibility that
Lysidice might just be a gifted amateur. For it is normally *professional*
tools that are dedicated.

IX

So it is an oversimplification to say that Asclepiades describes "the
antics, professional and otherwise, of the hetaerae".[70] When he does
write of hetairas he is content to focus on their traditional character-

istics: rapacity, promiscuity and sexual proficiency. But for the most part he is doing something more interesting: he is presenting us with a gallery of portraits of female *types*: the maiden who loves from afar; the reluctant virgin; the tease; the soft touch; the girl who can't say no; the transvestite with a taste for teenagers.

Just because they describe types, the relationship of poems to life if problematic. A new papyrus or inscription may one day solve the mystery of Propertius' Cynthia. But we cannot even look for *proof* in the case of Nicarete and Dorkion, because they never existed. All we can ask is how contemporaries would have interpreted the poems. And here we may compare a poem by another writer of the age, the first mimiamb of Herodas.

The bawd Gyllis tries to persuade a young woman called Metriche to be nice to a certain Gryllos who is desperately in love with her, on the grounds that Metriche's man Mandris has been away in Alexandria for five months and has probably forgotten all about her. Most commentators have assumed that Metriche is the wife of Mandris. The recent edition of I.C. Cunningham suggests that she is a hetaira.[71] Now it is true that in real life hetairas may have lived for long periods with one man — though hardly for five months without pay. And Metriche is indignant at Gyllis' proposition, cutting her off abruptly when she raises it again. Now an attractive girl who, in the face of strong temptation (Gryllos is wealthy and a double Olympic champion), is unswervingly loyal to a man who has been away overseas without word for five months does *not* fit the stereotype of the hetaira. On the contrary, she is being represented as the stereotype of the faithful wife. For example, it was at a festival, like some closeted New Comedy heroine, that she unwittingly inspired Gryllos' passion. So in so far as it matters for his appreciation of the poem, the contemporary reader was surely more likely to take her for Mandris' wife.[72]

Very few of the women described by Asclepiades fit the stereotype of the hetaira, an impression only heightened by his own occasional vivid use of this very stereotype. By contrast, the love epigrams of Callimachus, which are exclusively homosexual, lament with feeling the tricks of mercenary boys.[73] Even Fraser was struck by the fact that the theme of buying — or failing to buy — love was much more prominent in Callimachus than Asclepiades.[74] This is the more striking in that Callimachus was in some ways so clearly influenced by Asclepiades, who seems virtually to have invented the erotic epigram as we know it. Not only does this difference between their love poems surely reflect a real difference between the two men. More interestingly still, we see a reversal of the old Athenian attitudes: homosexual love has become more mercenary, heterosexual love less so.

With nothing in most of Asclepiades' poems to suggest the financial transactions assumed by modern commentators, why should ancient readers have assumed them? The truth is (as their tone reveals) that the commentators are often applying their own standards of respectability as much as the standards of fifth century Athens. Any woman who sleeps with or merely associates unchaperoned with a man to whom she is not married automatically excludes herself from the ranks of the respectable. Whether or not she actually charges hardly matters — especially if she is from the lower classes, 'women who sell bread and willing prostitutes' in the revealing phrase of the aristocrat Anacreon.[75] Yet obviously it makes a profound difference to the attitudes of both parties if it is a commercial arrangement rather than a love affair in which they are engaged. Prostitution may provide a temporary sexual outlet, but only in the most unusual circumstances could it provide a basis for love.

It is in the nature of things that young men in search of love rather than marriage are not going to find it among the truly respectable. But there have been few times and places where the only alternative was the whore, and Ptolemaic Alexandria, with its growing, fluid and often transitory population was surely not one. If perfume sellers and even neglected wives like Metriche are not allowed to have love affairs without being called hetairas, then the word has ceased to have a precise enough meaning to be useful. Some people prefer the old-fashioned term 'demi-monde'; but though less straightforwardly mercenary in its connotations, it nonetheless reflects the moralizing viewpoint of a respectable 'haut-monde'. The real strength and interest of Asclepiades' love poems is that he reaches beyond these polarities and stereotypes and draws his memorable because recognizable characters from the life.

Notes

1. See Jasper Griffin, 'Augustan Poetry and the life of luxury', *JRS* lxvi (1976) 103.

2. On its influence, see A.A. Day, *Origins of Latin Love Elegy* (Oxford 1938) 102–137; E. Schulz-Vanheyden, *Properz und das griechische Epigramm* (Münster 1970).

3. There are a few epigrams on boys (XXI–XXIV), but it is doubtful whether they are in fact pederastic: see Gow and Page's commentary (II.130–1).

4. There is no comprehensive critical study: see K. Schneider's article 'Hetairai' in Pauly Wissowa, *RE* viii. 1331–72 and H. Herter 'Dirne', in *RAC* iii. 1149–1213 and 'Die Soziologie der antiken Prostitution' in *JbAC* 3 (1960) 70–111.

5. Georgina Masson, *Courtesans of the Italian Renaissance* (London 1975), and Paul Larivaille, *La vie quotidienne des courtisanes en Italie au temps de la Renaissance* (Rome 1975), the latter with a concluding chapter on 'Le mythe de la courtisane' stressing the darker side.

6. Joanna Richardson, *The Courtesans: the demi-monde in nineteenth century France* (Cleveland and London 1967); Henry Blyth, *Skittles: The Last Victorian Courtesan* (London 1970); and Michael Harrison, *Fanfare of Strumpets* (London 1971), all with useful bibliographies.

7. See A.S.F. Gow's edition with commentary, *Machon: the fragments* (Cambridge 1965).

8. On prostitution in Ptolemaic Egypt see Lea Bringman, *Die Frau im ptolemäisch-kaiserlichen Aegypten* (Bonn 1939) 120–1.

9. E.g. Antiphanes, ap. Athenaeus XIII, 555 A; Harrison, *Fanfare of Strumpets*, 121–2 (a fist-fight between two aristocrats over Lily Langtry in Hyde Park); cf. Masson, *Courtesans*, 95.

10. The eye of the moralist may detect little difference between the mistress and the whore, but from the point of view of the woman, the element of choice and the possibility of fidelity, affection and permanence certainly raise the mistress above the level of the whore. Joanna Richardson deliberately omitted from her account of Parisian courtesans such colourful 'non-professionals' as Mme de Staël, George Sand and Sarah Bernhardt.

11. I shall be discussing the date and movements of Asclepiades in a forthcoming article 'Two Mistresses of Ptolemy Philadelphus.'

12. A.S.F. Gow and D.L. Page, *The Greek Anthology: Hellenistic Epigrams* i–ii (Cambridge 1965). I cite poems by their number in Gow–Page (though I often differ from their text). I have not given separate page references every time I quote their commentary on Asclepiades (ii. 114–151), which is the work of Gow.

13. *Ptolemaic Alexandria* i (1972) 564. D.H. Garrison, *Mild Frenzy: A Reading of the Hellenistic Love Epigram* (Wiesbaden 1978) 60, finds in Asclepiades a 'distrust of women' that he traces to 'the unsatisfactory nature of liaisons with hetairae.'

14. With some reluctance I use the conventional term 'respectable' to mean merely 'non-prostitute': see further p. 297 below.

15. A.W. Gomme and F.H. Sandbach, *Menander: a commentary* (Oxford, 1973) 32–4.

16. So stock a feature of Menandrean comedy did this become that the youth who rapes the girl usually even bears the same name, Moschion (W.T. MacCary, *TAPA* 101 (1970) 286–9). See, too, in general, Elaine Fantham, 'Sex, Status and Survival in Hellenistic Athens: a study of women in New Comedy', *Phoenix* 29 (1975) 44–74.

17. Sarah B. Pomeroy, *Goddesses, Whores, Wives, Slaves* (New York 1975) 120f.; there is much of value in Claude Vatin, *Recherches sur le mariage et la condition de la femme mariée à l'époque hellénistique* (Paris 1970).

18. Pomeroy, *American Journal of Ancient History* 2 (1977) 51–68. This pattern was to repeat itself at Rome. In the course of the second century B.C. aristocratic society was invaded by Greek courtesans, women possessed of a glamour and culture unknown to the respectable materfamilias (see the excellent account in R.O.A.M. Lyne, *The Latin Love Poets* (Oxford 1980) 8–18). But this Greek 'demi-monde' did not survive unchallenged the emancipation of Roman women in the first century: Catullus' Lesbia was the wife of a Roman aristocrat.

19. As for example Gow supposed (*Theocritus* II (Cambridge 1952) 252), on the analogy of fourth century texts, rightly criticized by K. Latte, *Gnomon* 23 (1951) 25. Even if the name is meant to be significant (Bitchy), that need not be a pointer to 'her profession' (Gow, and see now J. Stern, *GRBS* 16 (1975) 55); merely an indication that she has played Aeschinas false.

20. I think it is a mistake of emphasis to interpret this poem as merely a typical example of women attending a festival (as, for example, W. Headlam on Herodas I.56; or Vatin, *Recherches . . .* 263–7).

21. On Simaetha's status see the careful discussion in K.J. Dover, *Theocritus: Select Poems* (London 1971) 94–6.

22. J.U. Powell, *Collectanea Alexandrina* (1925 rep. Oxford 1970) 177–80.

23. Published by W. Ludwig, *Gnomon* 38 (1966) 22f. βληθείς in Meleager's imitation, *AP* xii. 72.3–4, lends-some support to βεβλημένον.

24. *Poetae Melici Graeci*, ed. D.L. Page (Oxford 1962) 390.

25. Pauly-Wissowa, *RE* xxii (1954) 1765.

26. See K.J. Dover, *Aristophanic Comedy* (Berkeley 1972) 192, 197.

27. An interesting selection of translations is quoted by W. and M. Wallace, *Asklepiades of Samos* (Oxford 1941).

28. According to Garrison, *Mild Frenzy*, p. 50, 'We have only the conventions of the genre to tell us that [Eirenion] is either a hetaera or a young music-girl destined to become a hetaera.'

29. See the discussion by G. Giangrande, *L'epigramme grecque* (n. 49) 150–2.

30. See the useful paper by W.G. Arnott in *Class. Rev.* 19 (1969) 6–8.

31. It is regularly so used of playful erotic behaviour: see J. Henderson, *The Maculate Muse* (New Haven 1975) 157; see too p. 284 below.

32. Gow has a characteristic note on whether the letters are 'embroidered in gold thread' or 'in thin metal appliqué.'

33. *Rev. Ét. Grecques* 86 (1973) 319–22. I agree with Gow and Page (ii. 122–3) that Platnauer's παρεόντα would mean much the same as P's παρεοῦσα, which I have therefore kept.

34. *Rh. Mus.* 114 (1971) 333–9.

35. In his note on Meleager LI.5 (ii.635). Both the similarities and still more the

differences between this poem and Asclepiades IX are instructive. The poet appeals not to the lamp but to Night, and all that he prays for is that, having made love and put out the lamp in the usual way, his rival will fall asleep and never wake up again. He is not so unrealistic as to imagine that there is any way of preventing them actually making love.

36.   It will be enough to refer to the full collection of references and bibliography on the lamp as both god and witness of lovemaking in K. Kost, *Musaios: Hero and Leander* (Bonn 1971) 126–132.

37.   Unless the climax of the poem is meant to be an *anti*-climax, a futile, impotent gesture.

38.   In a forthcoming book on the *Greek Anthology* I shall be showing, *inter alia*, that it is a mistake on principle to prefer the Palatine to the Planudean text.

39.   'πιβόητος is another of the ambiguous anticipatory epithets, but there is a complication. *AP* vii.345, by the (?) contemporary Aeschrion opens ἐγὼ Φιλαινίς ἡ 'πίβωτος ἀνθρώποις, 'I am Philaenis whom men talk about' — in fact the notorious whore/pornographer referred to below (n. 59). Now given their shared application of the same adjective, with prodelision (very rare in epigrams), to a dubious female, one of the two poems is presumably influenced by the other. Yet Aeschrion's purpose is to *defend* Philaenis against what he describes as slander: so his ἐπίβωτος is not straightforwardly derogatory.

40.   See N.J. Richardson, *The Homeric Hymn to Demeter* (Oxford 1974) 290.

41.   Fraser, *Ptol. Alexandria*, 191.

42.   I venture to think that Salmasius' ταὐτά and Hecker's ἐμοί improve the flat text printed by Gow–Page.

43.   See H.C. Youtie, *ZPE* 6 (1970) 105–16.

44.   *ZPE* 6 (1970) 245–6.

45.   P. Herfst, *Le travail de la femme dans la Grèce ancienne* (Utrecht 1922), 45, wonders whether the perfume-seller may not also have made the perfume she sold. On the perfume trade in Alexandria, see Fraser, *Ptol. Alex.* i.141.

46.   Merkelbach's διακλωπῶν, 'furtively', is based on a misunderstanding of the poem: see Tarán (next note) 88, n. 100, and my interpretation given above.

47.   *Exclusus Amator* (Baltimore 1956), and for a detailed analysis of the epigrams, see now Sonya Tarán, *The Art of Variation in the Hellenistic Epigram* (Leiden 1979) 52–114.

48.   See Appendix E of my forthcoming *Greek Anthology*.

49.   *L'Épigramme grecque* (Fondation Hardt, Entretiens xiv) 1968, 142.

50.   There are a number of examples in the plates to K.J. Dover's *Greek Homosexuality* (Cambridge, Mass. 1978): e.g. R 336; 373; 406; 458; 462; 494; 498.

51.   *Eranos* 65 (1967) 39–41, referring for support to the venerable but no less preposterous similar interpretation of εὐρώτας in *AP* v.60.6, on which see my paper in *GRBS* 22 (1981).

52.   Dover, *Greek Homosexuality*, p. 70. For some illustrations (mythological) of women shown in the short chiton, see M. Bieber, *Ancient Copies* (New York 1977), pl. I–III. It is presumably the short chiton that is meant when we read of women who attended Plato's lectures 'wearing male clothing' (Diogenes Laertius, III.46).

53.   *TGF*² 786 = Athenaeus XIII, 608 B.C.

54. Contrast Aristophanes, *Eccles.* 95–7 (with R.G. Ussher's commentary, p. 89), a warning to the women disguised as men not to hitch their chitons too high and betray themselves when clambering over others already seated in the assembly.

55. *L'Epigramme grecque*, 328.

56. 'Die sogennante Hetäreninschrift aus Paros' *Athen. Mitt.* 1899, 409–440; cf. *JOAI* 26 (1929) 59–65.

57. *L'Épigramme grecque*, 340–1; cf. *Bull. Epigr.* (1970) n. 200. The name 'Tryphera', for instance, borne by the alleged hetaira of poem XXVI, "n'évoque pas une orgie sardanapalesque; il est porté comme nom de reine en Cappadoce." K. Schneider's useful list of 300 hetairas in *RE* viii.1362–71 showed a bare 10% with what he considered "sprechender Hetärennamen"; the rest were all borne equally by respectable women.

58. See the examples collected in K. Mras' useful article 'Die Personennamen in Lucians Hatärengesprächen', *Wien. Studien* 38 (1916) 28.

59. *P. Oxy.* 2891. It seems to have been traditional to ascribe erotic manuals to female authors (M.L. West, *ZPE* 25 (1977) 118), and Philaenis' morals were defended by Aeschrion (Gow–Page ii.4–5). See K. Tsantsanoglou, *ZPE* 12 (1973) 183–195; D.W. Vessey, *Rev. Belg. Phil.* 54 (1976) 78–83.

60. E.K. Borthwick, *Class. Rev.* 17 (1967) 253.

61. *Class. Rev.* 17 (1967) 250–254.

62. *Ptol. Alex.* ii.805. I follow Ludwig, *GRBS* 4 (1963) 63, n. 9–10, in reading πρωτόβολοι (with the first hand in P and Plaudes) and ᾶς (first hand in P).

63. An adapted and more erotic version was later ascribed to Plato to blacken his name: cf. Ludwig, *GRBS* 4 (1963) 63–8; cf. too McKay, *Hermes* (1974) 369–71.

64. Schneider, *RE* viii.1344; Gow, *Machon*, p. 120; A.W. Gomme and F.H. Sandbach, *Menander: A Commentary* (Oxford 1973) 298, 430, 587.

65. The nineteenth century euphemism 'horsewoman' or 'horsebreaker', though it obviously carries this connotation, was in origin an 'innocent' continuation of the word 'whores' — though it also alludes to the fact that the most celebrated made sure that they really could ride well. According to Michael Harrison, this was a key factor in their success: 'The rigid Victorian mind simply could not accept that women demonstrating so aristocratic a talent could be anything but half acceptable' (*Fanfare of Strumpets*, p. 13).

66. J. Henderson, *The Maculate Muse* (New Haven 1975) 164–6.

67. *Ptol. Alex.* ii. 805, n. 98. Pace Fraser, τελεοδρόμος certainly does not imply that Lysidice 'has become the ἵππος'. Compare Dioscorides' imitation, where it is the girl who, ἥνυσεν . . . τὸν Κύπριδος δόλιχον,'completed the race of Love' (*AP* v.55.4). Note that δόλιχος, the long distance race, where στάδιον, 'sprint', would equally have fitted into the line, suggests that she skilfully prolonged the session. Gow (ad. loc.) has a meticulous note on the different lengths of race but fails to see the point.

68. In Dioscorides' imitation (v.55), a wonderfully sensuous piece of erotic writing, it is true that the couple do change positions, but there the poet makes the point explicitly. The lover begins by stretching Doris out on the bed (ὑπὲρ λεχέων διατείνας, 1.1) and then she straddles him (μέσον διαβᾶσα, 1.3). Only the innocence of the octogenarian Cambridge bachelor don could find

'difficulties' here (Gow, ii.239). But who would pay good money to a courtesan so gauche as to stay in one position all the time? πορφύρεα in 1.6 are (of course) the girl's breasts (Gow, 240; Fraser, i.597, translates 'limbs'). Did hetairas perhaps rouge their nipples?

69.   The list could easily be extended by selection from the list of -ητος adjectives in C.D. Buck and W. Petersen, *Reverse Index of Greek Nouns and Adjectives* (Chicago 1949) 480–490.

70.   Fraser, i.564.

71.   Herodas: *Mimiambi* (Oxford 1973) 57.

72.   In the real world she might also be considered a concubine (see Fantham, *Phoenix* 29 (1975) 64f.), but that would be to introduce an unnecessary complication here. All the poet needs is for her to be loyal and refuse so that Gyllis may continue her monologue.

73.   Fraser, *Ptol. Alex.* 790–2.

74.   *Ptol. Alex.* 791.

75.   Frag. 43, *PMG* 388. I am grateful to Beth Cohen, Sarah Pomeroy and Sonya Tarán for comments.

Women in Roman Egypt[†]

A preliminary study based on papyri

SARAH B. POMEROY

Hunter College and The Graduate School, C.U.N.Y.

In 30 B.C. CLEOPATRA VII, the last the of the Ptolemies to rule Egypt, chose to take her own life rather than march as a captive in the triumphal procession of the Roman general Octavian. Many aspects of women's daily lives in Egypt were not altered by the Roman conquest, nor are they different nowadays. However, there are ways in which women are affected by changes in political systems.[1] This paper will discuss those changes that Roman rule produced in the lives of women in Egypt, and in our own perceptions of the past, which resulted from the removal of restrictions on land ownership by women that had been in force in the Ptolemaic period.

In general works on Egypt, women in the Ptolemaic period have received more attention than women under the Romans. The same emphasis applies to specialized surveys on women. A few works treat women only in the Ptolemaic period, but the majority extend the time span to "Greco–Roman" Egypt.[2] I know of no previous study that is limited to women in Roman Egypt.

The system of land tenure under the Ptolemies has been much debated in recent years.[3] For the purpose of this paper it is sufficient to state that, in practice, some of the land was held by private owners, both women and men, some belonged to temples and cities, and

† Journal titles are abbreviated to the form in *L'Année philologique*. Papyrological abbreviations are those adopted by the American Society of Papyrologists and published in *BASP* 11 (1974). Accepted abbreviations will be used for other standard works.

A shorter version of this article was read at the annual meeting of the American Historical Association, Washington, D.C., December 28, 1980. Another version appears in *Aufstieg und Niedergang der Römischen Welt* (Berlin 1981) II, 10, 1.

the rest remained royal domain. The proportions of each varied through time and from place to place. Few statistics are available. However, it is known that in the village of Kerkeosiris in the Fayum in 118 B.C. 52% of the land was royal.[4] The Ptolemies allowed royal land to be leased to peasant farmers and also granted it as gifts to their favorites and as *kleroi*, or allotments, to men who could be summoned to serve in the king's army. Women were not permitted to own cleruchic land. Inetrestingly enough, no private land is known at Kerkeosiris; consequently, no women are recorded as land owners there.[5]

Women landowners are found elsewhere in Egypt. The ways by which they came into possession of such land, when these ways can be known, draw attention to another difference between Ptolemaic and Roman Egypt. Before the Roman conquest, land does not appear as a constituent of any dowry recorded in a Greek marriage contract.[6] The dowries are comprised solely of movables. These Ptolemaic dowries are thus different from dowries in many other areas inhabited by the Greeks at the same time, where the daughter might take as dowry her share of her parents' land.[7] The earliest example of a Greek marriage contract from Egypt showing a dowry that includes land comes from 42 A.D. (*P. Mich.* II 121 *recto* II 2, Tebtunis). In contrast to the marriage contracts, numerous wills — even in the early Ptolemaic period — show that parents and husbands bequeathed land to women. However, according to O. Montececchi's study of the testaments, sons are much more numerous than daughters as beneficiaries.[8] Married daughters are rarely mentioned, for they would have received their share of the patrimony as dowry, though, as mentioned above, land would not be a constituent of such a dowry before the Roman period. Obviously when women inherited as widows, they came into possession of their property later in life and owned it for a shorter time than they would if they had received it as dowry.[9]

In papyrology one hestitates to make an *argumentum ex silentio*, since the survival of documents is haphazard. Yet it is not only the lack of a dowry in land, but, on a larger scale, the exclusion of women from all land that was designated as cleruchic, which suggests that the Greek settlers in Egypt had brought with them attitudes about land ownership that had prevailed in some of the older Greek *poleis*.[10] In Athens only male citizens could own land. It was mortgaged by men as sureties for dowries of female citizens, but no woman actually owned land in Attica. Nor did any *metic* (resident alien), regardless of how many generations of his family had lived in Attica. In fact, the Athenians cherished a myth of *autochthony* (birth from the land itself) which entitled the men to exclusive possession of their land and simultaneously precluded an origin from women. Thucydides, who confesses that he is sceptical about earlier traditions, nevertheless reports that the same people had inhabited Attica continually, for this territory had not been subject to the waves of migration that had afflicted the rest of Greece before the Trojan War.[11] The exclusion of women along with *metics* in Athens indicates that political rights were intimately linked with land ownership.

In Egypt, the irrigation system functioned well only under a strong government. Consequently it had deteriorated in the last generations of Ptolemaic rule. The stringent system of land ownership had also weakened. The *kleroi* (land allotments) became hereditary in the male line. Finally, in the first century B.C., a brotherless woman inherited her father's *kleros*.[12]

The Romans restored the irrigation system, thus allowing more land to be brought under cultivation and thereby increasing their own opportunities for exploitation. As was their custom, they encouraged private ownership of land and had no reservations about permitting women to become owners. There was no restriction on land ownership by women, neither by category nor in amount. On some land registers from Roman Egypt the majority or a substantial minority of owners are women.[13]

The importance of land ownership in a country like Egypt that is based on an agricultural economy can not be overestimated. Land owners are fortunate people, even though land ownership in a conquered territory could not be the mark of privilege that it had been in an independent city-state like Athens. Under Roman rule, there was no differentiation between women and men in terms of political rights inasmuch as both sexes were equally subject to the Romans. But the release of all land to ownership by women conferred on them a share equal to men's share in the chief means of production. This economic power was also fraught with obligations to ensure that there was not any loss of income to the Romans. Countless *ostraca* (potsherds used to record tax payments) reveal that women and men paid the same taxes on crops and land.[14] In one category women paid at a higher rate. *P. Iand.* 137, a fragmentary list of taxes from Theadelphia from the first half of the second century, shows women paying at a higher rate on transfers of catoecic land. Sir Harold Idris Bell follows the editors of the papyrus in suggesting that the higher rate indicates that the origin of catoecic land as military *kleroi* had not been forgotten with the passage of time.[15] The tax rate did not discourage women from owning land in this category. Women constitute the majority of owners in *P. Lond.* II 193 (Fayum [?], first century), a register of catoecic land. They are numerous as well in *P. Upps.* 14, (Theadelphia, second century) a document recording the inspection of catoecic land.

Another Roman innovation was the institution of a capitation tax (λαογραφία). Strangely enough, although women in neighboring Syria were liable for this tax,[16] and although under the Ptolemies women had been liable for an analogous universal tax — the "salt" tax — women in Egypt did not pay the capitation tax. They were, however, listed in the house-to-house census. Scholars continue to disagree about whether women were counted in the Roman census.[17] They definitely were counted in Egypt, but in view of their exemption from the capitation tax one might wonder why they were included in the lists. The reason may have been simply the continuation of the earlier practice of counting women for the salt tax, just as the higher tax on catoecic land mentioned in the preceding paragraph simply perpetuated an earlier tradition. But a more compelling reason is that the census lists included not only the names, ages, and genealogies of household residents, but also indicated other property that they owned.[18]

Women landowners were exempt from the compulsory services, including work on the irrigation system, and the cultivation of crown land, to which male landowners were liable.[19] The jurist Ulpian (*Dig.* 50.4.3.3.) gives the reason succinctly: *corporalia munera feminis ipse sexus denegat* "Their sex alone precludes physical obligations for women". Yet it would have been inconsistent with their earlier practices if the Romans allowed men to dodge compulsory services by transferring land to the women in their families.[20] Spartan history served to warn the Romans of the consequences of land ownership by women free of obligations to the state. Aristotle saw a definite connection between the deterioration of Sparta and women's ownership of land. He noted that in his day women owned two fifths of the territory of Sparta.[21] The result was that fewer men met the property requirement for full citizenship and drifted away from Sparta. As I have observed elsewhere, the Romans, starting with the Lex Voconia in 169 B.C., attempted to curb the transfer of large amounts of capital to women when such ownership posed a threat both to the tax structure and to the military service that was coordinated with this structure.[22] These precedents lead one to look for an obligation that the Romans imposed on men to perform compulsory services on behalf of the women landowners in their households. The census records certainly made these family relationships perfectly clear.

Two petitions from women imply that compulsory services fell upon male next-of-kin. *BGU* 648 (164 or 196 A.D.) is a petition from a woman who had inherited property from her father. Her paternal uncle and her cousin had seized her inheritance, giving the excuse of the cultivation of crown land which she, being a woman, was not obliged to undertake. She states that she has no son (ἄτεκνος)) and cannot sustain herself. She petitions the *strategos* (a high-ranking official) to return the property to her, but to oblige her uncle and her second cousins to undertake the compulsory cultivation attached to the property. Doubtless the kinship relationship was too remote for her male relatives to take on the services in her behalf without actually taking over the property. The most detailed source for women's exemption from compulsory cultivation is *P. Oxy.* VI 899 (= *Chrest. Wilck.* 361, 200 A.D.). Apollonarion petitions the *strategos* to be relieved of the responsibility for cultivating crown land inherited from her father. Her plea is not simply that she is a woman, (γυναῖκα οὖσαν) but that she is a woman alone with neither husband nor helper (ἄνανδρον καὶ ἀβοήθητον). She is indeed so alone that she is not assisted by a male relative but must instead have a guardian appointed for her. The basis of her plea is that "men are the persons suitable for undertaking the cultivation . . . and it has been decided by prefects and epistrategi from time to time that women are not to be forced to undertake this duty."

Apollonarion states in her petition, that she cultivated her land as long as she could. Women, of course, did perform agricultural labor, yet that women were less enthusiastic than men about such work can be inferred from the fact that they appear in contracts far more often as lessors than as lessees.[23] The most desirable situation is described in *P. Ryl*. II 154, a marriage contract of 66 A.D. The wife's father turns over 10¾ arurae. The husband agrees to perform all the agricultural labor and pay the taxes on the property, bringing the harvest into their common abode.[24]

THE EFFECT OF LAND OWNERSHIP BY WOMEN ON FAMILY RELATIONSHIPS

A married daughter who acquired a piece of her parents' land and house through dowry[25] or inheritance[26] would tend to remain in close contact with her natal family. In the Ptolemaic period, in contrast, the bride, with her dowry of movables could be separated from her blood relatives forever. Accordingly, in the earliest marriage contract, *P. Eleph*. 1 (311 B.C.) the bride is protected by several stipulations which would have been superfluous if she could have availed herself of the aid of nearby kin. These protections included: the judgement of marital offenses by three men whom both wife and husband approve; an allusion to "those helping Demetria" (in effect, substitute kin) which implies that she will not be able to summon her father or other relatives for assistance; and, finally, the duplication of the contract so that Demetria may keep her own copy and produce it against her husband if she needs to, since they may be far away from the witnesses to the marriage.

Yet, in the Roman period, the proximity of kinfolk was not invariably beneficial to a married woman,[27] for her obligations and loyalties to her father on the one hand and her husband on the other could come into conflict. The petition of Dionysia (*P. Oxy*. II. 237 186 A.D.)

sets forth a history of business dealings and disputes between a father and daughter that could scarcely have occurred unless the two were living near each other. Demetria's father had attempted to take her away from her husband and to take back property he had given her at the time of marriage. The case was not unique, for Demetria cites precedents in which other fathers had attempted to interfere in the lives of married daughters, and where the official decision had been to limit the authority of a father over a married daughter and to allow the woman herself to decide with whom she desired to live.

Land ownership probably increased a wife's dependence on her husband, whereas a dowry of movables produced the opposite effect. For example, Demetria, the bride in *P. Eleph.* 1, has a dowry of clothing and ornaments valued at 1,000 drachmas. As S.D. Goitein has commented, when the dowry consists of a wife's personal possessions the husband must obtain the wife's full cooperation if he wishes to alter or spend it.[28] In contrast, the woman who owned land needed her husband's cooperation. In ancient societies labor was divided along gender lines, with complementary roles for women and men. The woman who had to rely on distant male relatives (*BGU* II 648), or the one who had neither husband nor son (*P. Oxy.* VI 899), was a pitiful creature. The arrangements in *P. Ryl* II 154 must have been the normal ones: the husband took charge of the agricultural labor and attendant taxes on his wife's land. Husbands most often acted as their wives' guardians in sales of land.[29] Doubtless as a result of bearing responsibility for the land, some of the husbands treated it as though it were their own.[30] They could hardly behave thus with a wife's property if it consisted of women's clothing and ornaments.

THE EFFECT OF LAND OWNERSHIP BY WOMEN ON THE LITERACY RATE

A minority of daughters acquired an education. Whether and how a girl was educated depended on many variables both general and specific in nature, including when and where she lived and her parents' wealth and social status. It is impossible to estimate the number of educated women and the extent of their education except in relative way. For this inquiry it will be useful to compare:

1) the Hellenistic period with the Roman
2) Egypt with the rest of the Roman world
3) women and men in Egypt.

Two categories of evidence will be discussed:

1) whether girls were given an education
2) the results of education, especially women's literacy.

As I have shown elsewhere,[31] the opportunities of Greek women to obtain an education began to expand in the 4th century and in the Hellenistic period. Parents paid tuition, except in places like Teos and Pergamum where private endowments had been established for children's education.[32]

Following the Greek precedent, the Romans too sent their daughters to school. The first Roman school was founded in the last quarter of the 3rd century B.C., and many others followed.

Recently Guglielmo Cavallo has repeated the consensus of earlier scholars that it was not until the first three centuries of the Empire that literacy was most widespread.[33] R.P. Duncan-Jones has also drawn attention to the persistance of illiteracy.[34] Although historians commonly assert that Egypt was different from the rest of the Roman world, in their discussion of literacy in the Roman Empire, Cavallo, Duncan-Jones, and others do not treat the evidence from Egypt (or from the rest of the Hellenized East) separately. Therefore it is necessary to explore whether the generalization about the increase in literacy in the first three centuries A.D. applies to Egypt, and, in particular, to women in Egypt.

In the Hellenistic period, Alexandria was a cultural center for women as well as for men. Ptolemy I established a precedent by engaging the scholar Philetas to tutor both Ptolemy II and Arsinoë II. Queens like Arsinoë II and Berenike II were well able to appreciate the erudite works of the poets and scholars in the Alexandrian court.

Although the efforts of male poets and scholars to obtain the patronage of the court were well publicized, female scholars and philosophers worked in Alexandria too. Agallis was the daughter of

Agallias who was himself a pupil of Aristophanes of Byzantium. She came from Corcyra, the island that was said to be the Phaeacia of the *Odyssey*. Her contribution may seem less silly in the context of Alexandrian scholarship that was engaged in a quest for the first person who did or invented something. Agallis patriotically attributed the invention of ball-playing to her countrywoman Nausicaa, doubtless because she was the first person in literature to be portrayed playing with a ball.[35]

There were two female scholars, each of whom wrote a single work. Hestiaea of Alexandria was a grammarian who wrote a treatise on a question which became an issue of scholarly debate: whether the Trojan War had been fought around the city which was named Ilium in her own day.[36] A woman named Diophila may have written a poem on astronomy. According to the scholia, a poem of Diophila may have been consulted by Callimachus for his writing of the *Aetia*.[37]

After the dazzling beginning under the earlier Ptolemies, intellectual life was not sustained at the same level. Nevertheless Neopythagorean treatises are extant that were written in Alexandria at the end of the first century B.C. Some of these treatises were written by women adopting as pennames the names of earlier female disciples and relatives of Pythagoras.[38]

Of course, these women scholars, philosophers, and literary patrons were exceptional. But they are important because they worked and lived in the cosmopolitan city of Alexandria, and were highly visible. Thus they served as models for other women not only in Alexandria but even beyond the boundaries of Egypt. The same sorts of evidence used to establish that girls were educated elsewhere in the Hellenistic world have been found also in Alexandria. These include terracotta figurines of girls reading and writing as well as an occasional depiction on a tombstone.[39] In the face of competition from other cities, and lacking the patronage of the Ptolemies, cultural life in Alexandria in the Roman period was never restored to the brilliance of the early Ptolemaic, and there is little information about learned women until we reach Hypatia. Although she is outside our chronological limits, it is interesting to observe that Hypatia continued the tradition of learned women in Alexandria inasmuch as she specialized in philosophy and wrote scholarly commentaries. The remarkable phenomenon of the history of Hellenistic women — the renascence of women poets — took place elsewhere in the Hellenistic world.

The next question is the relationship of Alexandria to other areas of Egypt settled by the Greeks in terms of education and literacy. The papyri, deriving mostly from villages and semi-rural areas, provide abundant testimony to the level of literacy and give information about educational practices. As a general rule, literacy rates are higher in urban than in rural areas, and there is therefore good reason to suppose that the literacy rate in Alexandria exceeded the level that appears in the papyri.

The range from literacy to illiteracy is broad and a straightforward interpretation of the data may lead to error. Scribes were commonly engaged to write public documents, but their use does not necessarily imply illiteracy on the part of their employers. Rather, the scribes were trusted to have some knowledge of the requisite legal formulas.[40] Moreover, wealthy people, who were themselves literate, might nevertheless employ slaves as secretaries to write personal letters. Some of the great Roman literary figures, like Cicero and Pliny, avoided this form of manual labor, and there is no reason to believe that people in Egypt who could afford them would not also employ scribes or secretaries.[41] Thus, the only definite evidence of illiteracy in papyri is the plain statement that a person is totally unable to write (ἀγράμματος) or is a slow writer (βραδέως γράφων).

It is impossible to compare the proportion of illiterates or slow writers in the documents from Roman Egypt to what it had been in the Ptolemaic period, since the total number of people, papyri, illiterates, and slow writers from each century has never been determined.[42] Rita Calderini did attempt some quantification.[43] The results are quite startling. Calderini surveyed 1,738 documents mentioning illiterates or slow writers. She found fewer women than men among the illiterates simply because women in antiquity participated less than men in activities requiring written documentation. However, she also discovered that the ratio of illiterate women to men increased in the first and second centuries A.D. Though illiteracy in general may have increased under the Romans, it is most unlikely that it increased at a faster pace among women than among men. Rather, I suggest that the rise in illiteracy in Roman Egypt which is perceived is exaggerated as a result of women's ownership of land. In an agricultural country like Egypt, with women participating freely in all the written documentation that ownership of land entails (e.g., leases, loans of seed, sales, and paying taxes), the documents will show an increase in illiteracy over what it had been when women were less active in this arena. In modern developing countries, the literacy rates of women are normally below those of men. Similarly, the women in papyri are able to sign their names in a much smaller proportion of their total number than the men.[44] This illiteracy was not burdensome, since unless a women enjoyed the *ius* iii *liberorum* (legal privilege of women with three children) she was always accompanied by a *kyrios* (guardian), most often a male relative. If he were literate, he would sign on her behalf, if both were illiterate, others would sign for them. In the usual situation where a woman was literate and a man illiterate, the woman did not sign on the man's behalf.[45]

In addition, since women were accompanied by guardians, borderline illiterates or slow writers were more likely to allow the men who were with them to sign on their behalf. This practice was fostered by the tendency, mentioned above on p. 309, for husbands to treat their wives' land as though it were their own. On the other hand, a man who was similarly a borderline illiterate or slow writer, being unaccompanied, would manage to affix his own signature. These considerations explain why Calderini could find only five female "slow writers" in the first and second centuries A.D., a time when, as she points out, the ratio of female to male illiterates increased.[46]

Some women in Roman Egypt were literate and, like women elsewhere in the Empire, most of them probably acquired their knowledge in school. Papyrus texts that must have been used by children learning to read and write are commonly referred to by papyrologists as "schoolboys' books."[47] However, girls must also have studied such texts.

In view of the number of men and women who did know how to read and write, there is surprisingly little explicit evidence about schools and teachers.[48] But a particularly rich source is a group of letters which talk about the education of a daughter in the second century A.D.[49] The girl is Heraïdous, daughter of Aline and of Apollonius, the strategos of Apollinopolis. In one letter, Aline asks that a gift of poultry be sent to Heraïdous' teacher so that he might make a special effort with his pupil (*P. Giss. Univ.* 80). The mother is also concerned that her daughter have the paraphernalia for school and a book to read (*P. Giss. Univ.* 85). Since Aline does not specify the book it is necessary to venture a guess at what it might have been by glancing at the literature preserved on papyri. There were more texts of Homer than of any other author. Since she knew how to read, Heraïdous doubtless already had her own copy. According to the survey of R.A. Pack, Euripides was next with 76 texts.[50] Euripides was probably chosen more frequently as a school text than Sophocles or Aeschylus for several reasons including the greater simplicity of his language. But apparently there was an interest in heroines like those of Euripidean tragedy. This taste is reflected in the fact that there are no less than twenty seven texts of [Hesiod] "Catalog of Women." (This work which gives the genealogy and deeds of mythical women seems to have been written later than the genuine works of Hesiod.) That a relatively large number of copies were found suggests an interest in the subject matter and the use of the work as a school text. Perhaps a work on mythical heroines was chosen for Heraïdous.

Not only social and economic class, but historical time and geographical place, helped to determine whether a girl would be educated. Claire Préaux places the education of Heraïdous in the context of the flowering of Greek culture under the patronage of Hadrian.[51] Calderini too found a small rise in the percentage of literate women in the second and third centuries (though, inexplicably, the percentage of men fell).[52] Local custom may also have played a role. In a survey of eighty three women empowered to act without a guardian by the *ius iii liberorum*, P.J. Sijpesteijn found only five who asserted that they were literate.[53] These five women, like Heraïdous, all come from Hermopolis, which was a center of education and Hellenisation second only to Oxyrhynchus in the second and third centuries.[54] On the other hand, it was not inevitable that women in Hermopolis be literate, for Sijpesteijn cities two who were not.

Most teachers, like Heraïdous', must have been men, as was the case in the rest of the Empire. Yet it was possible for a woman to be a teacher, for a female mummy from Memphis is inscribed "' Ερμιόνη γραμματική '."[55]

The letters from Aline are written in various hands, but, like other wealthy people, she may have employed secretaries even if she had been literate herself. Claire Préaux has drawn attention to the cultivated prose style that pervades Aline's letters. Yet it would be wrong to generalize from Heraïdous' situation and to suppose that her mother and other female members of families of high status or wealth would be literate. Heraïdous was definitely her mother's favorite. Aline refers to her other children collectively as *tekna*; Heraïdous is the only one she mentions by name. Doubtless more attention was given to her education than was ordinarily given to daughters even in the same economic and social class. Indeed, women who get into the documents tend to be a privileged class, including landowners and soldiers' 'wives,' yet their status is no guarantee of literacy. Although membership in a privileged class does not necessarily guarantee that women were literate, the converse is more likely to be true, for a girl's parents would have had to be able to pay for her tuition. Thus in an unusual case where sisters are described as literate, it is not surprising that their father was wealthy and served as a gymnasiarch, an archiereus, and a city councillor at Hermopolis.[56]

Parents who did not have sufficient wealth to send all their children to school probably did what parents in that predicament have always done — they invested in their sons' educations. A mother could profit more from educating a son than from educating a daughter, for she could use a son as her guardian when he was an adult and employ him to sign documents on her behalf. Attendance at school must have been responsible for the higher literacy of men; in addition, as people who continued to act in the public sphere where reading and writing could be practiced, they did not lose this ability as quickly as women did.

Literacy had no effect upon legal capacity. Under the Romans, women's legal capacity increased, for those who were granted the *ius iii liberorum* were permitted to transact business without a *kyrios* (guardian). Yet, as I have argued above, women's literacy rate probably was higher in Ptolemaic than in Roman Egypt. Literacy was not a prerequisite for the grant of the *ius* iii *liberorum*,[57] although illiteracy rendered such women incapable of exercising the independence that the law allowed. In 263 A.D., Aurelia Thaïsous, also called Lolliane, applied for the *ius* iii *liberorum* asserting that she was particularly eligible, since the law was especially suitable to "women who know how to write," and that she herself was "a writer able to write with the greatest ease" (*P. Oxy.* XII 1467). The intention of Thaïsous' statement needs to be clarified. H. Youtie abandoned his earlier opinion that Thaïsous was "somewhat boastful" and was introducing irrelevant information.[58] Despite Sijpesteijn's study, referred to above, which demonstrated a lack of correlation between literacy and the exercise of the *ius* iii *liberorum*, Youtie's revised opinion was that literacy, although not a prerequisite, would nevertheless enhance her plea.[59]

Thaïsous is merely drawing attention to the real difference that literacy makes to women who are granted the *ius* iii *liberorum*. Illiterate women were incapable of transacting business alone, and were most often accompanied by exactly the same men[60] who would have served as *kyrii* if they had been legally necessary. Only literacy enables women to make legally binding commitments without the assistance of men.

QUESTIONS AND CONCLUSIONS

Through the avenue of the *ius* iii *liberorum* the Romans eventually restored to women in Egypt the legal capacity to act without a male guardian that had been enjoyed by their predecessors before the rule of the Ptolemies. The guardian had been a Greek innovation, and was a requisite for any woman acting under Greek law. Before Ptolemaic rule, Egyptian women were not required to have a male guardian when they made legal contracts. Similarly, Jewish women did not need a guardian under Jewish law, but adopted the Greek rule in Egypt.[61] The employment of a guardian demonstrated assimilation to the ruling class. In contrast, under Roman rule, the privileged women were those who owned land, possibly the most precious possession in Egypt, and could dispose of it without a male guardian.

The study of women's land ownership raises several questions which can not as yet be definitively answered. First of all, it would be important to determine whether there was any relationship between endogamy and partible patrimony. In particular, to what extent were marriages — especially the extreme version of endogamy, those of brother to sister — motivated by a desire and need to unite parcels of land that had been fragmented by dowry and inheritance. It has been suggested that the requirement for metropolitan status (a civic status granting privileges and immunities) was responsible for consanguine marriages.[62] Because metropolitan descent had to be proven through both the maternal and paternal line, siblings married to assure the status of their children. This reason does not appear to me to be compelling. Metropolites could have married other metropolites who were not siblings. If, however, the need to preserve family plots were added to the desire to retain metropolitan status, then there would be a compelling reason for brother–sister marriages. The most extensive and uncontroversial evidence for consanguine marriage in Egypt outside the royal family comes from the Roman period.

The next question is whether the material presented in this article is indicative of increased hardship in Egypt under Roman rule. In the Ptolemaic period it would have been possible to dower daughters with private land that was not royal domain but such dowries are not found. Instead, parents managed to give daughters movables such as cash and jewelry, at the time of marriage. Later in life, some of these daughters added land and other items to their possessions through inheritance. The reason that daughters were not dowered with movables alone in the Roman period may have been that, owing to increased financial hardship, farmers had only a house and some land, but little movable capital.

Finally, we would like to know the relationship between the ownership of land by women and men's withdrawal into the countryside and abandonment of their obligations (*anachoresis*). The situation offers a parallel, though not an exact one to the emigration of men from Hellenistic Sparta, mentioned above. In Egypt, due to the dearth of men created by *anachoresis*, relatives as distant as uncles and second cousins could be held responsible for the compulsory sertvices attached to a woman's land. Such pressure would have induced even more men to take flight from burdensome services. Thus women's land ownership may not only be evidence of oliganthropy,[63] but also may have accelerated this phenomenon.

All the papyri from Roman Egypt will not be published in our lifetimes, and all these issues need further analysis before any definite judgments may be made. But from the material now available, the inevitable conclusion is that under Roman rule women gained in economic and legal capacity while the prosperity of Egypt as a whole declined.[64]

Notes

1. N. Lewis, " 'Greco-Roman Egypt': Fact or Fiction?", *Proceedings of the Twelfth International Congress of Papyrology* (Toronto 1970) pp. 3–14, maintained that the designation "Greco-Roman" should be eliminated, inasmuch as Roman rule introduced distinct changes in Egypt.
2. I. Biezunska, "La condition juridique de la femme grecque d'après les papyri", *Hermaion fasc.* 4 (1939). L. Bringman, *Die Frau im ptolemäisch-kaiserlichen Ägypten*, Diss. Bonn, (1939). F. Jeanquart, *La femme dans l'Égypte gréco-romaine. Lettres des femmes*, Thèse de licence (Brussels 1936). M. Mondini, "Lettere femminili nei papiri greco-egizi", *Studi della Scuola Papirologica* (Milan) 2 (1917) pp. 29–50. C. Préaux, "Le statut de la femme à l'époque hellénistique, principalement en Égypte", *Recueils de la société Jean Bodin* 11: *La femme* (1959) pp. 127–75. W. Schubart, "Die Frau im griechischen-romischen Agypten", *Internazionale Monatschrift fur Wissenschaft, Kunst und Technik* (1916) 10, pp. 1503–38. C. Vatin, *Recherches sur le mariage et la condition de la femme mariée a l'époque hellénistique* (Paris 1970).
3. See, most recently, J. Modrzejewski, "Régime foncier et status social dans l'Egypte Ptolemaique", in *Terre et paysans dépendants dans les sociétés antique (Colloque Besançon, 1974)* (Paris 1979) pp. 163–88.
4. D.J. Crawford, *Kerkeosiris. An Egyptian Village in the Ptolemaic Period* (Cambridge 1971) p. 103.
5. J.G. Keenan and J.C. Shelton, *P. Tebt.* IV, pp. 2, 6.
6. For Greek marriage contracts see O. Montevecchi, "Ricerche di sociologia nei documenti dell'Egitto greco-romano II. I contratti di matrimonio e gli atti di divorzio", *Aegyptus* 16 (1936) espec. pp. 4–6, 49. Apparently the same limitation on land in dowries appears in Demotic contracts, for land is not mentioned as matrimonial property in P.W. Pestman, *Marriage and Matrimonial Property in Ancient Egypt (Pap. Lugd. Bat.* IX, 1961).

7. See D.M. Schaps, *Economic Rights of Women in Ancient Greece* (Edinburgh 1979) pp. 4–7.

8. O. Montevecchi, "Ricerche di sociologia nei documenti dell'Egitto greco-romano I. I testamenti," *Aegyptus* 15 (1935) p. 116.

9. According to Deborah H. Samuel, "Women as Property Owners in Roman Egypt", (unpublished paper delivered at the annual meeting of the American Philological Association, New Orleans, December 28, 1980), women at Socnopaiou Nessos as well most frequently came into possession of land by means of inheritance; they are rarely found as purchasers of land.

10. Schaps, cited note 7 above, pp. 6–7, for the exclusion of women from land ownership in Athens and Delos.

11. Thucydides 1.2.5–6.

12. *BGU* 1734, Heracleopolis = *SB* VIII 9790; edited by W. Müller, "Bemerkungen zu den spätptolemäischen Papyri der Berliner Sammlung", *Proceedings of the IX International Congress of Papyrology, Oslo, 1958* (Oslo 1961) p. 190.

13. E.g. *P. Berl. Leihg.* 14 (second century), *P. Lond.* II 193 (first century), *P. Col.* V, 1, *verso* 6 (ca. 160–61 A.D.). However, in contrast, in *P. Col.* V, 1 *verso* 3 (155 A.D.), no women are named. On p. 109 the editors suggest that this tax was concerned with compulsory services from which women were exempt. See discussion below. For an example of a large property see the estate of Claudia Isidora in *P. Oxy.* VI 919, XII 1578, XIV 1630, 1634, 1659; for others, *P. Oxy.* XIV p. 14, note 3.

14. For these taxes see, S.L. Wallace, *Taxation in Egypt from Augustus to Diocletian* (Princeton 1938).

15. *CAH* 11, p. 653.

16. *P. Lond.* II p. 20, citing Ulpian, *Dig* 50.15,3.

17. For the evidence and the controversy see P.A. Brunt, *Italian Manpower 225 B.C.–14 A.D.* (London 1971) pp. 113–21.

18. Wallace, cited note 14, above pp. 101–02, M. Hombert and C. Préaux, *Recherches sur le recensement dans l'Egypte romaine, Pap. Lugd. Bat.* V (Brussels 1952) pp. 60–61.

19. See F. Oertel, *Die Liturgie. Studien zur ptolemäischen und kaiserlichen Verwaltung Aegyptens* (Leipzig 1917) pp. 105, 899, and N. Lewis, "Exemption From Liturgy in Roman Egypt", *Actes du Xe Congrès Internationale de Papyrologigues,* 1961 (Warsaw 1964) p. 70.

20. A.C. Johnson, *Roman Egypt to the Reign of Diocletian* (Baltimore 1936) p. 28 implies that there was a connection between women's land ownership and their exemptions "There was a tendency for private property to pass into the hands of women, who could not be appointed for liturgies nor be assigned land for forced cultivation."

21. Arist. *Pol* 2.6.11 (1270a). See also discussion in S. Pomeroy, *Goddesses, Whores, Wives, and Slaves: Women in Classical Antiquity = GWWS* (New York 1975) pp. 38–39, and James Redfield, "The Women of Sparta", *CJ* 73 (1977–78) pp. 158–60.

22. *GWWS*, cited note 21 above pp. 162–63 and "The Relationship of the Married Women to her Blood Relatives in Rome", *AncSoc* 7 (1976) pp. 22–25.

23. J. Herrmann, *Studien zur Bodenpacht im Recht der graeco-aegyptischen Papyri (Münchener Beiträge zur Papyrusforschung und Antiken Rechtsgeschichte* 41 (Munich

1958) p. 58.

24.   Similarly in *CPR* 24 (= *Chrest. Mitt.* 288, 136 A.D.) the husband is responsible for ἔργα and τελέσματα. The provision is reminiscent of the distribution of labor between husband and wife in Xen., *Oec.* 9–10.

25.   See O. Montevecchi, cited note 6, above, pp. 4–6 for a list of marriage contracts.

26.   See O. Montevecchi, "Ricerche di sociologia nei documenti dell'Egitto greco-romano I: I testamenti", *Aegyptus* 15 (1935) pp. 68–73 for a list of wills.

27.   N. Lewis, "On Paternal Authority in Roman Egypt", *RIDA* 17 (1970) pp. 251–58 and Pomeroy, "The Relationship of the Married Woman to her Blood Relatives in Rome", cited note 22, above.

28.   *A Mediterranean Society, The Jewish Communities of the Arab World as Portrayed in the Documents of the Cairo Geniza* III: *The Family* (Berkeley 1978) p. 180.

29.   O. Montevecchi, "Ricerche di sociologia nei documenti dell'Egitto greco-romano III: I contratti di compra-vendita", *Aegyptus* 23 (1943) p. 61.

30.   See *Pap. Lugd. Bat.* XIX, p. 26, note f, for a farmer who acts as if he were the owner of his wife's land, though he is actually only acting in her behalf. In *SB* 7188 (edited by P. Collart and P. Jouquet, *Aegyptus* 5 [1924] pp. 129–39), a husband leases a parcel of land which belongs to his wife. The woman herself does not participate in the transaction.

31.   "*Technikai kai Mousikai*: The Education of Women in the Fourth Century and in the Hellenistic period", *AJAH* 2 (1977) pp. 51–68.

32.   Susan Guettel Cole, "Could Greek Women Read and Write?", this volume, pp. 231–2 and notes 64, 71 objects to my interpretation of *SIG*³ 578, the inscription recording the endowment of the school at Teos. In *AJA*, 2 (1977) p. 52, I have argued that since the students are distinguished as girls (παρθένοι) and boys (παῖδες) in the second line of this lengthy inscription, both sexes must be included under the collective children (παῖδες) in the remainder of the inscription. Cole writes "if the sexes are distinguished in the first place, there is no reason to assume that the distinction is not maintained throughout the inscription". In fact, quite the opposite is the case in, e.g., *Thasos* I, number 141.5 where children of both sexes (παῖδες) are referred to three times collectively and then are distinguished as males (ἄρσενες) and daughters (θυγατέρες). Similarly Diodorus Siculus (20.84) refers to the children collectively (παῖδες) then distinguishes them as girls (παρθένοι) and sons (υἱοί). (See my discussion of these texts in "Charities for Greek Women", *Mnemosyne* [to be published]). Since the writer of the Teos inscription emphasized that girls were included by mentioning them specifically early in the text — rather than as a subgroup as is the case in the texts from Thasos and Diodorus Siculus — it is unlikely that they would be excluded from the provisions in the remainder of the inscription.

33.   "Del Segno Incompiuto al Segno Negato", *Alfabetismo e cultura scritta nella storia della società italiana*. Atti del seminario tenutosi a Perugia il 29–30 marzo 1977 (Perugia 1978) pp. 121–22.

34.   "Age-rounding, Illiteracy and Social Differentiation in The Roman Empire", *Chiron* 7 (1977) pp. 333–53.

35.   For Agallis see Athenaeus 1.14 d; *Suda s.v.* Anagallis. She is incorrectly named

Dalis by Schol. *Il.* 18.483. For Agallias see also Eustathius in Schol. *Il.* 18.491. I am grateful to Mary Lefkowitz for drawing my attention to Agallis.

36. Str. 13.599; Susemihl, *Gesch. d. gr. Lit. Alex.* II pp. 148–49, and n. 2. Eustathius, on B 538, 280, 19, notes that the name is spelled Histiaia or Hestiaia. That Hestiaea's work was a monograph is pointed out by Rudolph Pfeiffer, *History of Classical Scholarship: from the Beginnings to the End of the Hellenistic Age* (Oxford 1968) p. 250 n. 4.

37. R. Pfeiffer, *Call.* I, pp. 118–19, II, pp. 115–16.

38. Cole, cited note 32 above, p. 229 states that "the women's names used to identify the writers of the essays are almost certainly fictitious". It is not clear to me whether she is arguing that the authors were men rather than women or that women were the authors but that they wrote under pseudonyms. I have argued that considering the state of women's education in Alexandria at this time (see note 31, above, pp. 57–58) there is nothing inherently impossible in the notion that women actually wrote these treatises. Moreover, parents of a particular intellectual or religious persuasion in antiquity, as now, would tend to endow their children with the names of the founders or important figures in the movement. Thus the names of the authors are probably authentic.

39. For references see article cited note 31 above.

40. Aurelia Thaïsous who is unquestionably literate (see further discussion below, p. 316) employs a scribe in *P. Oxy.* XII 1475 (267 A.D.), an application to an archidicastes concerning a land sale. She seems to have no husband, since she identifies herself only by a patronymic in both documents. Thus she lacks the person who most usually acts as *kyrios* in land sales. See above, p. 309.

41. Thus Aline, the wife of a strategos employed a number of scribes or secretaries. See discussion below, p. 315.

42. For studies of literacy based on papyri, H.C. Youtie: "ΑΛΡΑΜΜΑΤΟΣ: An Aspect of Greek Society in Egypt", *HSPh* 75 (1971) pp. 161–76 = *Scriptiunculae* II 611–51; "Between Literacy and Illiteracy: An Aspect of Greek Society in Egypt", *Akten des XIII Internationalen Papyrologen Kongresses 1971* (Munich 1974) pp. 481–87 republished in a longer version as "Βραδέως γράφων: Between Literacy and Illiteracy", *GRBS* 12 (1971) pp. 239–61; "The Social Impact of Illiteracy in Greco-Roman Egypt", *ZPE* 17 (1975) pp. 201–21; and "Because They Do Not Know Letters", *ZPE* 19 (1975) pp. 101–10. In these studies, Youtie does not make a distinction between the Ptolemaic and Roman periods.

43. "Gli ἀγράμματοι nell'Egitto greco-romano", *Aegyptus* 30 (1950) pp. 14–41, espec. pp. 22–23.

44. E. Majer-Leonhard, Ἀγράμματοι (Frankfort 1913) pp. 74–77.

45. Youtie, *ZPE* 17, cited note 42, above, p. 216, note 41.

46. Calderini, cited note 43, above, pp. 34–35.

47. E.g. E.G. Turner, *Greek Papyri: An Introduction* (Princeton 1968) p. 89.

48. See P. Collart, "A l'école avec les petits Grecs d'Égypte", *CE* 11 (1936) pp. 250–51, 489–507 and H.-I. Marrou, *Histoire de l'Éducation dans l'Antiquité⁷* (Paris 1977) *passim.*

49. These letters have been discussed by C. Préaux, "Lettres privées grecques

322   SARAH B. POMEROY

d'Égypte relatives à l'éducation", *RBPh* 8 (1929) pp. 772–80. See also Mondini, cited note 2 above, p. 37.
50. R.A. Pack, *The Greek and Latin Literary Texts From Greco-Roman Egypt*[2] (Ann Arbor 1965), *sub nomine auctoris*.
51. Préaux, cited note 49 above, p. 772.
52. Calderini, cited note 43 above, p. 37.
53. P.J. Sijpesteijn, "Die χωρίς κυρίου χρηματίζουσαι δικαίω τέκνων in den papyri", *Aegyptus* 45 (1965) p. 176.
54. Préaux, cited noted 49 above, p. 775.
55. Now at Cambridge, Girton College. K. Parlasca, *Mumienporträts* (Wiesbaden 1966) pp. 81, 101–03, Plate 15.1 and *SB* 5753. According to Turner, cited note 47 above, p. 77, she may be a "literary lady" rather than a teacher.
56. *Pap. Lugd. Bat.* II 6.
57. Th. Reinach, "A propos de la question de l'enseignement primaire", *REA* 19 (1917) p. 32, had suggested that literacy was a requirement for the *ius iii liberorum*.
58. *HSPh* 75 cited note 42 above, p. 166 = *Scriptiunculae* II, p. 616.
59. *ZPE* 17 cited note 42 above, p. 221, note 62.
60. *Ibid.*, pp. 212–14, 219–20; *HSPh* 75 cited note 42 above, pp. 165–66.
61. *C. P. Jud.* I, p. 35.
62. M. Hombert and C. Préaux, cited note 18 above, p. 152.
63. J. Schwartz, review of J. Herrmann, *Studien zur Bodenpacht im Recht der graeco-aegyptischen Papyri (Münchener Berträge zur Papyrusforschuing und antiken Rechtsgeschichte*, 41), *CE* 34 (1959) p. 161 notes that the presence of a woman lessor in Theadelphia at the beginning of the Byzantine period is evidence of oliganthropy in this part of the Fayum.
64. I wish to express my gratitude for their comments on an earlier version of this article to E. Badian, S.M. Burstein, W.V. Harris, P.W. Pestman, and D.H. Samuel.

Etruscan couples and their aristocratic society

LARISSA BONFANTE

New York University

NON-ARCHAEOLOGISTS cannot easily imagine the difficulty of interpreting archaeological evidence so as to understand the role of women in an ancient society. By its very nature, archaeological evidence is incomplete, and must be interpreted with the help of literary sources in order to be used as history. The Etruscan situation is therefore particularly instructive as a test case, since we have none of their literature. What we know about this people is based upon their art, most of it funerary.[1]

In such a context, a particular feature of the representation of women in Etruscan art, the prominence of couples, deserves our attention as a historical question. This emphasis on couples, so strikingly persistent, and different from the contemporary representations of other societies, seems to be significant, reflecting the importance of couples in Etruscan society, and confirming the importance of Etruscan women suggested by Greek and Roman accounts, Etruscan monuments, and linguistic evidence. All of this evidence suggests that women in Etruria participated more fully in the public life of their society than Greek and Roman women. They had their own names, and apparently passed their rank on to their children — the frequent use of both patronymics and matronymics in Etruscan inscriptions attests to the mother's importance.[2] Their visibility, not only alone but together with their husbands, leads us to imagine that they played an important role in an Etruscan society where the family counted for more than the single individual male citizen. How much of what we imagine is true? And how justified are we in drawing further conclusions as to the type of society implied?[3]

There are two ways we can "test" the evidence of the monuments. In the first place, we can compare the Etruscan material with that of the people in the Mediterranean we know best, the Greeks and Romans at the same or similar periods of their history. In the second place we can look at what the Greeks and Romans had to say about their rich neighbors, and see how their accounts fit in with what we see represented on the monuments.

The question we will be dealing with is, basically, how much can we tell about a society from the way it represents itself in its art? It would be well to survey the Etruscan monuments first, before comparing relevant Greek and Roman monuments and literature.

Though Etruscan art is mostly funerary, some bronze statuettes of the seventh and sixth centuries B.C. serve as evidence of the importance of the married couple in Etruscan art and thought. These votive offerings, each consisting of a group of three bronze statuettes — a male figure with the attributes of a warrior, a female figure, and an animal statuette — have been convincingly identified not as divinities, but as a pair, a family unit, accompanied by an animal representing their property. This type of votive offering, popular in north Etruria, was widely exported into Europe, where it encouraged the diffusion of Etruscan artistic forms.[4]

We know that in the Orientalizing period, Etruscan women were honored as much as men after death, in graves often richer than men's. That female ancestors were heroized as much as male ones[5] is shown, for example, in a tomb in Cerveteri of the seventh century B.C., which yielded five statuettes, images of deceased ancestors, seated side by side, two women and three men.[6] Perhaps a man and a woman sat alternately, with two men framing the group on the outside; but we do not know.

By the second half of the sixth century the arrangement was definitely by couples. In Caere, the most famous example is the terracotta sarcophagus or ash urn of the "Bride and Groom," whose modern name emphasizes the affectionate gestures of the pair, the man's arm encircling his wife protectively (Figure 1), while the border of his mantle covers her leg symbolically.[7] Their hands, which seem today to gesture so eloquently the mute conversation, once held attributes. The symbols of their union, the bed and blanket, recur, as we shall see, in other depictions of married couples in southern Etruscan cities. The tradition of banquet couches like that of the "Bride and Groom" in the Villa Giulia Museum in Rome, and a similar one in the Louvre, recently restored and newly exhibited, was no doubt the creation of a great artist of Caere.

At Tarquinia a series of contemporary, late archaic wall paintings shows husbands and wives reclining together at banquets[8] (Figure 2), in a manner quite different from both the Greek and the Roman customs, and agreeing surprisingly well with Livy's description of the merry life of the Etruscan princesses of the Tarquin family.[9] A few representations, though somewhat different, seem to make the same point. The early fifth-century tomb of the Funeral Couch in Tarquinia shows, instead of a banqueting couple, a huge empty bed with the head-dresses of husband and wife. (Or are these, as has been recently suggested, two funerary *cippi* or grave markers, shown realistically placed on the bed at the time of the funeral banquet?)[10] Official or public appearances occasionally also include the couple's children.[11]

Much has been made, with good reason, of the existence of special forms of women's beds. In sixth- and fifth-century B.C. tombs in Cerveteri, different kinds of beds carved out of the rock distinguish male and female burials: a simple couch of *kline* was for a man, a *kline* placed inside a gabled chest or sarcophagus in the shape of a house was for a woman.[12] Later, in the fourth century, when the many-chambered family tombs had given way to the large hall, and the beds were no longer distinguished in this way, the house shape still differentiated the female grave markers or *cippi* representing the dead inside the tomb, from the pillar-, cone-, or phallus-shaped male markers. Many of these *cippi* have been found *in situ*, their inscriptions attesting to their owner's sex.[13] They are wonderfully illustrated on a well-known Etruscan vase-painting of this period, showing Admetus dramatically presenting his case to a dubious Alcestis, while behind them waits expectantly the demon of death, and beside them, their respective grave markers, male and female (Figure 3).[14] Here too, the Etruscan preference for couples dictated the artistic choice of theme, shown with sympathy and wealth of local color.

Male and female beds and male and female grave markers, appearing together, emphasize the equality, as well as the union of the couple in death as in life. As Heurgon has pointed out, however, the women's beds have something the men do not: the house-shaped chest enclosing the *kline* or couch, symbolically referring to the woman as "keeper of the house," responsible for the sphere of the family.[15] The gable-shaped chest is still in use in the fourth century for the two husband-and-wife sarcophagi from Vulci in the Boston Museum (Figures 4-5). (One of these contained only the wife, named Ramtha Visnai.)[16] Here we find illustrated those other symbols of the married couple, the bed and the blanket. The couples are shown in bed, privately, lying in each other's arms, not attending the banquet publicly, as in earlier Etruscan art. Though these two sarcophagi are unusual in their iconography, they are not unusual in the ideas they express. The blanket which covers both couples is the rounded toga, or mantle, symbolic of marriage, as we know from a tradition preserved for us in Roman literature.[17]

The group of the Bride and Groom, two hundred years earlier, alludes to this tradition, while a stone relief of the archaic period from Chiusi shows a wedding scene, its ritual covering of the pair with a blanket or cloth canopy reminiscent of the Jewish marriage ritual.[18] In fact, the iconography of the wedding is often repeated in a funerary context. The relief panel in front of the sarcophagus of Ramtha Visnai in Boston (Figure 5) shows the pair who have just come together, each followed by attendants bearing the proper attributes of rank, position and office. The man's stick shows he has been on a journey. Has he come back for his wife, in order to be joined with her once more? Is he about to lead her away, or to lead her in marriage (*in matrimonium ducere*), with the gesture of *dextrarum iunctio* touchingly rendered, as on Roman monuments?[19] On the side panels two carriages take them to the fated meeting, a prelude to their journey to the world of the dead.[20]

On the cover of the other sarcophagus in Boston a younger couple is depicted (Figure 4).[21] Again the two are lying in bed under the same blanket — the man's cloak — as a symbol of the marriage ritual renewed on their death bed. The classical style of the relief is closer to Greek models than the local, softer, expressive style of the older couple's faces and drapery. But the distance from its Greek models is striking. The monument would have shocked a Greek, for the couple lying in each others' arms is portrayed naked. This is a daring and unusual representation, and a conscious comment, I believe, on Greek nudity. Not only is the date, around 340 B.C., very early — even in Greece — to represent female nudity; the concept of a couple shown naked together is unknown in Greek art. Are we to think of them as naked, or nude? Are they naked because they are in bed together, and making love; or are they represented in "heroic nudity," husband and wife together sharing the Greek ideal of youthful, naked beauty?

Funerary monuments of the fourth century B.C. and slightly later echo the motif of the couple. An Etruscan man reclining on a *kline* is often accompanied by a woman seated at the foot of the bed (Figure 6).[22] (Usually this is his wife, although the motif is used also for the representation of the female angel or demon who will accompany him to the underworld.)[23] In the tomb of Orcus[24] and the tomb of the Shields at Tarquinia,[25] as well as in the François tomb at Vulci,[26] the family's ancestors are represented by couples, husband and wife each standing for a generation of an illustrious family.

This remarkable emphasis on couples is also found on a set of monuments of the archaic period (ca. 575 B.C.), whose interpretation has been much contested. On these terracotta relief decorations of a building complex at Murlo (Poggio Civitate), near Siena,[27] a group of seated figures appears (Figure 7). Georges Dumézil explains the first two seated figures — a man, and a woman holding out her veil in the customary wifely gesture — as a couple, husband and wife.[28] Cristofani agrees; denying the identification of the building complex as a sanctuary, he sees the figures as the lord and lady of the manor,[29] who sit, accompanied by their personal attendants and their following, friends, relatives, or colleagues. The number of servants attending the couple show their social position, like the liveried servants of eighteenth-century aristocrats, or the Roman *familia*. Related friezes show a carriage procession (Figure 8), a banquet (both apparently occupied by couples of the same sex rather than by husbands and wives), and a horse race. Everywhere there are the signs of an aristocratic way of life familiar to us from representations in Etruscan tombs. Unlike the monuments we have examined so far, these are not funerary. Whatever the rank or identity of the figures, gods, heroized ancestors, or lord and lady of the manor, they illustrate the family group as a couple.[30]

Even figures borrowed from the Greek repertoire are shown in pairs. Typical of archaic Etruscan iconography are Bacchic dancers on engraved Etruscan mirrors, entertainers or guests who appear in "bisexual groupings," partners or couples in the dance.[31] In the fourth century we have seen a (partly) naked couple in bed take the place, in Etruscan art, of the classical Greek male nude figure, alone or with another man. A man and a woman substitute (in this same period) for the traditional Greek group of two warriors carrying the body of their dead companion, on a bronze group once serving as the handle of a Praenestine cista (Figure 9);[32] while archaic terracotta painted plaques from Cerveteri show, in two contiguous scenes, Paris at his Judgment and the Toilette of Helen, thus maintaining the motif of the married (or common law) couple.[33]

Let us now see how the representations of couples in Etruscan art compare with monuments from Rome.

This insistence on showing people in pairs did not escape the notice of the early Romans, who borrowed Etruscan types for many of their representations of divinities. Hercules, who regularly appears in Etruscan art with a female companion, not always easy to identify,[34] was also given a partner in Roman ritual, perhaps in imitation of Etruscan custom. In 399 B.C. at a *lectisternium* in Rome — in which the gods' statues appeared, reclining on couches, at feasts held in their honor — he was paired off with Diana.[35] The infernal couple, Hades and Persephone, pictured on Etruscan wall paintings of the fourth century and later (Figure 10) was introduced into Rome as Dis and Proserpina.[36] Rome's gruesome sacrifice of two paired couples, male and female, of Greeks and Gauls, who were buried alive at the time of the war with Hannibal — a sacrifice repeated during other crises — has also been convincingly attributed to Etruscan influence.[37]

The Romans were willing to adopt external aspects of Etruscan civilization — rites, sacrifices, techniques of writing, *haruspicina*, and artistic representation.[38] But they never allowed Etruscan culture to impinge on their basic beliefs and customs. Throughout, Roman society remained strictly patriarchal. Divine couples — Dionysos and Ariadne, Hercules and Diana, Dis and Proserpina — might appear in art. But couples, human or divine, were not important in religion or law.[39] In Rome the *paterfamilias*, following most ancient traditions, alone carried the name and legal responsibility for the family.[40]

In Rome both literary and archeological evidence makes clear the contrast between the Romans' patriarchal structure and Etruscan society. The traditional Roman picture of the clash between Etruscan and Roman *mores* shows Roman awareness of the contrast between Etruscan royal couples such as Tarquinius Superbus and Tullia[41] and the all male cast of the early Roman Republican consuls and heroes. Women in Republican Rome were limited by custom to the private sphere, indoors:[42] Roman epitaphs illustrated women at home with their wool baskets beside them;[43] and Roman sources contrasted Lucretia's domesticity with the aristocratic social life of the Etruscan princesses.[44] The early third-century B.C. Roman tomb paintings of the Esquiline cemetery depicted the glorious deeds — battles fought and won — of the man, the heroic magistrate or victorious commander who brought nobility to his family;[45] on the nearly contemporary Francois tomb, noble couples and legendary exploits represented the Etruscan family's past generations.[46]

Like Republican Rome, democratic Athens limited women to the private sphere, indoors. Here monumental and literary evidence agree. Attic grave stelai showing women with their wool baskets repeat an ancient motif: Penelope sitting at her loom.[47] There was no lack of conjugal love and affection, but the intimacy of husband and wife belonged in the privacy of the home. Movingly portrayed in the farewell scenes of the grave stelai, conjugal love does not appear in Attic vase paintings because they belong to the public, purely male world of the *symposia*.[48] Even the grave stelai show surprisingly few married couples: the variety of relationships illustrated on the stelai more or less ignores the standard legal motifs of father and child or husband and wife. We see brothers and sisters, mothers and nurses and children of all ages (Figure 11).[49] A group which looks like mother and child turns out to represent grandmother and granddaughter, according to the epitaph.[50] The interpretation of the figures on Attic grave stelai has represented, not surprisingly, a scholarly problem of some difficulty.

Changes can be traced, but less easily explained. In Athens, on the earlier archaic stelai, women are conspicuous in their absence. Gradually, the emphasis on war and military life disappears after the aristocratic period of Peisistratid art. The quiet representation of everyday scenes comes with the democratization of the classical period, in which a greater part is played by women and older men. Later, in fourth-century Attic stelai, family groups reign supreme, as mother and children populate this quiet, private family life, a prelude to the world of New Comedy.[51] Throughout Attic art secular women play a private role, contrasting with the public role of Etruscan women both as individuals and as members of the couples who represent the family unit.

Of course the use of the iconographic motif of couples was not limited to the Etruscans. The couple, though absent or subordinate in classical Athens and Republican Rome, had appeared regularly in the art of the Mediterranean, in Egypt, and Asia Minor,[52] signifying divine or royal power. It also appeared in some archaic Greek art. In view of the similarities between archaic Sparta and the Etruscan cities,[53] the important series of Laconian reliefs which begin about 550 B.C. and continue into the Hellenistic period is very striking. Earliest and best-known is the stele from Chrysapha, near Sparta (Figure 12),[54] with a man and a woman seated together, the woman holding up her veil. The snake rearing near their thrones and the smaller figures of worshipers approaching show them to be the heroized dead, as in contemporary Etruscan tombs.

When on the oldest Laconian grave steles the dead are depicted not singly, but always man and woman together, like a married couple, this, in connection with the quite impersonal heroic characterization, is probably to be understood as implying that originally these monuments were devoted not merely to the single individuals but to the family as a whole, and served as the common resort for the family's ancestor worship. Gradually, however, they take on a more individual character. The married couples vanish, to be replaced by representations of the single dead.[55]

The archaic Etruscans and Spartans have in common — aside from the fact that we know very little about them — an aristocratic type of government, which finds expression in the representation of noble families through couples. Sparta, starting around 500 B.C., began to abandon the representation of married couples in favor of more clearly individualized single figures. What does this change mean? Can we assume that a movement away from an aristocratic society based on the family, towards an emphasis on the state, led to such a dramatic change in the monuments? It may be that Etruscan art, in contrast, continued or began once more to emphasize the motif of the married couple in the fourth century B.C. in conscious assertion of her aristocratic character.[56] For, despite the many changes in this period, in Etruria the married couple maintained its importance.[57]

Glimpses afforded us by literary sources suggest that other cities, like those of Etruria and Sparta, also retained aristocratic customs typical of archaic societies. Aristocratic Greek Sybaris — which was, parenthetically, tied to the Etruscans in the archaic period — had dinner parties which included ladies, in sharp contrast to the parties in Athens where men shared their couches with boys. The story is told of Mindyrides, a Sybarite, who came to Sicyon to ask for the hand of Cleisthenes' daughter. When a man approached to lie down beside him, at the dinner held after his arrival, Mindyrides rebuffed him rudely: he had no intention, he asserted, of sharing his couch with anyone but the lady he had come to marry.[58]

We have now come to the second type of evidence available to us. Literary sources, often in the form of such anecdotes, as well as other judgments concerning the place of women in archaic, aristocratic societies, are to be read within the context of a Greek topos or cliché. For Greek authors connected a number of non-Athenian customs, including Etruscan wealth and women's freedom, with barbarian luxury, or *truphe*.[59] They saw as a conflict of civilizations the wealth and sexual promiscuity, lust and luxury which the term *truphe* implied.[60] (Recently, scholars studying Etruscan history further read the term *truphe* to mean a feudal type of society: Posidonius' statement that the fertility of the Etruscans' land led to their *truphe* fits into such a focus.)[61]

Certain aspects of the life of peoples characterized by *truphe* are repeatedly emphasized by ancient authors: their manner of dressing, their banquets, their free and easy lovemaking. Plato's description of the luxurious city, the *polis truphousa*, in the *Republic*,[62] recalls the picture of Etruscan banquets on wall paintings of Tarquinia (Figure 2), and in Athenaeus' and Livy's descriptions.

Above all, however, *truphe* showed itself in the position of women and slaves, especially in their participation in public life. For *truphe* or luxury were especially connected, in the ancients' minds, with a way of life which also meant a type of government. Thucydides' account of nudity for men in Greece,[63] a part of his sociological scheme, also fits into a discussion of the *truphe* which he saw both in the Athens of an earlier generation and in contemporary barbarian societies. Such nakedness was indeed part of the egalitarian direction of the Spartan aristocratic society, of men together in the barracks; a kind of uniform. Certainly the Greek adoption of complete nudity for men marks a sharp break with the barbarian — and well-nigh universal — custom of advertising one's wealth by wearing many expensive clothes which make you look important and distinguished. Nudity also marks the difference, in Athenian art and daily life, between free Athenian men, who exercised in the gymnasium, and women, who stayed home.

Heroic nudity, a peculiarly Greek invention in the ancient Mediterranean world, characteristic of male society, constituted, with
language, the chief distinction between Greek and barbarian,
including the Etruscans. Eventually associated with democracy,
Greek nudity came to be seen as the opposite of barbarian *truphe*
and decadent luxury in an Athens where only male citizens
counted, and women, children and slaves were under their protection.[64]

In fact, the ancients wondered at the freedom of both women
and slaves in Etruscan society.[65] The Greek historian of the fifth
or fourth century, Theopompus, was amazed at Etruscan *mores*
which permitted women to banquet publicly with their husbands
and other men, and to toast in the presence of other men, and
even to propose toasts to whoever was present. Etruscan princesses attended banquets with their peers, other rich young people
of their set,[66] mingling freely with all their relatives and friends. In
contrast, in Greece "married women do not accompany their
husbands to banquets, or think of partying with strangers, or with
anyone who has just happened to come along."[67]

All Greek accounts of the loose, luxurious customs of the
Etruscans emphasize *truphe*, characteristic of barbarians, tyrants,
and women. Athenian male democracy clearly reserved a different
place for their women from that of the Etruscan feudal, aristocratic society of great families, and saw such *truphe* as a threat. No
one has understood this fear more clearly than Montesquieu, in
L'esprit des lois. A democracy, he says, must defend itself from
luxury, and from the consequent license that will lead to the
corruption and eventual destruction of this type of government.[68]
Montesquieu relates the government and laws in a state to the
position of women, connecting wealth and the liberty of women
with the type of government, just as the ancient concept of
truphe did.[69]

What does our brief survey of the evidence allow us to conclude
about Etruscan couples? Etruscan insistence on showing husbands
and wife together, which contrasts with both the classical Greek
and early Roman Republican custom, applies even to motifs
borrowed from Greek tradition, such as heroic male nudity, and

Greek mythological characters. Certain religious Roman rituals, like the *lectisternium*, and the sacrifice of paired couples of Greeks and Gauls, probably adopted from the Etruscans, also reflect the Etruscan tendency to represent figures together as couples, both human and divine. Such images seem to refer to an ideal different from both the Roman *paterfamilias* and the male citizen of Athenian democracy, but close to that of the image of the couple on Laconian funerary reliefs: an aristocratic society based on the family unit.

Although significant, couples in art do not have the same meaning at all times in all places.[70] Yet if we consider four peoples of classical antiquity, Etruscans, Spartans, Athenians, and Romans, as we know them in history and as they represent themselves in their act, and observe differences and similarities among them in terms of government, family structure, and the position of women, a certain pattern does seem to emerge. The masculine democracy of classical Athens was in some sense dependent on the separation of men and women for its characteristic expression: the public nudity of male citizens and the related relegation of women to the private sphere. In Rome, the situation as usual defies classification. There, from the beginning, in typical patriarchal fashion, women seem to have had no legal place, although by the third and second centuries B.C. of the Republic, when Rome was most aristocratic, they exercised plenty of influence. On the other hand the prominence Etruscans gave to couples in their art seems to be characteristic of Sparta and of certain other aristocratic cultures which Thucydides and later authors would have thought of as barbarian, or having *truphe*.

A recent study of archaic Greece emphasizes the importance of the aristocratic *ethos* and aristocratic ties in early Greece, 800-500 B.C., citing these aristocrats' passion for luxury as a stimulus for their own search for wealth, as well as for their patronage of crafts, arts and literature during the period 800-500 B.C.[71] The aristocratic character of the flourishing culture in the Etruscan cities of this period fits into this picture. What seems to set the Etruscans apart from Greeks of the classical period is the fact that in Etruria this structure continued. Is this not what Greek authors

meant, in effect, by calling attention to the *truphe* of the Etruscans, Ionians, Sybarites, etc.? The connotation of the word
changes, and becomes pejorative, when the concept no longer
refers to Athens, or Sparta. It refers to what we see reflected in
Etruscan art: a culture that does not change, socially and econo-
mically, along the lines of the Greek cities most familiar to us.
When the Greeks write contemptuously of Etruscan *truphe* and of
the freedom of Etruscan women, they are reacting against a
culture that is foreign to classical Greek society, but that is not so
different from their own culture in its period of greatest expansion,
the archaic period.

Notes

The present contribution is a sequel to my two articles: "The Women of
Etruria," *Arethusa* 6 (1973) 91-101; and "Etruscan Women: A Question of
Interpretation," *Archaeology* 26 (1973) 242-249. Full references, as well as
the most important discussion and interpretation of the material are to be
found in J. Heurgon, *La vie quotidienne chez les Etrusques* (Paris 1961),
translated as *Daily Life of the Etruscans* (London 1964) 95-122; A.J. Pfiffig,
"Zur Sittengeschichte der Etrusker," *Gymnasium* 71 (1964) 17-36, and
Einführung in die Etruskologie (Darmstadt 1972) 77-84.

    J.J. Bachofen, who first pointed out that Etruscan women were different
and attempted to explain why, is given due credit in W.F.J. Knight's review
of the new edition of *Das Mutterrecht* (1861; new ed. Basel 1949): "Italy he
regarded, perhaps brilliantly, as a home for lost causes." (*Journal of Hellenic
Studies* 72 (1952) 145-56). Cf. S. Mazzarino, *Historia* 6 (1957) 117, n. 2.

1.   O. J. Brendel, *Etruscan Art* (Pelican History of Art. Harmondsworth
    1978) hereafter cited as Brendel. M. Cristofani, *L'arte degli etruschi.
    Produzione e consumo*, hereafter cited as Cristofani (Turin 1978) 136.
2.   E. Peruzzi, *Origini di Roma* I (Florence 1970) 49-67. J. Le Gall, "Un
    critère de différenciation sociale: la situation de la femme," *Actes
    des Colloques, Caen 1969. Recherches sur structures sociales dans
    l'antiquité classique*, C. Nicolet, ed. (Paris 1970) 275-286. I. Kajanto,
    "Women's Praenomina Reconsidered," *Arctos* (Acta Phil. Fennica) n.s.
    7 (1972) 13-20. Kajanto's view is that women's *praenomina* disappeared
    in Rome; Giuliano Bonfante is preparing a study arguing that they
    never existed.
3.   For a recent survey on that status of women in various societies, see
    Rayna Rapp, "Gender and Class: An Archaeology of Knowledge Con-
    cerning the Origin of the State," *Dialectical Anthropology* 2 (1977)

309-315. For Greek and Roman women see Sarah Pomeroy, *Goddesses, Whores, Wives and Slaves: Women in Classical Antiquity* (New York 1975).

For the importance of ancient social contexts and attitudes for an understanding of the position of women in antiquity, see S. G. Pembroke, "The Last of the Matriarchs: A Study in the Inscriptions of Lycia," *Journal of the Economic and Social History of the Orient*," VIII (1965) 217-247; "Women in Charge: The Function of Alternatives in Early Greek Tradition and the Ancient Idea of Matriarchy," *Journal of the Warburg and Courtauld Institute* 30 (1967) 1-35 (on the traditions of Locri Epizephyri and Tarentum); *Annales, Economies* (1970) 1240-1270.

4. S. Boucher, "Une aire de culture italo-celtique aux VII-VI siècles av. J. Ch.," *Mélanges de l'Ecole de Rome* 81 (1969) 97ff.; *Gallia* 28 (1970) 190ff. Cristofani 127-129. See also Celtic figure types derived from Etruscan art, two figures embracing, "couples d'amoureux," and "the kiss": F. Benoit, *L'Art primitif méditerranéen* (Paris 1955) pl. 3; H. J. Eggers, E. Will, R. Joffroy, W. Holmqvist, *Les Celtes et les Germains à l'époque païenne* (Paris 1964) 210-211.

5. Cf. G. Colonna, *Civiltà del Lazio Primitivo* (Rome 1976) 28. On Greek Geometric scenes of heroization, see A. M. Snodgrass, "Towards the Interpretation of the Figure-Scenes on Geometric Vases," *Acta of the XI International Congress of Classical Archaeology, London, 1978. Greece and Italy in the Classical World* (London 1979) 188. On Roman ancestors, see N. D. Fustel de Coulanges, *The Ancient City* (Baltimore 1979); trans. of *La cité antique* (Paris 1864) with an introduction by A. Momigliano and S. C. Humphreys; F. Brown, "Of Huts and Houses," *In Memoriam Otto J. Brendel. Essays in Archaeology and the Humanities*, L. Bonfante, H. von Heintze, edd. (Mainz 1976) 5-12.

For Etruscan images of heroized ancestors, see G. Colonna, *Supplemento Annali Istituto Italiano di Numismatica* 22 (Naples 1975) 13; A. J. Pfiffig, *Religio Etrusca* (Graz 1975) 178-179, 187, and 372; F. Prayon, *Frühetruskische Grab- und Hausarchitektur* (Heidelberg 1975), and bibliography in L. Bonfante, *Dialoghi di Archeologia* n. s. 2 (1979) 73-94.

6. F. Prayon (above), 112ff., pls. 60-61; S. Steingräber, *Etruskische Möbel* (Rome 1979; hereafter Steingräber) No. 682, pl. 38, with full bibliography.

7. Brendel 230-232, 462; Cristofani 99-100. In the northern cities, e.g. Chiusi, women did not attend banquets: S. De Marinis, *La tipologia del banchetto nell'arte etrusca arcaica* (Rome 1961) 58ff.; Steingräber 181, Nos. 136-37, 143-45. The terracotta frieze from Murlo (Steingräber No. 131) probably shows two men.

8. M. Pallottino, *Etruscan Painting* (New York 1952) *passim*. Brendel 186-93; 189.

9. Livy 1.57.9; Dionysius of Halicarnassus 4.64. R. M. Ogilvie, *A Commentary to Livy. Books 1-5* (Oxford 1965) 222.

10. M. Pallottino, *Etruscan Painting* (New York 1952) 82. Brendel 264,

466, Figure 177; Streingräber No. 67; Pfiffig, *Religio Etrusca* 372, Figure 142. On the *cippi* as representing the deceased, J.-R. Jannot, "Une représentation symbolique des défunts. A propos de la tombe tarquinienne du lit funèbre," *Mélanges de l'Ecole Française de Rome* 89 (1977) 57988.

11. On the seventh-century oinochoe from Tragliatella (near Caere): G. Q. Giglioli, *StEtr* 3 (1929) 111ff. A. Alföldi, *Early Rome and the Latins* (Ann Arbor 1965) 280-83, pls. 19-21. Or the archaic tomba del Barone of Tarquinia: R. Bianchi Bandinelli, M. Torelli, *L'arte dell'antichità classica* II: *Etruria* (Turin 1976) No. 96: "una coppia maritale con i due figli: l'uomo riceve l'omaggio dei familiari."

12. The *klinai* were placed on the left side of the chamber, the "sarcophagus beds" on the right. R. Mengarelli, *StEtr* 1 (1927) 164ff.; 11 (1937) 85, etc.; Heurgon, *La vie quotidienne* 117-122; Prayon (*op. cit.*, note 5) 41: Steingräber 147. For a model with breasts, see Steingräber No. 490, and *Nuove scoperte e acquisizioni nell'Etruria meridionale* (Rome 1975) 5-7, No. 1.

13. R. Mengarelli, *Notizie Scavi* 1915, 347-386. Columnar *cippi* are inscribed *clan*, "son"; house-shaped ones, *sech*, "daughter." A few date from the fifth century B.C., most of them from the fourth century B.C. to the beginning of the Empire.

14. Museum of Fine Arts, Boston. Brendel 348, Figure 271. J. D. Beazley, *Etruscan Vase Painting* (Oxford 1947) 166-67, pl. 24, Figures 1-2.

15. J. Pitt-Rivers, "Women and Sanctuary in the Mediterranean," in *Echanges et Comunications. Mélanges Lévi-Strauss* (The Hague-Paris 1970) II, 862-875; quoted by C. Grottanelli, "Notes on Mediterranean Hospitality," *Dialoghi di Archeologia* 9-10 (1976-77) 186-194, esp. 187.

16. F. Matz, "Chronologische Bemerkungen zu einigen Deckelfiguren etruskischer Sarkophage," *Marburger Winckelmann-Programm 1973* (1974) 13-36, pls. 2-3, with bibl. M. Sprenger, G. Bartoloni, *Die Etrusker: Kunst und Geschichte*, hereafter cited as Sprenger-Bartoloni (Munich 1977), pls. 208-209. Brendel 389-390, Figures 299-300: the lids are transformed into marital beds, the *lectus genialis* (Brendel 389, 466), as in the Tomba del Letto Funebre (*supra*, note 10). L. Bonfante, *Etruscan Dress* (Baltimore 1975) Figures 84-85.

17. Varro, in Non. 867 L (14.541 M), quoted in E. Richardson, *The Etruscans* (Chicago 1964) 144. Cf. Heurgon, *La vie quotidienne*, 100ff. Aristotle (in Athenaeus 1.23d) referred to the Etruscan custom of men and women reclining together, under the same blanket; and Arnobius (*Adv. Nat.* 2.67) said the husband threw his toga over the marriage couch.

18. Chiusi, Museo Civico. M. Pallottino, *The Etruscans* (Harmondsworth 1978) 291, Figure 89; G. Q. Giglioli, *L'arte etrusca* (Milan 1935) pl. 109.2. Cf. L. Bonfante, *Etruscan Dress*, Figures 124, 127, with bibliography.

10. *Supra*, note 16. R. Herbig, *Die jüngeretruskischen Steinsarkophage* (Berlin 1952) 13-14, No. 5, pl. 40; G. M. A. Hanfmann, *Journal of*

Hellenic Studies 65 (1945) 47, pl. 8; Richardson, *The Etruscans*, 143-146, pls. 43-44. For the *dextrarum iunctio* see R. Brilliant, *Gesture and Rank in Roman Art* (New Haven, Conn. 1963) 18-21; couples, 31-35. A.M. McCann, *Catalogue of Roman Sarcophagi, Metropolitan Museum of Art* (New York 1979) 124-129. D..E.E. Kleiner, "A Portrait Relief of D. Apuleius Carpus and Apuleia Rufina in the Villa Wolkonsky," *Archeologia Classica* 30 (1978) in press.

20. For the symbolism of the carriage ride, see W. Weber, *Die Darstellungen einer Wagenfahrt auf römischen Sarkophagdeckeln und Loculusplatten des 3. and 4. Jahrhunderts n. Chr.* (Rome 1978).

21. Herbig, *Steinsarkophage* (*supra*, note 19) No. 6. Cf. *supra*, note 16.

22. Brendel 321, Figure 243: ... "reviving the ancient fantasy of the feasting dead." M. Cristofani, *Statue-cinerario chiusine di età classica* (Rome 1975), for the series.

23. Brendel 321-23, Figure 244.

24. M. Torelli, *Elogia Tarquiniensia* (Florence 1975) 54-55. Brendel 337-38, Figures 261-62; Sprenger-Bartoloni pls. 217, 223-224. Hades and Persephone rule jointly, as a couple, over this underworld.

25. Brendel 341, Figure 265; Sprenger-Bartoloni, pls. 218-222.

26. Brendel 412; Sprenger-Bartoloni, text to pls. 226-27. L. Bonfante, "Historical Art, Etruscan and Early Roman," *American Journal of Ancient History* 3 (1978) 136-162, esp. 138.

27. The excavator, Kyle M. Phillips, and Erik Nielsen, have identified the figures as two sets of triads: see T.N. Gantz, *StEtr* 39 (1971) 5-24; *Römische Mitteilungen* 81 (1974) 1-14, with bibl. Their interpretation has not been widely accepted: see Pfiffig, *Religio Etrusca* 36; G. Dumézil, *Archaic Roman Religion* (Chicago 1970) 685, n. 139; M. Cristofani, *Prospettiva* 1 (1975) 9-17, and *L'arte degli etruschi* 131-138; L. Bonfante, *Etruscan Dress* 118, n. 16, 179, Figure 72; and *Dialoghi di Archeologia*, n.s. 2 (1979) 81.

28. Dumézil (*op. cit.*, note 27) 685. Cristofani 146, n. 42.

29. Cristofani, *Prospettiva* 1 (1975) 9-17; *L'arte degli etruschi* 131-138. De Marinis, *La tipologia del banchetto* 58ff.; Steingräber, *Etruskische Möbel* 131, 143-145.

30. I. Edlund Gantz, *Dialoghi di Archeologia* 6 (1972) 167-235; R. Bianchi Bandinelli, *Dialoghi di Archeologia* 6 (1972) 236-247; L. Bonfante, *Etruscan Dress* Figure 121, and *Dialoghi di Archeologia* n.s. 2 (1979) 79-81.

31. Brendel 201-202.

32. L. Bonfante, *Etruscan Dress* Figure 87. G. Bordenache Battaglia, *Corpus delle ciste prenestine* I (Rome 1979) pl.x. Cf. Brendel 335, Figure 259.

33. Deborah Halsted will soon publish her theory, confirmed, in my opinion, by the prominence of the belt as symbol of love and marriage: Liddell and Scott, s.v. *zone*; *Iliad* 14, 187-228. See also A. Lesky, *Vom Eros der Hellenen* (1976) 18-19; F. Huemer, *Art Bulletin* 61 (1979) 573. For the "Boccanera" terracotta plaques, S. Haynes, *Römische Mitteilungen* 83 (1976) 227-231. Cf. F. Roncalli, *Le lastre*

dipinte di Cerveteri (Florence 1966) 28-33, 69-77; Bonfante, *Etruscan Dress* Figures 74-75.

34. J. Bayet, *Herclé* (Paris 1926) 79-120; Dumézil 680.
35. Livy 5.13.6. Dumézil 439, 567. The *lectisternium* itself was introduced into Rome from Etruria, probably from Caere. J. Gagé, *Apollon romain* (Paris 1955) 168-179. Cf. L. Ross Taylor, "The *Sellisternium* and the Theatrical *Pompa*," *Classical Philology* 30 (1935) 122-130. After the first *lectisternium*, at which the gods and goddesses shared their couches (did the goddesses recline, or sit at the foot of the bed?), there was a *sellisternium* reserved for goddesses, with chairs for them to sit on while male gods reclined alone.
36. Tomba Golini, Orvieto. Drawing by G. Gatti. Cristofani 171, Figure 152; in the same tomb were represented four couples on *klinai*. The games celebrated in honor of the *Di Inferi* were said to have been introduced by the last Tarquin: Servius, *ad Aen.* 2.140. Dumézil 571: "The Di Inferi must have been an Etruscan representation, like the rites themselves . . ." Until 249 B.C., when the *Ludi Tarentini* were first celebrated in honor of Dis and Prosperpina, "the Roman representation of the Other World had remained in a state of confusion, and the Di Manes had nothing to do with a king or a queen" (445). The form "Proserpina," from the Greek "Persephone," may be due to Etruscan pronunciation.
37. Plutarch, *Marcellus* 3.4: *Quaest. Rom.* 83; Livy 22.57.4. Dumézil 449-450, 479. Cf. L. Bonfante, *American Journal of Ancient History*, 3 (1978) 148. S. Mazzarino, *Pensiero Storico Classico* II (Bari 1966) 213-214.
38. Dumézil 625: L. Bonfante, *Etruscan Dress* 103.
39. Dumézil (576, 580) denies the centrality, once taken for granted, of famous Roman priestly couples (*flamen* and *flaminica*, Pontifex Maximus and Vestal Virgin, etc.). Plutarch, *Quaest, Rom.* 50: the *flaminica*'s duties are connected with those of her husband.
40. P. Bonfante, *Storia del diritto romano* (Milan 1923) 152-160. N.D. Fustel de Coulanges, *The Ancient City*. For Greek and Roman women, see S. Pomeroy, *op. cit.*, note 3.
41. Livy 1.34-41; 46-55. Ogilvie, *Commentary to Livy*, 140-144, 156-158, 184-199, with refs.
42. Dionysius of Helicarnassus gives a typically Greek view of the reason for Horatius' anger against his sister: "he was distressed that a young, marriageable girl should have left her household tasks at her mother's side and joined a crowd of strangers (3.21.2)." Livy's criticism of Tullia's behavior is also directed at her going out in public — as an Etruscan woman would, but a Roman should not —as much as at her driving the carriage over her father's body (1.46-48). Both historians express an Augustan ideal.
43. *Domum servavit, lanam fecit*. (Bücheler, *Carm. Cat. Epigr.* 52.8). M. Durry, *Eloge funèbre d'une matrone romaine* (Paris 1950). Ogilvie (*op. cit.*, note 9) 222. Bonfante Warren, *Arethusa* 6 (1973) 100, n. 20.
44. Livy 1.57.4-58. Ogilvie, *Commentary to Livy* 222.

45. A. Alföldi, *Der frührömische Reiteradel und seine Ehrenabzeichen* (second ed. 1979) Preface; F. Coarelli, *Roma Medio Repubblicana* (Rome 1973) No. 283. Torelli, *Elogia* 55-65. B.M. Felletti Maj. *La tradizione italica nell'arte romana* (Rome 1977) 145-152.

46. Bonfante, *Dialoghi di Archeologia* 2 (1979) 73-94.

47. A.C.L. Conze, *Die Attische Grabreliefs* (Berlin 1893-1922) Nos. 38, 40, 59, pls. 17, 19, 27. K. Friis Johansen, *Attic Grave-Reliefs* (Copenhagen 1951) 133. C. Clairmont, *Gravestone and Epigram* (Mainz 1970) 15, Nos. 22, 23, 51, etc., for mother and child in the classical period. Cf. Homer, *Odyssey* 2.96-102, 4.120-135; Aristophanes, *Lysistrata* 728-732, 572-586.

48. For the public, homosexual love of gymnasium and symposium illustrated on vase paintings (along with many other genre scenes and incidents from this part of life), see K.J. Dover, *Greek Homosexuality* (Cambridge 1978; New York 1980). The exception proving the rule is a representation of married love on a black-figure pelike by the Acheloos Painter, in the British Museum: a satyr carrying off a maenad is contrasted with a husband and wife at home, kissing sedately: J. Boardman, *Athenian Black Figure Vases* (New York 1974) 111, Figure 211. For the difference between references to lovemaking to a wife or a prostitute, see A.H. Sommerstein, "BINEIN," *Liverpool Classical Monthly* 5 (1980) 47. For the *termon* marking the site of the gymnasium, the place of the *eros* of young men, in contrast to the home, the place of women, see J.-M. Moret, "Un ancêtre du phylactère: le pilier inscrit des vases italiotes," *Revue Archéologique* (1979) 3-34.

49. Marble funerary lekythos: G.M.A. Richter, *Catalogue of Greek Sculptures in the Metropolitan Museum of Art* (Cambridge, Mass. 1954) 60-61, No. 89, pl. 73. Probably represents the father clasping his dead daughter's hand: the seated woman would be her mother, the child her little sister.

50. Clairmont, *Gravestone and Epigram* 61. On Clairmont No. 20, "which a loving husband has erected for his wife, the feelings of both are tenderly expressed in the epigram, but only the wife is represented." H. Diepolder, *Die attischen Grabreliefs des 5. and 4. v. Chr.* (Berlin 1931) pls. 22, 34, 54; cf. M. Robertson, *A History of Greek Art* (Cambridge 1975) 110-112; 563-582.

51. I have not seen F. Bourriot, *Recherches sur la nature du Genos: étude d'histoire sociale athénienne, périodes archaïque et classique* (Thèse, 1974; publ. Paris 1976).

   On social changes in Athens after 400 B.C. see J.K. Davies, *Democracy and Classical Greece* (Fontana History of the Ancient World 1978) 170-173.

52. Egypt, H.W. Müller, "Ancient Egypt," in *Encyclopedia of World Art* 4 (1958) pls. 342, 344. Asia Minor: W. Childs, *The City Reliefs of Lycia* (Princeton 1978) 7-9. Harpy Monument from Xanthos (ca. 480 B.C.): E. Berger, *Das Basler Arztrelief* (Basel 1970) 129-142, 187-189, with bibl.

53. M.M. Austin, P. Vidal-Naquet, *Economic and Social History of Ancient*

Greece: An Introduction (London 1977) 76, 80-81. On the use of the epithets "archaic" and "modern" reflecting the judgment of the Greeks of the classical period, notably Thucydides, see Austin p. 78. C. Mossé, "Sparte archaïque," *Parola del Passato* 28 (1973) 7-20.

54. In Berlin. H. Dressel, A. Milchhoefer, *Athenische Mitteilungen* 2 (1877) 303-307, pls. 2021; Robertson, *A History of Greek Art* (note 50) 114. J. Charbonneaux, R. Martin, F. Villard, *Grèce Archaïque* (Paris 1968) 148, pl. 183; J. Boardman, *Greek Sculpture. Archaic Period* (New York, Toronto 1978) 165, Figure 253. Two couples are depicted: the enthroned, heroized pair, and the approaching worshippers, a man and a woman. H. Stibbe is presently at work on a study of heroization in Sparta.

55. Friis Johansen, *Attic Grave-Reliefs* 86.

56. Torelli, *Elogia* 46-56, esp. 54.

57. In the late fifth and fourth centuries special Etruscan costumes serve as signs of status or rank (Bonfante, *Etruscan Dress* 39).

58. Biodorus Siculus, *Bibl.* 8.1S (C.H. Oldfather, *Diodorus of Sicily*, Loeb Classical Library 1939, vol. 3). Cf. Herodotus 6.126-127. Athenaeus, *Deipnosophistae* 12.519C. F. Jacoby, *Fr. Gr. Hist.* III (1955) 550, 650; the source is Timaeus.

All the sources emphasize the wealth of Mindyrides, who surpassed even the other Sybarites in *truphē*.

59. For Etruscan *truphē* see Athenaeus, *Deipnosophistae* 517D (XII.14); Posidonius, in Diodorus Siculus, *Bibl.* 5.40. J. Heurgon, "Posidonius et les Etrusques," *Hommages A. Grenier* II (1962) 799-808; *La vie quotidienne* 214. Bonfante Warren, *Arethusa* 6 (1973) 94, 100 n. 19, 101, n. 34.

60. A. Passerini, "La *truphe* nella storiografia ellenistica," *Studi Italiani di Filologia Classica* (1934) 35-56; J. Sekora, *Luxury* (Baltimore and London 1977). I thank Professor A.O. Hirschman for this latter reference, and for an interesting discussion of this topic.

61. W.V. Harris, *Rome in Etruria and Umbria* (Oxford 1971) 14-23, with refs.; Cristofani 39, etc.

62. Plato, *Republic* 372E. J. Adams' note on this passage (second edition, Cambridge 1965, p. 101) lists scholars who wanted to eliminate *hetairai*: but the presence of party girls was a standard feature of banquets in Athens. I thank my husband, Leo Raditsa, for the references to Plato and Montesquieu.

63. Thucydides 1.6.8; Pausanias 1.44.1. Cf. L. Bonfante, *Etruscan Dress* 20-21, 116-117.

64. P. Vidal-Naquet, "Esclavage et gynécocratie dans la tradition, le mythe, l'utopie," *Actes des Colloques. Caen 1969 (supra* note 5) 63-80. "[Dans] l'Athènes classique l'opposition entre le citoyen et l'esclave est nette, radicale, totale."

65. On Etruscan slaves, see J. Heurgon, *The Rise of Rome* (Berkeley, Los Angeles 1973) 48: "the country serfs, to the great astonishment of Roman jurists, enjoyed the right of property." Cf. Heurgon, *La vie quotidienne* 82; T. Frankfort, "Les classes serviles en Etrurie," *Latomus*

18 (1959) 3-22.
66. Livy 1.57. Heurgon, *La vie quotidienne* 102; Bonfante Warren,*Arethusa* 6 (1973) 100, n. 21.
67. Isaeus 3.14. P. Roussel, *Isée, Discours* (Belles Lettres, Paris 1960) 55. R.F. Wevers, *Isaeus, Chronology, Prosopography, and Social History* (The Hague 1969) 117, 103-105.
68. Montesquieu, *De l'esprit des lois* (Paris 1973, ed. R. Derathe) VIII.2.
69. *Ibid.* VII, "Conséquences des différents principes des trois gouvernements, par rapport aux lois somptuaires, au luxe et la condition des femmes," Chapter 9. For Rome, see Chapter 10.
70. C. Klapisch-Zuber, in *Annales. Economies, Sociétés, Civilisations* 34 (1979) 1216-1243. M. Meiss, *Painting in Florence and Siena After the Black Death* (1951; Harper Torchbook 1964) 60-61, 109-117. The importance of the family in non-aristocratic circles is also reflected in the funerary portrait reliefs commissioned by freedmen, who as slaves had not been permitted to marry: D.E.E. Kleiner, *Roman Group Portraiture. The Funerary Reliefs of the Late Republic and Early Empire* (New York and London 1977). On reclining couples in Roman art, and Etruscan influence: M. Collignon, *Les Statues funéraires dans l'art grec* (Paris 1911) 354-360.
71. Chester Starr, *The Economic and Social Growth of Early Greece, 800-500 B.C.* (New York, 1977) especially 139-145; and "The cult of masculinity" (130-132).

Sources for Illustrations

Figure 1. *DAI* 61.978; Figures 2 & 10. Alinari; Figures 3-5. Courtesy, Museum of Fine Arts, Boston; Figure 6. Sopr. Ant. Etr., Florence; Figures 7-8. Drawings courtesy Kyle M. Phillips, Erik Nielsen; Figure 9. G. Marchi, *La cista atletica del Mus. Kircheriano* (Rome 1848) pl. 2 (courtesy G. Battaglia); Figure 11. Metropolitan Museum of Art, Rogers Fund 1912; Figure 12. *Röm. Mitt.* 1877, pl. 20.

FIGURE 1.   Reclining couple, "Bride and Groom." Terracotta sarcophagus from Cerveteri. Rome, Villa Giulia Museum. Ca. 525 B.C.

FIGURE 2.   Banquet scene. Wall painting, tomb of the Leopards, Tarquinia. Ca. 480 B.C.

FIGURE 3.   Admetus and Alcestis. Red-figure Etruscan cup. Boston, Museum of Fine Arts, Fourth century B.C.

FIGURE 4.   Couple resting under a toga. Stone sarcophagus from Vulci.
Boston, Museum of Fine Arts. Fourth century B.C.

FIGURE 5.   Couple with attendants. Frieze on stone sarcophagus from Vulci. Boston, Museum of Fine Arts. Fourth century B.C.

FIGURE 6.   Banqueter and wife. Alabaster cinerary urn from Città della Pieve. Florence, Museo Archeologico. Late fifth century B.C.

FIGURE 7.　Seated couple with attendants and other figures. Terracotta relief frieze from Murlo (Poggio Civitate). Siena, Palazzo Comunale. Ca. 575 B.C.

FIGURE 8.　Carriage procession. Terracotta relief frieze from Murlo (Poggio Civitate). Siena, Palazzo Comunale. Ca. 575 B.C.

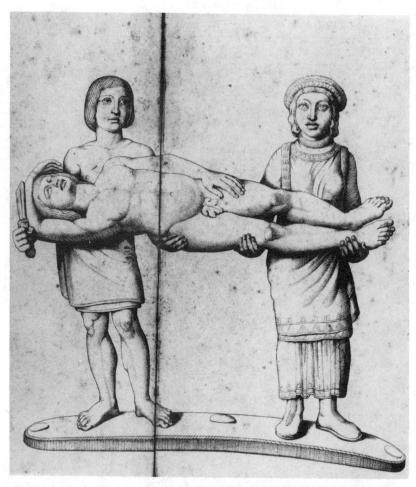

FIGURE 9.   Man and woman carrying a dead man. Bronze handle of a
Praenestine cista. Private collection. Fourth century B.C.

FIGURE 10.   Hades and Persephone. Wall painting from Tomba Golini,
Orvieto. Fourth century B.C.

FIGURE 11.   Family farewell to deceased girl. Gravestone in form of
a stone lekythos from Athens. New York, Metropolitan Museum of Art.
Fourth century B.C.

FIGURE 12.   Heroized couple enthroned. Stone relief from Chrysapha
(Sparta). Berlin, Staatl. Museum. Ca. 550 B.C.

Two matrons of the late republic

TERESA CARP

University of Oregon

IN A PROVOCATIVE ESSAY of some years ago, M.I. Finley spoke with conviction and disapproval of "the silence of the women of Rome."[1] In his view upper class Roman women, with a few scandalous exceptions, led passive, repressed lives in the shadow of their fathers, husbands, and sons to a degree unparalleled in subsequent periods of high culture in the West. This somber picture of the social reality of the life of women under the late Republic and early Empire has been questioned, more recently, by Sarah Pomeroy, who asserts rather: "The momentum of social change in the Hellenistic world combined with Roman elements to produce the emancipated, but respected, upper class woman."[2] She argues that Roman matrons had a range of choices in their roles and lifestyles as well as a demonstrable influence on the cultural and political life of their times.[3] While this view seems rather optimistic, a careful study of the lives of several aristocratic women, as revealed in Cicero's correspondence, suggests that it may be closer to an objective picture.

Two examples are Servilia and Caerellia. The former, mother of Brutus the Liberator and mistress of Julius Caesar, appears in the correspondence in a decidedly political role. Cicero seems, at any rate, to take her political influence for granted when he twice mentions her efforts to have the *curatio frumenti*, grain commission, removed from a Senate decree.[4] Caerellia was a *necessaria*, or intimate friend, of the orator. She seems to have lived quite independently — she had wealth of her own, including property in

Asia;[5] she engaged in large-scale financial transactions;[6] and she had intellectual pursuits as well.[7]

Women such as these acted in some instances with a surprising degree of independence of thought and action without at the same time going beyond the bounds of what was then defined as "respectable" behavior. Hence their lives belie the notion cherished by Roman moralists, and not a few classical scholars, that Roman matrons of the late Republic were either "bad women" as exemplified by Clodia, Sempronia, and Aurelia Orestilla,[8] or paragons of virtue as idealized in Latin literature, particularly in funeral encomia — the kind of women who, it was enthusiastically asserted, lived for no other purpose than to bear viable, legitimate offspring and to dwell with the same husband for decades *sine ulla querela*, without a single disagreement.[9]

Two prominent examples of the more independent type of matron are the wife and daughter of Cicero. The aim of the present discussion is to examine their biographies in greater detail in an effort to delineate the type of activities such women could and did engage in and the degree of independence attainable under the social circumstances of the late Republic.

Some cautionary remarks are in order concerning the sources on which this discussion is based, for we are dealing with at least two layers of bias. First, there is the generalized cultural bias resulting from the fact that we see Terentia and Tullia through the eyes of men only, Cicero and Plutarch chiefly. The interpretive problems created, however, are common to all examinations of the status of women in Roman antiquity since with few notable exceptions, such as the love elegies of Sulpicia, an indifferent poetess of the late Republic, little written evidence comes to us from the hands of women.

The more specific bias is the attitudes of the two main literary sources. Cicero in his correspondence from the period leading up to and including his divorce had a vested interest in vilifying Terentia so as to elicit pity and sympathy from his friends.[10] Plutarch, probably following the biography written by Tiro, shared this bias.[11] However, the hostile depiction of Terentia in these sources is more than adequately balanced by the earlier correspondence in which Cicero portrayed his family candidly and without rancor.

A more immediate problem is that of the degree to which the independence shown by Terentia and Tullia was peculiarly a function of Cicero's personality. Even a cursory reading of the correspondence reveals him to have been a man who, by the standards of his day and class, was somewhat irresolute. His indecisiveness in both political and personal affairs is manifest. Hence his failure to live up to the stern, authoritarian Roman male stereotype must be taken into account in examining the lives of his wife and daughter.

Yet it is also necessary to ask to what extent traditional notions of male authority and control were current in this age. In this period all members of a Roman family were in the *potestas*, power, of the oldest living male ascendant, the *paterfamilias*, who could, both in theory and practice, control almost every practical aspect of their lives. In addition to the well known *ius vitae et necis*, power of life and death over family members, he had control of marriage and divorce (all marriages required his consent; those already married could be forced to divorce); property (those *in potestate* could own no property, borrow or lend money, or make gifts); and partial legal jurisdiction (the *paterfamilias* with the aid of a "family court" could try family members on charges related to family reputation and could assess penalties up to and including death). This power was absolute and terminated only with the death of the holder or an act of emancipation on his part, voluntarily undertaken.[12] *Patria potestas* survived into the Christian era and was confirmed by the emperor Constantine.[13]

Once married, a woman would remain within her father's power unless he transferred it to his son-in-law. When this transfer did not take place, the marriage was termed a *conubium sine manu* and conferred a certain degree of freedom from the husband's control since the wife was under the control of her agnate male relatives. A woman became *sui iuris* (legally independent of the *paterfamilias*) if the *paterfamilias* died, leaving no other male ascendants. Nevertheless, she still had to have a *tutor*, legal guardian, the rest of her life; and *tutores* were, of course, male.[14]

The theory and practice of male control over women was

maintained not just out of a sentimental attachment to the *mos maiorum*, the way of the ancestors, but out of the social and economic interests of the state. The family was the basic unit of social organization and recognized as such, as was bound to be the case in a traditional society lacking the pervasive differentiation of social functions which characterizes so-called modern societies. There were, after all, no public agencies or institutions on any universal scale to see people through the practical realities of living. All ultimately devolved upon the family through its male head; and when Roman society grew in size and complexity, upon the system of patronage which was an extension of the same institution. In the supervision and regulation of a woman's life fundamental practical issues were at stake — the continuation of the family life and of domestic religion through the production of viable and legitimate offspring; and the maintenance of the family's financial resources through the regulation of property rights as a function of inheritance and dowering. Both the individual aristocrat and the state as a whole had a vital interest in maintaining a woman in her role as a *matrona* first and foremost. Even in moral and philosophical treatments the concern for marriage and the family was motivated primarily by this realization. These institutions were "the right thing" since they promoted social stability and cohesion. Companionship and sexual compatibility were desirable but hardly necessary.

Certain social and economic developments of the late Republic served to undermine these theoretical and philosophical traditions. The widowing of many upper class matrons during the Punic Wars and wars of conquest, for example, resulted in large amounts of capital devolving upon women. The diminishing size of aristocratic families may also have in some degree contributed to the accumulation of wealth in women's hands in spite of the *lex Voconia* of 169 B.C., which had limited the amount of property that women could inherit. Furthermore, men of public affairs were required by their military and political activities to spend long periods abroad, becoming in effect absentee *patresfamiliarum*. Aristocratic women also had more leisure time as a result of the rising standards of material culture and the abundance of slaves to perform the day-to-day tasks of domestic management. As a result of these and other factors, some women were in a position to make major decisions on their own initiative, as we shall see in the case of Cicero's family, for Cicero was certainly not the only Roman aristocrat who failed for whatever reasons to exercise tight control over the members of his immediate family.

Since, as we have noted, marriage was a matter of practical considerations, and in the upper classes, of political expediency, it comes as no surprise that Cicero most likely married in 79 B.C. for reasons other than romantic love. Terentia's family background and wealth would have been a definite advantage to this *novus homo*, or parvenu. She was related to the patrician Fabii and came to the marriage with considerable wealth of her own. Nevertheless, the marriage was not lacking in mutual respect and affection for over three decades. Cicero's letters until 48 B.C. are filled with expressions of love and gratitude. In them he calls her *mea vita*, my life, and *mea desideria*, my darling, and other terms of endearment. Terentia certainly kept to her end of the bargain, discharging her domestic duties competently and cheerfully, providing moral support, and enduring danger and humiliation on her husband's behalf. One incident reflecting her commitment to him occurred when she was compelled under duress in 58 B.C. to make a public declaration concerning Cicero's proscribed properties after the loss of their Palatine mansion to fire. Clodius, Cicero's arch-enemy, had apparently used this occasion to humilate Cicero *in absentia*. [15] For his part, Cicero never ceased to commend Terentia for her courage and resolve in the letters written from exile.

Yet there are also many indications that Terentia was loath to take a totally passive, unquestioning role; in fact, the marriage at times seemed to approach a notion of partnership. In three particular areas Terentia exercised considerable discretion — finance, politics, and match-making.

As regards the first, we have already noted that she came to the marriage with ample resources of her own. Plutarch seems to have underestimated her financial worth by a good deal.[16] The correspondence variously reveals that she owned in Rome two blocks of *insulae*, high-density apartment houses, which yielded a hefty annual income.[17] She also owned forest land near Tusculum,[18] and a farm which must have been of considerable value inasmuch as she considered putting it up for sale in 58 B.C. to alleviate the financial distress caused by Cicero's exile and the proscription of his property.[19] Furthermore, on at least one occasion, she had converted for her own use and gain, without paying the rents due, a portion of *ager publicus*, public land.[20] Terentia in all her financial dealings appears to have been free from Cicero's control, proceeding quite independently in the management of her properties with the able assistance of her freedman, Philotimus.[21] Some of her property did, however, eventually come into Cicero's hands as part of the divorce settlement.[22]

Just as she seems to have guarded her financial independence from Cicero, except for the offer to sell her farm in 58, so he in turn tried to keep his own financial dealings confidential from her. He continuously implored Atticus, his confidant and banker, to do so. Eventually Cicero ended up viewing his wife with outright distrust in matters of finance and even suspected her of theft. One letter, for example, alludes to the disappearance of income from some of his real property with the suggestion that Terentia is involved; he also hints that she may have diverted for her own use a portion of the first installment of the dowry for their daughter's third marriage.[23] Elsewhere we read that Terentia has allegedly cheated Cicero out of a small sum of money and that he suspects her of systematic embezzlement.[24] (Plutarch repeats the charges of financial irresponsibility on her part.[25])

After the divorce in 47 or 46 B.C., Terentia assigned her dowry, which Cicero was obliged to repay as initiator of the proceedings, to Balbus in repayment of a loan.[26] As a leading Caesarian, Balbus could have brought pressure to bear upon Cicero for prompt settlement, a situation which would have been onerous to Cicero, who was always capital rich and cash poor as a result of his personal extravagances. In addition, the situation must have caused not a little personal and political embarrassment. There were also other financial dealings of an obscure nature occasioned by provisions in her will.[27] Terentia even seems to have employed financial considerations to some degree in her dealings with her son Marcus. It would seem that she had at one point dangled the prospect of an allowance or inheritance before him as a means of gaining his loyalty and of inflating her settlement from Cicero.[28]

All these various activities reveal Terentia to have been a person of financial acumen as well as accomplishment. No doubt her wealth made her attractive to the subsequent spouse (or spouses) that tradition accords her.[29] She was clearly a Roman matron who did more than tend to her family and work in wool.

She also appears to have been involved in politics to some extent, in spite of Cicero's assertion at one point that her proper sphere of activity was religion, while his was the affairs of men:

> . . . neque di quos tu castissime coluisti neque homines
> quibus ego semper servivi nobis gratiam rettulerunt.

> . . . neither the gods whom you have worshipped so purely
> nor men whom I have always served have shown us gratitude.[30]

Plutarch preserves two accounts of her political involvement. The first was said to have occurred during the Catilinarian crisis of 63 B.C. when Cicero was undecided as to the course of action to take concerning punishment of the convicted conspirators. It so happened that the Vestals had been performing the annual sacrifice to the Bona Dea in his house by virtue of his position as consul for the year. A bright flame suddenly burst forth from the ashes on the altar. The Vestals promptly took this as a sign that Cicero should do what he had resolved for the good of the country. Terentia then related this and its interpretation to Cicero, using it to incite him against the conspirators. Plutarch here interjects a comment on Terentia's involvement in these terms:

> καὶ γὰρ οὐδ᾽ ἄλλως ἦν πραεῖά τις οὐδ᾽ ἄτολμος τὴν
> φύσιν, ἀλλὰ φιλότιμος γυνὴ καὶ μᾶλλον, ὡς αὐτὸς ὁ
> Κικέρων, τῶν πολιτικῶν μεταλαμβάνουσα παρ᾽ ἐκείνου
> φροντίδων ἢ μεταδιδοῦσα τῶν οἰκιακῶν ἐκείνῳ.

> . . . for she was otherwise by nature neither at all
> meek nor timorous but an ambitious woman and, as
> Cicero himself says, taking a larger role in his
> political affairs than she shared with him in domestic
> matters.[31]

The other incident which Plutarch reports involved Terentia's allegedly having goaded Cicero into the prosecution of Clodius because of her jealousy over Clodia's romantic designs upon the orator.[32] Here Plutarch characterizes Terentia as χαλεπὴ δὲ τὸν τρόπον καὶ τοῦ Κικέρωνος ἄρχουσα, ill-tempered and domineering over Cicero.[33]

If these accounts are at all accurate and not merely the biographer's attempts to shift the blame for Cicero's downfall away from Cicero himself,[34] then Terentia contributed to her husband's political demise by goading him into taking extreme measures in the first instance — he had the conspirators executed without allowing them recourse to *provocatio ad populum*, appeal to the people — and, more significantly, by making Clodius his implacable foe. As tribune of the plebs in 58 Clodius introduced the legislation which would have led to Cicero's prosecution and certain conviction, had Cicero not anticipated him by fleeing into exile.

Finally, in the area of match-making Terentia exercised a good deal of independence in the matter of Tullia's third marriage. There had been two previous marriages without issue. Cicero had been scouting prospects for the third only to discover that his wife and daughter had preempted him, choosing a candidate not only younger than Tullia but also notorious for his political radicalism and private profligacy. Cicero himself on two previous occasions had barely saved Dolabella from prosecution on capital charges.[35]

It seems that neither women took into consideration the fact that Cicero might be politically compromised. Certainly, if Terentia had been actively involved in Cicero's public affairs, she could not have been unaware of the political ramifications of the match. Dolabella had impeached Appius Claudius, with whom Cicero had assiduously been trying to ingratiate himself:

> Ego, dum in provincia omnibus rebus Appium orno,
> subito sum factus accusatoris eius socer!
>
> While in my province I was showing honor to Appius
> in every respect, suddenly I became the father-in-law
> of his accuser![36]

The marriage occasioned a written *apologia* to Appius in which Cicero disclaimed responsibility for the match.[37]

Cicero's undoing had been his unbounded affection for his daughter. Indeed his relationship with his Tulliola, his little Tullia, was so close as to have led in antiquity to baseless charges of incest.[38] Moreover, the Church Father, Lactantius, was so appalled by Cicero's expressed wishes for her apotheosis as to remark,

> Fortasse dicat aliquis prae nimio luctu Ciceronem delirasse.
>
> Perhaps someone may say that Cicero was delirious through excessive grief.[39]

Tullia's physical and temperamental resemblance to her father may have accounted to a great extent for the closeness of their relationship, for Cicero clearly saw himself mirrored in her as when he called her *effigiem oris, sermonis, animi mei*, the image of my appearance, speech and mind.[40] Relying on this intimacy, Tullia appears to have acted with a certain disregard for the personal and political consequences to her father of the marriage alliance with Dolabella. She was not likely to have been unaware of them, as her mother surely would have understood them. Yet Tullia and Terentia assumed that Cicero would pay the dowry in spite of his misgivings; and subsequent events confirmed their expectations. Moreover, after the marriage was clearly faltering, Cicero blamed not his daughter but himself for the disaster, even though he had previously labeled her attitude one of *fatuitas*.[41]

After her death Cicero kept her memory alive through literary and philosophical activity, chiefly in the writing of the lost *Consolatio*. He had originally planned a *fanum*, or shrine, in her memory and had spoken often of his hopes for her apotheosis.[42] The shrine was never built despite an initial flurry of negotiations; one suspects that it had been intended more as a monument to Cicero than to his daughter.

Both Terentia and Tullia, in the final analysis, departed in some significant respects from the traditional ideal of the *matrona*. We have seen that they acted with determination and independence in certain key areas and willfully disregarded the wishes and opinions of Cicero. In this regard a remark addressed to them by Cicero from exile is enlightening. In a burst of pride and gratitude he had asserted,

> Cohortarer vos quo animo fortiores essetis nisi vos fortiores cognossem quam quemquam virum.
>
> I would urge you to be stouter of heart were it not that I have recognized you to be stronger than any man.[43]

That remark, perhaps intended to be no more than a figure of speech, was confirmed in some degree by their conduct.

On the other hand, they did not radically exceed the traditional expectations of women of their class and time. Their concerns were still primarily those of hearth and home. Their independence was asserted in those areas and threatened neither the overall function of their households nor the larger social order; their choices and activities remained largely circumscribed. In spite of her financial and political activities, Terentia played the role of *matrona* above all. Twenty years into the marriage, as we have seen, she had been willing to some extent to subordinate her own financial interests to those of her family. After the marriage was dissolved, she went on, according to tradition, to marry again, choosing to forego a course of complete independence that her financial position could have made possible.

Tullia, even more than her mother, fulfilled traditional expectations in her course of life. Her main role seems to have been to act as an extension of her father's ego and a tool of politics, as the need arose. For all his fondness for her, Cicero, no less than other Roman aristocrats, did not fail to exploit her political value. Once it became obvious that Dolabella as a protégé of Caesar could prove more than a little useful, Cicero came to regard his son-in-law as a valued friend, even rejecting for a time the idea of Tullia's divorcing him. After her death in 45 B.C. Cicero maintained amicable relations with Dolabella in spite of his having to some extent contributed to her demise.[44] No doubt Dolabella's personal charm as well as the protection he could afford Cicero in those perilous times understandably inclined Cicero to maintain their friendship. Cicero even considered dedicating a political treatise to Dolabella, but Atticus advised against this measure.[45] Tullia, then, served her father as all good Romen women were expected to. Had she been able to choose an alternative, it seems unlikely that she would have done so.

Both women, in spite of their relative freedom, were defined and defined themselves in terms of their connection with a male figure. If by their behavior they affected contemporary events, it was by virtue of this connection alone. Their primary interests and activities remained in the domestic arena, the traditional environment of the *matrona*. Still, for all that, they were hardly "silent women." They did indeed speak up for themselves and make choices on matters which were of immediate concern to them; and Cicero clearly listened.

Notes

1. M.I. Finley, "The Silent Women of Rome," in his *Aspects of Antiquity: Discoveries and Controversies*, 2nd ed. (New York 1977) 132, first published in *Horizon* 7 (1965) 57-64.
2. Sarah B. Pomeroy, *Goddesses, Whores, Wives, and Slaves: Women in Classical Antiquity* (New York 1975) 149. See, more recently, Elizabeth Lyding Will, "Women in Pompeii," *Archaeology* 33 (1979) 34-43.
3. Pomeroy, *op. cit.*, p. 189.
4. *Ad Att.* 15, 11, 2; 15, 12, 1.
5. *Ad Fam.* 13, 72, 1.
6. *Ad Att.* 15, 26, 4.
7. *Ad Att.* 13, 21, 5.
8. On Clodia, see Cicero, *Pro Caelio, passim*; on Sempronia and Aurelia Orestilla, see Sallust, *Catiline* 25 and 15, respectively.
9. For a typical specimen, see *CIL* 6.1527, 31670.
10. The standard edition of the correspondence is R.Y. Tyrrell and L.C. Purser, *The Correspondence of Cicero*, 6 vols. and index (Dublin 1885-1901). See also D.R. Shackleton Bailey, *Cicero's Letters to Atticus* 6 vols. and index (Cambridge 1965); and W.W. How and A.C. Clark, *Cicero, Select Letters*, 2 vols. (Oxford 1925-26, rep. 1959-1962).
11. On Plutarch's probable sources for his biography of Cicero, see R.H. Borrow, *Plutarch and His Times* (Bloomington, Indiana 1967) 154-155.
12. For a discussion of *patria potestas*, see John Crook, *Law and Life of Rome* (Ithaca, New York 1967) 107-113.

13. Gaius, 1.55; 2.86-87; *Inst. Iust.* 1.9; 2.9; *Dig.* 1.6; 49.17; *Cod.* 8.46; 6.61; 12.30.36.
14. On *tutela*, see Crook, *op. cit.*, note 12, 113-116.
15. *Ad Fam.* 14, 2, 2.
16. Plutarch, *Cic.* 8.3, estimated the dowry at HS 1,200,000.
17. *Ad Att.* 12, 32, 2; 15, 17, 1; 15, 20, 4 (where reference is made to *mercedes dotalium praediorum*, or "rents of the dower property"; 16, 1, 5 (where the annual yield from the *insulae* is given as HS 80,000).
18. *Ad Att.* 2, 4, 5.
19. *Ad Fam.* 14, 1, 5.
20. *Ad Att.* 2, 15, 4.
21. If, as we might expect, Terentia had a *tutor* to help administer her finances, his name never appears in the sources, as Crook notes, *op. cit.*, note 12, 115.
22. *Ad Att.* 12, 32, 2.
23. *Ad Att.* 11, 2, 2.
24. *Ad Att.* 11, 24, 2-3.
25. *Cic.* 41.
26. *Ad Att.* 12, 12, 1.
27. *Cic.* 41; *Ad Att.* 11.16, 5, 24.
28. *Ad Att.* 12, 19, 4.
29. St. Jerome, *Adv. Iovin.* 1.48. Terentia's reported marriage to Sallust is dismissed as fiction by modern scholarship.
30. *Ad Fam.* 14, 4, 1.
31. *Cic.* 20.
32. Plutarch's ascription of jealousy as a motive is hardly credible, given Cicero's attitude toward Clodia as depicted in the *Pro Caelio*.
33. *Cic.* 29.
34. In general, Plutarch's criticism of Terentia's conduct must be viewed with suspicion, given his generally uncritical attitude toward Cicero.
35. *Ad Fam.* 3, 10, 5.
36. *Ad Att.* 6, 6, 1.
37. *Ad Fam.* 3, 12, 3.
38. Dio Cassius, 36, 18, 6; Ps.-Sallust, *In Cic.* 2.
39. *Divin. Inst.* 1, 15.
40. *Ad Q. Fr.* 1, 3, 3.
41. *Ad Att.* 11, 25, 3.
42. *Ad Att.* 12, 12 1; 12, 36, 1; 12, 37, 4.
43. *Ad Fam.* 14, 7, 2.
44. *Ad Fam.* 11, 11, 1; *Ad Att.* 13, 9, 1.
45. *Ad Att.* 13, 10, 2.

On Creusa, Dido, and the quality of victory in Virgil's *Aeneid*

CHRISTINE G. PERKELL

Dartmouth College

A CONTINUING CHALLENGE for readers of the *Aeneid* is to assess the moral quality of Aeneas' victory. Viktor Pöschl, in his extremely important work on the *Aeneid*, established that the moral poles of the poem are *imperium* and *furor* or, as he terms them, "order" and "the demonic" (violence, madness).[1] In his view Jupiter, Aeneas, and Augustus represent the higher moral principle of order. The triumph of these figures over their enemies is, therefore, morally legitimate and unambiguously edifying.[2] Subsequent critics have refined this reading by noting that it is not only Aeneas' enemies who are characterized by *furor* but Aeneas himself.[3] How, then, is this fact to be interpreted? Is Aeneas, like Dido, Mezentius, or Turnus, morally compromised by his *furor* — or is he not? This is an essential question to pose because Aeneas embodies the Roman imperial achievement. Through his picture of Aeneas, Virgil characterizes Rome.

Critics like G. Karl Galinsky and W. S. Anderson imply that there is a hierarchy of *furor* in the poem: some violence is good, "creative," while other violence is bad or destructive.[4] The reader may consequently distinguish between Aeneas, the exemplar of good *furor*, and his enemies, exemplars of bad *furor*. Some readers, however, may feel that this distinction risks being arbitrary and subjective. Michael Putnam, also an important critic of Virgil, does not observe such a distinction since he notes that in the poem's final scene Aeneas becomes identified with or parallel to Juno,[5] whose *furor* is incontrovertibly negative. Thus Aeneas would yield, finally, to that very *furor* against which he had struggled throughout the course of the poem. Most recently, W. R. Johnson, fully acknowledging Aeneas' flawed virtue, yet feels that the *Aeneid* is morally ambiguous, that it permits no final judgment on Aeneas and the Rome which he exemplifies.[6] The reader, then, confronts a substantive dilemma when excellent critics differ so widely on the moral quality of Aeneas' ultimate victory.

Certainly it is difficult to make unambiguous moral judgments about the *Aeneid*'s major figures. The final scene, for example, is splendidly problematic. Are we to damn Aeneas for his *furor*? or to praise him for his *pietas*? or perhaps for his political acumen in prudently eliminating a future adversary?[7] Or should we rather question even the political advisability of Aeneas' slaying the beaten, suppliant Turnus within the full view of his future subjects? Many factors — personal, political, moral — must occur to us when we attempt to evaluate Aeneas' actions. Consequently it is not surprising that no consensus has been reached about where the moral emphasis of the *Aeneid* lies. Yet it is unsatisfying, at least in the opinion of this writer, to assume that Virgil has no final conviction, that the problem must forever elude solution. Virgil shows Aeneas making choices; surely he intends us to evaluate those choices, not only to lament their difficulty.

If study of the motif of *furor* has not led to a secure judgment about Aeneas, we must then seek other indices of his humanity and morality which may help us to formulate a judgment. The hypothesis of this writer is that study of Aeneas' behavior towards Creusa and Dido, although it constitutes only a small part of the total picture of Aeneas, will shed light on his spiritual qualities and moral choices.

Aeneas' relationships with Creusa and Dido are parallel in several ways, a fact which suggests that Virgil shaped them deliberately and consistently. For example, both of these relationships end in the woman's death. This death is, at least partially, attributable to Aeneas, although in each case Aeneas attributes it to some cause or person outside himself. Each of the women perceives herself as abandoned by Aeneas. Finally, there is in each case a connection between Aeneas' departure and his *pietas*. First I should like to establish that this pattern does exist, and then I shall attempt an interpretation of it.

In order to set Aeneas' actions with women in appropriate perspective the reader must first consider the traditional epic heroes with whom Aeneas is implicitly compared. Hector and Odysseus constitute, in epic poetry, the most positive models of male behavior towards women. Neither is traditionally defined by his military role; each in his relationship with his wife is seen to be completely human, to have human feelings and needs. This human dimension makes them sympathetic figures.

Hector's relations with women are strongly developed in *Iliad* 6.[8] He appears, in contrast to both Paris and Achilles, as the hero of responsibility, of the cultural values of humanity, family, and love. Women are necessarily associated with these values since they are the life of the city, all able-bodied men being outside the walls at war. Hector's visits to Hecuba and Helen are dictated by the military situation since he must instruct his mother to lead sacrifices to Athena and direct Paris to return to battle. Remarkable by contrast is his visit to Andromache, whom he wishes to see purely for sentiment — and even before his loved son. The scene between Hector and Andromache in *Iliad* 6 is one of the most profoundly touching in all of classical literature, for Hector's interactions with his wife and infant son evoke powerfully the reader's sympathy.[9] Personal love and social responsibility coincide in Hector in *Iliad* 6 as he defends his family and city.

Odysseus similarly experiences compelling love for Penelope, for whom he rejects the goddesses Circe and Calypso, as well as the promise of immortality.[10] When Odysseus chooses Penelope over Calypso he affirms his humanity and mortality. Penelope's recognition of Odysseus, suspensefully delayed by the poet, is climactic, a significant mark of his return to a human, civilized, just society. Odysseus values Penelope because she suits ($\vartheta \upsilon \mu a \rho \acute{e} a$ *Od.* 23.232) and completes him.[11] His search for identity and "wholeness" overall is marked by his acceptance of positive female values. As Taylor writes:

Odysseus' quest for identity is in fact inextricably bound up with the feminine. In seeking the wholeness of his being, he (Odysseus) passes through intimate experience with various embodiments of archetypal woman, each reflecting some aspect of what he as masculine hero lacks.[12]

In sum, both Hector and Odysseus have strong, positive relationships with their wives and this contributes largely to their being human, sympathetic figures.

When we consider Aeneas in this regard we note that he seems not to be bound decisively to any female by love. Rather he is absorbed and driven by the political-military goal of founding the Roman empire. Love for Creusa and Dido remains subordinate to this goal. The destined marriage with Lavinia is a political act and does not signify affection.[13] While in Hector and Odysseus there is a convergence of personal and political goals, in Aeneas the personal and political are experienced as mutually exclusive. This dichotomy, typically although not exclusively Roman, is perfectly exemplified, for example, in the story of Brutus' execution of his sons for treason against Rome (Livy Bk. 2.5; cf. *Aeneid* 6.820 ff.). Love, whether for wives or children, is opposed to patriotic goals. Thus a love relationship with a woman apparently has no essential place in Aeneas' life's mission.

Let us first examine Virgil's treatment of Creusa's story.[14] As far as is known, tradition offered Virgil two variants of this story, the older of which represented Creusa as accompanying Aeneas into exile. This is the tradition which the Roman epic poet Naevius, for example, followed. It is illustrated on vases which show Aeneas departing from Troy accompanied by Creusa and other women; or which show him and Creusa exchanging a glance over the head of Iulus.[15] The other tradition, perhaps created by Stesichorus, tells how Cybele and Aphrodite conspired to rescue Creusa from Troy (Pausanias 10.26.1). This latter tradition is followed by Virgil, with the notable addition that, as Richard Heinze, an important critic of Virgil, puts it,[16] Aeneas allows Creusa to fall into danger, first by isolating her from the male family members and then by forgetting her altogether. Consider the following verses which illustrate Aeneas' concerns:

una salus ambobus erit. mihi parvus Iulus
sit comes, et longe servet vestigia coniunx
(2.710–711)

Whatever waits for us (Aeneas and his father),
we shall both share one danger, one salvation.
Let young Iulus come with me, and let
my wife Creusa follow at a distance.

succedoque oneri; dextrae se parvus Iulus
implicuit sequiturque patrem non passibus aequis:
pone subit coniunx.
(2.723–725)

and then [I] take up Anchises; small Iulus
now clutches my right hand; his steps uneven,
he is following his father; and my wife
moves on behind.

nunc omnes terrent aurae, sonus excitat omnis
suspensum et pariter comitique onerique timentem.
(2.728–729)

I am terrified by all the breezes, now startled
by every sound, in fear for son and father.

Because he forgets to look back for Creusa, Aeneas is unaware of
her fate (cf. 6.463–464).

hic mihi nescio quod trepido male numen amicum
confusam eripuit mentem. namque avia cursu
dum sequor, et nota excedo regione viarum
heu! misero coniunx fatone erepta Creusa
substitit? erravitne via seu lassa resedit?
incertum.
(2.735–740)

some unfriendly
god's power ripped away my tangled mind.
For while I take a trackless path, deserting
the customary roads, fate tears from me
my wife Creusa in my misery.
I cannot say if she had halted or
had wandered off the road or slumped down, weary.

And perhaps more significant:

⸴nec prius amissam respexi animumve reflexi,

> quam tumulum antiquae Cereris sedemque sacratam
> venimus . . .
>
> (2.741-743)
>
> I did not look behind for her, astray,
> or think of her before we reached the mound
> and ancient sacred shrine of Ceres;

If Aeneas appears careless of Creusa here, verses 712-720 show, in illuminating contrast, his attention to detail, his cool and effective planning for successful escape and reunion, and his concern for the safety and ritual purity of the *penates*. In this critical moment Aeneas plans effectively for his father, son, and household gods but not for his wife. May we infer that he is more concerned for them than for her?

Aeneas' neglect of Creusa has been overlooked by most critics. However, one must suspect that Virgil intended something significant by it since he is innovative and consistent (2.711, 725, 729, 735-742) on this point. Aeneas' isolation of Creusa (as in 729) evidently troubled some ancient readers for Servius *auctus* attempts to explain it away by understanding "son" to stand for "son and wife" (*"quidam comiti pro comitibus accipi volunt"*). This remedy does not, however, account for 2.741: "I did not look behind for her, astray/or think of her . . ." Consequently, the reader must consider the significance of Aeneas' remarks here. Heinze, alone among modern critics, studies this perplexing incident at some length: "For what purposes, one might ask, does Virgil complicate the causes of Creusa's loss, since, even without all this, the Great Mother could have taken Creusa to herself?"[17] Some critics think the purpose of the incident is to elicit sympathy for Aeneas.[18] Yet could one not plausibly argue that the incident must rather elicit sympathy for Creusa? She herself does not wish to perish, as she indicates clearly in her single speech as a living woman. As Aeneas rushes from home to futile (as he knows) battle, she addresses him on behalf of the survival of the entire family group, with herself emphatically included. She questions by implication the value of arms, asserts the value of family,[19] and expresses her sense that Aeneas is abandoning her:

'si periturus abis, et nos rape in omnia tecum;
sin aliquam expertus sumptis spem ponis in armis,
hanc primum tutare domum. cui parvus Iulus,
cui pater et coniunx quondam tua dicta relinquor?'
Talia vociferans gemitu tectum omne replebat . . .
                                    (2.675-679)

'If you go off to die, then take us, too,
to face all things with you; but if your past
still lets you put your hope in arms, which now
you have put on, then first protect this house.
To whom is young Iulus left, to whom
your father and myself, once called your wife?'
So did Creusa cry; her wailing filled
my father's house.

In her speech she is the final, hence emphatic, family member in the *tricolon abundans* (2.677-678). She values her person and, as it seems, she expects from Aeneas certain actions expressive of family responsibility, both as father and as husband. At this point (680) the portent appears and the reader cannot know if Aeneas would have yielded to Creusa's appeal of his own accord.

Once aware of Creusa's disappearance, Aeneas is frantic. He risks his life to search for her in the flaming city. Clearly he has much feeling for Creusa (cf. 2.784 *dilectae . . . Creusae*) and he does not wish to lose her now. Yet this search, although it shows courage and sentiment, does not undo the consequences of Aeneas' initial flight. Similarly, the vision which Aeneas experiences of Creusa's shade, with its deceptively positive prophecy,[20] does not restore to life the living woman who felt endangered and abandoned. Creusa — and what she represents to Aeneas of family, love, and personal values — is definitively lost to him and to the poem.[21]

Aeneas' view of his own responsibility here is interesting and seems to anticipate his view of himself at other significant points in the poem. On several occasions, of which this is one, he appears to attribute to an external force or to another person the responsibility for a negative action, which might otherwise be attributed to him. Here, although Aeneas, as seen above, forgets Creusa, he does not assume responsibility for her death. Rather he blames others:

quem non incusavi amens hominumque deorumque,
aut quid in eversa vidi crudelius urbe?

(2.745-746)

What men, what gods did I in madness not
accuse? Did I see anything more cruel
within the fallen city?

He blames implicitly even Creusa herself:

hic demum collectis omnibus una
defuit, et comites natumque virumque fefellit.

(2.743-744)

at last, when all were gathered, she alone
was missing — gone from husband, son, companions.

Fefellit means "disappointed" or "deceived."[22]

Finally let us note the connection of *pietas* (piety) with Aeneas'
loss of Creusa. Aeneas' flight from Troy with Anchises on his back
and Iulus at his side epitomizes the *pietas* of Aeneas.[23] It has become such a famous image that modern readers may be surprised
to learn that, as Galinksy has shown, Aeneas was not traditionally
associated with *pietas*. Rather Virgil, by defining Aeneas as *pius*
(pious) at 1.10 and throughout the poem, makes him into the
embodiment of *pietas*.[24] Modern readers may also assume without
question that Aeneas' *pietas* was meant to be admired in all its
features. Yet, as Galinsky has also shown, this was not so even in
antiquity.[25] In our passage Virgil shapes the image of Aeneas'
pietas to include only males: Aeneas, his father, and his son.
Since the exclusive maleness of Aeneas' *pietas*, as reflected in his
flight from Troy, was not demanded by the tradition Virgil
inherited but rather occurs as a result of Aeneas' forgetfulness of
Creusa, Virgil may have intended it to express Aeneas' own
unarticulated and unacknowledged values. The reader is invited
to consider the emotional implications of *pietas* so conceived and
so exemplified.[26]

Let us now consider Dido. As in the case of Creusa Virgil is
again innovative in his use of tradition. Tradition, as in Timaeus
(fr. 23 Mueller) and Macrobius (5.17.5-6), tells that Dido, still

honoring her dead husband, commits suicide rather than yield to marriage with a neighboring African king.[27] In these versions Aeneas plays no part at all in Dido's tragedy. Indeed, Dido and Aeneas are not even contemporaries in legend. Scholars have speculated that Naevius first linked the tales of Dido and Aeneas and that Virgil followed him in that version.[28] Since there is no persuasive evidence for this hypothesis we may provisionally assume that the love of Dido and Aeneas was original with Virgil. Macrobius (as cited above) relates that everyone knew that Virgil's story of Dido was false. Why then does Virgil tell the story as he does? Readers must consider this question with special care.

To many critics Aeneas' leaving of Dido has seemed a heroic assertion of resolve and responsibility against the temptation to self-indulgent, merely personal happiness.[29] The poet, however, does not show Aeneas, genuinely torn, deliberating over this choice: whether or not to leave Dido. Aeneas' vision of Mercury affects him powerfully and his decision to leave Carthage is instantaneous:

> ardet abire fuga dulcisque reliquere terras
> (4.281)

> He burns to flee
> from Carthage; he would quit these pleasant lands.

Rather Aeneas is shown deliberating over how to tell Dido of his leaving. Evidently the poet wishes the reader to consider not so much the question of Aeneas' departure but the manner of his departure:

> heu quid agat? quo nunc reginam ambire furentem
> audeat adfatu? quae prima exordia sumat?
> atque animum nunc huc celerem nunc dividit illuc
> in partisque rapit varias perque omnia versat.
> haec alternanti potior sententia visa est:
> Mnesthea Sergestumque vocat fortemque Serestum,
> classem aptent taciti sociosque ad litora cogant,
> arma parent et, quae rebus sit causa novandis,
> dissumulent . . .
> (4.283–291)

> What can he do? With what words dare
> he face the frenzied queen? What openings
> can he employ? His wits are split, they shift
> here, there; they race to different places, turning
> to everything. But as he hesitated,
> this seemed the better plan: he calls Sergestus
> and Mnestheus and the strong Serestus, and
> he asks them to equip the fleet in silence,
> to muster their companions on the shore,
> to ready all their arms, but to conceal
> the reasons for this change.

Aeneas' provisional decision is to postpone meeting with Dido and he retreats to a male world, as Virgil implies in 4.288, a verse entirely filled with men's names and epic epithet. We infer that Aeneas more easily faces battles and winter storms than he faces a difficult encounter with Dido. (We may compare Euryalus' bravura commitment of his very life to a dangerous mission and his simultaneous fear to tell his mother of it in *Aen.* 9.287-290.) Aeneas cannot with courage (cf. *audeat* 4.284) and honesty face Dido. *Dolos* ("deceit" or "guile") is the poet's term (4.296) for Aeneas' actions. As Page (*ad loc.*) notes, *ambire* ("to get round") and *exordia* ("openings") also imply deceit.

Many readers have felt Aeneas to be most ignoble in Book 4. He may hope to flee without ever having to face Dido (so Quinn).[30] His final speech to her is unsympathetic and not wholly honest. Troubled by Aeneas' lack of courage and nobility here, some critics attempt to defend him, saying that his love was so great he dared not voice it. Others argue that any negative judgment of Aeneas is anachronistically harsh: a Roman would have approved.[31] But Virgil clearly intended us to notice the unsympathetic quality of Aeneas' speech because he points the reader's attention towards it. Aeneas' speech to Dido is framed by his awareness, although unvoiced, of the necessity of being gentle and consoling to Dido. Preceding his speech to Dido Aeneas tells his men that:

> sese interea, quando optima Dido
> nesciat et tantos rumpi non speret amores,

temptaturum aditus et, quae mollissima fandi
tempora, quis rebus dexter modus
                    (4.291-294)

    while he himself —
with gracious Dido still aware of nothing
and never dreaming such a love could ever
be broken — would try out approaches, seek
the tenderest, most tactful time for speech,
whatever dexterous way might suit his case.

Following Dido's speech the poet expresses Aeneas' thoughts:

At pius Aeneas, quamquam lenire dolentem
solando cupit et dictis avertere curas,
multa gemens magnoque animum labefactus amore,
iussa tamen divum exsequitur classemque revisit.
                    (4.393-396)

But though he longs to soften, soothe her sorrow
and turn aside her troubles with sweet words,
though groaning long and shaken in his mind
because of his great love, nevertheless
pious Aeneas carries out the gods'
instructions. Now he turns back to his fleet.

The truly striking thing, then, is that while Aeneas does recognize
the necessity of being gentle and consoling, the words which he
actually utters to Dido are not consoling but inflammatory. In his
speech Aeneas acknowledges no fault of his own; expresses no love
for Dido, no sympathy for her pain, no regret at leaving her.
Instead he attempts to exonerate himself with the superficially
correct but substantively false legalism that he never actually
married her:

pro re pauca loquar. neque ego hanc abscondere furto
speravi (ne finge) fugam, nec coniugis umquam
praetendi taedas aut haec in foedera veni.
                    (4.337-339)

               I'll speak
brief words that fit the case. I never hoped
to hide — do not imagine that — my flight;
I am not furtive. I have never held

the wedding torches as a husband; I
have never entered into such agreements.

Aeneas evidently cannot openly confront the human issue which
entangles him and Dido. Dido, however, perceives instantly what
is missing from his speech, and that is, precisely, humanity.[32] As
she expresses it:

> nec tibi diva parens generis nec Dardanus auctor,
> perfide, sed duris genuit te cautibus horrens
> Caucasus Hyrcanaeque admorunt ubera tigres.
> (4.365–367)

> No goddess was your mother, false Aeneas,
> and Dardanus no author of your race;
> the bristling Caucasus was father to you
> on his harsh crags; Hyrcanian tigresses
> gave you their teats.

For Dido, what is intolerable in Aeneas' speech is the bleakly
absent assertion of care, for this is all that could solace her.
Aeneas' lack of sympathy is what most keenly wounds:

> num fletu ingemuit nostro? num lumina flexit?
> num lacrimas victus dedit aut miseratus amantem est?
> (4.368–370)

> For did Aeneas groan when I was weeping?
> Did he once turn his eyes or, overcome,
> shed tears or pity me, who was his loved one?

Aeneas' actions no less than Dido's determined the course of
their drama, yet Aeneas does not acknowledge this.[33] The reader,
however, knows that Aeneas allowed Dido's love and expectations
to develop inasmuch as Aeneas is entirely aware of Dido's passion
for him:

> with gracious Dido still aware of nothing
> and never dreaming such a love could ever
> be broken
> (4.291-292)

In action and dress Aeneas acted as Dido's husband, as we may infer from Mercury's term *uxorius* (4.266), which is corroborated later by Dido's phrase "the hand you pledged" (*data dextera* 4.307). Because of this Dido legitimately feels both rejected and betrayed.[34] Certainly Dido is a difficult character, tempestuous, fierce, passionate. The reader cannot be uncritically sympathetic towards her. "Her mind is helpless; raging frantically,/inflamed, she raves throughout the city — just/as a Bacchante . . ." (*inops animi, incensa* 4.300, *bacchatur*, 4.301). These verses suggest that Aeneas' view of her as "frenzied" (*furentem* 4.283) is justified. The flaws of Dido's character are not, however, of concern to us here but rather the truth of her accusations, which are exact. She catches Aeneas' thoughts and words with precision:

> *dissimulare* etiam sperasti, perfide, tantum
> posse nefas tacitusque mea decedere terra?
> (4.305–306)
>
> Deceiver, did you even hope to hide
> so harsh a crime, to leave this land of mine
> without a word?

Thus she echoes Aeneas' above cited *dissimulent* (291), *taciti* (289), and also *fuga* from *ardet abire fuga* (281) with *fugam* (328).

The effect of these passages is to make the reader question Aeneas' moral and emotional courage and honesty.[35] His legal (as connoted by the phrase *pro re*) argument, although technically correct, ignores the substance of his actions in Carthage which, as we saw, implied husbandly status. In addition he declines to make a statement of care or sympathy although he feels it to be necessary. Consider the following extract from his speech to Dido:

> me si fata meis paterentur ducere vitam
> auspiciis et sponte mea componere curas . . .
> (4.340–341)
>
> If fate had granted me to guide my life
> by my own auspices and to unravel
> my troubles with unhampered will, then I . . .

After this suspensefully elaborated protasis, both Dido and the reader surely expect that Aeneas will conclude (to paraphrase) ". . . I would remain with you." This is the moment to affirm love and care. Contrary to this expectation, however, Aeneas completes his condition by saying that, if he were free, he would not remain with Dido but would seek to restore Troy:

> urbem Troianam primum dulcisque meorum
> reliquias colerem, Priami tecta alta manerent,
> et recidiva manu posuissem Pergama victis.
> > (4.342-344)
>
> should cherish first the town of Troy, the sweet
> remains of my own people and the tall
> rooftops of Priam would remain, my hand
> would plant again a second Pergamus
> for my defeated men.

The reader may imagine how bitter this confession must be for Dido. And when Aeneas finally speaks of love it is not for Dido but for Rome:

> sed nunc Italiam magnam Gryneus Apollo,
> Italiam Lyciae iussere capessere sortes,
> hic *amor*, haec patria est
> > (4.345-347)
>
> > But now Grynean
> Apollo's oracles would have me seize
> great Italy, the Lycian prophecies
> tell me of Italy: there is my love,
> there is my homeland.

As Aeneas does not voice his own feeling for Dido, so he also implicitly discredits her feeling for him by suggesting that it is malice or envy which motivates her to detain him:

> > si te Karthaginis arces
> Phoenissam Libycaeque aspectus detinet urbis,
> quae tandem Ausonia Teucros considere terra
> invidia est? et nos fas extera quaerere regna.
> > (4.347-350)

> If the fortresses
> of Carthage and the vision of a city
> in Libya can hold you, who are Phoenician,
> why, then, begrudge the Trojans' settling on
> Ausonian soil? There is no harm: it is
> right that we, too, seek out a foreign kingdom.

Aeneas' accusations appear gratuitous[36] and are most certainly tangential to the real issue which troubles these two. Only when Aeneas speaks of his father, his son, and Jove (4.351-359) does his speech have genuine power and pathos. When Aeneas leaves the difficult topic of Dido and his actions towards her he speaks with feeling.

Dido warns that Aeneas' departure will have fatal consequences for her: "the cruel death that lies in wait for Dido" (*Moritura . . . Dido* 4.308), "a fallen house" (*domus labentis* 4.318), "this dying woman" (*me moribundam* 4.323). In the underworld, however, Aeneas claims to have been unaware of the consequences for Dido of his leaving her behind:

> nec credere quivi
> hunc tantum tibi me discessu ferre dolorem
> (6.463-464)

> And I could not
> believe that with my going I should bring
> so great a grief as this.

In sum, Aeneas does not voice responsibility for his affair with Dido, for his departure from her ("It is not my own free will that leads to Italy" *Italiam non sponte sequor* 4.361 and cf. 6.458-460), or for the consequences of his departure. One may usefully contrast the attitude of Aeneas' men who do apprehend the import of his leaving:

> duri magno sed amore dolores
> polluto, notumque furens quid femina possit,
> triste per augurium Teucrorum pectora ducunt.
> (5.5-7)

> And yet the Trojans
> know well the pain when passion is profaned
> and how a woman driven wild can act;
> their hearts are drawn through dark presentiments.

Following his final interview with Dido Aeneas is called *pius* (4.393). This is the first time in Book 4 that he is called *pius* and the first time since Book 1.378. Therefore we may infer that in leaving Dido, and even in so disquieting a fashion, Aeneas affirms his *pietas*. Again *pietas* is consonant with the loss of a female figure. While Aeneas pursues *pietas* and his mission he loses the opportunity of love from and for a woman. It almost seems as if loved women are introduced into the *Aeneid* in order that they may subsequently be lost from Aeneas' life. Thus Virgil is suggesting the emotional cost to the Romans of becoming an imperial people.[37]

What conclusions may we draw about the significance of Aeneas' actions towards Creusa and Dido? We note that Virgil has altered the traditional stories of Creusa and Dido in similar ways. This pattern suggests deliberation and purpose. Both of Aeneas' relationships with women end in female casualty and in Aeneas' departure. The women's deaths are at least partially attributable to the manner of Aeneas' departure although Aeneas does not acknowledge this. To Creusa Aeneas is fatally inattentive. To Dido he is also irresponsible, even treacherous. Each of the women perceives Aeneas as abandoning her. Creusa's criticism of Aeneas, while briefer and gentler than Dido's, is comparable in substance. Finally, there is in each case a connection between Aeneas' departture and his *pietas*. Thus each of the women becomes in some sense a casualty of the Roman mission.

My hypothesis is that this collocation of departure, female casualty, denied responsibility, and *pietas* is intended to reflect an incomplete humanity in Aeneas and in the *pietas* which he exemplifies. If Aeneas epitomizes *pietas*, as his repeated epithet would indicate, then perhaps Virgil is suggesting that *pietas* so conceived is a flawed ideal since it seems not to require humane virtues or any personal loyalty or affection which does not ultimately subserve what we might term political or military goals.[38] Love for Anchises and Iulus, as expressed in *pietas* towards them, is consistent with Roman political goals; love for Creusa and Dido is not. Thus, while Aeneas as a commander is entirely successful, as a human being — by comparison to the Homeric figures of Hector and Odysseus — he is incomplete.

It is not at all the intention of this paper to suggest that Aeneas has no virtues. He has many qualities which deeply move the reader. Viktor Pöschl is convinced of his nobility. Wendell Clausen's deservedly famous essay is a most beautiful and moving expression of a sensitive reader's identification with Aeneas. W. R. Johnson also gives eloquent voice to Aeneas' appeal.[39] Yet Johnson himself, Hunt, and Putnam have skillfully and variously pointed to Aeneas' disquieting actions and compromised *pietas*. Virgil's portrait of Aeneas is subtly considered. In the first book of the *Aeneid* we see Aeneas defeated and exiled. In his sorrow he is a sympathetic figure, noble, responsive to compassion. The tragedy of Aeneas' experience is that fate or history rewards his *furor*, not his humanity. His triumphs come from his *furor* which allows him to break the Latin siege:

> talia per campos edebat funera ductor
> Dardanius, torrentis aquae vel turbinis atri
> more *furens*. Tandem erumpunt et castra relinquunt
> Ascanius puer et nequiquam obsessa iuventus.
> (10.602–605)

> Such were the deaths dealt by the Dardan chieftain
> across the plains while he raged like a torrent
> or black whirlwind. The boy Ascanius
> and all the warriors break out at last
> and quit their camp site; now the siege is pointless.

Furor allows Aeneas to devastate his enemies and consequently to achieve victory. As Johnson points out, Aeneas, in order to conquer, is compelled to suppress love and pity but not *furor*.[40]

The significance for the *Aeneid* as a whole of Aeneas' behavior towards Dido and Creusa is that it reveals his otherwise astonishing brutality in Books 10 and 12 to be not entirely anomalous. Otis feels that Aeneas' cruelty in these books is unbelievable, inconsistent with his character.[41] An alternative is to imagine that Aeneas has within him from the start the capacity for inhumane action. This capacity, partially revealed in his actions towards Creusa and Dido, is nurtured by success and allows him ultimately to achieve the victory he both envisions and embodies. As Aeneas pursues his vision of Rome his actions must trouble the reader's sympathy, however great it was initially. Aeneas' killing of the noble Lausus (10.811-815), his cruel boasting (10.531-532, 557-558, 592-593), his slaughter of a priest (10.537-541), his sacrifice of live youths to Pallas (11.81-82) are all cases in point.

Aeneas' final action in the poem is the killing of Turnus. This action was difficult for Aeneas, as his hesitation shows. Certainly the death of Pallas was a grievous loss to Aeneas and the reader shares his sorrow. Yet when Aeneas declines to spare the beaten and suppliant Turnus, he not only falls short of Anchises' ideal of sparing the vanquished, but he does so in the full sight of his future subjects. This is a spectacularly public killing. To the Latins Aeneas appears not a figure of compassion but of murderous fury.

Here it is critical to note that, as previously with Creusa and Dido, Aeneas attributes responsibility for this difficult action to another. As he kills Turnus he cries:

'. . . Pallas te hoc vulnere, Pallas
immolat et poenam scelerato ex sanguine sumit.'
(12.948-949)

'It is Pallas
who strikes, who sacrifices you, who takes
this payment from your shameless blood.'

As Anderson observes, these words do not hide the real identity of the killer — at least not from the reader.[42]

At the poem's close Virgil leaves the reader to ponder the implications of Aeneas' victory. What place is left in Aeneas' spirit and in his empire for those humane values which would legitimize his conquest and the losses it required? It may be useful for us in seeking an answer to this question to return to Homer and to contrast the final scene of the *Aeneid* with the conclusions of the *Iliad* and *Odyssey*, Virgil's often recalled epic models.[43] In the conclusions to these poems the hero comes together with other human beings. There is for him a moment of shared experience and intelligibility.[44] *Iliad* 24, in particular, concludes with Achilles' heroic magnanimity to an enemy and his reflective acceptance of his own humanity as he yields to Priam's plea (*Iliad* 24.486-551). Aeneas, on the contrary, declining Turnus' almost identical plea, stands victorious and alone, passionate for conquest and private vengeance.[45]

Acknowledgements

I wish to thank the anonymous readers of *Women's Studies*, Holly Wolff, and my colleagues James Tatum and Christian Wolff, whose suggestions greatly improved this paper.

Translations of the *Aeneid* are from Allen Mandelbaum, *The Aeneid of Virgil: A Verse Translation* (Berkeley 1971). All others are my own.

Notes

1. Viktor Pöschl, *The Art of Vergil: Image and Symbol in the Aeneid*, trans. by Gerda Seligson (Ann Arbor 1962) 18 (hereafter cited as Pöschl).
2. See, e.g., Brooks Otis, *Virgil: A Study in Civilized Poetry* (Oxford 1964) (hereafter cited as Otis); Pöschl 15, 18.
3. E.g., Michael C. J. Putnam, *The Poetry of the Aeneid* (Cambridge. Mass. 1966) 192-193 (hereafter cited as Putnam); J. William Hunt, *Forms of Glory: Structure and Sense in Virgil's Aeneid* (Carbondale, Illinois 1973) 77-78; William Nethercut, "Invasion in the *Aeneid*," *G & R* (1968) 82-95.
4. G. Karl Galinsky, "The Hercules-Cacus Episode in *Aeneid* VIII," *AJP* 87 (1966) 18-51, especially 41-42; William S. Anderson, *The Art of the Aeneid* (Englewood Cliffs, N.J. 1969) 63 (hereafter cited as Anderson).
5. Putnam 200-201.
6. W. R. Johnson, *Darkness Visible: A Study of Vergil's Aeneid* (Berkeley 1976) 1-22 (hereafter cited as Johnson). The *Aeneid* is an "uncommitted meditation on man's nature and on the possibilities and impossibilities of his fate" (22). One could, however, argue that the overall effect of Johnson's compelling book is to suggest rather Virgil's despair in the face of his experience.

7. See, e.g., Otis 378 f., Pöschl 133 f., Putnam 192-201, and Anderson 98-100.

8. See James M. Redfield, *Nature and Culture in the Iliad* (Chicago 1975) 119-127.

9. See James M. Redfield (*ibid*) and E. T. Owen, *The Story of the Iliad* (Toronto 1946) 56-72.

10. See George deF. Lord, "The *Odyssey* and the Western World," *The Sewanee Review* 62 (1954) 406-427, reprinted in Charles H. Taylor, ed., *Essays on the Odyssey* (Bloomington, Indiana 1963, repr. 1969) 36-53; William S. Anderson, "Calypso and Elysium," *CJ* 54 (1958) 2-11 (also reprinted in Taylor 73-86).

11. Ann Amory, "The Reunion of Odysseus and Penelope," in Taylor (*ibid*) 121.

12. Charles H. Taylor, Jr., "The Obstacles to Odysseus' Return: Identity and Consciousness in the *Odyssey*," *The Yale Review* 50 (1961) 579; reprinted in Taylor (*op. cit.*, note 10) 87-99.

13. See, e.g., Putnam 186.

14. See Richard Heinze, *Virgils Epische Technik* (Leipzig 1915; repr. Darmstadt 1972) 57-63 for the most complete discussion of Virgil's treatment of Creusa.

15. See R. G. Austin, *P. Vergili Maronis Aeneidos Liber Quartus* (Oxford 1955, repr. 1966) ad 708.

16. Heinze (*op. cit.*, note 14) 60.

17. *ibid.*

18. See, for example, K. Büchner, "P. Vergeilius Maro," *RE* 8 A2 (1958) 1357; Kenneth Quinn, *Virgil's Aeneid: A Critical Description* (London 1968) 120.

19. Quinn (above) 7 notes that Hecuba in *Aeneid* 2, similar to Creusa in this passage, represents human values and doubt of arms (2.519-522).

20.   "but you will reach
    Hesperia, where Lydian Tiber flows,
    a tranquil stream, through farmer's fruitful fields.
    There days of gladness lie in wait for you;
    a kingdom and a royal bride."

                    (2.781-784)

    See Sara Mack, *Patterns of Time in Vergil* (Hamden, Connecticut 1978) 57 on the disparity between the reality of Aeneas' experience and the prediction which he hears from Creusa's spirit/shade. Thus this pro-phecy, among others, becomes "the vehicle of a terrible irony not fully revealed until the poem ends."

21. Putnam 47: "The hell of Troy, and the presence of Creusa therein, offer in subtle conjunction an attraction for all that is human in Aeneas . . ."

22. On the connotations of *fefellit* see T.E. Page, *The Aeneid of Virgil* (London 1894; repr. New York 1967) ad loc. against Austin (*op. cit.*, note 15) ad loc.

23. See G. Karl Galinsky, *Aeneas, Siciliy, and Rome* (Princeton 1969) 21: *Aeneid* 2.721-725 is "supposed to be emblematic of *pietas*."

24. Galinsky (above) 3-61, especially 4, 20, 61.
25. Galinsky (*op. cit.*, note 23) 4.
26. Cf. Quinn (*op. cit.*, note 18) 6: "He [Virgil] leaves it to us to formulate, if we choose, the moral implications of his narrative; his form does not deal in express moral judgment."
27. On the history of the Dido tradition see Arthur Stanley Pease, *Publi Vergili Maronis Aeneidos Liber Quartus* (Cambridge, Mass. 1935; repr. Darmstadt 1967) 14-21.
28. For a convenient bibliography of sources see Pease (above) 19; also Heinze (*op. cit.*, note 14) 115-117.
29. Cf. Austin (*op. cit.*, note 15) *ad loc.*, Anderson 46: "The apparent coldness and rationality of his words, then, represent a heroic achievement . . ."
30. Quinn (*op. cit.*, note 18) 343-345.
31. E.g., Austin (*op. cit.*, note 15) 106: "His speech, though we may not like it, was the Roman answer to the conflict between two compelling forms of love, an answer such as a Roman Brutus once gave, when he executed his two sons for treason against Rome." See also note 29, above. Pöschl (44) assumes that the gods forbade Aeneas to comfort Dido, but this is not expressed in the text.
32. Cf. Friedrich Klingner, *Virgil: Bucolica, Georgica, Aeneis* (Zurich 1967) 449: "She must, however, be enraged that he denies human feeling." The earliest model for this passage is Patroclus to Achilles (*Il.* 16.33-35). See Pease (*op. cit.*, note 27) *ad loc.* for an exhaustive list of parallel passages in Greek and Latin.
33. Klingner (above) 449: "It remains obscure, however, how Aeneas could have indulged Dido so long in the belief that he acquiesced in her desire." Contrast Aeneas' behavior here to Odysseus' restraint when confronted with Nausicaa's youthful interest in him (*Od.* 8.457-468).
34. See Büchner (*op. cit.*, note 18) 1371: "Aeneas must allow himself to be reproached — justly — not only with harshness, but with transgression of the highest Roman value (*perfide* 366, *nusquam tuta fides* 337), if one accepts Dido's purely human interpretation, that faith (*fides*) is established through a natural bond, without expression in words." Aeneas has violated an implicit bond.
35. See Otis 268-269.
36. Cf. Francesco Arnaldi, cited by Otis (269, note 1): "He accuses because he is afraid of himself." Aeneas' inner conflict may also be implied by Virgil's change of Homeric precedent in making Mercury visit Aeneas. In *Od.* 5.21-115, Hermes visits Calypso, not Odysseus, since she is the obstacle to Odysseus' departure.
37. See Wendell Clausen, "An Interpretation of the *Aeneid*," *HSCP* 68 (1964) 143-145, reprinted in Steele Commager, ed., *Virgil: A Collection of Critical Essays* (Englewood Cliffs, N.J. 1966) 75-88 on the emotional costs to Aeneas and to the Roman people of founding Rome.
38. Cf. Hunt (*op. cit.*, note 3) 60: "Certainly the *pietas* of Aeneas is clearly established; but its connotations in the course of the epic come to suggest less of goodness than of devotion or commitment to his mission through

all acts good or evil." Cf. W. R. Johnson, "Aeneas and the Ironies of
Pietas," *CJ* 60 (1965) 362: In killing Turnus Aeneas "yields, constrained
by anger, to the lesser claims of revenge (lesser, that is, if *humanitas* is
the prime virtue in the poem; greater, of course, if politics is of the
essence) . . . His claim to *pietas* as compassion is here destroyed . . ."
It is perhaps revealing of Virgil's purpose here to note that the *pietas*
of Augustus was perceived by some of his contemporaries as merely
an excuse to legitimize the elimination of political enemies. Cf. Tac.
Ann. 1.9; Ronald Syme, *The Roman Revolution* (Oxford 1939, repr.
1971) 147, 201 on self-serving claims of *pietas* by Augustus.

39.   Pöschl 41-42; Clausen (*op. cit.*, note 37); W. R. Johnson 15: ". . . he is
a deeply humane and profoundly good man; he is also fearless and
courageous, as powerful and as energetic as he is compassionate and
gentle."

40.   Cf. W. R. Johnson (*op. cit.*, note 38) 360 on Aeneas' achieving significant advances through *furor*, while his effort at peaceful control fails
(362). He cites 10.525, 10.556–560, 10.597–600, 12.932–934 as instances of Aeneas' ignoring compassion (363). The correlation between
violence and success occurs also in *Georgic* 4. See Büchner (*op. cit.*,
note 18) 1310 on the *"Brutalität"* of *bougonia*; cf. my "A Reading of
Virgil's Fourth *Georgic*," *Phoenix* 32 (1978) 219–220.

41.   Otis 361.

42.   Anderson 100.

43.   See especially Otis 215–392 on Virgil's recalling of the Homeric epics.

44.   See Redfield (*op. cit.*, note 8) 210–223, especially 215 on "reconciliation" with Priam. Achilles' sense of mortality "here becomes a bond
with others, even with his enemy" (216). With respect to intelligibility
Redfield writes that Achilles "states the concluding synthesis of the
poem . . . Achilles is able, for the first time, to reflect upon himself
and his own fate as one instance of a universal pattern" (217). See
Michael S. Nagler, *Spontaneity and Tradition: A Study in the Oral Art
of Homer* (Berkeley 1974) 185–198 on Achilles' reaffirmed humanity
and vision. On Odysseus's humanity and vision see Taylor (*op. cit.*,
note 12) 580 and John H. Finley, Jr., *Homer's Odyssey* (Cambridge,
Mass. 1978) 185–186, 195–200, and 211–217. On lack of "intelligibility" in Aeneas see Robert A. Brooks, *"Discolor Aura*: Reflections
on the Golden Bough," *AJP* 74 (1953) especially 279–280 (reprinted
in Commager [*op. cit.*, note 37] 143–163), who writes of Aeneas'
"success in action/frustration in knowledge" (278). This is true not
only of Aeneas' experience with the Golden Bough but, I would
suggest, in the poem overall.
        Aeneas' final speech in the *Aeneid* is emphatic in its *furor* because
Aeneas' emotional direction in the poem is the inverse of Achilles' in
the *Iliad*. While Turnus' plea echoes Priam's, to which Achilles yields,
Aeneas' final words in the *Aeneid* recall the raging Achilles in *Iliad*
22.261–272 (cf. Pyrrhus in *Aen.* 2.547–550) and not the compassionate, reflective Achilles of *Iliad* 24.
        For a systematic and illuminating examination of the nature and

direction of Aeneas' utterances throughout the poem see Gilbert Highet, *The Speeches in Vergil's Aeneid* (Princeton, N.J. 1972) 29-43. Aeneas' first speech in the poem recalls Odysseus, his last Achilles of *Iliad* 22.

45.   Cf. Putnam 193. See 151-291 ("Tragic Victory") for a powerful study of this book as a whole.

Approaches to the sources on adultery at Rome

AMY RICHLIN

Dartmouth College

THERE HAS BEEN a good deal of speculation as to the amount of sexual freedom enjoyed by Roman men and women. This freedom certainly involved many types of liaison: homosexual as well as heterosexual; from casual use of prostitutes to established concubinage. In a society where marriage was common, many of these relationships entailed adultery. The purpose of this study is to present different sorts of evidence on heterosexual extra-marital love affairs, especially evidence which reflects societal attitudes towards such affairs, and to draw attention to problems in the evaluation of this evidence.

To the Romans, the concept of marriage was full of heavy moral and social significance; it follows that their reactions to adultery were not simple. This study will lay out five categories of evidence on Roman attitudes toward adultery — law, history, moral anecdote and *exempla*, slander, and satire. After all five categories have been described fully, and the picture of adultery given by each has been outlined, then the contradictions among them will be set forth, and suggestions made as to the ways in which they can be reconciled. From the whole can be seen the way in which a profound social problem projects multiple images in literature.[1]

A few facts can be relied on as landmarks. The most important is that before the time of Augustus there was no criminal law about adultery; and that Roman law from its earliest times was the custom of a very public community, where everyone knew everyone else's character and social standing. The family had great jurisdiction over its members, the *paterfamilias* at the head, the males in direct line under him, the women under them, and the freedmen, clients, and slaves under all. Execution of the law depended at all times on self-help, since there was no police force; therefore, the concerned parties had to decide among themselves whether to go to court, settle within the family, use force, or do nothing, and the Twelve Tables are full of the most physical instructions — for haling your adversary to court, keeping debtors in chains at your house or cutting them into bits, noxal surrender. A thief caught in the act could be killed; runaway slaves were branded F for *fugitivus*, on their foreheads, for all to see.

It is also important to keep track of changes in manners. The late Republic and early Empire were characterized, at Rome, by a certain flamboyance of behavior; the end of the Julio-Claudians and the beginning of the Flavians seems to have marked a general return to a love of respectability, and it is clear that, by the time of Trajan, the Senate was no longer flamboyant, but pleased to observe decorum in its social life. Under the Julio-Claudians the senators and *equites* were aristocrats or bohemians; later, they were elevated bourgeoisie.

A final point to bear in mind is that all the literary sources here surveyed were written for Rome and the Senate, while the legal sources to be considered later were compiled in the fifth century for the benefit of the entire empire.[2] Furthermore, all the material was written by men, so that whatever picture of Roman sexual mores can be established must be without any direct evidence from women themselves.

LEGAL SOURCES

The legal sources are largely limited to those of the late Empire, especially *Digest* 48.5 and *Codex* 9.9. Yet this includes two earlier bodies of writing: the comments of the jurisconsults who wrote under Severus, and some of the original words of the *lex Julio de adulteriis coercendis*. Here and there in the legal sources are rescripts by emperors of the first and second centuries. Paulus'

Sententiae (2.26) also devote space to the *lex Julia*, and clarify a few points mentioned nowhere else in the legal sources.[3]

The comments of the jurists are unfortunately ambiguous. Rarely do they give a direct quotation from the Julian law; on the other hand, they often use the phrase "the law says . . ." Whether this refers directly to the *lex Julia* or to the body of commentary surrounding it is not possible to say; it seems likely that what the jurisconsults say can be accepted as at least consistent with the tenor of the law for the period between the passage of the *lex Julia* and the reign of Severus.

The *lex Julia de adulteriis coercendis* was passed by Augustus as part of his campaign for the moral reform and eugenics of the Senate and *equites* in 18 B. C.,[4] and was complemented by the later *lex Papia Poppaea*, which, among other things, forbade a senator to marry a convicted adulteress. The law on adultery seems to have included a great deal of regulation of procedure. Most important was its establishment of a *quaestio perpetua* for the hearing of accusations of adultery, similar to those already in existence for the hearing of other *iudicia publica* (parricide, acts of violence, murder, treason). This alignment of what is essentially a civil or victimless crime with crimes of violence should be noted as an impractical touch and a serious weakness in Augustus' approach to moral legislation.[5]

The law delineated the steps to be taken in the *quaestio*. The husband was to divorce his wife as soon as he found out she was adulterous, or he would himself be liable for prosecution for *lenocinium*, pimping.[6] He had sixty days in which he or the woman's father had the exclusive right to accuse her of adultery.[7] However, the adulterer had to be accused first, and his trial would be first. If he were found guilty, the woman would then be tried. If he were found innocent, and the woman had re-married, she could not be tried.[8]

The law further delineated the circumstances in which the husband or father could kill the wife and/or the adulterer. Any killing had to be done *in flagrante delicto*[9] and only in the husband's or father's house. The father had unlimited rights, but had to kill both parties. The husband could only kill the adulterer if the adulterer was *infamis*.[10]

When two months had passed after the act of divorce, any third person could bring the accusation of adultery, within the next four months. There was a five-year statute of limitations on the accusation.[11]

Neither the *Digest* nor the *Codex* makes any mention of the penalties to be imposed by the court on those found guilty of adultery. To sum up, the *Digest* does cite the following penalties: the ability of the father to kill the wife and adulterer caught *in flagrante delicto*; the ability of the husband to kill the adulterer, within limits; the limits of the severe punishment of a husband who killed his wife *in flagrante delicto*; an opinion by Papinian that a husband, who can kill the adulterer, can certainly inflict injury (*contumelia*) upon him; the husband's risk of being accused of *lenocinium* if he does not divorce his wife; and the culpability of any accessories to the adultery as adulterers themselves, which seems to be an amendment to the original law (*Dig.* 48.5.8, 8.1, 9, 9.1, 9.2, 12, 32.1).[12]

Paulus' *Sententiae* give the legal punishment for adultery (2.26.14): the wife and the adulterer were subjected to *relegatio* (exile), to different islands; the woman lost half her property and a third of her estates, and the adulterer lost half his property.[13] Women found in adultery, with other women of low moral standing, were prohibited from re-marriage to freeborn Romans by the Julian marriage laws.[14]

It will be noticed that the only situation legally considered to be adultery was sexual intercourse between a *matrona* and a man not her husband. A married man could legitimately have intercourse with any man who was not freeborn or woman who did not have the status of *matrona* and was not either married or in concubinage, and could keep concubine(s) of either sex in his household.[15] If he did have intercourse with a married woman, his own wife did not acquire the explicit right to prosecute him for this until the late Empire; of course there is no reason why she or her representative should not have been eligible to prosecute the adulterous pair as third parties after the husband and father.[16]

That the *lex Julia* was revived by Domitian, though this is mentioned in only extra-legal sources (see below), may be noted here. There is no legal description of what was entailed by this revival.

The jurisconsults themselves represent a stage in the history of the law on adultery. Each of the excerpts in the *Digest* and *Codex* is taken from a book or section of a book by that jurist on adultery or on the *lex Julia* itself. The chief concern of each jurist seems to have been to define the rules as to the time allowed for bringing accusations, and occasionally to define the circumstances under which the husband or father could kill the adulterer and/or the wife. It might, then, be postulated that the chief area of confusion and concern for those wishing to accuse under the law was when they might do so; perhaps this is more naturally a question for a third party wishing to accuse.

HISTORICAL SOURCES

The historical sources extend back to the early Republic, although from no earlier than the standpoint of Augustan Rome; the skewing of their evidence is thus certain but not consistent. The earliest statement is Cato's (recorded by Aulus Gellius, 10.23) that a wife can do nothing to her husband if she catches him in adultery, while the husband may kill her if he finds her so. Cato is expounding on the husband's general *imperium* over his wife. The adultery law cited by Dionysius of Halicarnassus as instituted by Romulus (2.25; cf. Plut. *Rom.* 22.3) resembles Cato's description of current custom.

Livy shows no concern for factual cases of adultery in the extant books. Instead, in the stories of Verginia and especially of Lucretia (1.58), he depicts an idealized version of the embodiment of chastity — outraged *matrona*, staunch husband, slain seducer — which has little to do with history and much in common with the moral tales of a writer like Plutarch. The tales of Lucretia and Verginia are so much more *exempla* than historical episodes that they cannot be compared with the narratives of adultery found in other historical sources.[17]

Still, it is possible to sift a good deal of reliable information out of sources of all kinds. Cicero and his correspondents mention many scandalous divorces, some of which found their way into later biographies.[18] One of the great sensational divorce cases of the late Republic was Caesar's divorce of his wife Pompeia on suspicion of adultery with Clodius, involving his intrusion at the rites of Bona Dea;[19] this *cause célèbre* was one factor in Clodius' hatred of Cicero, who was the witness who destroyed his alibi.

The double standard which prevailed in society at Rome is suggested by two cases, one famous. Antony flaunted his affair with the actress Volumnia Cytheris, freedwoman of Volumnius Eutrapelus; it was one of the things which galled Cicero most bitterly about Antony (*Att.* 10.10.5, 10.16.5, 15.22). Yet it was only the parade of it that was so bad; Cicero could tolerate Cytheris, although he disapproved, when Eutrapelus gave a dinner party and had her seated next to himself (*Fam.* 9.26.2; cf. 14.16.1). It seems that Cytheris and her function were acceptable, as long as she stayed in her place.[20] On the other hand, a married woman could have no such concubine; when Caecilius Epirota, Atticus' freedman, was suspected of seducing his patron's married daughter, the liaison was, as a matter of course, not tolerated. Epirota, dismissed from his job as Attica's teacher, landed on his feet under the patronage of Cornelius Gallus, which tolerance later influenced Augustus against Gallus (Suet. *Gramm.* 16). As will be seen, some *liberti* who seduced the wife or daughter of a *patronus* experienced much more serious reprisals.

After the passage of the *lex Julia*, the limited evidence suggests only that the law's application was irregular, although the possibility must be kept in mind that only irregular cases were recorded by contemporary writers. Of the three main stages prescribed by the law — divorce, trial, and exile — there is very little evidence that is not in some way aberrant. Divorces in the royal family included that of Julia and Tiberius (Suet. *Tib.* 10.1, 11.4), Nero and Octavia (Suet. *Ner.* 35.1-3) and Domitian and Domitia (Suet. *Dom.* 3.1, 13.1; especially hypocritical, cf. *Dom.* 8.3). As for the trial, most recorded by Tacitus were held before the Senate, most in Suetonius before the *princeps*; the emperors had a special interest on the *equites*,[21] and (perhaps following Caesar's example as dictator, Suet. *Iul.* 43.1) set themselves up as censors (*Aug.* 37,

39; *Tib.* 35.1; *Claud.* 15.4, 16.1; *Calig.* 16.2; *Dom.* 8.3). The *quaestio perpetua* established by Augustus could have disappeared completely, for all the sources have to say about it. It must be assumed that it existed and heard normal cases (those not involving senators or *equites*), but was dying gradually, and (unfortunately) being replaced by the process of *cognitio* administered by the urban prefect. In this court, the punishment was left to the discretion of the judge, thereby allowing a great deal of room for irregular sentences.[22] A further factor in this confusion is that Tiberius reaffirmed the jurisdiction of the family council over unchaste married women (Suet. *Tib.* 35.1).

Most of the exiles on record are involved with offenses to the reigning dynasty. That of the two Julias[23] was implemented by Augustus himself as *paterfamilias*, without recourse to the *lex Julia*; the poet Ovid (whose poetry was itself too favorable to sexual activity to jibe with the Julian laws) was perhaps exiled as an accessory under the law, if he was officially charged at all. Seneca the philosopher was likewise implicated in a royal adultery (said to have been trumped up, Dio 60.4-6). The most heinous example of such an exile was that of Octavia by Nero (Suet. *Ner.* 35.1-2).

Adulterous relations between freedmen or slaves and upperclass women were severely punished by Augustus, as they had been by Caesar (*Iul.* 48; *Aug.* 67.2, cf. 45.4; *Vesp.* 11).[24] It is clear from this and from the case of the Julias that the *lex Julia* did not abrogate the rights of the *paterfamilias* to act for himself; Augustus was a strong proponent of the *mos maiorum*. and in addition seems to have considered himself *paterfamilias patriae* as well as *pater patriae*. In general any Roman who offended against a class above his own was in an especially bad position; cf. the case of the *laticlavius'* wife who committed adultery with a centurion (Pliny *Ep.* 6.31.4-6) and that of T. Vinius with his commanding officer's wife (Plut. *Galba* 12).

On the other hand, this very Vinius exemplifies one great recourse from legal sanctions: amnesty. He was released from prison when Gaius died; if, then, an exile could survive, he or she might come home when the new emperor took over, just as Gaius called home all who had been exiled under Tiberius (Suet. *Calig.* 15.4).

Tacitus' accounts of adultery must be read carefully, since they are closely related to some of his most personal interpretations of the history of the early Principate; thus they are here considered separately. Where one would expect to find scattered accounts of cases of adultery and of the normal procedure, Tacitus records only stories which depict the immorality of upperclass women, the cruelty of the *princeps*, or the savage greed of *delatores* (informers) — all three, if possible. The cases he reports are irregular and inconsistent, probably because most of the people involved were senators and/or relatives of the royal house.[25] In the case of Appuleia Varilla, granddaughter of Augustus' sister, Tiberius intervened to lessen the penalty (*Ann.* 2.50); he also brought D. Silanus, adulterer of the younger Julia, back from his *relegatio* (*Ann.* 3.24). Yet he later intervened to make penalties more rigorous, as in the case of Aquilia (*Ann.* 4.42).

Irregularities for the senators and *equites* were fostered by the boom in *delatio* under the Julio-Claudians. *Delatores* were attracted by the sanctions of the *lex Papia Poppaea* (*Ann.* 3.25):

Nor, therefore, were marriage and the bringing up of children made popular, childlessness prevailing: meanwhile the great number of those endangered was increasing, when every home was undermined by the legalistic machinations of informers, and as previously trouble came from immoral behaviour, so now it came from the laws.[26]

This law was used by Tacitus as the premier example of the invasion of private life by the principate through the agency of *delatio* (*Ann.* 3.28). *Delatores* received a substantial cut of escheated property; the ability of a third party to prosecute under the *lex Julia de adulteriis coercendis* provided a perfect opportunity. A husband who wished to allow his wife sexual freedom risked a great deal.

That some husbands were flagrantly complaisant is seemingly evidenced by the case of Vistilia (*Ann.* 2.85; cf. Suet. *Tib.* 35.2):

In the same year the wantonness of the women was put under control by severe decrees of the Senate, and provision was made that no one whose grandfather, father, or husband had been a Roman knight should prostitute herself. For Vistilia, born of a praetorian family, had publicly registered with the aediles her availability for sexual intercourse, in the traditional manner, which held that there was enough punishment of unchaste women in the very profession of their flagrant crime. Moreover, it was demanded of Titidius Labeo, Vistilia's husband, why he had neglected the revenge of the law in the case of a wife openly guilty. And when he gave as his excuse that the sixty days allowed for consultation had not yet gone by, it seemed enough to make a decision about Vistilia; and she was put away in the island of Seriphos.

Vistilia's tactic would have exempted her not only from prosecution for adultery, since she was now *infamis*, but from the provisions of the *lex Papia Poppaea* penalizing celibacy.[27] It is striking how cynically the husband shelters behind the letter of the law; clearly the whole business is as irksome to him as it is to his wife.

Tacitus perceives an ominous connection between the use of charges of *maiestas* (lèse-majesté) and of adultery as a political weapon. The very first example he gives of the abuse of *maiestas* is the case of Appuleia Varilla, cited above; the charge is linked with adultery in a most sinister way (*Ann.* 2.50):

Meanwhile, the treason law was coming of age. An informer summoned even Appuleia Varilla, the granddaughter of Augustus' sister, on a charge of *maiestas*, since she had made fun of the deified Augustus and Tiberius and his mother in indecent speeches and, a relative of Caesar, was held for adultery . . .

Other cases where Tacitus suggests a link between *maiestas* and adultery, or that evidence of adultery was manufactured, include those of Antistius Vetus (*Ann.* 3.38), where Tiberius intervened drastically; Aquilia, who appears in a list of those charged with *maiestas* (*Ann.* 4.42); Claudia Pulchra, Agrippina's friend (*Ann.* 4.52); and Faenius Rufus, at the time of Nero (*Ann.* 15.50).[28]

The case of Albucilla (*Ann.* 6.47-48) demonstrates how freely a *delator* could use the law as a political lever, implicating as many eminent co-respondents as suited him:

Then Albucilla, notorious for love affairs with many men, and who had been married to Satrius Secundus who informed on [Sejanus'] conspiracy, was denounced for disloyalty to the emperor; Cnaeus Domitius, Vibius Marsus, and Lucius Arruntius were linked with her as her accessories and adulterers ... But accounts sent to the Senate indicated that Macro had presided at the interrogation of witnesses and the torture of slaves, and the fact that no letter of the *princeps* was attached led to the suspicion that most of it was made up, the *princeps* being ill and perhaps unaware of the whole thing, because of Macro's well-known grudge against Arruntius.

Domitius and Vibius survived, Arruntius killed himself, and Albucilla ended up in prison; in the end, three more men were exiled or degraded on her account. The lurid case of Nero's wife Octavia (*Ann*. 14.60) is an extreme example of what the law meant to Tacitus — a perversion of moral law by a vile *princeps* and his unscrupulous henchmen, for the persecution of a hunted nobility.

Tacitus expresses his feelings about moral ideals and, indirectly, his conviction of the inappropriateness of the *lex Julia* in Chapters 18-19 of the *Germania*. He is in the midst of praising the Germans, whose military prowess he has earlier touted in a manner reminiscent of Livy writing of early Rome:

However marriage is very strict there, nor would you give more praise to any part of their *mores*. For, almost unique among barbarians, they are content with a single wife, except for only a few, who undertake many marriages, not for the sake of lust but because of their nobility ... By these means the women live their lives with their chastity firmly girded, corrupted by no lures of extravaganzas, no unsettling excitements of dinner parties. Men as well as women know nothing of secrets in letters. Adulteries are very rare in such a numerous people, for which the penalty is to hand, given over to the husbands: the husband drives the wife naked from home, her hair cut off, in the presence of her relatives, and drives her through the whole village with a crop; for there is no mercy for a virtue that has become public property: she will find a husband not by looks, youth, or money. For no one there laughs at vices, nor are corruption and being corrupted called "the times." Indeed, still better are those states in which only virgins marry, and put an end to speculation and utter their wife's pledge at one and the same time ... And good *mores* have more force there than good laws elsewhere.

Here Tacitus combines the castigation of common Roman vices, a stock piece in contemporary rhetoric, with an unusual and oddly wistful description of a sort of physical punishment which at Rome was reserved for slaves.

MORAL ANECDOTES AND RHETORICAL EXEMPLA

Tacitus' parable in the *Germania* makes a good introduction to another genre which often concerned itself with adultery, that of moral anecdote and rhetorical *exemplum*. Here we leave sources which tell the truth as they see it — law and history — for sources which tell of ideal cases, the truth as they would like it to be.

Valerius Maximus' rhetorical handbook does include several cases which are realistic rather than idealistic. The account of the trial of Fannia before Marius (8.2.3; cf. Plut. *Mar.* 38), although suspect in several details, seems to be an account of a common republican procedure — the *actio de moribus* (suit for immoral conduct) brought as a counter-suit by a husband in an effort to retain part of his wife's dowry after a divorce. The case of Calidius Bononiensis (8.1. *Absol.* 12), on the other hand, shows an adulterer (presumably after 18 B.C.) making an ingenious, if disreputable, excuse in court as to why he was found in a married woman's bedroom. Finally, Val. Max. 6.1, *De pudicitia*, includes an account of cases of adultery in which the husband resorted to "self-help" punishments (6.1.13):

> But if I might quickly also run through a list of those men who resorted to their own feelings instead of the public law in vindicating their honor: Sempronius Musca horsewhipped Gaius Gellius caught in adultery, Gaius Memmius beat Lucius Octavius, caught in a similar situation, with a . . .,[29] Carbo Attienus (caught by Vibienus) and Pontius (caught by Publius Cerennius) were castrated. And the man who caught Gnaeus Furius Brocchus handed him over to his slaves to be raped. That these men had given in to their anger was not grounds for a lawsuit.

But *exempla* generally are unrealistic, and their characters are often famous men and women or people proverbial for especially virtuous actions. Val. Max. 6.1 begins with Lucretia and Verginia, and ends with three non-Roman *exempla*. These relate marvelous tales of the extremes to which chaste women have gone in the defence of their honor. This is the pattern of a sort of moral tale of which not only Livy (Lucretia (1.58) and Verginia (3.44f.)) but pre-eminently Plutarch was very fond; Plutarch *Moralia* 258-261 tells several stories in which the slain seducer plays a leading role. In 258C, Camma poisons an unwanted admirer; Chiomara's is beheaded (258 EF; this is the same story as Val. Max. 6.1. *Ext.* 2, in which the woman is not named); Timocleia of Thebes pushed hers down the well, 259D-260D (= *Alex.* 12); Eryxo's brothers stabbed her would-be adulterer, 260E-261B. At 261F Plutarch describes a tyrant who preys on women and young boys. (In this context, Plutarch's attitude elsewhere towards adultery is to be noted: in his advice to prospective brides, he notes that it is better to shut one's eyes to a little philandering than wreck your marriage, and advises a sweetly indulgent attitude (*Mor.* 140B, 144F); though he does exhort the husband not to enrage his wife unduly (144D) and both to consider the holiness of procreation (144B).) Apuleius' story of Charite (*M.* 8.13) repeats the pattern, with gruesome embroideries of blinding and suicide. The moral principle seemingly so appealing to Greco-Roman society of the first century is surely closely linked to the ideal of the *univira* and the death of Dido,[30] and so it is possible to see here the familial relation of the most vapid and jejune of literary material, the moral *exempla* of Valerius Maximus, to the noblest expression of Roman sentiment.

Such situations were popular in another genre — the exercises of the rhetorical *scholae* which flourished from the time of Cicero onwards. The *controversiae* of the elder Seneca and the *declamationes* of Quintilian and Calpurnius Flaccus favored gruesome crimes as subject matter for their mock trials, as being most challenging[31] — and, presumably, most enjoyable. Of these crimes, adultery was a favorite, especially the situation in which a husband found his wife *in flagrante delicto* and killed her, or tried to. Of seventy-four *controversiae* in Seneca's collection, fourteen deal with adultery and other sexual crimes (rape being the most common: 1.5, 2.3, 3.5, 4.3, 7.6, 7.8, 8.6). This preoccupation seems to have continued strongly through the years; of the fifty-three *declamationes* of Calpurnius Flaccus preserved by his editor, eight (2, 11, 17, 23, 31, 40, 48, 49) are concerned with adultery, and several others with rape and other sexual offenses (one, *decl.* 3, is directly taken from Val. Max. 6.1.12). Quintilian has at least fourteen cases of adultery (*decl.* 277, 279, 284, 291, 335, 347, 379, 244, 286, 273. 275, 357, 310, 249), out of 145 cases.

It should be noted that, where *exempla* are supposedly real cases for reference in speeches, all *controversiae* deal with unusual circumstances, conflations of bizarre events that would give scope for rhetorical virtuosity. Most of the situations are made up for the occasion, the characters usually being anonymous ("the soldier who found his wife . . ."). Moreover, Seneca presents high points of all the speeches given, so that the result is a kaleidoscopic series of arguments for all viewpoints, one more ingenious than the next.[32]

GOSSIP AND SLANDER

The fourth category to be considered here merits special consideration for two reasons: partly because it is important to keep it carefully separate from accounts which purport to tell the truth about current *mores*; and especially because it represents one practical form of the *infamia* which resulted from behavior classed as immoral. As rhetorical *exempla* demonstrate a conscious presentation of idealized behavior, so gossip shows what the Romans said when they were being malicious. Of all the ephemera of antiquity, conversation is the most thoroughly lost to us; still it has its fossil form in insults, scandal, and rumors recorded in all genres.

Cicero's letters are surprisingly rich in gossip about sexual misconduct; in fact, he was renowned as a wit in his own time and long afterwards, and many of the jokes attributed to him are sexual. One such joke he preserves himself; in a letter to Atticus (2.1.5), he boasts of a retort he claims he made to Clodius, not only insulting but obscene. Clodius had complained that his influential sister would not even give him one foot of room at the games; Cicero says he replied, "Don't complain about one of your sister's feet — you can always raise the other" (= Eng. colloq. "you can always get her to spread her legs"). Even if this is only what Cicero wishes he had said, it gives some idea of the possibilities in Roman slander. It has been shown above that these letters, and later biographies, talked about then verifiable information, divorces and attendant circumstances; but they did not stop there. As Cicero said in a letter to Atticus, "we are both great gossips" (*Att.* 6.1.25), and it was true.[33]

Smutty stories clung to the great, as they always have; not only the dissolute Antony (Plut. *Ant.* 6) but Pompey (Plut. *Pomp.* 2, Suet. *Gramm.* 14) and even Cato the Elder (Plut. *Cat. Mai.* 24) had their names bandied about. There were stories in circulation about the profligacy of every emperor, although it is noteworthy that there are few about Vespasian and Titus. The pages of Suetonius are full of shocking anecdotes, but the similarities between stories about different emperors (e.g. *Aug.* 69.1 and *Calig.* 36.2) ought to warn the reader.

It has likewise always been popular to make up jokes about those in power. Among others, there is a series of jokes about Augustus' daughter Julia, in which she plays the part of the clever protagonist; her clothing, her companions, her method of birth control, and her sexual attitudes all provided matter for amusement (Macrob. *Sat.* 2.5, esp. .2-3, .5, .6, .9, .10). A particularly Roman kind of joke was the jingle set in an elegiac couplet, which might have been painted up as graffiti as well as passed around in oral circulation; Suetonius preserves one about Otho and Nero (*Otho.* 2.2):

> You ask why Otho is in exile, under the semblance of an honor?
> He had begun to be the adulterer of his own wife.

Otho had married Poppea so that Nero could enjoy her, but then kept her to himself; Nero sent him off to Lusitania on government business.

That so many of these stories concern the most eminent Romans of their time is sometimes the result of the deliberate spreading of propaganda, as, perhaps, with Antony's smearing of Octavian; on the other hand, it is a commonplace in oral literature that apocryphal jokes proliferate about well-known and powerful people. Thus such stories must be treated with extreme caution as information about their subjects. Still, one can perceive in such generalized rumors of misconduct a culture-wide attitude about what constituted bad behavior. It is hard to know how far beyond court circles such stories would have circulated; that they reached at least Italy is suggested by the sling-bullets from the siege of Perusia with obscene messages on them,[34] the soldiers' songs at Caesar's triumph (Suet. *Iul.* 49.4), the popular reaction against Octavia's suffering (Suet. *Ner.* 35.1-2). What is perhaps most revealing, the existence and preservation of these stories shows that at least some parts of the current audience found them, not disgusting, but titillating.

SATIRE

Satire paints a lurid picture of adultery and those involved in it; it is important to note the formal relation of this picture to that of the rhetorical *locus de saeculo*, and to remember that the picture is intended to amuse. On the other hand, it is not probable that any humorous genre could have amused its audience without being recognizable, if exaggerated.

The two largest areas of sexual humor in Latin literature are those related to heterosexual intercourse and those related to male homosexuality. Of the heterosexual jokes, one very large sub-group deals with adultery, with a balanced division of the comic roles among wife, lover, and cuckolded husband; the reverse situation (husband, mistress, and jealous wife) is much more rarely used. The rest of heterosexual humor is generally concerned with wanton women, some of whom are prostitutes or concubines and hence not involved in adultery; thus, although the brutality of the jokes about common prostitutes in Roman satire is interesting, it will not be considered here.[35]

The depiction of adultery in satire bears a family resemblance to a sort of bedroom farce which was a common skit in mime, as attested by several direct references in satire. The episode involved a stupid husband, a buxom wife, and a dashing adulterer. The adulterer, although he proverbially hid in a chest, afraid for his life (Juv. 6.44), at some point turned around and buffeted the hapless husband, Panniculus ("Little Rags") (Mart. 2.72.3-4, 3.86.3, 5.61.11-12). The husband was always jealous of the wife (Juv. 8.197), who may have been the type of the naïve country girl (cf. Juv. 6.66). These scattered references convey the impression that, in mime, the husband was despised, the adulterer was a successful villain, and the wife, though appealing, was upstaged by both.

This situation is the focus of Horace S. 1.2, in which the poet exhorts his audience not to bother with coy, troublesome married women, but to stick to willing slaves (male and female) and freedwomen. This idea recurs in the *Satires* (1.4.27, 111-115; 2.7.45-57, 72), along with the cynical generalization that adultery came into being along with the dawn of civilization (*S.* 1.3.105-110). This idea, in turn, is the take-off point for Juvenal's sixth satire, which is all one enormous argument to a putative prospective bridegroom as to why he had better not marry; Juvenal gives many special types of disagreeable wife, but again and again returns to the way wives cuckold their husbands.

A special satirical persuasion against adultery were the horrific punishments visited on the adulterer by the cuckold. The adulterer ran the risk of castration, being beaten, or paying a fine,[36] mutilation,[37] death,[38] anal rape,[39] or simulation of it,[40] or irrumation, in which the husband forced the adulterer to fellate him.[41] The only punishment of adulteresses mentioned in satire is that they had to abandon the dress of a respectable woman, the *stola*, for the toga worn by prostitutes.[42]

One legalistic vignette in satire is that of the husband who pimps his wife, as at Juvenal 1.55-57:

> . . . when the pimp accepts the adulterer's bequest,
> if the wife has no right of taking — he's well-trained
> at looking at the ceiling, trained to snore in his cups
> with wakeful nose . . .

This goes back to a proverbial passage in Lucilius (1223 Marx); Cicero twice (*Fam.* 7.24, *Att.* 5.39.2) uses the tag from it, "*non omnibus dormio*" ("I don't close my eyes for every man").[43] Such action is sometimes referred in satire to *captatio* (legacy-hunting), as at Hor. *S.* 2.3.231, 237-238, or at *S.* 2.5.75, where Teiresias advises Ulysses to hand over Penelope on demand; or to perversion (Juv. 9.40-86).[44]

The hapless cuckold appears, if rarely, as the butt of jokes in epigram (Mart. 3.70, 6.31, 10.69, 12.93); Claudius is the most eminent model cuckold (Juv. 6.115f., 10.329-345), asleep while his wife prostitutes herself and commits bigamy, although perhaps the noblest evocation of cuckoldry is the anonymous innocent (addressed as *tu*!) who walks unknowing through the traces of his wife's debaucheries at Juv. 6.312-313.

The favorite picture is simply that of the adulteress. She entraps even effeminates (Mart. 2.47), divorces her husband for her lover (Mart. 3.70, 4.9, Juv. 6.100) or just cheats on her husband, in many ingenious ways (Lucilius 680 Marx, 781 Marx; Mart. 1.73, 2.56, 3.26, 4.58, 6.90, 11.7, 11.71; Juv. 6.140-141, 277-279. *O.* 31-34, 464-6, 487-9, 548, 567). An elaboration on this theme is the idea that the chastest of women is a whore at heart; the most famous presentation of this idea is the story of the widow of Ephesus, told by Eumolpus to the party on board Lichas' ship (Petr. *Sat.* 110.6-112.8). This surely is an inversion of the ideal of pure womanhood put forward by rhetoric. A similar idea is that upper class women enjoy low lovers; in the *Satyricon* (126.5-11), Circe's maid gives a cynical account of her mistress's preference for base men (slaves, messengers, gladiators, muleteers, actors), while she, the maid, turns up her nose at any but men of rank. Both Habinnas and Trimalchio recall how, when they were slaves, they used to perform sexual services for their mistresses (69.3, 75.11). Such women appear in Martial (6.6, 12.58) and throughout Juvenal 6.

A topic peculiar to the reign of Domitian is the revival of the *lex Julia*. Some of Martial's epigrams on this subject are seriously laudatory (6.2, 6.4, 9.6), but many more attack women (rarely, men) whose behavior undermines the intent of the law.[45] Juvenal mentions the law only to sneer at Domitian's hypocrisy (2.29-33) or that of those who accuse women (2.36-78).

The only author to make a stock villain of the adulterer corrupting an innocent wife is Juvenal. At 3.45-6 he wants no part of such goings-on — "let others carry what the adulterer sends to the bride . . ."; at 3.109-113 the Greek parasite is the lover of everyone in the house. The infamous Crispinus was interested only in adultery (4.2-4), and had actually seduced a Vestal Virgin (4.8-10).

It will be seen that the male bias in Latin literature is most obvious in sexual humor. Married women are, in satire, always unchaste, just as prostitutes are either wanton or teasing; they are all always described as they would be seen by the male lover. The places where the poet, as narrator, talks of his own sexual feelings are rare, and limited to laments over impotence; a poem like Martial's exhortation to his "wife" to be more abandoned (11.104) is even more unusual. The only area in sexual humor in which the woman does not play the central role is in the depiction of punishments of adulterers; here, the woman sits and shrieks in the background while the husband and adulterer fight it out.

CONCLUSIONS

There are obvious contradictions in the evidence presented here. If any one of the five categories were used alone to illustrate Roman sexual attitudes, the picture would be a false one. The law lists clear sanctions against all who commit adultery and are accused and found guilty; one assumes that such people were often brought to court, found guilty, and punished according to the law. From historians and other sources offering factual information, it seems that the Julio-Claudian emperors used the law exactly as they wished, that it was a great opportunity for *delatio*, and, overall, that it was imposed on a nobility which had enjoyed great sexual freedom, and caused a long and deeply-felt resentment. It is startling to turn to contemporary rhetoric and *exempla* and find that the law is not mentioned, or appears only in a distorted and hardly recognizable form; on the other hand, the speakers of these set-pieces espouse moral ideals which would make one think the *lex Julia* could hardly have been necessary. (At the same time, however, the speakers of the *controversiae* seem to take these ideals less seriously than do writers like Plutarch; they wallow in murder and adultery.) Then again, despite the terror caused by the *delatores* according to Tacitus, we find that people must have been happily spreading scurrilous rumors about each other not only before but after the *lex Julia*. Finally, satire describes a wholly different situation. Here, adultery is common, even rife, but the sanctions of the *lex Julia* are unheard of and the law itself not mentioned until the time of Domitian, when it is often broken. Instead of legal appeal, outraged husbands exact their own vengeance, raping, mutilating, fining, even killing the unlucky adulterers.

How is it possible to reconcile these accounts, and why should they disagree so wildly about a fact of everyday life? The first, obvious, answer is that each obeyed the conventions of a genre, and told the portion of the truth which its audience had come to hear. This, however. leaves us weighing the reliability of genres, a false analysis of the problem. What can really be studied here are the special ways in which each author views the situation, and the possible motives in each case.

The factors which will have allowed the different accounts to evolve were those which allowed irregularities in the administration of the law. It is ironic that, although the *lex Julia* may have been intended to improve the senators and *equites*, the most flagrant cases in these classes were subject to special treatment by a variety of *principes*. The law was gradually eroded by the process of *cognitio* and would always have existed in tandem with the jurisdiction of the family; the tradition of self-help punishments would have been hard to regulate. Exile was administered in varying degrees, sometimes not at all, sometimes for a term of years, sometimes to a pleasant place and sometimes to a desert island; the powerful will always have been favored, especially against a weak plaintiff. And most of the inhabitants of the empire, not being Roman citizens, will have been subject to harsh and sometimes arbitrary treatment. So it is easy to see how notorious adulteresses may have continued to live at Rome, or in the resort towns around Naples; it is also easy to see how famous people might have either evaded the law, or been hurt badly by it; clearly, the degree of sexual freedom and attendant risks depended on who, when, and where you were.

At the same time, the great variety in the sources is a sign that adultery was an enormously important subject in Roman society.

The number of books interpreting the law, the amount of gossip, testifies to a practical, everyday concern with sexual goings-on from the late Republic on. Nor were women excluded from hearing of such things, even if they did not participate.

It is still puzzling that four contemporary sources — Tacitus, Pliny, Plutarch, and Juvenal — wrote so strongly and so differently at a time when society at Rome was settling down to a happy home life. The change in manners in Pliny's time is exemplified by the story of the gay old lady Ummidia Quadratilla, a veteran of the Julio-Claudian decadence (*Ep.* 7.24), and her priggish nephew. Tacitus and Juvenal, then, both in their different ways express a sort of literary nostalgia for the scandals of the early Principate, Tacitus deliberately flagellating his readers with stories of earlier oppression. Plutarch, in his moral tales, extols an ideal that the *lex Julia* never managed to make a reality. Clearly, there was a great variety of sexual behavior in Roman society; clearly, it had its hazards, only some of which were a product of the Augustan law. It also seems likely that the wide range of literary depictions of adultery, and the preoccupation with it, was spurred by two societal traumas — not only the Augustan marriage legislation, but the change in attitudes at the end of the first century A.D.

Acknowledgement

I want to give special thanks to Professor Gordon Williams for many criticisms and suggestions.

Notes

1. I have generally, in this paper, not included specimens of the attitude of serious poetry toward sexual behavior. On the whole they can be aligned with the fantasies and idealizations of rhetoric described below, and in any case I think it is hard to generalize about societal attitudes from Roman epic, elegy, and lyric. The period under consideration in this paper runs from the second century B.C. to the early second century A.D. Useful sources on adultery at Rome include the following: W. Rein *Das Criminalrecht der Römer* (Leipzig 1844) 835-856, a clear list of the ancient evidence; Mommsen *Römisches Strafrecht* (Leipzig

1899) 688-699, a technical discussion of points of the law; P. Corbett, *The Roman Law of Marriage* (Oxford 1930, reprinted 1969), 127-46; J.E.B. Mayor *Thirteen Satires of Juvenal* (London 1877) *ad* 10.314-317, an extensive list of literary sources on the punishment of adulterers. Special studies: P. Garnsey, "Adultery Trials and the Survival of the *Quaestiones* in the Severan Age," *JRS* 57 (1967) 56f., and *Social Status and Legal Privilege in the Roman Empire* (Oxford 1970) esp. 21-24, 103f., on the administration of the *lex Julia*; D. Daube, "The *lex Julia* concerning adultery," *The Irish Jurist* 7 (1972) 373f., on the culpability of accessories; S. Bonner, *Roman Declamation* (Berkeley 1949), is informative and imaginative on the relation between the legal situations described by the *controversiae* and those of real life. H. Brockdorff, *"Lex Julia"* in *En Kvindes chancer i oldtiden*, H. Salskov Roberts, ed., *Opuscula Graecolatina* 13 (1977) 118 f. (in Danish) lists sources of various kinds on adultery and the *lex Julia*, with translations, brief notes, and commentary on the reasons for the lack of success of the Augustan marriage legislation.

2. The problem is well defined by Garnsey, *Social Status*, 8-10.
3. *Coll.* 4 consists of selected points, especially from Paul's commentary on the *lex Julia*. For parallels in modern law, cf. S.P. Scott, *The Civil Law*, Cincinatti 1932, vol. 1, p. 281.
4. *Dig.* 48.5.1; for arguments regarding the date of this legislation, and a general account of its content, see H. Last in *Cambridge Ancient History* 10. 443-447. The law used the terms *adulterium* and *stuprum* interchangeably; *stuprum* was illicit sexual relations with a virgin or unmarried woman (*Dig.* 48.5.6.1), but then surely in the *lex Julia stuprum* is used to mean "adultery." The law does not seem ever to have been intended to outlaw all sexual relations outside marriage, nor can the procedure under the law very easily have been applicable to unmarried women.
5. Last (above) notes that one aim of the law is to transfer the punishment of the wife from the control of the family to the control of the court, so that it will be less harsh (i.e. limiting the family's power to kill the woman). This may have been in Augustus' mind, but in all the evidence surveyed there was not a single mention of any real woman ever having been killed by her relatives, and it may be assumed to have been a rare occurrence. It seems to me rather to be the case that Augustus was trying to legislate shame into the upper orders — an endeavor doomed to failure — and that this is borne out by the treatment of the compliant husband legally as a *leno* — as if, by making this moral judgment true in law, Augustus could instill it in the conscience of the nobility.
6. *Dig.* 48.5.2.2, 2.5, 2.6, 2.7, 12(11).13 (specifically under the *lex Julia*), 15(14).pr., 30(29); Paul. *Sent.* 2.26.8. If the husband took no action against a wife he knew to be adulterous, there was no case against his wife (*Dig.* 48.5.2.3); the *adulter* could try to bring action for *lenocinium* to ensure this, but not once he himself was accused (48.5.2.4). The law was particularly concerned with husbands who took money for their compliance, connivance, or mercy (48.5.15(14), 48.5.30(29).3), and

was lenient towards those who concealed their knowledge gratis (48.5.30(29).2) or who were simply ignorant (30(29).4). Women came to be covered under this law (48.5.11(10).1), and Marcianus opines that a woman who receives money for her husband's adultery can be accused as an *adultera* (48.5.34(33).2). A soldier who acted in this manner was released from his oath and deported (48.5.12(11).pr.).

7. *Dig.* 48.5.4 12(11).6, 15(14).2. The sixty days were computed from the date of divorce, in the case of a woman who re-married, or from the date of the act, if she remained single (48.5.30(29).5). The husband had priority over the father, and could bring an accusation even after a third party had begun proceedings, if he had not delayed through negligence (48.5.2.8, 3, 4.2).

8. *Dig.* 48.5.2, 12(11).11, 20(19).3. At 48.5.5 it is stated that the *lex Julia* itself made the following provision: that if the woman were unmarried, the prosecutor could begin with either her or the *adulter*; if she were married, he had to start with the *adulter*. Hence the jurist opines that a divorced woman can certainly be prosecuted (also at 48.5.16(15).8). It is pointed out that even if the *adulter* is convicted, a married woman accused of adultery with him might still win her case, if he had been falsely convicted (48.5.18(17).6).

9. The term is modern, not classical.

10. The father's right to kill the daughter and her lover was superior to the husband's, considering that the father would be the more likely to show mercy (48.5.23(22).4). This right, over adulterers of all ranks, was stated in the second chapter of the *lex Julia* (Paul. *Sent.* 2.26.1). The law originally gave the right to the father of a daughter who was in his *patria potestas* (48.5.21(20)), although Paulus' opinion is that a *filiusfamilias* should have the right to kill his daughter (*Sent.* 2.26.2). Killing had to be done *in flagrante delicto* (48.5.24(23)) and only in the father's or husband's house (48.5.23(22).2). The father had to kill the *adulter* and his daughter as simultaneously as possible (48.5.24(23).4). If the father did not kill both, he could be prosecuted under the Cornelian law (48.5.33(32).pr.).

The husband could not kill his wife, and could only kill certain kinds of adulterers (48.5.25(24).pr., Paul. *Sent.* 2.26.4) and only in his own house, not his father-in-law's (also Paul. *Sent.* 2.26.7). The husband, under the law, could kill anyone who was a pimp, a singer or a dancer, one convicted of a criminal offence and not restored to full civil rights, or a freedman of his immediate family. Once he had killed such an *adulter*, he had to dismiss his wife immediately (*Dig.* 48.5.25(24).1) and announce the circumstances publicly (Paul. *Sent.* 2.26.6) within three days.

The right of a man to kill an *adulter* who outranked him was a sticky point; cf. *Dig.* 48.5.25(24).3, 48.5.39(38).9.

A husband who did not wish to kill the *adulter* found *in flagrante delicto* could detain him for up to twenty hours in order to bring in witnesses (*Dig.* 48.5.26(25).pr., 48.5.26(25).5; Paul. *Sent.* 2.26.3 places this rule in chapter five of the *lex Julia*).

The husband who did kill his wife was recommended to the court's mercy in a rescript of Antoninus Pius (*Dig.* 48.5.39(38).8); he was not to suffer the death penalty, but if of inferior rank, was to be sentenced to hard labor for life; if of superior rank, to *relegatio* to an island. Paulus also recommends leniency (*Sent.* 2.26.5).

Finally, Papinian notes that anyone who may kill an *adulter* has *a fortiori* the right to "treat him with contumely" (48.5.23(22).3). In conjunction with the rules about the husband's right to kill, this would seem to indicate a modified liability if the husband assaulted the adulterer, if the adulterer should choose to go any further; in the *Institutes* (4.4, concerning injuries) it is noted that the customary penalties in lawsuits for injury are "honorary" — that is, that "the estimate of the injury is increased or diminished in proportion to the dignity and honorable position in life of the person injured . . ." This principle is a late one; still, if the adulterer were *infamis* to begin with, his "dignity" would not be very high. Of course, the question remains as to how the husband was to ascertain the rank of a naked stranger in bed with his wife. An explicitly stated distinction as to rank is likely to be later than Hadrian, but the principle may well have been implicit earlier; see Garnsey, *Social Status*, 103f., esp. 156-157.

11.   *Dig.* 48.5.2.9, 48.5.4.1 (four-month period), 48.5.14(13).4, 48.5.16 (15).5. Anyone could be prosecuted within five years of the committing of the act, even if the woman had died (48.5.12(11).4). It is not clear why the four-month period for third parties was indicated at all, if the statute of limitations was five years; perhaps the five-year period was important if the husband did not divorce, and the evidence of adultery came to light much later than the act (I am indebted to Professor S. Treggiari for this suggestion). It was also not clear how much freedom to accuse a third party had if the husband chose not to prosecute. Ulpian (*Dig.* 48.5.27(26).pr., 48.5.27(26).1) states that a third party may not accuse at all unless the husband accuses first, or unless he first accuses the husband of *lenocinium*; Papinian (48.5.40(39).1) gives as his opinion that the third party can accuse even if the husband has not accused of *lenocinium*.

Although a man could not accuse his concubine of adultery as a husband, since he was not her husband, he could accuse her of adultery as a third party, as long as she was of good standing (e.g. a freedwoman who was the concubine of her patron; *Dig.* 48.5.14(13).pr., 48.5.14 (13).1).

Other limitations, or lack of such: the woman could be prosecuted even after the death of her husband (*Dig.* 48.5.12(11).8); the adulterer could be prosecuted even after the death of the woman (*Dig.* 48.5.40 (39).2). A woman who had been raped could not be accused of adultery (48.5.14(13).7); a married woman under the age of twelve had to be accused as a fiancée rather than as a wife (48.5.14(13).8). By marrying a woman, a man cancelled her previous wrongdoings and lost his ability to accuse her of adulteries previous to their marriage (48.5.14(13).9-10). The *lex Julia* specifically prohibited the accusation of anyone away on legitimate Senate business, while they were away (48.5.16 (15).1), as well as action by certain persons, e.g. those under age 25 (48.5.16(15).6).

12. On the fine points of the culpability of accessories, cf. Daube, *IJ* 7 (1972) 373f.

13. It seems probable that, by the second century, this punishment applied only to culprits of the senatorial and equestrian orders, and that people below those orders found guilty of adultery were punished corporally; cf. the rescript of Pius cited above. Garnsey discusses this question at length, *Social Status*, 103f.; see especially 103 n. 2, 111 n. 3, 136, 152, 167, 222. It is important to realize that it would have been normal for the "servile" or harsh physical punishments to have been inflicted upon any non-citizen below the rank of decurion — i.e., on most people. For the different sorts of exile, see Garnsey, *op. cit.*, 55, 111-122. The penalty implied by the *lex Papia Poppaea*, that a convicted adulteress cannot take under a will (as *caelebs* and *infamis*), is no small one. Though denial of the *ius capiendi* was used as a club by this legislation in an age of *captatio*, nevertheless it would have been a real deprivation for someone in exile, whose comforts and possibly hopes of return depended on money.

14. See A. Greenidge, *Infamia in Roman Law* (Oxford 1894) 171-6, for discussion.

15. According to Papinian, the *lex Julia* applied only to free persons who were victims of adultery or *stuprum*; slaves were covered by the *lex Aquilia*, laws covering *iniuria*, or the praetor's action for corruption of a slave (*Dig.* 48.5.6.pr.). If the slave was not harmed, there was no *iniuria* (Paulus *Sent.* 2.26.16); and Paulus further states that adultery cannot be committed with women who have charge of a business or shop (*Sent.* 2.26.11).

16. Despite *Codex* 9.9.1; cf. *Codex* 9.9.34(35); though a woman or her family did have the right to start proceedings for divorce, at the risk of losing the dowry — cf. Bonner, 95 n. 1, on the *actio malae tractationis* and the *actio rei uxoriae*, 124 on the *actio de moribus*. A woman could plead in court, but this was not usual and enough of a prodigy that Val. Max. has several anecdotes on such women; see Bonner, 52.

17. There are, however, a few points worth noting in the story of Lucretia. The means by which Tarquin forced her into compliance was a threat to rape her, then kill her, placing the body of a male slave beside her, so that it would look as if she had been caught in adultery and killed with her lover. It might be assumed that adultery with slaves was the thing most feared; hence the republican custom allowed the killing of the wife not only in revenge but so that she would not bear the child of a slave. There are few jokes on bastards in Roman satire, but several of these do elaborate on the shame of a man whose children resemble his slaves (Mart. 6.39; cf. Juv. 6.76-81).

18. Cic. *Fam.* 8.72, 2.15.5; Memmius and the wives of the Luculli, *Att.* 1.18.3; Lucullus' other marital problems, Plut. *Luc.* 38, *Cic.* 29; the affair of Milo's wife Fausta with the historian Sallust, Gell. 17.18,

cf. D.R. Shackleton Bailey's commentary *ad Att.* 1.18.3; Pompey's divorce of Mucia for adultery with Caesar, Suet. *Iul.* 50.1; Dolabella as adulterer, Cic. *Att.* 11.23.3, 12.52.2, 13.7, Plut. *Ant.* 9; Cato's divorce of his wife Atilia, Plut. *Cat. Min.* 24.

19. Cic. *Fam.* 1.9.15; *Att.* 1.12.3, 1.13.3, 1.18.2-3; Suet. *Iul.* 6, 74; Plut. *Cic.* 28-29, *Iul.* 9-10.

20. For other famous republican courtesans, see S. Treggiari, *Roman Freedmen During the Late Republic* (Oxford 1969) 140, 142.

21. P. Garnsey, *Social Status*, 85, 88-9.

22. Garnsey, 103f.

23. Suet. *Aug.* 34.1, 65.4, 101.3, *Tib.* 11.5, 50.1, *Calig.* 16.3; cf. G. Williams, *Change and Decline* (Berkeley 1978) 58-61, for other sources and sound discussion. This was certainly a test of the new laws which Augustus would not have wished or contrived.

24. On these cases, see Treggiari, *Freedmen*, 72-3.

25. The legal and political aspects of these cases are discussed fully by Garnsey, *Social Status*, 21-24.

26. Translations throughout are my own.

27. Greenidge, *Infamia*, 171-2.

28. On the political importance of sexual liaisons within the royal family, see Sandra Joshel, paper presented as the Berkshire Conference on Women's History, 1978.

29. I hope to examine the corruption in this passage, along with all the evidence here surveyed that relates to the self-help punishments, in a future article.

30. As it was in the passage cited above from Tacitus *Germania*; see G. Williams, *JRS* 48 (1958) 23-24.

31. So Bonner, *Roman Declamation*, 38-41, 83.

32. On the validity of the "laws" on adultery cited in the *controversiae*, see Bonner, 119-121, 131-132; Quintilian *inst. orat.* 3.6.17, 27; 5.10.36, 39, 104.

33. Cf. *Att.* 5.21.9, 2.24.3, 9.22.4; Plut. *Cic.* 26; Clodius and Clodia, *Att.* 2.4.2, 2.9.1, but cf. Plut. *Cic.* 29, for a counter-rumor; Servilia and Caesar, *Att.* 2.24.3, cf. Suet. *Iul.* 50.2, Macrob. *Sat.* 2.25.

34. For a discussion of these at length, see J. Hallett, "*Perusinae glandes* and the Changing Image of Augustus," *AJAH* 2.2 (1977), 151-171.

35. See A. Richlin, *Sexual Terms and Themes in Roman Satire and Related Genres* (diss. Yale 1978) 233-253.

36. Plautus *Curc.* 25-38, *Mil.* 1395-1426, *Poen.* 862-3; Ter. *Eun.* 957; Hor. *S.* 1.2.41-6, 132-4; Mart. 2.60, 3.85, 3.92, 6.2.

37. Mart. 2.83, 3.85.

38. Petr. *Sat.* 45.79, Juv. 10.316.

39. Mart. 2.49, 2.60, Hor. *S.* 1.2.132-3.

40. Cat. 15.19, Juv. 10.317.

41. Cat. 21.7-13; Mart. 2.47, 2.83; A. Richlin, "The Meaning of *Irrumare* in Catullus and Martial," *CP* 76 (1981). These punishments are similar to the threats against thieves made by the god Priapus in the *Carmina Priapea*, esp. *Pr.* 13, 22, 28, 30, 35, 44, 56.5-6, 59, 70.13, 74; for

Roman machismo and interest in Priapus in the first century A.D., see
H. Rankin, *Petronius the Artist* (The Hague 1971) 52f., esp. 58-63.

42. Mart. 2.39, 10.52; Juv. 2.65. For a description of the humiliation entailed in such a change of dress, see Pliny *Ep.* 4.11.

43. This idea has a close parallel in serious poetry at Horace *C.* 3.6.25-30.

44. Women, too, corrupt their daughters: Petr. *Sat.* 140.1-11, Juv. 6.232-242, 14.25-30.

45. Mart. 1.74, 5.75, 6.7, 6.22, 6.45, 6.91.

Index